Salvador Bernal

MSGR. JOSEMARÍA ESCRIVÁ DE BALAGUER

A Profile of the Founder
of OPUS DEI

SCEPTER
London – New York

SCEPTER LTD
1 Leopold Road, London, W5 3PB
505 Fifth Avenue, Suite 1402, New York, NY 10017

First published in English in 1977, this is a translation of *Mons. Josemaría Escrivá de Balaguer — Apuntes sobre la vida del Fundador del OPUS DEI*, Madrid, 1976

ISBN 0 906138 00 0 (paperback)
ISBN 0 906138 01 9 (hardback)

Printed in Great Britain by
Staples Printers Ltd., at The Stanhope Press, Rochester, Kent, England.

CONTENTS

CONTENTS

FOREWORD

On 26 June 1975 around midday Monsignor Escrivá de Balaguer died in Rome. Some hours later his mortal remains lay in the oratory of Our Lady of Peace in the central offices of Opus Dei. Don Alvaro del Portillo, who was then Secretary General of Opus Dei, came to place some red roses at the feet of the Founder, whilst quietly repeating some words of St. Paul: Quam speciosi pedes evangelizantium pacem, evangelizantium bona! *(Rom 10: 15), how fair are the feet of those who bring news of peace, who bring good tidings!*

It would have made a splendid epitaph. All who have met him and been with him, even for a few moments, are unanimous in singling out his happiness. His peaceful, open look was cordially welcoming. He was a man of God who overflowed with attraction and human warmth. He infused peace and cheerfulness, serenity, contentment and the desire to serve others.

"I can think of no one," Manuel Aznar wrote a few days later, "who combined as intimately as he did, and with such spontaneity and such admirable naturalness, the natural with the supernatural, God with man and man with God. He accomplished that hardest of tasks of keeping supernatural inspirations present in the midst of the tiniest trivialities of human existence, and did so without apparent effort, with no jarring as the yearnings for higher things engaged with reality here below."

He lived for God, and was also marvellously human. To carry out the Work entrusted to him by Our Lord, he received gifts that made him humanly attractive. And at the same time surprising, since people often expect a "founder" to be somewhat "special" or different. "I had to keep making acts of faith, to remind myself that I was in the presence of the Founder of Opus Dei. He is so straight-forward and easy to get on with," was the comment made by a priest from Jaén when he met him in Pozoalbero, near Jerez de la Frontera (Spain), on a November day in 1972. Another priest remarked on "how naturally he hides the depth of his spirituality". But, he added: "it just bubbles out. He can't hide God's presence within him."

And so it is not easy to explain what he was like or how he acted. His personality and his teaching are rich and many sided. Besides, they dovetail so neatly in the simple and strong unity of his life that it is hard to separate them out and analyse them. One cannot take to pieces a life so richly threaded with human and divine significance even in its tiniest details.

Nevertheless I have tried to sketch in here some aspects of his rich personality. A sketch then, for in all honesty I would find it very difficult to attempt a full portrait of the person I first met on 8 September 1960. That meeting took place in the little garden of Aralar University Residence in Pamplona. A hundred or so students had gathered there and we fired questions at him for nearly an hour. I learned a lot that afternoon, and was changed inside. His sense of humour took me by surprise. We laughed a lot. I knew I had been brought very close to God. On top of this, and perhaps by way of summing it all up, I had a great time: it was a delightful hour.

I had never imagined that Msgr. Escrivá de Balaguer could be so attractive, nor that he could "win over" university students as he did. He evidently shared our deepest concerns. He spoke our language, our jargon even; and he used this gift to demand a lot from us, to push us upwards, to draw us out of our small-mindedness. (Seven years later, I witnessed a similar reaction in the Vallecas suburb of Madrid: a manual worker whose children were studying at the Tajamar Institute said to me: "This priest is easy to understand; he talks like one of us. . . .")

But his inborn ease for making himself understood, the speed of his replies, his human charm and attraction had nothing to do with a desire to please. He was strong, spontaneous and true. And it was a genuine confidence that he placed in us (at the time, in that summer of 1960, I was half way through my university studies) when he spoke to us about things very close to his heart. That too was his way of showing his unlimited capacity for loving, which ranged from the most lofty concerns (he spoke to us about our conversation with God, about loving Our Lady, and about spreading the Church to countries in Asia and Africa) to the most everyday things: as when he scolded us for neglecting to close a window shutter (we could see it was open from the garden) which meant that the furniture in that particular room was being exposed to the beating rays of the midday sun. He had affectionate words for one in the crowd who had an arm in plaster, a not infrequent sight in a numerous crowd of young people; and he seasoned all he did with stories that were really amusing.

The life of the Founder of Opus Dei does not fit into neat compartments. He did not drink, yet he liked to joke about a well known Spanish brandy (Fundador), saying of himself that the only good founder he knew came in a bottle. He considered himself, in all humility, a Founder without foundation.

José Ortego, a professor of criminal law, was quite right when he answered a journalist on 26 June 1975 saying: "I have read a biography of Don Josemaría Escrivá. Then, thinking it over, I have come to the conclusion that you cannot write his biography. His vigorous personality escapes any attempt to capture on paper what he was like. However many and well ordered the facts, however significant the anecdotes, his life which was so rich and intense inevitably eludes us: nothing can make up for direct knowledge of the man."

For many years he resisted outright any suggestions to film aspects of his life. Fortunately, he finally yielded and, as a result, a number of episodes from the last years of his life are now on film. I feel that half an hour of film of the Founder of Opus Dei, speaking about God and answering questions from all kinds of people, gives a clearer knowledge of him than anything I can say here.

Then there are the books he has written, which have achieved an enormous circulation all over the world, and his unpublished writings: for, as he often said, punning on his surname, Escrivá escribe, Escrivá writes. In those texts, rather than in these pages, can be found the true dimension and depth of his life.

However, I felt the urgency of making some attempt at a written sketch of this priest of God. There was a risk of offering just a partial view of a reality that was brimful with meaning, but I felt the risk worth taking. So, after some weeks of reading background material, I wrote these pages quickly and almost without interruption in November and December 1975. I thought that what I had written was inadequate and that many things were missing, so I decided to go over it again, taking time to fill in the gaps, even though my publisher was keen to send the book to print, as he thought it could be useful. During 1976 I touched it up in a number of places, but have added very little and the original approach and plan of the book remain the same.

So the reader must not expect a finished biography. This is just a profile, a few impressions which, though based on historical fact, do not follow a chronological order. Events and writings from different periods have been brought together and intermingled freely as a way of sketching with a few rapid brush strokes those particular features of the Founder of Opus Dei which I have highlighted at any particular moment. Whoever has met him in the flesh, or through his writings or on film, will soon realise that many important aspects of his personality do not appear in these pages.

These impressions may, however, help the reader to rethink his experiences and to meditate anew the writings of the Founder of Opus Dei. That is my hope and it would fulfil the aim of this book, which is to shed a little more light on the rich personality of Msgr. Escrivá de Balaguer, who delighted in passing unnoticed, following his lifelong motto: **I have to pass unnoticed and disappear, so that Jesus alone may be in the limelight.**

Many years ago an English journalist wrote in a profile of him in The Times: *"His most striking characteristic, in all circumstances, is that of absolute normality. There is nothing fanatical or domineering in his manner, none of the expected marks of a great originator or a leader of men. The suggestion of personal magnetism or of spiritual energy may easily be missed. He is of middle height and weight, with a pallid rounded face more often smiling than not. There is a warmth of expression in his brown eyes, and a nervous energy in him betrayed by the rapidity and play of his voice and gesture. He is direct and personal in his approach, but impressionistic rather than factual; a man that deals in broad lines and bold strokes, delegating detail with ease and confidence: the independence and individual responsibility of members is always stressed. A lasting impression is of a humane and happy character who would have much in common with Sir Thomas More, whom, indeed, he has chosen as a patron saint of his movement."*

This journalist has hit upon a fundamental trait of the extraordinary personality of the Founder of Opus Dei: he breathed an air of normality. This is perhaps one of his most precious bequests. He showed that in order to be truly godly one has to be very human. He taught thousands of people the world over how to imitate the naturalness of Jesus Christ. Jesus is perfect God and perfect Man and is so in his ordinary life, in his years of hidden work. Christ was always the only Model for those who seek genuine sanctity, without concessions or excuses, in the ordinary circumstances of each day. Msgr. Escrivá de Balaguer could hardly have hoped to preach this message if God had not made him profoundly human, welcoming and straightforward; though it is true that he suffered at times because others misunderstood him or made little effort to understand him; and he had to beg pardon for possessing **the peculiarity of not being peculiar.** *It seems that men have a constant tendency to set their sights on what is showy, artificial or extraordinary, and they find it difficult to appreciate the depths, both human and divine, of what is ordinary and everyday. He would sometimes explain the problem by pointing out how some people react when they* *see beautiful freshly cut roses, with perfectly shaped and graceful petals:* **They look like plastic!** *such people exclaim, because they prefer artificiality.*

The human and divine are so utterly fused together in his life and teaching that often it is not easy to distinguish whether we are witnessing a trait of his character or the workings of divine grace, acting in an apparently natural manner. Fr. Sancho, O.P., puts it very accurately with deep theological insight when he writes: "My impressions of him are of a man of very great virtue which, in his simplicity, he did not show. I cannot single out any specific detail of his profound humility, because his simplicity filled his life with naturalness. There was nothing surprising about him, because what he did all the time was to supernaturalise everything, with simplicity and with cheerfulness, which is even harder to achieve."

God's grace always acts that way. It makes men's lives supernatural, without annihilating the human side or putting it out of joint. Indeed, only the man who is faithful to God's grace can be fully a man.

CHAPTER ONE

A CHRISTIAN FAMILY

1. FROM BARBASTRO TO LOGROÑO

From the foothills of the Pyrenees of Aragon there extends at some fifteen hundred feet above sea level a wide shelf of undulating upland which eventually drops sharply towards the south. This region, which appears as a kind of buffer zone between the mountains and the plains, is called Somontano, and geography has conferred on it an important place in history as a natural passageway for trade and, consequently, as the setting for much political intrigue.

Barbastro, the main town of the Somontano region, has had a long history. Already well known in Roman times, it was conquered by the Moors and, in the year 1100, retaken by Peter I of Aragon. At that time the nearby city of Roda became an episcopal see, which seat was later transferred to Barbastro, a distinction which it still retains. Over the troubled centuries of Spanish history Barbastro quietly prospered, so that by 1900, with 7,000 inhabitants and a well developed local administration, it stood out as the most important commercial centre between the two provincial capitals of Huesca and Lérida.

It was in Barbastro that Don José Escrivá y Corzán, the father of the future Founder of Opus Dei, had set up in business. In 1894 he was one of the three partners of a firm called "Successors of Cirilo Latorre". The family had originally come from Balaguer (Lérida) where Don

José's paternal grandfather had been born. Some of them had moved to Peralta de la Sal and later to Fonz, a village situated on the left bank of the River Cinca, halfway between Barbastro and Peralta de la Sal. It was there that José Escrivá was born on 15 October 1867. His brother, Fr. Teodoro, and sister, Josefa, also lived there for a number of years.

In Barbastro, on 19 September 1898, Don José married María de los Dolores Albás y Blanc, the twelfth of thirteen children. The Albás family was well known in Barbastro, where they occupied a large house. The presence of this family was so notable that the locals referred to that household as "the house full of children".

Martín Sambeat, who still lives in Barbastro, remembers Don José as a man of great goodwill and integrity, always well dressed in the fashion of the period, with a top hat and a cane which he changed every day. Martín's father was also in business, and every Wednesday several businessmen of the town used to gather in a room over his shop for a *tertulia*, that typical Spanish get-together in which good conversation is often spiced with wine and a game of cards. Martín recalls how he was sometimes sent by his father to remind Don José of this weekly *tertulia*, which was also occasionally held at *La Amistad*, a local bar in the Town Hall Square.

Don José worked at 10 Ricardos Street. There was a chocolate factory in the basement. The shop itself was on the ground floor with a spiral staircase leading up to a storeroom for merchandise. The two upper floors were occupied by the family of Juan José Esteban, a Barbastro notary until 1925, who had married a niece of Cirilo Latorre, the founder of the business.

It is interesting to form a mental picture of this shop on Ricardos Street where the Founder of Opus Dei spent so much time as a child. It was very typical of a textile dealer's establishment in Spain at the turn of the century: stacks of great wooden shelves with large drawers underneath, a huge plank of wood which served as a counter, containing the special box with a slot into which coins were dropped during business hours, and, of course, a weighing machine and scales in the corner. Business was good. When the "Successors of Cirilo Latorre" was wound up in May 1902, the assets came to the equivalent of several million pesetas in today's money. In fact, the money they received from the liquidation of the firm enabled two of the original three members of the company, Don José and Juan Juncosa, to carry on the business under the new name of "Juncosa and Escrivá".

Not long before this, on 9 January 1902, Josemaría, the Escrivás' second child, was born at the house in the Mercado Square, next door to that of the Argensola family. He was christened José María Julián Mariano at the baptismal font of Barbastro Cathedral. His elder sister, Carmen, was born on 16 July 1899. After them were born María Asunción (1905), María de los Dolores (1907), María del Rosario (1909) and Santiago (1919).

Life in the Escrivá home was normal and uneventful. The mother, Doña Dolores, looked after the house with the help of a cook, María, a maid and, when circumstances required it, a nanny. There was also a manservant to take care of the heavy work.

Those who knew Doña Dolores in Barbastro have described her as a woman of great dignity and refinement: a great lady, who was very beautiful and elegant, and yet at the same time calm, simple and kind, with a very good sense of humour. Her children's friends would often come and play in the house, and she used to give them clothes to dress up in, though she preferred them to keep their games to the lumber room. When teatime came round there was always plenty of bread and chocolate — a common children's treat in Spain — and oranges.

Very naturally and good-humouredly, Doña Dolores took advantage of every opportunity to instil in her children a true christian outlook on life. Some of the practical lessons she taught them remained indelibly impressed in Josemaría's mind, and he was to repeat them time and again throughout the course of his life. He would tell, for example, how as a child he used to react to the social custom of family calls which was then much in vogue. As the son of the family he was supposed to greet the guests, but when his mother's friends wanted to kiss him he would try to avoid them, especially a distant relative of his grandmother who had a prickly moustache.

Nowadays, you ladies know how to use make-up, he once joked to a large gathering in Argentina. **You weigh up the circumstances, and you don't make up for a formal visit in the same way as you would for a party ... and cosmetics these days have come a long way. But at that time, ladies either didn't use make-up at all, or else they put it on in such a way that I heard my mother say jokingly: "Mrs. So-and-so will be stiff with make-up when she comes" (and indeed she had put on a lot when she came) "so we mustn't make her laugh because it could crack and peel off."**

Nor did Doña Dolores like her small son to be bashful when he had to put on a new suit for the first time. She made a point, which he recalled many times: **I hid under the bed and stubbornly refused to go out into the street when I was dressed in a new suit ... until my mother gave a few light taps on the floor with one of my father's walking sticks. I came out then because of the walking stick, and for no other reason. She then affectionately told me: "Josemaría, the only thing to be ashamed of is sin." Many years later I realised what a depth of meaning these words contained.**

His mother taught him to say his prayers, and it was from her that he learned "O my Lady, O my Mother, I offer myself entirely to you . . . ," his morning offering. In one of his homilies, given on 26 November 1967, he recalled: **Morning and evening I never omit to renew that offering which my parents taught me.** In Buenos Aires in 1974, to show how the most trifling of things can sometimes hinder a person's complete surrender to God, he mentioned what he had once been told by a mother who had also taught her infant son to make that self-same offering: **He was a little boy who was tired of toys — one of those children who are refused nothing — until one day a friend of the family gave him a little pet rabbit. And he was so delighted with this little bunny — is that what you call it here? — that when the time came to say with his mother: ". . . and I offer you my eyes, my ears, my tongue and my heart, in a word, all that I am . . ." he suddenly repented and added: ". . . except my little bunny rabbit".**

Under his mother's direction, a life of simple unaffected piety was taking root in Josemaría's heart. He called this fact to mind on his visit to Argentina in 1974 after a lady from Cordoba had told him about her five-year-old son who, when they were out on an excursion one day, noticed a statue of Our Lady in the bus. The little chap waved to the statue and immediately began talking to the driver about the sort of things he could say to the Blessed Virgin while driving: "Our Lady, we have to stop now; the traffic signal is red. . . . Now we can go on again because it's turned green. . . ."

When he heard this story, Msgr. . Escrivá de Balaguer paused for a moment in thought, and then said to the child's mother: **That is contemplative life. When I was that age I was very devout, but I didn't have contemplative life.**

Many people remember the Josemaría of that time in Barbastro as just another little boy, cheerful and mischievous, who used to play with a big toy horse on wheels. He used to let the young ones ride on it, as he pulled it round the house on a string. Like other boys of his age he had lead soldiers, and *birlas* — sticks with soldiers painted on them — which they used to knock down by throwing balls at them.

When the weather was fine, he used to get together with his friends in the square to play "cops and robbers", or to race with hoops. At other times he would go to the shop on Ricardos Street where his father worked. There he used to meet the Esteban children, whose father was the public notary, and other friends such as the Cajigós, the Sambeats and the Fantobas. María Esteban Romero, who still lives in Barbastro, was one of those children, although she did not have all that much contact with him because the girls did not often play with the boys. She thinks they used to come over to play especially on Thursday afternoons when there was no school. One of Josemaría's favourite pastimes was making soap. In those days it was made with ash, not lye, and the houses used to have barrels of very fine ash which was used for washing. The children used to knead it with water and then boil it in pots so as to turn it into soap. On some nights, after the shop was closed, the children would stay behind "helping" to count the day's takings. They thought it great fun to sit on the counter and count the coins.

"But what he used to like most of all when he was with his friends," says Adriana Corrales, who also knew him as a child, "was to sit in a big rocking chair and tell them horror stories which he made up himself." He really must have enjoyed stories. In Buenos Aires on 16 June 1974, before thousands of people in the San Martín congress hall, he recounted how, when he was little, he used to steal into the kitchen, even though he had been told not to: **There were two wonderful things in that kitchen, a cook called María, who was very good and who knew a story — it was always the same story — about some very likeable robbers; and on top of that, there were the most delicious fried potatoes you could imagine. Both things were banned: listening to the story.... Because we never asked her to tell us 'a' story. No, it was: "Come on, María, tell us 'the' story." We knew she didn't know any other, but she told it so well that it always seemed new.**

The atmosphere of that house in Mercado Square had a flavour of its own: full of mutual respect, simplicity and elegance, happiness and christian piety. There too Josemaría learned to pray the Rosary. On Saturdays the Escrivás used to go down to St. Bartholomew's, a church that no longer exists, with other families of their acquaintance to say the Rosary and the Hail Holy Queen. (It was to this church that Josemaría and Carmen also went to Mass with their parents.)

Doña Dolores herself prepared her son for his First Confession. She fixed the date with her own confessor, Fr. Enrique Labrador, a saintly Piarist father, and on the appointed day, after giving him some last minute instructions, she took him by the hand to the church. In 1972 he told how it happened: **I was very happy after I made my First Confession — I was six or seven at the time — and I always look back on it with joy. My mother took me to her confessor, and . . . do you know what he gave me as a penance? I'll tell you, you'll be very amused. Even now I still hear the chuckles of my father, who was devout but never sanctimonious. The good priest — he was a really kind little friar — could think of nothing else than to say: "Tell mama to give you a fried egg." When I told her this she exclaimed: "Good heavens! He could have told you to eat a sweet. But a fried egg!" Obviously he was very fond of fried eggs, that priest.**

But isn't it wonderful for a child, who still knows nothing about life or about its sorrows, to be told by his mother's confessor that she is to give him a fried egg? It's marvellous! That priest was worth his weight in gold.

His mother taught him to say his morning and night prayers, and his father often used to join him at his night prayers. Doña Dolores also helped him to learn his catechism until he was ready to make his First Communion, which he did on St. George's Day (23 April 1912), because it was the custom in Upper Aragon to make it on that day:

I was then ten years old. At that time it was unheard of to make one's First Communion at such an early age, in spite of the dispositions laid down by Pius X. Now it is customary to make it even earlier than that. An old Piarist father, a good, simple and devout man, prepared me for it, and it was he who taught me the formula for the spiritual communion.

This prayer is now familiar to thousands of people throughout the entire world:

I wish, Lord, to receive you with the purity, humility and devotion with which your most Holy Mother received you; with the spirit and fervour of the Saints.

When Josemaría made his First Communion in 1912, he was already at the school of the Piarists in Barbastro. There were not many pupils at the school. According to Aurelio Español, a pharmacist in Jaca, who also did all his *Bachillerato* (secondary studies) there between 1900 and 1912, at the beginning of the century it was the exception rather than the rule to do secondary studies, at least in Barbastro. The school had a certain prestige. It was run by about twelve Piarist Fathers, which is not surprising, for Saint Joseph Calasanz, their Founder, had been born in nearby Peralta de la Sal, and had begun his apostolic work as a priest under the guidance of the Bishop of Barbastro, Felipe de Urríes, who was the Saint's protector during his student days.

A manservant called Faustino went to collect the schoolboys every morning. The boys wore navy blue coats with brass buttons. Their corduroy caps with patent leather peaks were also navy blue. The school badge was fitted on the centre of the peak. As a scarf they wore a folded neckerchief of a lighter colour. Indoors at school they wore striped blue overalls, with buttons down the front; collar and belt were also blue.

At first, in order to qualify for the official *Bachillerato*, the pupils at the Piarists' school had to go to the Institute of Huesca for their examinations. They usually went by train (with stops at Barbastro, Selgua, Tardiente and Huesca). Afterwards they went instead to the Institute of Lérida. Josemaría went to Huesca for his *Bachillerato* Entrance Exam in 1912, that is, when he was ten, which was at that time the age at which the exam was normally taken.

According to Martín Sambeat, Josemaría was noticeable at school for his calm; he was not a trouble-maker. Another schoolfellow of his, José María Muñoz, son of the veterinary surgeon in Barbastro, and now a Piarist Father in Logroño, recalls that he was studious and pensive; neither noisy nor rough; well mannered: "You could see that his parents had brought him up carefully." According to Fr. Mur, who was two years ahead of him at school, he stood out — together with Mariano Esteban, Leopoldo Puig and Ricardo Palá, all now dead — for his talent, his good marks and his piety. Together with another schoolfellow, Miguel Cavero — a well-known engineer when he died — he won a prize in elementary arithmetic and geometry at the Institute of Lérida in the year 1912–1913, that is to say, in his first year of *Bachillerato* (it appears in the weekly magazine *Juventud*, Barbastro, 13 March 1914, quoted by Fr. Liborio Portolés Piquer, a Piarist, in an article published in the old boys' magazine of the San Antón College in Madrid).

He also did the second-year examinations at the General and Technical Institute of Lérida. *Juventud* (Barbastro, 12 June 1914) published the results obtained by the pupils from the Piarist school. In that same number there was an article written by J. Argente Llanas about the atmosphere in those exams at the Institute. Argente mentioned how the pupils went happily together towards the Institute, until they were suddenly confronted by a door, at the end of a long narrow street. That door led to the "scaffold": "After walking up and down the sombre corridors, a bell rings. Their faces become even more dismayed. Panic takes hold of them. They are examined by three men who inspire fear rather than respect or admiration. The schoolboy trembles, goes red in the face, his body seems to stop functioning, his senses are deadened, except for his hearing, as he anxiously awaits the questions he is going to be asked by the man in the academic cap. . . ."

There were then three different ways of going through secondary school: a) "Official Education", for which the pupils had to attend classes at the Institutes; b) "School Education", for which the pupils went to recognised Schools, instead of the Institutes; the Schools then sent the pupils to be examined at the Institute, with the marks they thought each boy deserved: furthermore, a teacher from the pupils' school was one of the three examiners; and c) "Free Education": in this the pupils were not presented by any school.

In fact, however, the students in this last category (the "free students") used to go to the Institute sometimes during the year to meet the teachers who were to examine them; so that the candidates who were usually most afraid of the Institute were the boys educated at other schools, since their only visits to the official Centre were for the examinations.

In June 1914, Josemaría did well. According to the lists of the magazine *Juventud*, he turns out to be the second-year pupil with best results. He was given *notable* in Spanish geography (no one obtained higher marks) and *sobresaliente* in Latin, arithmetic and religion. Like everybody else he had obtained a pass in physical education.

As he progressed through school, however, his family suffered successive blows. The most painful were the deaths of his three younger sisters. Rosario, the youngest, died first on 11 July 1910, before she was one year old. Then Dolores, also called Lolita, on 10 July 1912, when she was five. And finally Asunción, who was nicknamed Chon, died on 6 October 1913, shortly after her eighth birthday. When she died,

Josemaría was eleven and his eldest sister, Carmen, was barely fourteen. Both were deeply affected by these tragic events.

Their childhood friends realised it all too well. It was then the custom for some girls chosen by the family to attend the funeral, holding the handles of the litter on which the coffin was laid, or the ribbons attached to the coffin if the child died before doing his or her First Communion, which was the case of Josemaría's three sisters. Adriana Corrales, for example, held the ribbons for Rosario and Lolita, but when Chon died, as she was already eight years old, Adriana held the handles. She has never forgotten what Josemaría went through because of these family tragedies. After Chon died, Josemaría started saying that it was his turn next, since his sisters had died in ascending order from the youngest upwards. He stopped when he realised that he was hurting his mother. She assured him:

"Don't worry, you have been offered to Our Lady of Torreciudad."

The family had, indeed, a great devotion to Our Lady of Torreciudad and, when Josemaría had fallen ill at the age of two and the doctors had given up hope for his recovery, his parents offered him to Our Lady to be cured of his illness. That is why they later took him on a pilgrimage to the shrine of Torreciudad.

The Baroness of Valdeolivos also remembers those times: "I cannot recall exactly how soon it was after the death of Dolores, it must have been the following summer, that Chon fell ill. It's as if I were seeing her now: she was a very pretty, fair-haired girl." She describes how one afternoon Josemaría had told her outside his house that he was going upstairs to see how his sister was. She had died. His mother told him that she was very happy now, because she had gone to Heaven; but seeing Josemaría so disconsolate she had to insist:

"Now, now, Josemaría, don't be like that, don't cry. Can't you see that Chon is already in Heaven?"

The news also hurt the Baroness of Valdeolivos — who was a small child then — because it was the third sister who had passed away in a short time, and they were great friends. But in spite of that sad scene of sorrow which was deeply impressed on her memory, the image she preserves of Josemaría is that of a "cheerful, optimistic boy, with a great heart".

The Valdeolivos saw a lot of the Escrivás, for although they lived in Lérida, they spent their summers in Fonz, and went to Barbastro in September, to their grandmother's house, which was in the same square as that of the Escrivás. There, under the arches, or at home, they spent many hours playing together, even though Josemaría was five or six years older than she was. She remembers him as "a rather tall, strong boy, who wore long socks up to his knees and short trousers, like all the other boys of his age then". Rather than playing with her and her cousins, Joaquín Navasa and Julián Martí, he spent his time keeping them amused because they were younger. When they went to his home he would bring out his toys for them to play with. He had many puzzles. The girls liked to build castles with playing cards. One afternoon (Rosario and Dolores had both died by then) they were gathered round the table and holding their breath as the last card was being placed on one of those castles, when Josemaría, uncharacteristically, toppled them all with his hand. They were on the brink of tears, and Josemaría said to them very seriously: **That is exactly what God does with people: you build a castle, and when it is nearly finished, God pulls it down.**

His little friends did not understand a thing; but now, the Baroness of Valdeolivos thinks that those words "could well have been a result of the mark left in this boy's soul by the sad events that had occurred in his family and that had made him suffer".

To these bitter experiences were added the progressively worsening financial difficulties which the family had to endure. Towards the end of 1913 his father's business was nearly ruined. It was said of Don José Escrivá in Barbastro: "He is so good that people have played a dirty trick on him."

The Escrivás' household went through difficult times. They had to do without the cook, the parlour maid and the rest of the servants: they had already dispensed with the nanny soon after Chon died.

The Baroness of Valdeolivos was still very young but what she heard made a deep impression on her. That is why she was surprised to see Josemaría eating a ham sandwich one afternoon, and she remarked to her mother:

"Why do they say the Escrivás are so badly off? Josemaría had a very good snack today."

Her mother pointed out that things were not as bad as all that, to the point of their not being able to eat.

Doña Dolores managed with her daughter Carmen's help to do the housework, even though her health was not very good. Her children's friends used to see her in the afternoons nearly always doing the ironing, sitting on a chair because, they surmised, she had a heart complaint. They admired her permanent smile: she never complained, despite all the financial worries through which she had to go.

It was thus, working from morning till night, that the members of Opus Dei found her years later. One of them, Pedro Casciaro, met her in Madrid in 1936. He went with Francisco Botella to the rector's house of the Patronato of Santa Isabel, where she lived with her son — who was the Rector — to help her move to what would be her new house in the Rey Francisco Street, carrying trunks and suitcases and parcels. It was the first time that he had seen her and he did not know how to address her. He opted for calling her *señora*. She was, he recalls, very ladylike. He was impressed by her soft, sweet tone of voice.

When she said goodbye to them she thanked them, and Pedro Casciaro was left with the feeling that "there was a special relationship between her and us. Perhaps it was after meeting her that day that I began to call her Grandmother." Her daughter Carmen and her other son, Santiago, also lived with her, but Pedro Casciaro only remembers her on that day in 1936: "Her face was still young. She radiated serenity, and at the same time, there were traces of interior suffering. I had the impression that her eyes were tearful." In 1936 the country was going through very difficult moments. After the February elections, social instability had increased and anticlericalism was growing. Once more Doña Dolores had to move house in humanly difficult circumstances. But the serene cheerfulness with which she had accepted right away the financial disaster of Barbastro, more than twenty years before, had continued to grow.

Don José had also borne it all with the same fortitude. All agree that his business failed because some people took advantage of his trust and his good faith. He was always a real gentleman in everything. He soon found work in another town in the same textile trade. Early in 1915 he went to Logroño to begin working, to find a house for his family, and to set it up before they moved in.

Their two children, Carmen and Josemaría, finished their year at school. They spent the summer at Fonz. At the beginning of September they went back to Barbastro and a few days later, early in the morning, they took the Huesca stage coach, bound for Logroño.

The lesson of faith and fortitude of his parents in that difficult situation made a deep impression on the young mind of Josemaría. He recalled their example years later in a letter, dated 28 March 1971, to the mayor of Barbastro, Don Manuel Gómez Padrós, answering his greetings for St. Joseph's Day and thanking him for the news he had sent about social improvements in "our town":

Allow me to tell you that although my parents had to leave this city, they instilled in us, together with faith and piety, a great love for the banks of the rivers Vero and Cinca. Thinking now particularly of my father, I recall things which make me feel proud and which have not been erased from my memory, even though I left there when I was thirteen: anecdotes of a generous and hidden charity, a strong, unostentatious faith, an abounding fortitude in the hour of trial, closely united to my mother and their children. Thus it was that Our Lord prepared my soul, through those examples that were full of christian dignity and of hidden and ever-smiling heroism, so that later it would be the poor instrument through which — with the grace of God — He could carry out a design of His Providence which in no way separates me from that beloved town of mine. Forgive this outpouring. I cannot hide from you that these memories fill me with joy.

In Mercado Street — now General Mola Street — in Logroño, Don Antonio Garrigosa y Borrell owned a clothes shop called "The Great City of London". Don José Escrivá had come to an arrangement with him to have a share in the business, while at the same time working there looking after the clients. Manuel Ceniceros, a godson of Garrigosa, who took up a job in that shop in 1921, was impressed by the dignity and elegance of his behaviour and especially by the way in which he accepted his change in fortune. "One could see he was a happy man, and extremely methodical and punctual. He dressed very smartly." He remembers him with his bowler hat and cane, going for his Sunday walk through the centre of Logroño.

He was also a genuinely religious man, and was not afraid of admitting it in front of people who bragged about being anticlerical. He went to Mass frequently, which did not prevent him from getting to work on time. He said the Rosary with his family: his house was a real christian home. Don José, according to Manuel Ceniceros, went about his life with great naturalness, without any show. At work he fitted in easily. He was always kind and ready to help. His change of fortune never led him to complain or bear a grudge against anyone.

When Manuel Ceniceros was interviewed by a journalist in June 1975, he repeated what he had often commented with his fellow workers:

"If the son's sanctity is like that of his father's, I am sure he will be raised to the altars."

The first months in Logroño must have been especially hard for the Escrivá family, for they hardly knew anyone there. They lived at 18 Sagasta Street (now number 12), on the fourth floor. It had a low ceiling, and was only partly separated from the roof by a loft: the flat was hot in the summer and cold in the winter.

Doña Paula Royo, whose father worked in the Garrigosa shop, still lives in Logroño. She has told us how Sr. Garrigosa asked her father to help the Escrivás to settle into their new surroundings. A good friendship developed between the Escrivás and the Royos as a result. On Sundays they often went out for walks down the roads of Laguardia or Navarra, after crossing the Iron Bridge over the Ebro. She remembers Josemaría being strongly built, tall, handsome and full of good humour. He looked very much like his father, "a very gentle, kind and good person". His sister Carmen was more like her mother. Paula Royo thought her a bit more serious, "but also charming".

Some time later, the Escrivás moved to 7 Canalejas Street, and another fourth-floor flat. Sofía de Miguel got to know them there. She is now over eighty years old, but still has a lively and open character. She was living on the fifth floor at the time. Fernando, one of her sons, was two years older than Santiago Escrivá, who was born on 28 February 1919, and they often played together.

The flat in Canalejas was nothing to write home about. When the postman arrived and there was mail for the Escrivás, Sofía often volunteered to take the letters up to them. "You can't imagine how kindly they thanked me for this service," she says, and adds: "I remember that one day I arrived when they were eating and I noticed how beautifully the table was laid. They were real gentlefolk! Young Santiago was also always very well dressed; you should have seen how well brought up he was. . . ." After so many years, she can still picture Doña Dolores: "She had very bright eyes, not very big, but slanting; she always wore her hair in a bun pinned up high." She likewise praises Don José as being a very "penetrating" man — meaning that he was intelligent and cultured — and she cannot imagine why he was working in Garrigosa's shop: "I can't think why it was . . . , at times things don't turn out too well. . . ."

Another friend of those years writes: "They were a marvellous family, and I can honestly say that, if I have ever in my life seen a united couple, it was Josemaría's parents. Josemaría's father was a real

saint. He was very much in love with his wife. He was very patient and
accepted everything: he always looked cheerful. The mother was also
a great lady. I remember perfectly — even though the detail might
seem trivial — the teas she prepared for us. She knew how to do it
very well and prepared everything with great care."

Don José worked hard all day in the shop on Mercado Street, and
then, when he arrived home, in spite of feeling tired, he carried on
working. He was very responsible; and he learned to live with the
sobriety that circumstances had imposed upon him. For his afternoon
break he had just one sweet. Manuel Ceniceros has not forgotten this
because he often went out to buy his sweets: they were ten for a penny.
And Don José smoked little: he smoked six cigarettes a day, which he
carried in a silver case. As was usual then, he rolled the cigarettes
himself.

By then Josemaría had finished his *Bachillerato* at the Logroño
Institute. With his third year (1914–1915) and the exams in Lérida
behind him, he did the fourth year as a non-official pupil at the
Institute. He did the fifth and sixth years as an official pupil. In the
14 subjects he took during those three years in Logroño his marks were
two *sobresalientes* with Distinction, eight *sobresalientes*, and four *notables*.
The Distinctions were for literary composition, in the fourth year, and
ethics and rudiments of law, in the sixth year.

At that time, many of the official pupils used to go to the Institute
in the morning, usually from nine to one. Then after lunch, they would
go until eight to tutorial schools, where they had revision classes, periods
of study, and activities of human and religious formation. There were
two such schools in Logroño. One was run by the Marist Brothers. The
other, St. Anthony's College, was run by laymen, although it had a
resident spiritual director. Josemaría attended St. Anthony's.

His school friends recall that he was like so many other boys,
sensible, not rowdy, "the type that never pulls a fast one" (Eloy Alonso
Santamaría); "tall, on the stout side, smiling and kind" (Antonio
Urarte); "somewhat reserved, but cheerful" (Julián Gamarra); joining
with all the others in the get-togethers at the "casino", which is the
name they gave to the gatherings before class in the school playground.

Antonio Royo's daughter says that Josemaría was tall for his age,
on the strongish side and good-looking, with an infectious smile.
"However," she adds, "his cheerfulness was not boisterous: it was
intimate, true, very pleasant, and catching." Paulo Royo insists that
there was never anything in his external behaviour that would make

one think he was called to the priesthood. When he decided that he wished to become a priest, "his parents talked about it with mine in amazement, but they never made things difficult for him. We did not expect him to want to be a priest. He was a boy of excellent character, and very refined . . . but very normal, that's all."

At that time boys with a possible vocation to the priesthood usually entered the seminary when they were about ten years old. Agustín Pérez Tomás, who was at school with Josemaría in Logroño, recalls the occasion when another schoolboy said to Josemaría that he could be a priest, and he answered quite convinced: **Don't be silly.**

Josemaría had never thought the priesthood was for him; but he willingly changed his plans when he began to sense that God wanted something of him. When he made up his mind to follow that way, he spoke to his parents, and he was given the advice one would expect from a deeply christian family. In October 1918 he began to study in the seminary of Logroño as an external student. Later, in September 1920, he moved to Saragossa. It was there, a few months before he was ordained a priest, that tragedy once more afflicted his family. His father died.

Don José died in Logroño on 27 November 1924, in the same house in Sagasta Street where they had lived before, though now they were no longer on the fourth floor, but on the second. It was all over in a matter of hours. When he got up that morning he was feeling very well. He had breakfast, he prayed for a good while in front of an image of the Miraculous Virgin, which they had at their home those days, and he played for a while with young Santiago. He then got ready to leave, and when he had reached the door he felt unwell. He leaned on the frame of the door, and then collapsed on the floor. Two hours later he peacefully surrendered his soul to God, without regaining consciousness.

When nine o'clock came and went and he had not arrived at the shop, they immediately guessed that something serious must have happened, for he was always punctual. The owner asked Manuel Ceniceros to go and find out what had happened. When Manuel reached Sagasta Street, Don José was still alive. He died a short while later, Ceniceros relates, "with a sanctity that spread to the whole family". The family asked him to send a telegram to Saragossa to inform Josemaría that his father was very ill, and to ask him to come. Manuel went to meet him at the station. On the way home, he had to tell Josemaría the whole truth: "He took it so calmly that it surprised me in a way that is difficult to explain."

Many years later, the Founder of Opus Dei gave this summary of his father's life: **I can never recall having seen him look severe. I remember him always calm, with a smiling face. And he died worn out: he was only fifty-seven years old, but he was always smiling. I owe my vocation to him.**

A few months after that, the Escrivá family moved to Saragossa.

2. THE EXAMPLE OF A CHRISTIAN HOME

On the morning of Sunday, 1 October 1967, the Founder of Opus Dei was in Madrid meeting parents of the pupils of Tajamar School. He talked to them about the ideals of youth and love of God; about affection and work, about their families and their homes, **those homes of yours which I bless with both hands, as I bless the home — that is no longer — of my parents.**

Msgr. Escrivá de Balaguer always carried in his heart the memory of his family home and he was especially grateful to his parents for making his vocation possible. Even though Don José never came to know the plans God had in store for his son, God's Providence had nevertheless used the example of his life to form the Founder of Opus Dei from his childhood days for the mission that was to be entrusted to him in 1928.

He often referred to that home, which prepared the soil where the seed of God's call would yield fruit. In 1970 he commented: **Our Lord prepared things so that my life would be normal, ordinary, without anything exceptional.**

He brought me to life in a christian household which is normal in my country. I had exemplary parents who practised and lived their faith. They allowed me a lot of freedom from an early age, yet kept a close watch on me at the same time. They endeavoured to give me a christian upbringing, and I owe more of it to them than to my schooling, though I was sent to a convent school when I was three and to one run by religious fathers when I was seven.

Above all they taught him what a truly christian home was like. On 4 July 1974 in Chile he summarised it in the following words: **They loved each other very much, and life brought them many sufferings, because Our Lord had to prepare me (. . .) I always** saw them smiling. They didn't caress in our presence, but it was obvious that they had great affection for each other (...) I can now say this with gratitude on the five continents, and I can add, as you heard me say the other day, that I am "paternalistic".

In Buenos Aires, a few days before, he had been asked why he repeated that he blessed human love with both his priestly hands. He began by quoting some texts from Holy Scripture, and then continued:

I cannot but bless that human love which Our Lord has asked me to renounce. But I love it in others, in my parents' love, in yours, in that between spouses. So, love each other, really! And my advice is always: husband and wife, have few quarrels. It is better not to play about with happiness. If you, wives, give in a little, he will give in as well.

Certainly, never quarrel in front of the children: they notice everything and soon make their own judgements (...)

I often repeat with great joy that I am paternalistic. Take a good look at me, for I might seem to you to be very antiquated. I am paternalistic, because I cherish wonderful memories of my father and mother. I never saw them quarrel. They loved each other very much...so no doubt they quarrelled occasionally.

But they quarrelled when we children were not around. Nor did they behave foolishly: a kiss now and then. Be modest in front of your children.

He thus learned a great lesson: that of a deep human and supernatural affection. But that was not, by any means, the only lesson. As a child in his parents' home the Founder of Opus Dei learned to practise most of the human virtues, without which the way to sanctity in the middle of the world would be unthinkable.

They helped him, for example, to make good use of his freedom and to respect that of others. They were understanding with their children's mistakes which they would correct whenever necessary. **They never imposed their will on me,** he would often say in their praise. They learned how to **make friends** with their children, as he explained to a large group of married people in Buenos Aires in June 1974:

It gives me great joy to be able to say that I do not remember my father hitting me except on one occasion. I was very, very small. It was on one of those few occasions when I sat at

**table with the grown-ups, on one of those high chairs. It must
have been something to do with my stubbornness. I am very
stubborn; I come from Aragon. If this is taken to the supernatural plane, it is of no consequence; on the contrary, it can
be good, because in the interior life one has to keep on insisting, isn't that so? Anyway, he gave me a . . .** (and he imitated a
slap).

**Never again in all his life did he lay a hand on me; never.
He was always gentle with me, and it did me a world of good.
I have the most wonderful memories of my father, who was
my friend. And that is why I recommend what I have experienced: you must become your children's friends.**

Another way in which they taught him how to use his freedom well
was by keeping him **short of money, very short, but free.** Yet his
father was deeply concerned about the welfare of those who worked
under him, and had a deep sense of charity towards the needy. **He was
a great almsgiver,** was how the Founder of Opus Dei liked to sum up
the way his father practised christian poverty and charity.

His father's hard work was also a constant example. Josemaría saw
him wearing himself out day after day, untiringly, with a constant
smile, first in the shop in Barbastro, then in Logroño, always concerned
for the material and spiritual welfare of his family. He was reliable and
punctual. He never skimped in his efforts to serve others, and, at the
same time, he faced life's contradictions with resilience and good
humour, even though they were heavy and difficult to bear. He was
always unruffled, as if these problems did not really matter.

Josemaría's parents accepted the will of God generously. They
accepted without any complaint, as we have seen, the trials that
God's Providence permitted. The Holy Spirit was thus, in a hidden
manner, preparing the Founder of Opus Dei. Years later he humbly
admitted:

**I have always made those around me suffer very much.
I have not provoked any catastrophes, but the Lord, to shape
me who am the nail — forgive me, Lord — gave one blow on
the nail and a hundred on the horse-shoe. And I came to see
my father as Job personified. I saw him suffer cheerfully,
without showing it. And I saw his courage. It was a constant
lesson to me, because afterwards I have felt so often the ground
giving way beneath me and the heavens falling on top of me,
as if I were about to be crushed between two steel plates.**

Humanly speaking, the life of the Escrivás was difficult. God wished Opus Dei to be born without earthly backing or support, as its Founder later acknowledged with deep conviction:

My father was ruined, and when Our Lord wished me to begin work at Opus Dei, I had not a single resource, nor a penny to my name. I only had the grace of God and a good sense of humour. Can't you see how good this was? Now I love my father all the more, and I give thanks to God that my father's business didn't go at all well, because that is how I came to learn what poverty is; if not, I would never have known. I feel a holy pride: I love my father with all my heart, and I am sure he is enjoying a very high place in heaven because he learned how to bear the humiliation of being left in the street. It hurt him deeply, but he bore it in such a dignified, marvellous and christian way.

In the same way, divine Providence made use of his family so that Msgr. Escrivá de Balaguer, even as a child, might learn to love God and his Blessed Mother, the Virgin Mary, and be led along the paths of christian prayer in a completely normal way.

Human love was the channel for the love of God. The Founder of Opus Dei stressed this on countless occasions when he spoke of how souls in love with God should behave:

When there is love, I'm not afraid to affirm that it is not even necessary to make resolutions. My mother never had to make a resolution to love me, and you should have seen how affectionate she was to me!

She also was a living example of hard work, an especially important virtue for her son, who was to preach that Christians must seek sanctification through ordinary work:

I cannot remember ever having seen my mother empty-handed. She was always busy with something: knitting, or sewing, or mending clothes, or reading ... I cannot recall having ever seen her idle. And she was not a strange person; she was normal, kind (. . .) She was a good mother who cared for her family, a christian family, and she knew how to make good use of her time.

The Founder of Opus Dei used to say that a good way of measuring christian detachment from material goods is to check if one is using them as does **a father of a large and poor family.** That is what his parents did: they put a lot of work into running their home, keeping it neat and tidy. When they fell on bad times financially, they still lived with dignity and good taste, trying to avoid undue fuss about their difficulties and making up for the lack of goods with imagination, affection and ingenuity.

They had always taught their children that it was important to make things last so as to avoid unnecessary expense; that they should think over any purchase carefully and commonsensically before buying it, "without making the arm stretch out further than the sleeve"; to make use even of things which might appear to be useless: "with the threads one throws away, the devil makes a rope" was a phrase Doña Dolores often said to her daughter Carmen when she was learning to sew in Barbastro. . . .

An anecdote illustrates Doña Dolores' gentle dignity in their family life. Their traditional dessert on Friday of Passion Week, Our Lady of Sorrows, was *crespillos*, spinach leaves coated with flour, milk and egg, fried in olive oil and sprinkled with sugar. They were served plentifully, piping hot, with a lot of sugar, on an enormous porcelain dish covered with a white linen napkin. Doña Dolores liked these *crespillos* very much, but she realised that she could not serve them too often: so she chose her feast day. It was always a great occasion in that house, which the children awaited with greater eagerness than if it had been the most expensive sweet on earth.

3. THE FAMILY ATMOSPHERE OF OPUS DEI

Not only the Founder personally but the whole of Opus Dei owes much to the Escrivá de Balaguer family. Without the affectionate upbringing that the Founder received from his parents, Opus Dei could not have had one of its most important features: its warm atmosphere which is that of a simple and happy christian family, where charity means affection.

Opus Dei is an **unorganised organisation,** alive with spontaneous responsibility. It is not a set-up, nor a regiment, but a family that has grown and multiplied through love, and has kept the same family air even when it has become so widespread and has been enriched with such a variety of races and temperaments.

On 26 July 1975 Cardinal Baggio wrote in the *Avvenire* of Milan, that in 1946 he had "the good fortune of meeting Monsignor Escrivá de

Balaguer and of beginning a steady friendship, that was full of respect and discretion, but nevertheless truly affectionate and deep". One of the things which impressed Cardinal Baggio was the external appearance of the central offices of Opus Dei, which "had nothing in common with conventional ecclesiastical buildings". It is like any other building in the Parioli district of Rome. There are no nameplates or showy symbols. There are bushes and flowers. The Founder of Opus Dei had explained to him that this was also part of the lay spirituality of the Association, which aims to sanctify everyday life to a heroic degree, yet without in any way altering its own specific nature.

The family atmosphere fits the human tone of Opus Dei, as its Founder saw from the beginning. He was also helped by the example of his parents who were docile to the will of God. When they were faced with the fact of their son's vocation, they responded generously and were ready to help him in every way they could.

Josemaría was ordained in 1925. The event filled the family with joy and gratitude to God. At the same time Doña Dolores was quick to accept the renunciation that his vocation involved. Her son had to devote himself fully to his priestly ministry.

Later he went to Madrid to carry on with his priestly duties. There in due course he was joined by his mother, and Carmen and Santiago. Opus Dei was born in Madrid and when the time came he explained to them what God wanted of him. His mother then, without any hesitation or dismay, put all her energy into helping the Work that God was doing through her son. Hers was a silent self-surrender. It was in no way striking, but it was very effective. **Without her help,** the Founder of Opus Dei declared, **it would have been difficult for the Work to develop.**

From 1932 onwards they lived at 4 Martínez Campos Street. Don Josemaría continued from there the apostolic work he had been carrying out with young people. Many members of Opus Dei learned its spirit there. They would go to Martínez Campos in the afternoon, and spend time with him chatting or in a get-together. Many began to receive spiritual guidance from him in that flat. Before they left he used to read out to them from a large missal the Gospel of the day, and then make a practical, incisive and brief commentary on it. This custom, the commentary on the Gospel, is now practised at the end of each day in all the Centres of Opus Dei.

Little by little the members came to realise what their **family tone** should be like. Without Doña Dolores' gentle guidance it would perhaps have been very difficult, not to say impossible, to get that family spirit across. She treated them as sons. She cared for them with motherly tenderness and loved to keep sweets or goodies for them.

Juan Jiménez Vargas sometimes stayed for the *merienda*, or afternoon tea. It might seem a rather irrelevant fact, but it helped him to understand what real family life was to be like in Opus Dei. Because of its distinguished human tone, although the family was not at all well off, it was not easy at first to realise that such invitations meant quite a sacrifice. Such meals were also an opportunity to present things well despite the lack of means. Juan Jiménez Vargas mentions how he personally found them a stimulus to improve not only from a spiritual point of view, but also in moderation and refinement in his dealings with others: "really it helped to 'groom' us in every way, so much so that some of us can say that we even learned our manners there."

A little later on they began the first Centre of Opus Dei — the DYA Academy. It was in a small flat in Luchana Street, very near Martínez Campos. Doña Dolores provided many of the basic necessities to set up the flat. As the years went by, many pieces of furniture from her house ended up in different Centres of the Work. The Founder's family even sold their own lands to raise money for the Centres. The Baroness of Valdeolivos recalls how the Escrivás had gone to Fonz in September 1933 when Fr. Teodoro, Don José Escrivá's brother, died. Fr. Teodoro had been chaplain to the Morers, and the family sold all they had been left in his estate, which was quite substantial: "I remember that the family had a fairly large farm in Palau. The people of the village found it strange that they should want to get rid of it all. As time goes on one understands better. It must have been a sad blow for them, but it was a tangible proof of their detachment from the goods of this earth."

A lot of work had to be put into running the first Residences of the Work in Madrid. Funds were very short. Doña Dolores was also concerned for her son and would get cross with him when, for instance, she saw him using old shoes that had been thrown away by the residents. He walked all over Madrid on his daily apostolic work wearing shoes with large holes in the soles. She had to refuse to patch up his cassock, which had been mended countless times.

After the Spanish war — which meant three years of immense suffering for the whole family, with Doña Dolores keeping writings and documents of the Work sewn into the mattress on her bed, with all the risk that it entailed — she and her daughter Carmen, at Don Josemaría's request, looked after what the Founder of Opus Dei would later call the **apostolate of apostolates:** the domestic task of administering the Centres of the Work.

I see it as God's Providence, he would recall, **that my mother and my sister Carmen should have helped us so much to have a family atmosphere in the Work. Our Lord wanted it that way.**

The two of them supervised all the domestic work in the Jenner students' residence in Madrid. Afterwards, in 1940, they went to live in the house at 14 Diego de León.

They were hard times for all Spaniards. A member of Opus Dei expresses her admiration for the amount of work the mother of the Founder and, above all, Carmen managed to get through in Diego de León: "It was really incredible that they should have managed to get girls and teach them to do the housework and to be presentable. We never saw Carmen run, although she moved and worked quickly; you wouldn't see her tired either, or with her hair untidy, or her clothes stained." A few years later some members of the Work took over that job. One of them recalls: "Sometimes we had to stay until late at night doing accounts or finishing jobs that were pending. Carmen had run the house on her own." Obviously the spirit of hard work was a family "disease". "At night, in her room, she would darn socks. There just wasn't time for it during the day. And as even darning thread was scarce, when a pair of socks had to be discarded, she would undo them, and use the wool for darning."

With her generous heart — another family "disease" — Carmen was always concerned to ensure that everybody ate as well as possible, which was not easy on a very tight budget and buying very cheap foodstuffs. If she saw someone not eating out of a false sense of sobriety, she would find a way of getting him to eat. Those who lived with her have described her — and the description sounds familiar — as hardworking and strong-willed, with a very big and noble heart, giving herself unstintingly. They also remember her frankness — she always called a spade a spade — and her spontaneity. She was so natural in her behaviour that it seemed no effort for her to be constantly kind to everyone in a variety of different ways. That is the way she is always remembered.

In the old house in Diego de León, Doña Dolores occupied a room on the second floor with a balcony that opened on to the corner of Lagasca Street. She had some flower pots there, which she herself looked after. The last months of her life were spent in that room which was not big, but well lit. She worked tirelessly as she had always done. A picture of Our Lady presided over her last moments on earth. It is an Italian oil painting, where a rosy-cheeked Child with neatly-combed hair is being offered a tea rose by his Mother. This image of Our Lady accepted her last sacrifice. She had offered everything for the Work, including her death in 1941.

The Founder of Opus Dei left his sick mother in Madrid, as he wrote fifteen years later, **to go to Lérida to preach a retreat to diocesan priests. I did not know how serious the illness was, because the doctors did not think that my mother's death was imminent, or that she could not be cured. "Offer your discomfort for the work I am going to do," I asked my mother as I said goodbye. She agreed, even though she could not help saying in a low voice: "This son of mine! . . ."**

I went to the Tabernacle when I arrived at the seminary of Lérida where the retreat for priests was being held and said: "Lord, take care of my mother, for I am looking after your priests." The retreat was half-way through. It was midday and I had just given them a talk commenting on the unique supernatural role a mother has at the side of her priest son. When I had finished I decided to remain recollected for a moment in the chapel. Almost immediately, the bishop apostolic administrator, who was also doing the retreat, approached me, his face drawn and pale, and said: "Don Alvaro is on the 'phone for you." I heard Alvaro say: "Father, Grandmother has died."

I returned to the chapel without a tear. I understood immediately that the Lord my God had done what was best: and then I cried, as a child cries, reciting out loud — for I was alone with Him — that long ejaculatory prayer, which I so often recommend to you: Fiat, adimpleatur, laudetur . . . iustissima atque amabilissima voluntas Dei super omnia. Amen. Amen. **Since then, I have always thought that Our Lord wanted that sacrifice of me, as an external proof of my love for diocesan priests, and that my mother especially continues to intercede for that work.**

She died on 22 April 1941. Don Josemaría called the civil governor of Lérida, whom he had known in Saragossa, for they had often gone together to teach catechism in Casablanca, one of the suburbs of the town:

Juan Antonio, my mother died a short while ago. How can I get to Madrid quickly?

"I'll send my car right away with the chauffeur."

He arrived in Madrid at three o'clock in the morning. His mother's body lay before the altar in the oratory. Many came to pay their last respects. He wept like a child, like a young son who has lost his mother. A mother whom he had not been able to accompany at her death, because Our Lord had asked that sacrifice of him, for love of His priests.

The death of his sister Carmen was different. He was able to be with her in Rome, when God called her. Carmen had arrived in the Eternal City, already very experienced in self-sacrifice in many things and still as simple and cheerful as ever. Also, because it was God's Will, she welcomed death calmly and joyfully. After a very trying illness, which lasted for two months from when it was diagnosed, she suffered an agony lasting forty-six hours, during which she never lost her union with God. Guided by her brother and by Don Alvaro del Portillo, she turned her agony into a continuous prayer. "We are with you," Don Alvaro was saying to her a few minutes before she died, "and above all God is with you, giving you strength. All your life you have been working for God, and now you are going to meet Him."

She died at dawn on 20 June 1957 on the Feast of Corpus Christi. Not long before, in mid-April, the doctors' diagnosis had been that she had an incurable cancer. She received the news "like a saintly person of Opus Dei," in the words of Don Alvaro to the Founder of Opus Dei. And from that moment on, with peace and joy, she prepared herself for a good death. A member of Opus Dei wrote years later: "When we heard about her illness, we looked after her as if she were our mother, keeping her company and doing everything we possibly could to make her last days more bearable." They prayed for a miracle: "Lord if you want, you can." She prayed "for the Will of God to be done". And everyone, with a firm heart, accepted whatever Our Lord would ordain, repeating the words: **May the most just and most lovable Will of God be done, be fulfilled, be praised and eternally exalted above all things. Amen. Amen.** The faith of the Founder of Opus Dei was comforted by a **taste of honey** which he received from God, and which, because it concerned a supernatural happening, he wrote down in a document which he left in a sealed envelope with instructions that it should not be opened until after his death. The members of Opus Dei heard him say at the time:

The tears were over the very moment she died: I am happy now, my sons, and grateful to Our Lord who has taken her to Heaven and I rejoice with the joy of the Holy Spirit. You must congratulate me, because she is already in Heaven. She was looking forward to Heaven, looking forward to it very much. She is already there praying for us.

Her sufferings were over and so were the sufferings of those who had accompanied her so affectionately. The peaceful expression on her face reflected her life of serene and self-sacrificed surrender to the service of God. Her remains now rest close by those of her brother Josemaría, in the crypt of the oratory of Our Lady of Peace, in the central offices of Opus Dei. It is quite proper that it should be so, for though she was not a member of Opus Dei, she too is part of the foundations of the Work.

4. A VERY UNITED FAMILY

God wanted Opus Dei to be a family in the literal sense of the word. And, as we have just mentioned, he deliberately used the human and supernatural virtues of the home of its Founder for this purpose. But the Founder was always and truly "the Father" of that family. He brought it up, humanly speaking, with a fatherly and motherly heart, which went out to all the members of Opus Dei, both when they were few and when they had become tens of thousands, of all colours and races.

They had already been spread over the five continents for many years when Msgr. Escrivá de Balaguer made his last journey to Spain. He went to his native town to receive the gold medal of Barbastro. The investiture took place on 25 May 1975. When the time came for him to read his short speech in the town hall, he had to interrupt himself:

Please forgive me. But I am very moved for two reasons: first, because of your affection; and secondly because late yesterday evening I received the news from Rome that one of the first people I sent to carry out the Work of God in Italy had died. He was a pure soul, with a first-class mind. He had a doctorate in civil law from the University of Madrid (then the Central University) and another in canon law from the Lateran University. He was a Lawyer of the Rota. Later, during the

pontificate of John XXIII, he was appointed an Auditor of the Rota.

He served the Church with his virtues, his talents, his effort, his sacrifice, his cheerfulness, and with the spirit of Opus Dei which is one of service. I ought to be happy to have another son in Heaven, because this kind of thing must needs happen often in a large family. But I feel very tired and weary. I am sure you will forgive me and you will be glad to know that these things affect me. I now continue.

This way of reacting as a father of a family who has a human heart and a divine faith was the way he had always reacted to the deaths of members of Opus Dei. Fr. Sancho, O.P., testifies that when Isidoro Zorzano died in 1943 the Founder of Opus Dei was both sorry for the separation and happy because Isidoro had died like a saint.

This Dominican priest adds: "His tireless zeal for all souls went hand in hand with a deep paternal affection and concern for his children. They were the apple of his eye. He was tough with them, demanding that they strive for sanctity, but he also treated them as kindly as a father treats his children. I was surprised by the way he dealt with them, especially with those members of the Work whom I held in high esteem because they were university professors: for him they were first and foremost his sons. He had a great respect for their freedom, and he loved them all very much; which is natural, because after all they were his sons."

Don José Luis Múzquiz, one of the first three priests of Opus Dei (the others being Don Alvaro del Portillo and Don José María Hernández de Garnica) writes: "Very often, even though he had a lot of work to do, I saw the Father spend long periods with someone who was ill, helping him to see things supernaturally, telling him things to entertain him, or doing some norm of piety with him."

In the seventies, when Don José María Hernández de Garnica (who was always called Chiqui, his family nickname, by Msgr. Escrivá de Balaguer) became seriously ill, Don José Luis Múzquiz received a letter from Don Alvaro, telling him "Chiqui is very ill" and "the Father has asked me to write to you personally for your prayers". On reading this, Don José Luis remembered when Isidoro Zorzano had fallen ill and the Father — just like mothers who are the first to sense when their little ones are ill — had felt that it was serious even before the doctors' diagnosis. The same had happened on this occasion: Don José María Hernández de Garnica had gone to Rome, and as soon as the Father saw him, he immediately asked him to get a complete medical check-up.

Don José María died in Barcelona on the eve of the Feast of the Immaculate Conception, 7 December 1972. Not long after, Don José Luis Múzquiz received a letter from Rome:

A few moments ago I received the very painful news of Chiqui's death (may he rest in peace). Our Lord has wished to take him well purified. I cannot hide from you that I have suffered, and am suffering a lot, that I have wept.

Please offer many suffrages for him, and ask everyone else to do the same, although I am sure he does not need them any more. Pray to him for all those things we hold close at heart — I have done so from the very first moment — for Chiqui will continue helping, very close to the Blessed Virgin, as he has always done.

Be calm and at peace: the Lord knows best.

He was like that in life as in death. Encarnación Ortega stresses the Father's gentle tenderness: "He had an intuitive knowledge of our worries and of our moods." She gives some very practical examples of how he made his affection — his maternal affection — compatible with energetic corrections and the fortitude of a father who knows how to make demands on his children, precisely because he loves them: for instance, when women members of the Work went to Rome, usually for their studies, he was concerned that they be helped to settle in, especially if they came from very different and distant countries. He wanted them to be safeguarded from the change of climate, to be helped to adapt gradually to the Italian food, and to have the company of people who spoke their own language.

Encarnación Ortega was in London in September 1960. A little earlier some women members of Opus Dei had gone to Osaka and Nairobi to start the apostolic activities of the Work there. As always they were very short of material means. The Founder was in London at the time and wanted to telephone them so that he could hear news from them directly. He asked how much it would cost and calculated that if they did without other things, they could afford it. And he telephoned. His fatherly heart had got the better of him.

But affection did not exclude fortitude, which was a different way of expressing that same affection. He never failed to make a correction; be it in serious matters, in which fundamental aspects of the spirit of Opus Dei were involved, or in some minor and apparently unimportant question.

He knew how to correct because he knew how to love. His warnings did not hurt, nor did they crush. He loved so much that, no matter how direct or how strong the correction was, everyone felt understood and encouraged to put things right.

It is this care and affection that makes Opus Dei a family, in the true sense of the word. And this affection extends in a very special way to the families of the members of the Work.

As a result of his meditation on the fifth joyful mystery of the Holy Rosary, the Finding of the Child Jesus in the Temple, the Founder of Opus Dei had written: **And as we are consoled by the joy of finding Jesus — three days he was gone! — debating with the doctors of Israel (Luke 2: 46), your soul and mine will be left deeply impressed by the duty to leave our home and family to serve our heavenly Father.**

It was a clear obligation, which the Church has always practised in that way; but at the same time, whenever possible, the Founder of Opus Dei wanted the members of the Work who did not live with their parents to be with them when they were going through hard times, or at least — when it was not possible for them to be physically present — that they should accompany them with their constant prayers and letters, and with visits from other members of the Work.

He lived this spirit himself; and he taught it to the younger people, who because of their temperament — indeed almost as a law of life — tend to hide the love and gratitude they feel for their parents, with an apparent remoteness, which at times is simply laziness.

As Don Remigio Abad, who for many years has been the chaplain of Xaloc, an apostolic work run by Opus Dei in Barcelona, recalls: "He taught me how to love my parents with a deeper affection; on a number of occasions he asked me, for he knew I was a lazy writer: **How long is it since you last wrote to your parents?** He prayed for them every day in the Mass."

When people talked to him about parents who did not feel too happy about their children being in the Work, he usually, and quite rightly, blamed the children because it was they in fact who had not been faithful to the spirit of the Work. A mother from Brazil wrote to her son in 1974, after having met Msgr. Escrivá de Balaguer:

Dear son,

After seven years, I can again look at you face to face and tell you that really it is better this way. It had to be this way.

I can now look at a crucifix or a church, without feeling sorrow in my heart. Yes, I can now see that you have not been stolen away from me. That you had to go. And that yours is a marvellous world.

You, my son, are very privileged. How the Father has changed me! He has given you back to me. He has also given God back to me. I can now love Him again.

My son, try to follow the teaching of the Father. For me it's as if his is the very Love of Christ.

The heart of the Founder of Opus Dei was really fatherly. That is why he could understand so well the sentiments of all parents; and that is why he always kept in mind the families of the members of the Work. When their work required the children to go far away, he always encouraged them to write frequently to their parents, to give them good news and help them share in their happiness, for the greatest source of joy to parents' hearts is the happiness of their children.

He lived this with everyone, even in the extremely difficult circumstances of the Spanish war. Enrique Espinós Raduán, who spent a few hours with the Father in Valencia in October 1937, when he passed through on his way to Barcelona, was very impressed by him. Enrique went to see him off at the station with his cousin Francisco Botella. He recalls being very struck by the Father's peace and calm, and his immense trust in God. Francisco (or Paco as he was called) was later to join Don Josemaría in Barcelona and to accompany him when they crossed the Pyrenees. A few months later Enrique Espinós began to receive letters from Isidoro Zorzano giving him details of their journey from Valencia to Burgos: "It was proof of a refined charity towards me and Paco's parents: there is no doubt that Isidoro wrote at the Father's suggestion, for I did not know Isidoro."

Pedro Casciaro also had the same experience around that time. He had frequently spoken to the Founder of Opus Dei about his father's spiritual life. His father was a man of human virtues and great good will, but his desire to improve the lot of working men led him to join a political party which adopted an increasingly anticlerical stance. As a result he had begun to give up the outward practice of religion. Don Josemaría encouraged Pedro to invoke the Blessed Virgin with confidence. In December 1937, after reaching Andorra, he went to Lourdes before returning to Spain. Pedro was going to serve his Mass there. When they were already at the foot of the altar, Don Josemaría turned gently towards him as he was kneeling at the step, and said to him in a low voice: **I suppose you will offer the Mass for your father, so that Our Lord may grant him many years of life as a Christian.** Pedro Casciaro was amazed: "Really at that moment I had not made any such intention, but I answered in the same tone: 'I will, Father.' " When the war ended, his father had to go into exile. He suffered great deprivation, but Our Lord moved him to live as a fervent Christian with a sincere piety. During the last eleven years of his life — he died very peacefully on 10 February 1960, on the eve of the feast of Our Lady of Lourdes — he was a man of daily prayer, Mass and Holy Communion. He loved the Founder of Opus Dei very much and was a Cooperator of the Work.

When Opus Dei spread over the world, the Founder's affection did not diminish. This cannot be attributed to purely human causes: people of very different temperaments and races, who did not speak Spanish and who perhaps had never actually seen Msgr. Escrivá de Balaguer, considered him and loved him as a real Father — and that is what he was, a real Father. Víctor García Hoz, a distinguished educationalist who first met him in 1939, made special reference to this: "One of the things that struck me most during the last years of the Father's life was to see how he succeeded in keeping an intimate atmosphere when he catechized multitudes in get-togethers with hundreds and even thousands of people. I cannot explain it except as a special grace of God."

The Founder of Opus Dei had always recommended and practised an apostolate of friendship and trust, but as the development of the Work began to make it impossible for him to receive and talk to each and every one of those who wanted to listen to his teaching, there arose spontaneously those "get-togethers", some of which drew more than five thousand people around him. What was astonishing about them is that the people there never had the impression of being in a crowd. They felt as intimate as in a family gathering. Everyone felt "at home", very much in tune with whoever was asking a question or telling things, whether it was a grandmother in her eighties, or a fifteen-year-old boy; a married man with many children, or a young girl; a worker, or a university professor, or a film actress. The topics of these conversations were sparked off by their own personal problems or worries. The Father kept the atmosphere personal and intimate. And all found themselves sharing the same concerns and receiving his answers as if they were addressed to each one individually.

Some of those get-togethers have been filmed in colour. Any one of those films would describe much better than these pages can record what the Founder of Opus Dei was like, and how much he loved each and every one of those people who came to listen to him. On 16 June 1974 thousands of people gathered in the San Martín congress hall in Buenos Aires. First there were a few brief words of his:

You will not be surprised if I tell you — because you will think it quite natural — that I remembered you very much this morning in the Holy Mass; and also in my thanksgiving. I prayed to Our Lord for each one of you; for your worries and concerns, for your affections and interests, for your temporal, material health, and for your spiritual health. Because I want you to be happy. And I imagined what this was going to be like and how it would seem as if we were a great multitude. We are quite used to this in Opus Dei, and we know we are not a crowd: we are a family. Give us a couple of minutes and the multitude becomes a cosy little group. We speak as affectionately as if we were just half a dozen people who love one another and who understand one another.

A little later a young man from Paraguay spoke of his mother's death. She was in the Work and he told how she died praying for the Founder. A woman, whose husband belonged to Opus Dei, wanted to know what she needed to do to make up her mind to join. Someone else was worried because his work was sometimes so absorbing that he found it difficult to give it a supernatural meaning. Then a member of the Work stood up. His widowed mother was with him and he explained that she was concerned about what would happen to her son when he grew old:

"She says that I will have no family . . . and as she is here by my side, I would like you to explain to her that we are a family, that we love one another very much, and that furthermore we are always young, as you are. . . ."

Msgr. Escrivá de Balaguer illustrated his answer with an old story about a prominent person who had once attacked a member of Opus Dei because the latter, acting as a free citizen, had disagreed with him. Among other things, he had said that this member of the Work "had no family". The Founder of Opus Dei went straight to see him and told him: **He has my family, he has my home.** That person asked to be forgiven. Then the Founder continued: **You know that your son has a family and that he has a home, and that he will die**

comforted by his brothers with all their affection. Happy to live, and happy to die! Not afraid of life, nor of death! (...) Opus Dei is the best place for living and the best place for dying! How fortunate we are, my children!

That day many commented that there, in that congress hall, they felt they were in the atmosphere of early Christianity, united in heart and soul and in affection. They understood that Opus Dei is truly a home, full of human warmth and holy refinement.

Two years earlier, on 22 November 1972, in a similar gathering in Barcelona, a little girl said to the Father:

"The other day I was in another get-together with you. On the way out, a friend of mine said: 'Did you notice those priests who were in the get-together with the Father? I am sure they have heard him say the same things a thousand times. And yet, how affectionately they looked at him. How the people of Opus Dei love one another!' "

He answered immediately and with great feeling:

Yes, we love one another! Yes, we do love one another! And it is the best compliment we can receive. Because it is what the pagans used to say of the early Christians: "See how they love one another!"

5. THE SANCTITY OF HUMAN LOVE

The Founder of Opus Dei has taught people all over the world to love the family. At a time when sanctity seemed to have become more or less the preserve of the religious and priests, God made use of him to make many married couples see that married life is a true path to sanctity on earth.

Juan Caldés Lizana met him during a retreat in September 1948. He wrote in *Mundo Cristiano* (September 1975): "A marvellous world was opened to me when I contemplated matrimony (a great Sacrament) as a real vocation, a new divine way on earth." It was an utterly novel panorama: everyone called to the same sanctity, the plenitude of christian life; the family, a **bright and cheerful home,** and an appropriate starting point from which to **convert the prose of each day into heroic verse;** parents, **sowers of peace and joy,** and children, *gaudium meum et corona mea* ("my crown and my joy"). This last phrase was the one that the Founder of Opus Dei wrote on the back of a photograph of Juan's ten children. The ideas which Juan heard in 1948 marked a deep innovation in the role of the laity in the Church.

In the thirties, when he talked about **matrimonial vocation,** and presented marriage as a way to sanctity, Msgr. Escrivá's words sounded newer still. Dr. Jiménez Vargas, who attended the circles and meditations given by the Founder of Opus Dei, stresses this. He also points out that his talks on the virtue of purity sounded tremendously original and new. "Nowadays," he says, "after so many editions of *The Way*, it sounds familiar, but it is important to imagine oneself back in 1933, bearing in mind the way devout young people used to think then, and how widespread were certain forms of preaching on chastity, which led more than anything else to a deformed and even Freudian view of the matter. For a start, he preferred to talk about purity rather than chastity, and did so with that positive and optimistic outlook of his which is now so well known." His teaching on matrimony caused even more surprise. It was later summarised in three points of *The Way* (numbers 26, 27 and 28). Professor Jiménez Vargas notes that "when he said that marriage was for the rank and file (neither *The Way* nor *Consideraciones espirituales* had yet been published) I can assure you that his words fired those who thought they had a 'rank and file' vocation just as much as those who thought that they had another vocation. It never crossed anybody's mind to get the wrong idea and nobody felt hurt by this remark, which, besides, was very amusing when you heard it from him directly."

His way of presenting the christian virtue of purity encouraged people to fight, because he always stressed the positive side of purity. It came across as something attractive and affirmative, to be practised by someone in love. This is how the Founder of Opus Dei defined it in a homily given on Christmas Day 1970: **Chastity — not just continence, but the decisive affirmation of a will that's in love — is a virtue that maintains the youthfulness of love in any state in life.**

Msgr. Escrivá de Balaguer had long before prepared the path along which countless members of Opus Dei would struggle for sanctity in their marital vocation. It would take years to obtain legal recognition for this vocation. But the Founder of Opus Dei waited, trusting in the Will of God. In the meantime he was forming souls so that when the time came they would be ready to receive God's explicit call.

One such person was Antonio Ivars Moreno, who began attending apostolic activities run by Opus Dei in Valencia in 1940. They were held in a house at 16 Samaniego Street, which was soon to become a students' residence. Antonio Ivars remembers: "The Director was Don Pedro Casciaro and he was helped by Don Amadeo de Fuenmayor, who has been a friend of mine for many years. One day they called me and Pedro told me briefly that there were people in the Work who had given themselves with complete dedication to God. But he added that the Father had said that I had **a vocation for marriage,** and that they should leave me be. I was lucky because the Father was in Valencia then and I was able to tell him what Pedro and Amadeo had said to me. He confirmed what they had said, adding that when I got married he would be delighted to perform the ceremony."

He urged each and every one, whether single, engaged, married, or priest, to explore the depths of love, warning them against the great temptation of selfishness, which rendered the problems created by that very passion insoluble. He encouraged them to flee from sensuality because, as he often repeated, sensuality cuts back the wings of love, and debases the great ideals of which the human heart is capable.

He taught young people what he had written in *The Way* and what he repeated with other words in 1974 to a large group of young men in São Paulo: **I pray to Saint Raphael the Archangel that, as with Tobias, he may lead those of you who are to form a family, to find a good and clean love on earth. I bless this earthly love of yours, and I bless your future home. And I ask John the Apostle, who fell so deeply in love with Jesus Christ and who was courageous at the foot of Christ's Cross — the only man: the others fled — when the Redeemer was conquering and seemed conquered; I ask that young but strong disciple, to help you, if Our Lord is asking more of you.**

The Founder of Opus Dei said farewell to those young people with the blessing given to those who are going on a journey: **We are all on our way in this life. . . . My blessing is the blessing that Tobias gave to his son when he went, accompanied by Saint Raphael the Archangel, to collect the money due to his father. The fact is he also went, without realising it, to find a bride, and found one who was good and pretty and rich. It is a beautiful story of clean and noble love, a chaste and fruitful love, such as the love your parents have, which I bless.**

A few days earlier, also in São Paulo, he encouraged married people — as he had always done throughout his life — to take the affection of courtship as a model for their own love: **Love one another**

very much. The love of christian spouses — especially if they
are children of God in Opus Dei — is like good wine. It im-
proves with time, and appreciates in value. . . . Well, your love
is far more important than the best wine in the world. It is a
splendid treasure that Our Lord has wished to grant you. Keep
it carefully. Do not throw it away! Look after it!

Later on, in that same conversation, answering another question
Msgr. Escrivá de Balaguer insisted: **There is nothing wrong in
showing the pure affection you have for each other in front of
the children; it would be wrong not to show it. For the sake of
modesty, don't be over-affectionate in front of the children;
but love each other very much, because Our Lord is very happy
when you do so. And when the years go by — you are all still
very young — do not be afraid: your affection will not lessen;
it will increase. It will even become more enthusiastic; it will
become once again the affection of your courting days.**

He had a gift for treating **divine things in a human way, and
human things in a divine way.** He drew examples from human love
to open people's eyes to the love of God. When he preached on the Holy
Eucharist (where, he would exclaim, Christ is a **prisoner for Love!**),
he would speak about how a good mother washes and perfumes her
baby, and presses it to her heart, and almost devours it with kisses.
Well, Christ succeeds where men fail: he becomes food, life of our life:
"take and eat" he tells us.

In his homily on Maundy Thursday 1960, he evoked the human
experience of two people who love each other and yet are forced to
part: **They would like to stay together forever, but duty — in one
form or another — forces them to separate. They are unable
to fulfil their desire of remaining close to each other, so man's
love — which, great as it may be, is limited — seeks a symbolic
gesture. People who make their farewells exchange gifts or
perhaps a photograph with a dedication so ardent that it seems
almost enough to burn that piece of paper. They can do no
more, because a creature's power does not match its desire.**

**Where we fall short, Our Lord succeeds. Jesus Christ,
perfect God and perfect Man, leaves us, not a symbol, but a
reality. He himself stays behind. He will go to the Father, but
he will also remain among men. He will leave us, not simply
a gift that will make us remember him, not an image that
becomes blurred with time, like a photograph that soon fades**

and yellows, and has no meaning except for those who were the protagonists of that loving moment. He is really present under the appearances of bread and wine, with his Body and Blood, with his Soul and Divinity.

He encouraged everyone he met to be straightforward with God, to talk to him with the same heart and the same words one uses when talking to people one loves on earth; or **without saying any words out loud, while you are in the street, at a meal, smiling at someone, studying. . . .**

On more than one occasion, when asked the question "Father, teach me an ejaculatory prayer", he reacted spontaneously:

I should give you a good spanking. . . . An ejaculatory prayer? Is it possible that you do not know how to speak with your heart? How would you have spoken to your girl friend? What do you want: to be "prompted" as to what to say to your girl friend? Well, it is just the same when you are speaking to God Our Lord.

Human love was his point of departure for helping others understand the sanctifying treasure buried in the thousand details of daily life which a soul in love knows how to unearth. It is not surprising, therefore, that in explaining the meaning of marriage, he stressed aspects which might appear trivial.

A conversation which took place in São Paulo reflects exactly the tone with which Msgr. Escrivá de Balaguer used to address all who were called to sanctify their married life. It was a very lively dialogue and practically impossible to reproduce in writing. The woman who was asking the questions was so moved that her emotion once or twice got the better of her. The first interruption came from the Founder of Opus Dei, when he heard her saying that she was twenty-three years married and had five children. . . .

Really! You can't be telling the truth. . . . Twenty-three years! So young and so pretty!

She had asked how she could maintain and increase in her daily life the enthusiasm of the early days of her marriage.

Sit down, my daughter, sit down. You will be . . . How do you say sweetheart in Portuguese?

Namorada, they answered him.

. . . enamoured for ever, always. You have to win over your husband each day, and he you.

(. . .) You will be able to do this if you see your husband as

he really is: a great part of your heart, all your heart! If you bear in mind that he belongs to you and you to him; if you remember that you have an obligation to make him happy, to share in his joys and his sorrows, his sickness and his health. . . .

And Msgr. Escrivá de Balaguer, as if addressing all the wives who were in the packed hall of the Palace of Conventions in the Anhembi Park, continued:

You know more than anyone in the world, because love is most wise. When your husband comes back from work, from his job, from his professional tasks, don't let him find you in a temper. Do yourself up, look pretty, and, as the years go by, decorate the facade even more, as they do with old buildings. He'll be so grateful to you! Very often, when he's been annoyed at work, he will have thought about God and about you, and he will have said: "I'll be going home, and . . . what a relief! There I will find a haven of peace, of happiness, of affection and beauty." For in his eyes there is nothing in the world more beautiful than you. (. . .) The day he comes in tired, and you notice it, or foresee it, you remember that dish he so likes: "That's what I'll prepare for him." And you don't tell him, so as not to make him feel embarrassed. You give him a surprise, and he looks at you with such affection. . . . And that's the way! That's the way!

The Founder of Opus Dei gave parents plenty of helpful advice, full of common sense and supernatural outlook. Much of it is to be found in his writings, but some has to be gleaned patiently from among his words to numerous gatherings and the personal conversations with those who visited him in Rome, or who had known him more intimately when he was in Spain. He really loved families, of all types — large families, families with fewer children, and those with none at all, because God has given them none even after they — and that includes **the husband,** he would always add — have tried all honest human and supernatural means. Only rarely did there escape from his lips words he had no relish to utter:

I am no friend of those families who for selfish reasons cut back the wings of love and make it sterile and barren . . . !

He advised parents to bring their children up in a christian manner, above all by good example: teaching them to pray, but without forcing them to say **long prayers: a little, but every day** (in this he was addressing mothers, of course, but fathers too); teaching them the value of money, but not giving them too much. He would add **it is better for them to have money only when they have earned it.** Children's freedom should be respected prudently. They should be encouraged to help others in ways suitable to their age, filling each day with little acts of service. In a word, parents should be aiming to make their house a **bright and cheerful home.** (In the last years of his life, how often he would bless **your children's guitars!**)

Msgr. Escrivá de Balaguer helped parents understand that their mutual affection is strengthened by the sorrows and difficulties of life. This is what he had to say to the editor of the women's magazine *Telva* in February 1968:

Anyone who thinks that love ends when the worries and difficulties that life brings with it begin, has a poor idea of marriage, which is a Sacrament and an ideal and a vocation. It is precisely then that love grows strong. Torrents of worries and difficulties are incapable of drowning true love because **people who sacrifice themselves generously together are brought closer by their sacrifice. As Scripture says,** aquae multae — **a host of difficulties, physical and moral** — non potuerunt exstinguere caritatem (Cant. 8:7) — **cannot extinguish love.**

Another journalist, Luis Ignacio Seco, published a very moving article after the death of his seven-year-old daughter, Martha. She had fallen ill with leukaemia in 1970, and Luis Ignacio had written to Msgr. Escrivá de Balaguer to ask him to pray for her. "His reply came very soon. He spoke to me about the **most lovable Will of God,** and assured me of his prayers. And he made me understand immediately that what we had at home was a hidden treasure, a marvel placed in our hands to help us to live our vocation as parents to the full, as direct and willing collaborators of Providence, as common or garden Christians who try to materialise without any show the wonderful love God has for all his children, for all mankind."

It was not necessary, however, to be an intellectual to grasp the Father's teaching about the duty to sanctify human love. His message found an echo among people of all levels of society. María is a member of Opus Dei who lives near Pozoalbero in the south of Spain. Her husband, a simple farm labourer who met Msgr. Escrivá de Balaguer in Pozoalbero in November 1972, provides us with an example. She says that her husband had said to her at the time:

"Now I'll have to fold my clothes tidily, because Monsignor is here. . . ."

That was his way of practising what he had learned from the Founder of Opus Dei. María was also very happy because she had noticed that "since he had seen the Father" her husband was making a real effort not to get annoyed even with the small domestic matters that crop up in all families.

Msgr. Escrivá de Balaguer had encouraging words for all who were going through trying circumstances. When it was humanly impossible to find a solution, he helped them at least to bear them. His interview with the editor of *Telva* offers a fairly comprehensive account (which is worth re-reading) of his attitude to the wide range of situations that can arise in married life: a married woman's work, its social value, marriage as a vocation, the number of children, childless couples, separation of husband and wife, quarrels and differences of opinion, the "generation gap", how to teach piety, child guidance, "trial marriages", the monotony of housework, comfort and sobriety, etc. Perhaps it would be true to say that one question was missing. It is one he was asked in São Paulo in May 1974:

"Unfortunately, today there are many divorcees. What attitude should a Catholic take towards such families, and towards the children of those families?"

First, understanding, my children. Nothing is gained by ill-treating people. When they are souls who need help, good advice, words of affection, we are not going to treat them badly. They are spiritually sick, just as there are others who are mentally or physically sick.

First step: don't ill-treat them.

Next, if they ask: "What do you think of my situation?" — give a clear answer: "Well . . . lamentable! I am very sorry but it is lamentable." What's the point of lying? But don't despair, because with the grace of God it can be put right. As they are often sentimental matters and there are children involved, it is difficult. However, such situations often find a solution, and, at the end of their lives, always.

Don't ill-treat them ever. Is that clear? And help the children of those families in whatever way you can. Let them not be ashamed, although the poor creatures cannot be very satisfied. It is a tremendous shock, but that is all the more reason for treating them well, affectionately, with a super-

natural sense, and showing them that we are Christians. So be very human and understanding as a first step, and be christian too. We are first of all human beings; and after that, with Baptism, comes the grace of being children of God. In your lives, in your relations with people, both the human virtues and the supernatural virtues should come through: your affectionate and friendly behaviour, because you try to be gentle and kind, and then the supernatural medicine you give with your good christian advice and with your example.

CHAPTER TWO

CALLED TO THE PRIESTHOOD

1. INTIMATIONS OF A SPECIAL DIVINE CALLING

I had never thought of becoming a priest, or of dedicating myself to God. The problem had not arisen, because I did not think it was for me. Furthermore, it annoyed me to think that I could one day become a priest, so much so that I felt anti-clerical. I loved priests very much, because my upbringing at home was profoundly religious; I had been taught to respect and venerate the priesthood. But it was not for me; it was for others.

That was how Msgr. Escrivá de Balaguer explained it. What is more, no one who knew him as a boy thought he would be a priest. God's calling, however, was making itself felt, little by little, without any overtly extraordinary happenings. What has happened to so many souls, seems to have been especially providential in the case of the man who was later to be the Founder of Opus Dei, and who would teach people to sanctify the normal things of each day, warning them to guard against the **temptation of seeking the extraordinary:** for ordinary Christians sanctity is not to be found in doing peculiar or "difficult" things, but rather in turning **the prose of each day into heroic verse.**

The temptation to do extraordinary things appears several times in the course of the Gospel. After Christ's forty-day fast in the desert, the devil tries to draw him away from his redemptive mission by pressing him to shun human sufferings (hunger, thirst, pain), the very instruments with which he is to carry out the Redemption. It is not just Satan who does this sort of thing. Jesus' relatives keep urging him to go to Judea to win fame during the Feast of the Tabernacles. His own disciples, too, incite him to do something striking for the people to admire. When John and James ask him to send down fire from Heaven to consume the inhabitants of a Samaritan village, Our Lord once again has to lead them away from this temptation of relying on the abnormal: "You do not understand what spirit it is you share." So it continues right up to the dramatic moment on Calvary, when the chief priests and scribes deride him, telling him that if only he will come down from the Cross, they will believe. Christ rejects the temptation. He has come to redeem the human race by suffering and death, not by spectacular exploits. If this was not so, what was the purpose of his thirty years of hidden life and work in Nazareth?

God uses ordinary events to attract souls to his love. On occasions he may work great miracles, which may pass unnoticed to the human eye. But the greatest miracle continues to be the normal, simple operation of his ordinary providence. It was along paths such as these that Josemaría Escrivá de Balaguer's vocation came. He often repeated this to the members of the Work to warn them against the temptation of seeking what is spectacular and striking:

There come to mind so many manifestations of God's Love during my adolescent years, when I sensed that Our Lord wanted something of me, though I didn't know what it was. Ordinary events and happenings, seemingly without significance, and yet He used them to place within my soul a divine restlessness. And so I well understand that love so human and yet so divine of Theresa of the Child Jesus, whose heart is moved when, in turning the pages of a book, she comes across a picture of the wounded hand of the Redeemer. Things of this kind happened to me as well, and they stirred me and they led me to daily Communion, to purification, to Confession and to penance.

When he met people who showed clear signs that God was calling them, yet were afraid or lacked generosity, he helped them to consider how God goes about things. He was asked about this in Buenos Aires in 1974. Someone referred to several friends of his who only needed a tiny, little push. . . .

I won't be the one who gives it. . . . Because a vocation to Opus Dei is divine. And because, my son . . . I resisted as best I could. Mea culpa, mea culpa. **I resisted. I can distinguish two callings from God: one at the beginning, when I did not know what it was for, and I resisted. Later on . . . , later on I resisted no longer, once I knew what it was for.**

God was preparing him gradually, even against his own personal inclinations and plans:

I remember that when I was in secondary school, we studied Latin. I did not like it. In a silly way — how it hurts me now! — I used to say: "Latin is for priests and monks. . . ." You see how far away I was from wanting to be a priest?

On 1 July 1974, in Santiago de Chile, the Founder of Opus Dei was encouraging a large group of people to struggle generously, for love of Jesus Christ, and to draw many souls to God. To help them overcome temptations of cowardice, or a false respect for the freedom of others, he concluded: **Jesus Christ did not ask me for permission to enter my life. If anybody had told me, years ago, that I was going to be a priest. . . . And yet, here I am!**

He would often come back to this idea: **I never thought of dedicating myself to God. The problem had not arisen, because I did not think it was for me. But Our Lord was preparing things. He gave me one grace after another, overlooking my defects, my errors as a child, and my errors as an adolescent.**

One very frosty winter's day, in Logroño, Josemaría, still an adolescent, saw the bare footprints of a Carmelite in the snow. Those footprints so moved his heart that the desires of a great love were enkindled. Seeing what the friar had sacrificed for the love of God, Josemaría asked himself what he was doing for God.

Josemaría felt these **intimations of Love** when he was fifteen or sixteen years old. He was perfectly aware that Our Lord wanted something of him, but at the same time he did not know what it was. That winter, in the early months of 1918, he went to talk to Fr. José Miguel on several occasions. He was one of the friars who lived next to the convent of Discalced Carmelites and looked after their church.

It was then that Josemaría thought of becoming a priest: **Why did I become a priest?** he was to reflect years later. **Because I thought it would be easier that way to fulfil something God**

wanted, which I did not know. For about eight years before my ordination I had intimations of it, but I did not know what it was. And I did not come to know until 1928. That is why I became a priest.

From that time he prayed constantly for that intention which he still did not know. As the years went by, a clamour of ejaculatory prayers poured out of his soul: *Domine, ut sit! Domina, ut sit!* (Lord, may it be! Lady, may it be!); and he would proclaim aloud, as if singing, those words of Our Lord: *Ignem veni mittere in terram, et quid volo nisi ut accendatur?* (I have come to spread fire over the earth; and what better wish can I have than that it should be kindled?) The answer made itself felt unmistakably: *Ecce ego quia vocasti me!* (Behold me Lord, because you have called me.)

Josemaría talked with his father about it. Don José Escrivá listened with surprise to his son's plans. As he had always been quick to accept the Will of God, he respected and loved the way Our Lord was tracing out for his son. It must have cost him a lot because he had other plans, but he backed up his son's decision: **I owe him my vocation,** the Founder of Opus Dei used always to say.

The Baroness of Valdeolivos recalls a story that took place in the summer of 1919. Don José Escrivá went to Fonz to spend a few days with relatives and he showed them some photographs of his children: there was Santiago, who had just been born — "he is the Benjamin," he remarked — with Carmen and Josemaría. He was unashamedly proud of them. Showing a photograph of Josemaría, he commented pensively: "He has told me he wants to be a priest, but at the same time he is going to study law. It will mean a bit of a sacrifice for us. . . ."

The Founder of Opus Dei tells his side of the story:

One fine day I told my father that I wanted to be a priest: it was the only time I saw him cry. He had other plans in his mind but he did not object. He told me:

"My son, think it over carefully. A priest has to be a saint. . . . It is very hard to have no house, no home, to have no love on earth. Think about it a bit more, but I will not oppose your decision."

And he took me to speak to a friend of his who was a priest, the administrator of the Collegiate Church of Logroño.

The Collegiate Church of Logroño, commonly known as *La Redonda*, is now the Cathedral of the diocese of Calahorra, Logroño and La Calzada. The administrator at the time was Don Antolín Oñate

Oñate, who was in 1943 to be Master of Ceremonies of Calahorra. Don Antolín was a real institution in Logroño.

Don Albino Pajares, an army chaplain stationed in Logroño from February 1917 until May 1920, also helped Josemaría at his father's request.

Don Antolín and Don Albino encouraged him in his vocation and tutored him in philosophy, Latin, and in the first year of theology, which he did as an external student of the seminary of Logroño. The Founder of Opus Dei was always very grateful to these two priests.

We know, however, that he was not interested in an ecclesiastical "career"; he was not attracted by the idea of being a priest in the usual sense that this word had for the general public: **That was not what God was asking of me, and I knew it: I did not want to be a priest just for the sake of being a priest,** el cura **as they say in Spain. I felt a great veneration for the clergy, but I did not want to be a priest in that way.**

From October 1918 he was an external student of the seminary. He also studied at home with a private tutor, Manuel Sanmartín. In the academic year 1919–1920 he finished the first year of theology. His marks were *meritissimus* in all subjects but one, in which he got *benemeritus*.

A fellow student of his, Don Manuel Calderón, declares that he was a good student, and showed he had good general knowledge: "clean, elegant, refined, it all went to show that he came from a first class family". Another companion, Don Amadeo Blanco, remembers distinctly his blue jacket, high collar, and bow tie; however, what really caught his attention was his smile, his pleasant, kindly character and his affable temperament. Don Máximo Rubio has similar memories: he remembers Josemaría as a well-mannered young man, who dressed with care and was refined in the way he dealt with others; a good student, serious, but — in Fr. Rubio's opinion — with a rather reserved character: "he was a man of few words, very dutiful and pious." On the other hand, Don Pedro Baldomero Larios — the son of a bookbinder who was a great friend of Josemaría's father — recalls him as "likeable, communicative, cheerful and very agreeable to talk to. I was very impressed by him because I considered him to be very talented."

Don Pedro Baldomero Larios was an external student of the seminary, a year or so below Don Máximo and Don José María Millán, who, though now dead, was at that time, it seems, the closest friend of the future Founder of Opus Dei. Josemaría's life was shared between his family and his classes, and little else. The students used to meet sometimes in the house of the Larios, or the Escrivás, or the Rubios. Sometimes they would walk to Lardero — which seemed a long way to them in those days — or they went crab-fishing in the river.

Larios, perhaps because he was the youngest, does not have anything special to say about their life of piety: "We used to go to daily Mass at the seminary even though we were external students. We then went back home for breakfast, and then to class." Máximo Rubio confirms that Josemaría, for a time, often went to the Carmelite convent and spent long hours there. Máximo Rubio also refers to the apostolic drive of Josemaría: in their conversations after class, he helped them see how much could be done for the pupils of the Institute, and he showed the sorrow he felt for the apparent lack of christian spirit among those young people.

The boarders at the seminary gave catechism classes which were very well attended. It would seem that the external students did not help much with the catechism, because Don Amadeo Blanco — who was a boarder — was impressed by the way Josemaría cooperated. Though under no obligation, he was there every Sunday in the church of the seminary where the catechism classes were held, and made himself available "for whatever they wanted him to do".

Josemaría was not an external student of the seminary of Logroño for long. In September 1920, he moved to Saragossa to continue his theological studies in the Pontifical University of San Valero and San Braulio.

2. THE YEARS IN SARAGOSSA

Time passed, and many hard and distressing things happened, which I will not tell you about, because they do not make me suffer, but you would be saddened by them. They were axe blows struck at the tree by God Our Lord. From that tree, he was shaping a beam that would be used, in spite of its weakness, to do his Work. Almost without realising it, I kept repeating: Domine, ut videam! Domine, ut sit! **I did not know what it was He wanted, but I went on and on, without fully corresponding to God's goodness, waiting for what I was later to receive: a succession of graces, one after another, which I**

did not know how to describe and I called them operative, because they so dominated my will that I hardly needed to make any effort. I carried on, without doing anything unusual, working with just average intensity.... Those were the years in Saragossa.

In that city Josemaría began a way of life which was very different from that which he had led up to then. It was divided between the seminary of San Carlos and the Pontifical University of San Valero and San Braulio.

The Pontifical University was in the Square of La Seo, next to the Archbishop's House. There were courses leading to the degrees of licentiate and doctor in philosophy, theology and canon law. The seminarians attended lectures at the Pontifical University, while the rest of their priestly training — their study, life of piety, and discipline — was provided in the seminaries.

Towards the end of September 1920, Josemaría joined the seminary of San Francisco de Paula, which occupied two floors of the building belonging to the San Carlos seminary, but had an independent oratory and refectory. The seminarians wore a sleeveless black tunic, with a red sash and a metal badge with the sun on it and the word *charitas*. From San Carlos they went to class along El Coso to the Square of La Seo. They walked in double file, accompanied by an inspector. In San Carlos they did half an hour of meditation and attended Mass before breakfast. After morning lectures, normally for three periods, they went back to the seminary for lunch. In the afternoon they went to the university again. When they came back there was recreation, study and Rosary. Between supper and bedtime, they said prayers and listened to a short talk which outlined some points for the following day's meditation. On Thursday afternoons they went for walks, all in line, through quiet districts or to the countryside. On Sundays those who had relatives, in Saragossa could go out to spend the day with them.

One of the reasons why Josemaría had moved from Logroño was that in Saragossa he could also study for a law degree at the university. As we have just seen, his father had mentioned this possibility in Fonz in the summer of 1919. While he was waiting to see clearly what God wanted of him, Josemaría thought that he would be better prepared, humanly speaking, to fulfil God's will if he had a civil degree as well. His father also advised him to study for a law degree, in spite of the financial sacrifice involved in his moving to Saragossa.

A number of close relatives and intimate friends of the family lived in Saragossa. Among them was an uncle of his, Canon Carlos Albás, who was Archdeacon at La Seo. However, the friends Josemaría had at that time point out that Don Carlos and the family of his nephew were not on particularly close terms, through no fault of the Escrivás. It seems that the canon did not think too highly of his brother-in-law and more or less blamed him for the reversal of the family fortunes. A contemporary witness, referring to the canon's intransigent attitude towards Josemaría's father, observes: "It was a great injustice not to have appreciated the constantly honest and upright behaviour of that man, which led him to wind up his business, because he was more concerned about keeping his christian conscience clear, than about his own material interests." The fact is that Don Carlos did not go to Logroño in 1924 when Don José died, nor did he attend Josemaría's first Mass in 1925.

Life in the seminary was not easy for Josemaría. He must have found it hard to settle into the San Carlos establishment, for until then he had had no experience of the ordinary channels of clerical training. The atmosphere of the state Institute and of St. Anthony's College in Logroño had been very different to what he now found among the seminarians of Saragossa.

A fellow student of his in the seminary, who today is a notary in a Spanish city, has described in precise terms the atmosphere of the place. He would not have done so if he had not been asked to do so expressly. In recalling those years, he would be hurt to think that his words might be misinterpreted. He states that, as a notary, he only wants to give the facts, which are justifiable and reasonable, and says that he fully realises that very holy men were trained in that seminary.

Many of the pupils came to San Carlos with the traditional virtues of the rural areas of Aragon, but also with some defects that were well known at that time: very elementary education, a certain contempt for appearances due to a misguided notion of sincerity, a disregard for personal hygiene, etc. Christian virtues made up for much of this. In fact, whenever the Founder of Opus Dei referred to his time in the seminary, he said that all he could remember about his companions were their virtues and their desire to serve the Church.

Some students from the beginning did not understand Josemaría's bearing, deportment and manners. When he was appointed superior of the seminary, José María Román Cuartero was assigned to him as his attendant. Cuartero always considered him very correct and more refined than the other seminarians. Cuartero mentions, for instance, that Josemaría washed daily from head to foot, something which the others did not do. This fact and other things about Josemaría made Cuartero suspect that Josemaría would never end up as a priest. Cuartero felt Josemaría had the human qualities to make a better career for himself. Another fellow student, Don Francisco Artal Luesma, comments on that contrast in a more positive way. He feels that Josemaría's stay in the seminary was a clear manifestation of his response to God's will. His external cleanliness and the care with which he dressed were a proof of his love for priestly dignity and a reflection of the refinement of his soul and of his interior life.

Naturally enough not everyone saw things in that light: some interpreted them in a completely opposite way; but this lack of understanding had no effect on him. Another companion remembers him saying: **I do not think it is a virtue to be dirty.** He argued his case "gently, without bitterness, with his typical sense of humour". Don Agustín Callejas Tello, now parish priest of Magallón, makes similar observations: Josemaría was very understanding and had a great sense of humour; he was witty and could see the amusing side of things; he knew many jokes and told them well: "Those of us who were his friends greatly admired his witty commentaries, and the festive or satirical tone of his epigrams. These epigrams quite surprised us, because they indicated a fluent command of the language, and reflected his familiarity with the classical authors."

Also, Josemaría's motives in going to the seminary were, up to a point, different from those which brought many other seminarians: he was not "seeking a career", and that is why churchy subjects — a frequent theme of conversations — were not his only concern. Furthermore, especially after he had been appointed superior, it was easy for him to be absent from the seminary, even though, as one of his fellow students recalls: "he went out very little and when he did he came back soon, for he always had something to do". This, however, did give rise to misunderstandings, although Josemaría was kind with everyone and sought to be friends with all. Fr. Agustín Callejas describes him as "a pioneer, forward-looking, with a free and independent spirit, and it was this which on occasions some, through their own lack of maturity, could not understand and which, unjustly, they took as a sign of arrogance".

Even one of the teachers formed this impression of him. Some of this teacher's notes are still preserved and in them, referring to the academic year 1920–21, he describes Josemaría as "inconstant and arrogant, but well mannered and polite". The teacher observes that his piety is good, but his application and discipline poor. The following year he writes "good" under these two headings. (As a matter of fact in the year 1920–21, Josemaría got *meritissimus* in four subjects, and *benemeritus* in another; in the following years he got *meritissimus* in all subjects.) But the teacher did not change his opinion on Josemaría's character, even though it did not fit the results: top marks in all subjects is hardly a sign of inconstancy.

There is also a marginal note on that manuscript, though unfortunately it bears no date. It refers to what must have been the period of greatest tension. The note says literally: "He (Josemaría) had a row with Don Julio Cortés and received due punishment, the acceptance and fulfilment of which was to his credit. In my opinion it was his opponent who attacked him first and hardest, uttering against him (against Josemaría) coarse words improper for a cleric, and insulting him in my presence in the Cathedral of La Seo." I have not been able to find out anything else for certain about this incident; only that many years later, on 8 October 1952, in a way which does him honour, Don Julio Cortés wrote to the Founder of Opus Dei from Jaén — where he later died as the chaplain of the El Neveral tuberculosis sanatorium — asking for forgiveness, "repentant in the most submissive and unconditional way, *mea culpa* . . . !"

It might have been the most disagreeable incident, but it was by no means the only one. Josemaría's soul was being forged to face far graver difficulties which he would meet throughout his life.

Nobody has ever doubted that his was a life of intense, pleasant, cheerful and attractive piety, which was not only compatible with, but was the basis of his constant good humour and optimistic outlook; but he did not give any importance to what he did, nor did he brag about anything: with naturalness he did what he could to pass unnoticed. One day, a companion of his discovered a cilice in his room, and he told others about it. This time Josemaría became serious, and he showed them that it was not in good taste or prudent to gossip about the piety of others.

Don Agustín Callejas admired the way he did his daily meditation in the seminary: his attitude was one of intense prayer, concentration and recollection. Don Agustín was also struck by the way in which he received Holy Communion. He was devout, but without doing anything peculiar, "with his hands joined together over his breast, his body erect, and a firm step".

His relationship with his fellow students changed somewhat in the year 1922–23, because in that year he was appointed superior of the seminary. Some recall that Cardinal Soldevila — then Archbishop of Saragossa — made a lot of him. When he met the students in the seminary, or the Cathedral or elsewhere, the Cardinal used to single Josemaría out in front of the others and ask him how he was and how he was getting on in his studies. Sometimes he would add: "Come and see me when you have time." Fr. José López Sierra, the rector of the seminary, affirmed that the Cardinal had appointed Josemaría superior of the seminarians "because of his exemplary conduct, no less than his application". In the rector's opinion, he stood out among the other seminarians "for his refined manners, his kindness and simplicity in his dealings with others, and marked modesty". He further adds: "He showed respect for his superiors and was understanding and affable towards his companions. He was held in high esteem by the former and admired by the latter."

To be a seminary superior or inspector — official documents use the two terms indiscriminately — it was necessary to be a tonsured cleric. That was why Cardinal Soldevila conferred the tonsure on Josemaría on 28 September 1922, on his own, in a chapel of the Archbishop's House in Saragossa, which is no longer in existence.

The superiors, or inspectors, were chosen from among the more promising and pious pupils. Their task consisted in directing studies, seeing that discipline and rules were observed, and accompanying the pupils when they went out to class or for a walk, etc. Although the inspectors were seminarians as well, they were considered in the rules to be superiors and had to be obeyed and respected. They were also given some external privileges. They had a single room which was rather larger than the rest, and an attendant or servant. (These attendants were seminarians on a scholarship and they had to clean the rooms of the superiors and serve the seminarians at table. Something similar still exists at some famous schools and universities in Britain and America.) At San Carlos, there were two inspectors, one for arts and philosophy, and the other for theology students. Their job, according to an old boy of the seminary, "was difficult, because the younger boys used to give a lot of trouble, as could be expected from boys of that age. Josemaría never lost control or became flustered. He was always kind, prudent and well-mannered."

José María Román Cuartero, the attendant assigned to Josemaría when he was appointed inspector, remembers those times when, among other services, he used to make Josemaría's bed each morning and serve him at the separate table for superiors in the refectory. He was always impressed by "his kindness and patience". When Josemaría saw Cuartero was annoyed, he would help him get over his annoyance with some kind words or a joke. And he shared his food with him, for the superiors had special meals. "I now realise that he did these mortifications without anyone noticing, in a very natural way."

Don José López Sierra, the rector of the seminary, always praised Josemaría's apostolic zeal as director of the seminarians. He wanted to win them all for Christ; that they should all be one in Christ; and he succeeded because he did things well. He was not fond of punishing. He formed the young seminarians with a "charming simplicity and gentleness"; "his sympathetic and attractive appearance was enough to contain the most rebellious; a simple, welcoming smile would come to his lips when he noticed some edifying detail in one of his seminarians; a discreet, penetrating look, at times sad, and very compassionate, was enough to quell the dissident".

The years in the seminary passed by. We also know that he spent many hours in prayer on the balcony which overlooked the right hand or epistle side of the church of San Carlos.

He spent his holidays in Logroño, and most likely also went back to Fonz, where his uncle Fr. Teodoro lived. Some summers he went to Villel (Teruel) to stay with the family of Don Antonio Moreno, then vice-president of the seminary of San Carlos. We are told this by Carmen (*née* Noailles), the widow of another Antonio Moreno (a nephew of the former), who was more or less the same age as Josemaría and studied medicine at the University of Saragossa. His life in that village was very normal. They chatted, and went for walks. They went fishing or crab-catching. They also went on the occasional excursion. Carmen Noailles mentions several details which indicate the refinement with which Josemaría practised the virtues of purity and modesty.

He never went out with girls there. His elegant manners, fine figure and agreeable personality made him very attractive to them. When Antonio or some other friend made some comment to him on the subject, he would cut them short, saying something like: **If they knew me on the inside, as I really am . . .** If someone told jokes that were in poor taste, or smutty, he would stop them affectionately but firmly with a very forthright answer. "I never saw him make the slightest concession. He did not allow any banter or loose commentaries on this matter."

The members of that household cared a lot for him, because Josemaría was very likeable: "he was very gentle, discreet and prudent, but affectionate, and his natural good humour was constantly apparent". They considered him as one of the family.

These memories of Carmen Noailles refer to the summer of 1921 or 1922, perhaps to both. In the summer of 1923 Josemaría began his law studies and sat his first examinations in September. He was already a tonsured cleric when he matriculated at the faculty for the year 1922–23. He started fourth-year theology in October 1922. On 17 December 1922 he received the minor orders of porter and lector from Cardinal Soldevila, and on the 21st (also in the Archbishop's House) those of exorcist and acolyte. The Cardinal was to die on 4 June 1923, assassinated by anarchists.

In the meantime, Josemaría had still not seen what the other thing was that he felt the love of God had in store for him. He studied and prayed and placed himself in the hands of the Virgin Mary. He made daily visits to Our Lady of Pilar. In the newspaper *El Noticiero* of Saragossa, he wrote on 11 October 1970: **I continue to have a filial love for her. And to invoke her with the same faith as in the early twenties, when Our Lord made me sense he had something in store for me.**

He appealed to her to solve what was taking shape in his soul for, as he explained on another occasion, he felt he was going about **half blind, always wondering why: why am I becoming a priest? Our Lord wants something, what is it? And in a not very classical Latin, using the words of the blind man of Jericho, I repeated again and again:** Domine, ut videam! Ut sit! Ut sit! **"May that which you want, and I don't know, be."**

A prayer which he repeated for years actually found its way on to a statue of Our Lady, which was later found by someone:

Years, many years, went by, and one day, when I was in Rome, the Central Directress came to me and said: "Father, we have received a statue of Our Lady of Pilar, which you had in Saragossa." I answered: "No, I don't remember." She went on: "Yes, look at it: there is something written by you." It was such a horrible statue, that I did not think it possible that it could have been mine. She showed it to me, and on the base of this plaster image there it was, written with a nail: Domina, ut sit! **with the exclamation mark I always put after the Latin ejaculations I write. "Lady, may it be!" And a date: 24-9-924.**

In June 1924 he had finished the fifth year of theology. On the 14th of that month he was ordained subdeacon in the church of the seminary of San Carlos, by Don Miguel de los Santos Díaz Gómara, a man who had a great affection for him. Don Miguel was the president of the seminary of San Carlos and he usually chose Josemaría to accompany him at functions which he had to preside over or when he went to administer the Sacraments.

Josemaría studied very hard in the summer of 1924 and took seven subjects in the September law examinations. That June he had only taken Spanish history, which was a subject he knew well from his secondary studies and from his wide reading. He always had a passion for history and a genuine scholarly love for the subject. Although during that academic year he had concentrated on his priestly training — it was only during the summer months that he studied for his civil career — he had applied to be examined in June because he had an excellent grounding in history. However, the professor let him know through mutual friends that should he sit the June exam he would be failed, because he had not attended lectures, and the professor considered this a personal affront. Josemaría was astonished as he had a keen sense of justice, and as an external student he was under no obligation to attend lectures. Besides, he knew the subject very well, so he went to be examined. He was failed without being allowed to do the examination.

In September, the professor acknowledged that he had acted unjustly, and assured him before the exams (through the same mutual friends) that all he had to do to pass was to do the exam. At the same September examinations Josemaría obtained *matrícula de honor* in Roman law and canon law; *sobresaliente* in political economics; *notable* in natural law; and a pass in history of law and civil law I.

The following academic year, 1924–25, he did very little in regard to his civil studies. Although he put his name down for four subjects, making use of the two scholarships obtained with the *matrículas de honor* of the previous year, he sat only for the civil law II examination. He obtained *notable* in this, but took no other exams either in June or September.

This is not really surprising for many important things happened that year. On 27 November 1924 Don José Escrivá died in Logroño. On 20 December, Josemaría was ordained deacon by Don Miguel de los Santos Díaz Gómara, in the church of the seminary of San Carlos. On 28 March 1925, the same Don Miguel de los Santos, who had been the auxiliary bishop of Cardinal Soldevila, ordained him priest. His first Mass was celebrated on the 30th at El Pilar, in Our Lady's Chapel. There were only a few people present at this Mass, about a dozen altogether. The new priest offered it for the repose of his father's soul. It was Monday of Passion Week, and the following day Don Josemaría was already in the small village of Perdiguera, where the parish priest had fallen ill. He supplied for him until 18 May.

In 1925–26, though he registered as an external student, he did attend lectures in the faculty of law. In June 1926 his subjects and marks were: international public law (*matrícula de honor*), mercantile law (*notable*), political law (*notable*), administrative law (pass). In the September examinations he got passes in criminal law, public finance and judicial procedures; and obtained *notable* in private international law. At this stage he had only one subject pending to get his law degree. It was on court practice and the issue of public documents. He availed himself of a royal ordinance published on 22 December 1926, by which students with only one or two subjects pending could take special examinations, and he passed the subject in the special examinations of January 1927. He thus qualified for the degree of *Licenciado en Derecho*, for a royal decree of 10 March 1917 was still extant by which all the general exams and practicals which hitherto had been required to obtain titles, had been abolished. It was enough to pay the fees— 37.50 pesetas — and he did this on 15 March 1927, at the same time as he asked to transfer to Madrid to do his doctorate there.

David Mainar Pérez remembers those years well, especially 1925–26 in which Don Josemaría, by then a priest, went regularly to the law faculty. He has not forgotten the bench in the patio of the university on which they sat and talked during the intervals between lectures. Don Josemaría "was very open in his dealings with others". He became a firm friend of the students, even with some who had grave doubts of faith. He adapted himself easily to the students' conversations, the language and content of which could have given rise to awkward situations for a priest. But, as David Mainar adds, "he had a special knack of coming out on top, with his wonderful sense of humour. There might be a moment of embarrassment; then, without losing his dignity, he would gently make himself respected. He was never abrupt."

Another fellow student, Juan Antonio Iranzo Torres, also mentions that they felt a bit uneasy with him at first, but his trust and frankness soon made them look on him as one of themselves. Iranzo Torres praises

Don Josemaría's simple and frank character. He was not at all conceited or self-important. Domingo Fumanal stresses this point: "It has been said that he was vain, which is absolutely false: it was just the opposite . . . ; he was an upright man, who stuck to his principles with a smile." He adds that he showed special care in his dealings with women.

He told Domingo Fumanal one day that he might be going to Madrid. Fumanal thought it a natural decision, because "in Saragossa he didn't have enough scope, nor did he get the help he deserved". Don Josemaría was wondering about applying for a job as a tutor, and Fumanal gave him some advice, in forthright student language, as to how he would have to change his attitude towards women from what it had been until then. His friend feared that the young priest would not get on in this type of work given the very refined manner in which he lived chastity.

Don Josemaría had planned to leave Saragossa, because he wanted to second God's wishes and he thought that what God was asking him (he still did not know exactly what it was) could be carried out more easily in a city like Madrid. In the meantime, awaiting new lights from God, he continued his priestly work in the diocese of Saragossa.

The day after his first Mass in the chapel of El Pilar, he left Saragossa for the village of Perdiguera, 24 kilometres away. It is in the extreme west of the district of Los Monegros and lies between the Sierra Alcubierre and the lower valley of the river Gállego. He lodged there with a family of country folk, who have all since died: Saturnino Arruga, his wife Prudencia (*née* Escanero) and a son. His priestly zeal was very much alive in the two months he spent there:

I lodged in the home of a very good countryman. He had a son who took the goats out every morning, and I felt for him, seeing him spend all day out there with the herd. I did my best to give him a few catechism lessons, so that he could make his first Holy Communion. Little by little I taught him a few things.

One day, to see how much he was learning, it occurred to me to ask him:

"What would you like to do if you were rich, very rich?"
"What does being rich mean?" he answered.
"To be rich is to have a lot of money, to have a bank. . . ."
"And . . . what is a bank?"
I explained it in a simple way and continued:

"To be rich is to have a lot of land, and instead of goats, very big cows. And to go to meetings, change suits three times a day. . . . What would you do if you were rich?"

His eyes opened wide, and then at last he said:

"I would like to eat lots of bowls of soup and wine!" All our ambitions come down to that; nothing is worth while. Funnily enough I have never forgotten that story. It struck me and it made me think: "Josemaría, it is the Holy Spirit speaking."

The Wisdom of God did this to teach me that the things of the earth, all of them, come to that: very, very little.

He worked in Perdiguera until 18 May 1925. His example impressed Teodoro Murillo Escuer, then an altar boy and now the sacristan of the parish. Don Josemaría's work consisted of confessions, Holy Mass, Rosary in the afternoon, Holy Hour on Thursdays, catechism classes, and first Holy Communions. He showed special concern for the sick. He visited them frequently and if he was asked for the sacraments he was always ready to oblige. "At that time," Teodoro recalls, "Holy Communion was only taken when people were seriously ill and it was taken in procession. Don Josemaría took it privately to all the sick who asked for it."

When Don Josemaría left, Teodoro Murillo really missed him. In such a short time he had become very fond of him, because he was "cheerful, very good natured, refined, simple and affectionate".

Don Josemaría returned to Saragossa. He put more time into his studies in order to finish his law degree. He was living with his mother, sister and brother in a house in San Miguel Street, which has since been pulled down. It was a little beyond the crossing with Santa Catalina Street. He taught Roman law and canon law at the Amado Institute, perhaps to help keep his family.

The director of that Institute, which was in 44 Don Jaime Street, was Don Santiago Amado Lóriga, an army captain with a science degree. Like similar academies in other Spanish towns, it offered classes in *Bachillerato* and in certain pre-university subjects. There were also some students preparing for the entrance exams to the engineering schools and the military academies, and for certain competitive examinations for state lawyers, judges, notaries, and registrars of property, and for other exams for entry into the civil service. Students of law, arts, science, commerce and education also studied there.

It must have been an educational establishment of some prestige, for in 1927 it began to publish a monthly magazine, in which, together with items of general information there appeared articles on law and on military, engineering and scientific subjects. People who were later to be university professors or well-known personalities of Spanish life figured among the teaching staff. The third issue of the magazine, dated March 1927, contains, for example, a note by Don Santiago Amado, explaining that there is no article by Luis Sancho Seral, one of the lecturers of the centre, because he had just been appointed professor of civil law at Saragossa University. This issue also contains an article by Fr. Josemaría Escrivá on "The form of marriage in current Spanish legislation". It is the first known published work of the future Founder of Opus Dei.

In Saragossa he usually said Mass at the church of San Pedro Nolasco which was run by the Jesuit Fathers. They lived in Torres de San Ildefonso but went to San Pedro Nolasco for their acts of worship (all the Fathers and Brothers of that community have now died). He went with young people to teach catechism in several places. One of them was in the district of Casablanca. In Holy Week of 1927 he was posted to Fombuena. In the register of the Archdiocese of Saragossa there is an entry (30 March 1925) recording his appointment as curate of the parish priest of Perdiguera. His name does not appear again in that register until 17 March 1927 when he is given permission to go to Madrid for two years for study reasons.

While he confidently awaited further light from God, Don Josemaría was — as he would be all his life — a priest through and through, dedicated to his ministry.

3. PRIESTLY SOUL AND LAY MENTALITY

"He was a priest, very much a priest, down to the last consequences. That was the indelible impression he made on those of us who knew him at the time," affirms Juan Jiménez Vargas, now a professor of medicine, who met the Founder of Opus Dei in 1932. In these pages we shall have ample opportunity to note the great diversity of "consequences" which flowed from Msgr. Escrivá de Balaguer's identification with his priesthood. All of them stem from one root: his love for the Holy Sacrifice of the Mass.

In 1967, Msgr. Escrivá de Balaguer commented: **I am in my sixty-fifth year and have made a marvellous discovery. I love to celebrate the Holy Mass, but yesterday I found it a tremendous effort. How hard it was! I then saw that the Mass is truly Opus Dei, work, as His first Mass — the Cross — was for Jesus Christ. I saw that the priest's job, celebrating Mass, involves the work of making the Holy Eucharist; he experiences pain and joy and tiredness. In my flesh I felt the exhaustion of a divine work.**

It was also an effort for Christ. His most Holy Humanity resisted having to open out his arms on the Cross, with an Eternal Priest's gesture. I have never found it so hard to celebrate the Holy Sacrifice as on that day when I felt that the Mass, too, is Opus Dei. It made me very glad, but it left me completely worn out.

Cardinal Marcelo González, the Primate of Spain, has written: "His whole life was, as it were, the prolongation of an uninterrupted Mass that gave glory to the Father, sought to obtain pardon for sin through the grace of the Sacrament and put professional work and family concerns as a purified host on the altar. All this is what I have seen in the conversations he had, what I have gleaned from his writings and seen verified in those priests of Opus Dei I know."

The Founder of Opus Dei has written some wonderful pages on the Holy Mass and on the Eucharist. They reflect his loving heart. For him the Mass was an **epithalamium,** a nuptial song, an expression of love.

These writings have influenced many souls all over the world to savour the divine fact that the Holy Mass is **the centre and root of the interior life,** as Msgr. Escrivá de Balaguer has constantly taught ever since he was a young priest, and as was to appear textually many years later in documents of the Second Vatican Council.

The descriptions by the Founder of Opus Dei of the Holy Mass are moving and exciting, because they transmit an experience into which he put his whole heart and soul. "I believe that his great love was the Holy Eucharist," says Don Joaquín Mestre Palacio, the Prior of the Basilica of *Nuestra Señora de los Desamparados* in Valencia. He adds: "I recall with what affection, veneration and piety he showed His Grace the Archbishop (Marcelino Olaechea) and myself the oratories of Bruno Buozzi (the central offices of Opus Dei), paying special attention to the Tabernacle. He showed it to us with the same awe and reverence with which a young priest, in love with his ministry, would show the chalice for his first Mass."

Many people have been present at a Mass celebrated by Msgr. Escrivá de Balaguer. There is a unanimous agreement about the intense, caring and profoundly devout way in which he said it.

Don Laureano Castán Lacoma, the present Bishop of Siguenza and Guadalajara, has never forgotten the Masses said by the recently-ordained Don Josemaría at Fonz in the summer of 1926 or 1927. Don Laureano was then a seminarian and was spending his holidays in his native town of Fonz. They coincided there when Don Josemaría and his family visited their uncle, Fr. Teodoro, the chaplain to the Morer family. Don Laureano sometimes served his Mass in the chapel of the Otal family (the Barons of Valdeolivos) who were great friends of theirs. Don Laureano praises "the piety and fervour with which he celebrated the Holy Sacrifice of the Mass, which I followed with great piety and devotion, and this did not pass unnoticed by Msgr. Escrivá, as Don Alvaro del Portillo recently told me by letter. No doubt he was already practising what he was to put into writing later on: **The Mass is a divine action, trinitarian, not human. The priest who celebrates serves Our Lord's designs, lending Him his body and voice. The priest does not act in his own name but** in persona et in nomine Christi, **in the person of Christ and in the name of Christ."**

Pedro Rocamora was another who served the Mass of the Founder of Opus Dei. He did so in Madrid in the chapel of the Patronato de Enfermos, in Santa Engracia Street (now García Morato Street). He used often to go to early Mass before going to university: "Each word he said had a profound meaning and a special tone. He savoured the concepts. . . . Don Josemaría seemed to be detached from human surroundings and was, as it were, tied to the divinity by invisible bonds." Rocamora knew the Latin text of the Mass by heart, and could therefore follow the liturgy well. Although so many years have elapsed, for this took place in 1929, he still recalls those Masses with emotion: "After Mass on those mornings in the chapel of Santa Engracia, those of us who had served Fr. Escrivá sometimes couldn't contain our tears." For the record, Rocamora adds that he considers himself a normal man, neither over-sensitive nor exaggeratedly emotional.

Later, the Founder of Opus Dei would have to live his love for the Holy Eucharist in circumstances as adverse as those during the periods of religious persecution in republican Madrid. Julián Cortés Cavanillas has written in an article in *ABC* that, on the morning of 11 May 1931, while churches and convents were burning in Madrid, "I was with him when he took the Blessed Sacrament, holding it tightly to his breast, from the chapel where he was chaplain in Manuel Cortina Street, to the military quarters near Cuatro Caminos Circus, where he deposited the divine treasure of the Eucharist in the house of some Aragonese friends."

Then and later in Madrid and Barcelona, between July 1936 and December 1937, he had to overcome great difficulties to live his eucharistic piety. He had to celebrate Holy Mass in hiding and to carry Holy Communion in secret from one place to another, risking his life as he did so. There were many holy priests in Madrid and other cities in Spain who had no fear of death. Msgr. Escrivá de Balaguer was later to comment that during those months he frequently thought of the persecutions of the early Christians. From different hiding-places, wearing borrowed clothes and having become very thin because of all the weight he had lost, as soon as he was able to move around Madrid, he carried out an intense priestly apostolate: he heard Confessions, he gave spiritual guidance to individuals, or to small groups in meditations (he even preached a retreat) and he celebrated Holy Mass and took Communion to different people.

During the days he spent in Barcelona prior to his escape through the Pyrenees via Andorra, his priestly work was performed under similar circumstances. Some members of the Work and a few of his friends joined him in a general expedition conducted by guides who knew the route to escape from the Red zone.

He celebrated Mass on 28 November 1937 up in the mountains. The travellers had just reached the escarpment of Ribalera, after walking all night. Without delaying any longer, they found a suitable place which formed a sort of circle and was protected from the wind. They chose the stones that could best be used as an altar. He was worried that there might be some irreverence, for some blasphemies had been uttered during their night march, but he announced that he was going to say Mass and said that all those who wished to attend could do so.

There were more than twenty people there who had not been able to go to Mass since July 1936. There was great expectancy. They were very moved by the way he celebrated Mass. Antonio Dalmases, a student, was with another group that had joined their expedition. He noted in his diary: "I have never been to a Mass like to-day's. I don't know whether it is due to the circumstances, or because the priest is a saint."

A few days later Don Josemaría celebrated the Holy Sacrifice in Andorra, with all the proper vestments and sacred vessels. He had been nearly seventeen months in hiding. Even after thirty-seven years the priest there, Fr. Pujol Tubau, has never forgotten that group of men. One of them came up to him and greeted him with outstretched arms: **Thank God we see a priest at last.** It was in fact Don Josemaría who introduced himself as a priest. He explained that they had just crossed the frontier and that he wanted to celebrate Holy Mass in thanksgiving. He did so the following day, one of the first days of December, at the high altar of the church of St. Stephen. Fr. Pujol was impressed by his profound piety, "by the devotion with which he said Mass, as well as by the length of time he and his companions spent in giving thanks and praying before the Blessed Sacrament".

Many other people have made similar statements. Antonio Ivars Moreno was a student when he heard Mass one day in 1939 in a small first-floor flat of Samaniego Street, where the first Centre of Opus Dei in Valencia had been established: "I didn't miss a word. Not a single gesture. When he celebrated Mass he made all of us there feel that he had penetrated the depths of the great mystery of our Redemption. That Mass was truly the same Sacrifice of Calvary without the shedding of blood. There was no room for distractions."

A well known Valencia architect, Vicente Valls Abad, has expressed in writing in the newspaper *Levante* his impressions of his stay at the Jenner students' residence in Madrid. It was in 1942 and Don Josemaría was looking after the spiritual direction of the residents, and the preaching of meditations and retreats. Not without certain reservations, Vicente attended a day of recollection. He was struck by Don Josemaría's direct, specific and penetrating preaching. It encouraged him to improve. What really won him over, however, was the way Don Josemaría gave Benediction: "The respect and devotion with which he held the Blessed Sacrament, the way in which he pressed it to his breast at the end, and the constant moving of his lips as he silently spoke to Our Lord right to the end of the ceremony: here, I thought, is a priest in love with God."

The Founder of Opus Dei celebrated Mass like a man in love. His affection reached even the most minute details. Don Vicente Jabonero, a histopathologist from Oviedo, noticed one such detail during the Mass Msgr. Escrivá de Balaguer said in 1967 on the campus of the

University of Navarre. Dr. Jabonero was struck by the pause made at the *Ideo, precor* in the *Confiteor*. Dr. Jabonero then considered that it was logical for him to pause as he did, in the same way as when one says: "therefore, I pray . . .". He adds: "the comma or pause was just right. It was then that I understood why he had written in *The Way* with reference to vocal prayer: **Consider what you are saying, to whom it is being said . . ."**

Don Juan Antonio Paniagua, who lectures in history of medicine, remembers the tiny flat in Valladolid which they called *El Rincón* (The Nook). It was used in the early forties for apostolic work with university students. It was there that he learned from the Founder of Opus Dei to appreciate the importance of the tiniest expressions of love towards the Holy Eucharist, and to avoid any improvisation in divine worship. Juan Antonio Paniagua noticed that those details revealed — or concealed — his love: a crazy love such as is described in *The Way* (number 438):

Crazy! Yes, I saw you in the Bishop's chapel — alone, so you thought; as you left a kiss on each newly-consecrated chalice and paten: so that He might find them there, when He came for the first time to those eucharistic vessels.

It's crazy, isn't it?, Paniagua recalls the Founder of Opus Dei saying to Javier Silió, the youngest of those who were there then. "Yes Father, it's crazy!" Javier said. He replied: **Well you must be crazy too, my son.**

On the death of Msgr. Escrivá de Balaguer, the Bishop of Aachen, Msgr. Pohlschneider, commented: "The sixty thousand members of Opus Dei weep for the death of the Father who has left them. But after his death they will be interiorly faithful, because they know what they owe him. Well may they say, in the words of Lacordaire: 'The greatest happiness a man can enjoy on earth is to have met in his lifetime a real man who is truly a priest after God's heart.' "

We would, however, be giving an inaccurate picture of his priesthood if we separated it from his **lay mentality.** From a negative viewpoint a person with a lay mentality is one who is not clerical; that is to say, he does not take advantage of church structures for worldly ends, or to look for better treatment than normal citizens get. The Founder of Opus Dei found privileges and exemptions repugnant. Instead he delighted in working within the framework of civil law, fulfilling his obligations and, also, insisting on his rights, a citizen's rights and not priestly privileges.

Another example of clericalism of the wrong kind is a form of mimicry which results from an inferiority complex: as, for instance, when activities which belong properly to priests are presented as the ideal for the laity; or, vice versa, wanting to bring priests into secular activities as a way of impregnating those activities with christianity. The priest who acts like a layman and the layman who is "clerical" in his behaviour and speech are unhealthy products of bad clericalism. They take people away from reality and turn them into "displaced persons"; whereas a person with lay mentality knows how to be "in his place".

It was characteristic of Msgr. Escrivá de Balaguer to "give his decided support to secularity". This was inseparable from "his full and consequent priestliness which he lived so coherently down to the very last detail" (Msgr. Francisco Hernández, in *La Religión*, Caracas, 26 July 1975).

The cleric's role in the world is to be of service to everyone without exception. The priest has to be another Christ, who came to serve, not to be served; and the great service that priests render to men, today as yesterday, is to speak to them about God, to make God present to them in their lives. There is no doubt at all that the most "lay" thing for a priest to do is to "talk about God".

The Founder of Opus Dei was often asked about lay mentality. On 19 October 1972, in Madrid, he stated: **I am anticlerical because I love the priesthood.** His was a **good anticlericalism,** because he wanted priests to be faithful to their own unique mission. He wanted to convince them that priests who do not speak about God are all "clerical" in the bad sense of the word.

Practically everything in the life of the Founder of Opus Dei was directed towards making laymen sanctify themselves in their ordinary work: the work with which they earn their living, maintain their families and fulfil their social duties. The priestly ministry he also saw as an **ordinary professional job.** He looked upon it as a **work of God.**

Msgr. Escrivá de Balaguer was a priest who spoke only about God. In him this was immediately evident, and clear for all to see. He also lived in depth that "lay mentality" about which he preached so much, with all its consequences: for priests, not to be "dictatorial" with souls, not to poke their noses into other people's business, respect for the freedom of consciences, abhorrence of privileges and exemptions. . . .

He took this attitude to the extreme of not wanting to "live off his cassock". There were times when he was very hard pressed for money. Among many others there was the occasion when he went to Madrid in 1927. He taught Roman law and canon law at the Cicuéndez Academy, for the simple reason that he needed money to support his mother, sister and brother.

After the Spanish war he accepted a teaching post at the Madrid School of Journalism, doubtless because he still needed money, though he cannot have earned very much there. He went to the School at the request of a friend, Giménez Arnau, who was then the Director General of the Press, and also because to lecture on ethics and deontology to future journalists was a way of giving doctrine, of speaking about God. That was the real reason for his being at the School of Journalism.

The first Secretary of that School, Pedro Gómez Aparicio, wrote in the Madrid *Hoja del Lunes*: "I have a feeling that the memory of Don Josemaría still lingers among his former pupils. His manner was simple, respectful and kind; his character open, optimistic and generous, and always ready for a friendly dialogue. I think he would have made a great journalist if he had not been fully absorbed by his apostolic activities."

Though he fulfilled his commitments as a lecturer with a sense of duty, he always made it clear that he was not "professionally dedicated" to that job. All he wanted was to be a priest pure and simple. Many encouraged him to apply for academic posts, but he always declined. His answer was that if he did that, there would be just one more professor, but that if he continued being a full-time priest, there would as a consequence be many priests and many professors, and many workers and many holy married couples dedicated to God.

It is easy now to see why he insisted so much on priests' wearing cassocks (or whatever clerical garb is approved by the bishops), for to do so immediately advertises the presence of a minister of Christ. He saw the priesthood as a ministry, a public service, and he considered that others — be they Catholic or not — had a right to be able to recognise priests by the way they dressed, so that their services could be requested in any place or circumstance. He used to tell priests to dress as priests out of a sense of charity or justice, and also as a consequence of their lay mentality.

Don Josemaría practised this even to the point of heroism in times when it was dangerous to walk about the streets of Madrid in a cassock.

After the burning of churches and convents in May 1931, priests who were ready for decisive and, when necessary, courageous action usually went about the streets of Madrid dressed in lay clothes. Dr. Jiménez Vargas' recollections of the Founder of Opus Dei, ever since he had met him in 1932, are that he "never wanted to go about in lay clothes. Furthermore he wore a cape, which was even more striking than an overcoat."

Archbishop Cantero of Saragossa summed up these and other features of Msgr. Escrivá de Balaguer's priestly soul and sterling personality in the homily he preached at the Mass celebrated in Saragossa for the repose of his soul: "there was balance and harmony which allied prudence and courage in his life and works; an Aragonese determination and an unstinting openness to the thought of others; and a respect and love for freedom combined with discipline and obedience. He had a sense of humour and a resilience under the cross of physical and moral sufferings; a debonair and unshakable optimism, and an understanding of human miseries and limitations. There was, in addition, his fidelity to orthodoxy, and a hunger and thirst for creativity in the service of God, His Church and of all his brother men, because he loved God, the Church and men with the same heart."

Msgr. Escrivá de Balaguer was indeed above all else a man of God, a priest.

4. THREE LOVES: CHRIST, MARY, THE POPE

May you seek Christ, may you find Christ, may you love Christ. Madrid 29-V-33. Don Ricardo Fernández Vallespín still has a copy of the *History of the Sacred Passion* by Luis de la Palma with this dedication written by the Founder of Opus Dei.

It could be said that Msgr. Escrivá de Balaguer did nothing else from his youth until his death, but to introduce souls to Christ, to that Christ who is *heri et hodie, ipse et in saecula*, "the same yesterday and to-day and for ever" (Heb 13:8). Christ, who is the only Victim, the only Model. Christ, who is not a character lost in history, but who is alive now and has been waiting for each and every Christian for twenty centuries.

Probably if a theologian were to analyse all his writings he would most likely come to the conclusion that his doctrine is, above all, thoroughly *Christological*; but without entering into theological considerations — this will be for others to do — we can say here that it is clear that his Christocentricity is inseparably united to his devotion to Mary and his unconditional affection for the Pope, the Vice-Christ, the sweet Christ on earth, as he liked to say in the words of St. Catherine of Sienna.

Anyone who talked with him, no matter how briefly, realised immediately that his whole life revolved around Christ, Mary and the Pope. Don Alfonso Casas, Chancellor of the Cathedral of Tuy, was introduced by the Bishop of Tuy to the Founder of Opus Dei in 1945. He observes: "I do not know if it was then (or later, through his writings) that I was able to appreciate his profound devotion to the Blessed Virgin and to St. Joseph, and his unceasing and intense love for the Pope."

Cardinal Marcelo González, the Primate of Spain, wrote in the *ABC* newspaper: "Three great forces influenced his interior life; they were always in his soul and were essential for living as a son of the Church in its twofold dimension: mystical (love for the mystery of Christ's spouse) and apostolic (the dynamism of a faith that aspires to renew the world). They were the Eucharist, especially the Holy Sacrifice of the Mass (the idea of redemption); love for the humanity of Christ, child and adult, dead and risen (the incarnation of faith in the world); and a very deep love for the Blessed Virgin Mary, who is not to be separated from St. Joseph (the idea of a family of children of God who have every reason for joy on discovering the spiritual beauty and motherly help of Mary)."

His devotion to Our Lady was indeed inseparable from that to St. Joseph. Significantly he expressed this even in the way he brought together in one word his christian names, Joseph and Mary. Canon Mariano A. Taberna in the *Diario de Avila* (28 June 1975) wrote: "I have written the full name, because he never tolerated being called only Don José. **Please don't take Our Lady away from me,** he would say immediately."

Another priest, Fr. Ramón Cermeño, remembering the retreat he attended just after the Spanish war in the seminary of Avila, says that Don Josemaría insisted on the importance of fostering presence of God during the day, and that he called the Virgin Mary "the Lady" and "Holy Mary" and recommended invoking her before study with an ejaculatory prayer: *Sancta Maria, Mater Dei et Sedes sapientiae, ora pro me*, "which custom, in my case, became second nature". He concludes: "He also inculcated the need to have a great devotion for 'the lord St. Joseph'. It was something he clearly had."

The Founder of Opus Dei practised what he preached, and talked about what he practised. All who knew him point this out. This is also true of his devotion to St. Joseph and Our Lady. Fr. Sancho, O.P., affirms: "He had a very great devotion to Our Lady. I cherish his book on the Holy Rosary, every word of which is a living proof of his Marian devotion. If he hadn't had so much devotion, he could not have written that book which is so full of tenderness for our Mother."

Many different expressions of affection for the Blessed Virgin have been incorporated into the daily life of the members of Opus Dei. They are ways of expressing tenderness for the Mother of God and Our Mother, as he liked to put it. He culled them from the treasury of firm, centuries-old christian traditions: the Holy Rosary, the Angelus, the Memorare, the three Hail Marys at night, the scapular of Carmel, the images of Our Lady which preside over so many places of work and prayer.

Together with his devotion to Our Lady, and inseparable from it, was his constant recourse to St. Joseph, whom he invoked from very early on as **Father and Lord.** He always looked upon St. Joseph as the master of the interior life. He has written beautiful passages about St. Joseph, commenting upon his working life, his docility in carrying out God's plans, his humble sense of responsibility, his loving and gentle manner towards Mary and Jesus. The members of the Work were encouraged to learn from the Holy Patriarch how to get to know — to contemplate — Jesus Christ and the Virgin Mary.

During the last years of his life, awareness of the presence of the **trinity on earth** — Jesus, Mary and Joseph — which had been second nature to the Founder of Opus Dei since his days as a young priest, became day by day more intense and more intimate. During those final years of his sojourn on earth he proclaimed with all his strength his love for St. Joseph, with whom he established a special relationship which coloured everything he did. There are two particular ideas which the Founder of Opus Dei proclaimed in season and out of season, and which without doubt are at the centre of his later preaching on the Holy Patriarch. They have deep theological significance and, above all, an inexhaustible flow of practical consequences. They left a deep impression on a Brazilian member of Opus Dei who was with the Father on the plane that took him from Rio de Janeiro to São Paulo in May 1974. On that journey, the Father began to speak about St. Joseph and of a resolution he had made for that month of May to **put St. Joseph into everything.** The two ideas which he sketched briefly on that flight and which form the framework of a whole programme of contemplative life, were:

After the Blessed Virgin, he is the most perfect creature that has come from the hands of God; I am certain of that.

Bear in mind that one could apply to St. Joseph, what theologians say of the Virgin Mary: that God Our Lord could fill her with his grace, and if he could, he did. . . .

Together with St. Joseph, Mary his Spouse is present in the most decisive events in the life of Msgr. Escrivá de Balaguer and in the history of Opus Dei: before its foundation, in his confident prayers to Our Lady of Pilar; on 2 October 1928, in the peal of bells of the Madrid church of Our Lady of the Angels, which were ringing out in honour of their Patron, and which he heard while he was praying; in the first approval that Opus Dei received from the Holy See, on 11 October 1943, the feast of the Motherhood of Our Lady; on 2 February 1947, the feast of the Purification of Our Lady, when Pius XII promulgated the Apostolic Constitution *Provida Mater Ecclesia*, through which Opus Dei was to obtain the Church's solemn approval; on 15 August 1951, in the Holy House of Loreto, when in very difficult moments he consecrated the Work to the Most Sweet Heart of Mary; and then at the time of the Angelus on 26 June 1975, when he felt Our Lady's gentle kiss accompanying him on his way towards the eternal presence of her Son.

His filial recourse to Our Lady was constant: he went to her for big things, and also for those that might appear insignificant. All the praises of the Virgin Mary found an echo in his heart.

Lorenzo Martín Nieto, an architect from Seville, coincided with Msgr. Escrivá de Balaguer one Maundy Thursday in the forties. The Founder of Opus Dei had arrived in Seville the day before. A place was needed where some members of Opus Dei could live and carry out their activities in that city:

Pray that we soon have a house, because so far we are here only on credit, he told them. **I have asked this favour from your Patron** La Virgen de los Reyes, **and I have told her that if she arranges for us to have a students' residence here soon, her image will preside over the oratory we shall set up there.**

On 15 November 1972 he consecrated the altar of the oratory of Guadaira University Residence, which had been set up a few years before in a newly-built residence. The oratory is presided over by a statue of *La Virgen de los Reyes*. It is a new carving, better finished than the one which had been in the first premises of Guadaira since the forties.

The same day, after consecrating the altar, he stayed for a good while with the residents. He stressed how Christ forgives from the Cross, and he recalled how his first visit to Seville had been during Holy Week. He had begun to pray before one of those processional statues of Our Lady:

I forgot what was happening around me. Looking at such a beautiful image of the Blessed Virgin, I forgot I was in Seville or even in the street. Then someone touched me like this, on my shoulder. I looked round and I saw a country man who told me:

"Father! You haven't seen 'nothing'! Ours is the best one!"

At first it sounded like blasphemy. But afterwards I thought: "He is right; when I show portraits of my mother, even though I like them all, I also say: this one, this is the best one."

How well you love Our Lady here, my sons! May she bless you and keep you. May she make you clean and straightforward and cheerful — which you are already. May she make you happy on earth; even though you might have some little sin or other. . . . Jesus will forgive you because when you go back to her, you go back to her Son.

Besides, we are all so very weak. . . . I hope you will also pray that I, too, may always go back to my Mother, with the love you have for her. I have come to Seville, once again, to learn to love the Virgin Mary. I have not come to teach: I always come to learn. And I love the Virgin in all your images, which are so marvellous. Yesterday they were telling me:

"Won't you go to see the statue of Our Lady of . . . ?"

And I replied:

"Look, I like all the images of Our Lady. I would have to go and see them all, and that isn't possible; so I won't be able to go and see that statue you have mentioned."

In a distant corner of Aragon we are building a great shrine for Our Lady. I love Our Lady so much that I will not do any publicity for the Virgin of Torreciudad, none at all (. . .) .

Because I love all the portraits of my Mother, all the images of the Virgin Mary.

In the early years of his life shrines and sanctuaries of Our Lady all over Spain had heard the compliments — the Holy Rosary — of the Founder of Opus Dei, as, later, did those of the whole world, such as Lourdes, Fatima, Loreto, Einsiedeln, Willesden (London), Guadalupe (Mexico), Aparecida (Brazil), Luján (Argentina), Lo Vázquez (Chile), or any hidden image of the Virgin Mary, in some street corner of Madrid or Rome, or in churches — Catholic or not — over most of Europe.

Pedro Casciaro, who had met Don Josemaría early in 1935, asked him to be his spiritual director. Under his guidance he learned to do mental prayer, and to strive to be always in the presence of God, even in the street. As a way of helping him, Don Josemaría asked him one day what his usual route was from his home in Castelló Street to the school of architecture (the classes were held in the Areneros building, which had been confiscated from the Jesuits by the government) or to the faculty of sciences, which was still in San Bernardo. Then Don Josemaría listed the images of Our Lady that he could find on his way.

These were more or less his words: **In Goya Street there is a pastry shop, just round the corner from Castelló, which has a figure of the Immaculate Conception in a niche; when you reach the statue of Christopher Columbus, as you cross the Castellana, you will find on one of the bas-reliefs of the pedestal of the statue a scene of the** Reyes Católicos, **where there is an image of Our Lady of Pilar; as you go up the Boulevards . . .**

Pedro Casciaro was amazed when he realised how limited his own powers of observation had been for, as an architectural student, he made a point of noticing ornamental details. In fact, he adds: "only a soul in love with Our Lady could have detected them. From then on my working hours acquired a new motive for sanctification, and my walks through the streets of Madrid, new contemplative perspectives."

Then, there was the Pope, the sweet Christ on earth.

Encarnación Ortega remembers in detail her arrival in Rome on 27 December 1946, with three other members of the Women's Section. They were the first who were going to stay in Italy. The Founder arranged that their itinerary from the airport to the small flat in Piazza della Città Leonina should include the Colosseum. There they recited the Creed, slowly, asking the martyrs, who had died there, for faith and fortitude in order to be good instruments to serve the Church and the Roman Pontiff. On the following morning, they renewed their petition with filial love at the tomb of St. Peter, the first Pope, and prayed intensely for the Roman Pontiff who then occupied the See of Peter.

This event was no exception. Quite the contrary: the Founder of Opus Dei always taught souls to love and pray for the Holy Father, whom he regarded as **the Vice-Christ,** the representative of God on earth. That is why he wanted every member of Opus Dei who came to Rome to go immediately to St. Peter's to renew his faith and pay homage to the reigning Pontiff.

His love and veneration for the Pope, whoever he might be, was manifest. It was certainly not necessary to be a member of Opus Dei to notice it. On 27 August 1972, to give one example among many, Cardinal Frings preached in Cologne at the first solemn Mass of a new priest of Opus Dei: "To be a priest in the Catholic Church you have to be firmly convinced — and, I would say, convinced with a divine certainty — that the Church is directed from its summit by Peter and by his successor, the Pope. Msgr. Escrivá grasped this a long time ago. He has gone ahead leading his sons and daughters with his faithful loyalty to the Pope, and he has always remained unshakably faithful to the Pope."

Don Florencio Sánchez Bella, the Counsellor of Opus Dei in Spain, gave a homily at a Requiem Mass for the soul of Msgr. Escrivá de Balaguer celebrated at the beginning of July 1975 in the Basilica of St. Michael in Madrid. At one point, Don Florencio spoke of his passionate love for the Church:

"You will have read in the press that the Founder's last words were words of love for the Church and the Pope.

"Allow me to open my heart to you as a friend. I want to tell you something that happened very recently, last Saturday. We were doing our prayer early in the morning in the oratory of the General Council of Opus Dei in Rome. It was only hours after we had buried the body of Msgr. Escrivá de Balaguer. There was an atmosphere of peace and serenity, while the priest, sitting at a small table, read passages from a book of meditations, written some years ago. Then he came to a quotation from the Father which had been included there. I will read it to you: **When you are old, and I have already rendered my account to God, you will tell (...) how the Father loved the Pope with all his soul, with all his strength.**

"The sobs which were heard at this point underlined how our Father was already leading us along paths of faith, hope and charity, keeping us inseparably united to the Church and to the Pope."

This spirit of the Founder of Opus Dei could be summed up in one adjective: "Roman". Cardinal Poletti, the Vicar General of the diocese of Rome, wrote to Don Alvaro del Portillo, then the Secretary General of Opus Dei, on 27 June 1975:

"The diocese of Rome owes much to so many founders of religious institutes, associations and apostolic activities that have worked in the city. Msgr. Escrivá de Balaguer, a personality of inexhaustible spiritual richness, joins this admirable list of men of God.

"He, who had lived in Rome since 1946, prided himself on being 'very Roman', and he has inculcated this love of his for Rome, the Pope's diocese, in his sons and daughters all over the world. (. . .) On recalling the personality of the Founder of Opus Dei, I desire as Vicar General of the Holy Father to express my gratitude for his zeal and that of his sons, which has been a leaven of apostolic life in the most varied aspects of life in Rome."

The complete text of this letter appeared in the July–August 1975 issue of the *Rivista Diocesana di Roma*. In that same issue, Francesco Angelicchio published an article with the expressive title "A 'very Roman' Spanish priest". He asks: "Why did Msgr. Escrivá de Balaguer wish to be 'very Roman'? Why was it that, as he repeated to his sons and daughters, he wished with all his might to 'Romanise' the Work he had founded? Undoubtedly it was so that he himself would have and would be able to give to this new foundation a spirit identical to that which Christ wished to give his Church and to his Vicar, when he established him in Rome. For the Founder of Opus Dei, 'Roman' is synonymous with unity and universality. It is a manifestation of love and obedience to the Pope, the Bishop of Rome. It is an expression of docility and service to the apostolic see. It is a desire to be drenched in the spirit of the early Christians and of the Church of the martyrs who made a major contribution in Rome to the work of salvation and to increase men's fidelity to the Spouse of Christ and the Primacy of Peter."

The Founder of Opus Dei wished to impress on the members of the Work and on all the faithful, the love for the Vicar of Christ which welled up in his christian heart. Once again he spoke and taught what he practised. His first journey to Rome was in 1946. After a difficult crossing from Barcelona to Genoa, where Msgr. Escrivá de Balaguer celebrated his first Mass on Italian soil in a church that was partly destroyed by bombs, he went from Genoa to Rome by car, together with Don Alvaro del Portillo and Don Salvador Canals, who had gone to Genoa to meet him. Don José Orlandis, who accompanied him from Madrid, describes their arrival in the Eternal City:

"There was still light in the sky in the twilight of one of the longest days of the year when we reached the outskirts of the city along the Via Aurelia. At a particular moment, after a bend in the road, the dome of St. Peter's appeared before our eyes. The Father was visibly moved and said the Creed out loud. Shortly afterwards we stopped at the Piazza della Città Leonina, where a flat had been rented. It was to be the first domicile of Msgr. Escrivá de Balaguer in Rome. The flat had a terrace that opened out on to St. Peter's Square. On the right you could see the large building of the Vatican Palace, with a light shining from the window where the Roman Pontiff worked. The Father naturally was tired after such a long, hard journey, but in spite of our pleadings he did not want to rest and he spent the whole night in prayer on that terrace, looking towards the house of the Vicar of Christ on earth.

"I would also like to point out another fact which, without doubt, meant a heroic and silent mortification for our Founder. He had looked forward all his life to doing his pilgrimage to Rome *videre Petrum* (in order to see Peter). It so happened that his first residence in Rome was a stone's throw from St. Peter's Square. But our Father must have decided then to offer to God what for him must have been a very hard sacrifice. He allowed a day to go by, and another, and another, up to six, without crossing the square and kneeling at the tomb of St. Peter. Finally (we had observed all this with silent respect) on the 29th, the feast of the Apostle, he said: **Let's go to St. Peter's.** We went out, crossed the square, and entered the Basilica, and our Founder spent a long time praying on his knees at the Altar of the Confession. Then, we returned to the flat in Città Leonina."

Francesco Angelicchio has something similar to say, in the article just quoted above: "He loved to go — sometimes for many days running — to St. Peter's Square to say the Creed and the prayer *pro Pontifice*. When he came to the words 'I believe in One, Holy, Catholic and Apostolic Church' he introduced a small variation, which he prayed with great intensity: **I believe in my Mother the Roman Church,** and he used to repeat this act of faith three times. Then he carried on: 'One, Holy, Catholic and Apostolic'. We could see how he meditated on these words and how he tried to engrave them as if by fire upon the minds and hearts of those who accompanied him."

Msgr. Escrivá de Balaguer prayed and asked all the members of Opus Dei to pray daily, for the Pope and his intentions. The Counsellor of Opus Dei in Italy, Don Mario Lantini, emphasised the point at the Requiem Mass celebrated on 28 June 1975, in the Roman Basilica of St. Eugenio:

"Christ, Mary, the Pope. Have we not just indicated, in these three words, the loves that sum up the Catholic faith? Msgr. Escrivá de Balaguer, the Father, wrote these words in 1934, when he was thirty-two years old and Opus Dei had only been in existence for six. These three words form a programme that has guided his whole life, that of all the members of Opus Dei, and that of hundreds of thousands of people throughout the world."

5. ZEAL FOR ALL SOULS

The Founder of Opus Dei showed his love, his passion, for the sanctity of all priests, until the very moment of his death. On the morning of 26 June 1975, just two hours before he died, the Founder was speaking in a Centre of the Women's Section of Opus Dei in Castelgandolfo:

I will tell you as I do whenever I come here that you, by the simple fact of being Christians, have priestly souls. With your priestly soul and with God's grace, you can and should help the priestly ministry which we priests carry out. Together, we shall work effectively.

In everything you do, find a motive to talk to God and to his Blessed Mother, who is our Mother, and to St. Joseph, our Father and Lord, and to our Guardian Angels, so as to help this Holy Church, our Mother, which is in such great need, and which is having such a difficult time in the world these days. We should love the Church and the Pope very much. Ask Our Lord that our service on behalf of the Church and the Pope may be effective.

This was a very original theme of his and he preached it unceasingly down the years. No one before him had given precise expression to the theological fact that all the faithful, including women, have a **priestly soul.** Once again he was asking for cooperation.

His love for priests, and also for men and women called to the religious life, was a constant feature of his life, though he always pointed out that he himself had no vocation to be a religious. Msgr. Cantero, the Archbishop of Saragossa, underlined this love in his homily at a Requiem Mass for the Founder of Opus Dei with a very expressive anecdote:

"I will never forget one of my personal encounters with my beloved and mourned friend Josemaría Escrivá. Late in the afternoon of 14 August 1931, he called in unexpectedly at my house in Madrid. The heat was oppressive. Even after three months it seemed as if the smoke of burning convents still floated in the sky. That visit and conversation with Josemaría Escrivá was a turning point in my life and in my pastoral ministry."

Msgr. Abilio del Campo, Bishop of Calahorra, La Calzada and Logroño, also gave testimony to his unconditional and unconditioned love for the Roman Pontiff, his veneration for the Hierarchy and his brother priests, and his affection for the religious. He stressed especially Msgr. Escrivá de Balaguer's love for diocesan priests, for whom he had providentially made room in Opus Dei, and in whom he always instilled complete obedience to their respective Ordinaries. Bishop del Campo said that in his diocese he knew several priest members of Opus Dei who were really exemplary and "have always been my obedient sons and zealous collaborators in pastoral tasks".

Msgr. Méndez, the Archbishop of Pamplona, declared in a newspaper interview as soon as he heard of the demise of the Founder of Opus Dei: "I was impressed by his priestliness. He spoke of the priesthood in vivid, loving tones. He was passionately interested in everything that had to do with the priesthood."

Msgr. Escrivá de Balaguer manifested his care at all times, even under very difficult circumstances. In the forests of Lérida, for instance, while he waited during the winter of 1937 for the right moment to set off on the journey through the Pyrenees that would take him to Andorra, he welcomed a priest from Pons who was hiding in the hamlet of Vilaró. This priest went to see the Founder of Opus Dei and chatted with him on several occasions. About an hour's distance away, there was a group of priests who had taken refuge in a hut since the first day of the war. He made a point of visiting them, to strengthen their optimism and their supernatural outlook.

He was convinced that the sanctity of many souls depended on the sanctity of all priests. Don Manuel Martínez Martínez, a priest from

León, noticed this when he heard him preaching a retreat to the priests of León, shortly after the Spanish war. Msgr. Ballester, then Bishop of León, had invited him to preach. One day the Bishop remarked: "Have you seen how they listen to you?" Msgr. Escrivá de Balaguer answered that he tried to take special care of priests, because they in turn had to foster the piety of the faithful; he added that if you manage to increase the faith and virtues of the priests, you have done everything.

It is because he loved all mankind that the Founder of Opus Dei, in the forties, gave so many retreats to priests all over Spain. He had no time to spare, because at that time his task of developing the Work was enormous and, until 1944, he was the only priest of Opus Dei. He had to prepare the members of the Work for the apostolate, and besides he was also very busy giving spiritual direction and encouragement to many other people who came to him. As if this were not enough he was invited by bishops from all over Spain to preach to priests and religious. He was thirty-seven years old when the Spanish war ended, and many prelates held him in great esteem. That is why they asked him to help them train their priests.

Don Jesús Enjuto, who was seventy-three years old in 1975, had attended, in 1942 or 1943, the retreat given by the Founder of Opus Dei in the diocesan seminary of Segovia, at the invitation of Bishop Platero. As the bishops, until recently, used to organise retreats for all the clergy of their dioceses, it would not be unreasonable to suppose that some priests attended just to please the bishop, rather than through a real desire to profit from this traditional means for renewing the interior life; but that summer Fr. Enjuto was very struck by the fact that the unanimous verdict was: "The best retreat we ever had", because of the strength of the preacher's words, which were full of affection and love and spirituality; and also because "he did not go in for exaggerated alternatives which were very common then and were so disheartening at times, for they made sanctity seem inaccessible". By contrast, his "preaching was stimulating, and it moved and enthused all of us, without exception". It was noticeable that the preacher loved the religious, but he did not love his brothers in the priesthood less, and he wanted them too to be saints, as saintly as the most observant religious. (It is worth stressing that this idea was not usual then, for sanctity and perfection were associated only with the cloister and with the religious vocation.)

Many priests still today express their appreciation of the retreats and recollections they attended thirty years ago. Some, like Jaime

Bertrán Crespell who went to one held from 13 to 18 October 1941 at the Conciliar seminary of Lérida, have kept the notes they took. He was then the curate at the parish of Saint John the Baptist and taught religion in the official secondary school in Lérida. He remembers that the basic idea of the retreat was "to fall in love with Jesus Christ". His two main resolutions, prompted by the preacher, were "to feel a hundred per cent a priest" and "to appear everywhere as such".

One of the most expressive appreciations was published by Fr. Juan Ordóñez Márquez in the Seville *ABC* newspaper. His article started: "We do not yet know if a saint has died. The Church will pronounce judgement in due time. We only know that a priest has died who showed the way. And what a priest!" He then went on to describe the limitless priestly activity of the Founder of Opus Dei. The article ended: "he was a priest, indeed, capable of passing on his priestly enthusiasm to the very priests of the Church".

He obtained that sympathy and enthusiasm without seeming to do anything extraordinary. He was just one more, a brother among his brothers, whom he loved to distraction, and that is why he always felt a sense of unworthiness when having to preach to them. More than once he would say it was like trying to **sell honey to a bee-keeper.** There was nothing odd or extraordinary about his retreats. Don Francisco Alvarez Rodrigo, the parish priest of San Francisco de la Vega in León, attended one. He did not know, nor did he deduce then, that it was the Founder of Opus Dei who was preaching. He simply thought it was a friend of the bishop, Msgr. Ballester, who had brought him to preach to the priests of his diocese. "What is more, judging by his expressions and the examples he used, I formed the opinion that he was from Avila or Segovia. And the same thing happened to many others."

Don Gumersindo Fernández García also went to that retreat. He still has the notes he took. Among the many things he heard about Our Lady and St. Joseph, about devotion to the Holy Eucharist and love for the Holy Mass, etc., he mentions above all the preacher's stress on the life of prayer and the life of faith: "He talked very, very much about faith. It is there that I heard more than anywhere else about the life of faith: in that retreat." Don Gumersindo was amazed by his command of the Sacred Scriptures, the ease with which he quoted from memory passages from the Gospels and facts from the Epistles, with every detail and without hesitating: "He relived the Gospel, and made us relive it."

That retreat left an impression on him which time has not cancelled. Every year he goes over those notes and meditates on them: "The day I received the news of the death of the Father I was reading the notes I had taken from the meditation on death he gave on that retreat."

Only a year before his death, the Founder of Opus Dei had been recalling in Buenos Aires his work with priests in the forties. He was addressing a numerous group of priests from Argentina:

I began to give many, many retreats — they used to last seven days at that time — in a number of Spanish dioceses. I was very young and it embarrassed me. I always began by going to Our Lord and saying to him: "You'll have to see what you are going to say to your priests, because I . . .". I felt so ashamed! And afterwards if they didn't come to chat, I called them one by one. Because they weren't used to talking to the preacher.

The Founder of Opus Dei went to practically all the dioceses of Spain. He had an unquenchable zeal for his brother priests. After moving to Rome in 1946 he still continued, as far as possible, preaching to priests. Msgr. Infantes Florido, the present Bishop of the Canary Islands, met him there in 1957 when he attended a retreat for secular clergy in Castelgandolfo. Msgr. Infantes was impressed by his insistence in urging them to foster a serious and responsible priestly sanctity, which would be reflected in their faithful allegiance to the Hierarchy (*nihil sine Episcopo*), and in their fraternal concern for all priests, and would be a way of eliminating despondency and isolation.

Prelates from all over the world, from Cardinal Enrique y Tarancón, the President of the Spanish Episcopal Conference, to Cardinal Parecattil, Archbishop of Ernakulam (Kerala, India), or Cardinal Cooke, Archbishop of New York, have publicly expressed their gratitude to Msgr. Escrivá de Balaguer for his apostolic zeal which has done so much good for the priests of their dioceses and rendered magnificent service to the Church. Msgr. José María Guix, an Auxiliary Bishop of Barcelona, paid a moving tribute to the Founder when he conferred the diaconate to fifty-four members of Opus Dei a few days after the death of Msgr. Escrivá de Balaguer. He urged them to love him more, so that from Heaven he would continue to help them to be ever-better sons of the Church: "good priests, who love the Holy Church, the Roman Pontiff and the Hierarchy as he loved them."

Msgr. Escrivá de Balaguer reminded the faithful how important it was for them to pray for all priests. He told them that they had a duty not to "leave them on their own" and an obligation to look after them, also in their material needs. On occasions, when addressing lay people, he would raise his voice in emphasis as he did in the Coliseo Theatre in Buenos Aires, on 23 June 1974:

Pray for all priests — sinners like myself — so that we don't do anything crazy, and so that, at the altar and away from the altar, we behave as Jesus Christ and our Mother the Church would wish. There are no bad priests, they are all good. They would be better if we prayed more. Let us pray more!

To diocesan priests, he would always insist in terms similar to those he used one day in May 1974 in Brazil: **I have the same vocation as you have. I have never had any other. That is why I do not give offence to the religious — whom I love very much — if I love you in a very special way. I am under a special fraternal obligation to do so.**

"I also know how much he loved the religious, and in particular the contemplative life, for it comes across clearly in his letters. He also instilled in his sons and daughters an esteem and appreciation for the prayers of contemplative souls." It is Sister María Rosa Pérez, a Poor Clare, from a monastery in Valencia who affirms this.

In these pages we have already quoted a number of religious who testify to a profound affection for Msgr. Escrivá de Balaguer, and recall the great esteem he had for the religious state, even though God had given him a totally different calling. The task of the Founder of Opus Dei was to foster and spread the desire for sanctity in the middle of the world; he spoke to those who lived and worked in ordinary circumstances. The great means he counted on for this was prayer. This included the prayers of the religious from whom he **begged** for the **alms** of their prayers with noteworthy perseverance. "In his letters," says that same Poor Clare from Valencia, "he asked me to pray both for him and for the Work."

He did not remember them only to obtain the prayers he needed. In his concern and zeal for the whole Church, he prayed and got others to pray for the religious. He also obtained vocations for the religious life (as, for instance, the Carthusian of Porta Coeli, to whom Aurelio Mota refers in the newspaper *Las Provincias* of Valencia, of 2 July 1975). When asked to do so, he worked directly on their behalf.

Eduardo Zaragüeta, an Augustinian, spoke of this in *La Voz de España* of San Sebastian (8 July 1975): "We Augustinians know his affable character and his simplicity for he preached a retreat in the monastery of San Lorenzo, at El Escorial. Escrivá loved St. Augustine and the rich tradition of this Order founded by him sixteen centuries ago in circumstances very similar to those that obtain today."

The Franciscan Joaquín Sanchís Alventosa, who has held important posts in his Order and who took an active part in the Second Vatican Council, has not forgotten the first steps of Opus Dei in Valencia, in 1939. The house in Samaniego Street, where the students' residence was, was near his convent of San Lorenzo, and the director of the residence asked the friars if they would say Mass for the residents and give Benediction on Saturdays. A very friendly relationship was thus established, which Fr. Joaquín praises for "the affection and deference which those university students, who had begun to live a lay spirituality, had for us Franciscans. That veneration was a proof of the love for the religious state that Msgr. Escrivá had infused in those sons of his, who sought sanctification in the midst of their professional commitments."

It was clear then, as the Church was to sanction some years later, that life in Opus Dei is very different from the religious vocation; but this clear-cut distinction, far from being a motive for separation, leads to mutual admiration and affection. If Fr. Joaquín was delighted by the affection with which young undergraduates treated him, it is also moving to note the christian magnanimity of this Franciscan priest rejoicing at the sight of the mercies of God in the activities of Opus Dei: "Many old boys of our Franciscan schools," he recalls, "have spoken to me about the decisive part the apostolate of Opus Dei has played for them on their arrival at university. Quite a few received a vocation to Opus Dei. I recall how happy I was to meet in Rome one of my much-loved old boys, who had been ordained to the priesthood in Opus Dei."

The Founder of Opus Dei spread the message of the universal call to sanctity throughout the whole world, especially to lay people. But, as Fr. Aniceto Fernández, a former Master General of the Dominicans, acknowledges, that reality never meant for him, or for the members of the Work, that they "undervalued or found fault with the religious life, or in any way failed to appreciate the excellence of the religious vocation".

Another practical manifestation of his love for the religious appears in the decisive help he gave from 1940 onwards to restore the order of Hieronymites at El Parral (Segovia). José María Aguilar Collados, a monk of that order, who today is chaplain to the monastery of San

Bartolomé in Inca (Majorca), testifies that he owes his religious vocation to Msgr. Escrivá de Balaguer and he lists names of some students who were also confirmed in their religious calling by the Founder of Opus Dei.

Dom Pío María, who today is a Camaldolese monk at the Yermo of Santa María de la Herrera (San Felices, Logroño), met him at the monastery of El Parral. Msgr. Escrivá de Balaguer preached a retreat to them into which he put his best human and supernatural efforts to move each one of the retreatants, even though he reminded them frequently that he was not a monk. . . . Dom Pío María points out as well that he never interfered in any way in the running of the Order. He heard him say more than once: **each must govern according to his own spirit.**

From El Yermo, in a remote corner of Logroño, Dom Pío María testified in 1975, twenty-nine years after his last meeting with Msgr. Escrivá de Balaguer: "To have heard now that Opus Dei has spread to the five continents has filled me with joy, but it has not come as a surprise."

These are some examples of how the Founder of Opus Dei felt for the religious and of the mutual affection that resulted, in spite of the difference in vocation. He never ceased to pray for them and, whenever he could, visited them to respond to their affection, their prayers, and their constant invitations to spend some time with them.

Thus, when he went catechizing all over the Iberian Peninsula in October and November 1972, he visited several convents of contemplative nuns. In Navarre he was with the Cistercian nuns of the monastery of San José in Alloz. One afternoon in Madrid he visited the Augustinian Recollect nuns of Santa Isabel, of whose Royal Patronato he had been rector many years before. He went to the Carmel of Coimbra; in Cadiz, to a community of Discalced Carmelites; then, in Valencia, to the Carmelites of Puzol. Finally, in Barcelona, nearly at the end of those two months of unceasing activity, he talked to the Poor Clares of the monastery of Pedralbes. He had words of gratitude and supernatural encouragement for all.

You are the Church's treasure, he would say very often. In Puzol, the Carmelite convent surrounded by orange groves which he visited during his stay in Valencia, he added:

The Church would be arid without you, and we would not be able to say: "Draw out with joy the waters of the fountain of the Saviour." It is here that you draw the waters of God, so that

we can convert the dry land into an orchard full of orange trees. Without you we could do nothing; that is why I have come to thank you. I am convinced that many priests who now suffer and weep in the world, on hearing your canticles — including those you sing at recreation — will be filled with joy. May you be a thousand times blessed!

In these visits he insisted that the nuns should be lovingly faithful to their vocation, and he promised he would pray that they should have many vocations:

I am not a religious, but I love the religious with all my soul, and I suffer when I see them without vocations. I will pray a lot so that this community will also have young people.

Many religious expressed their affection and gratitude to the Founder of Opus Dei when they heard of his death. Sometimes, as the Superior General of the Servants of the Poor pointed out, it was because his writings had encouraged them to struggle for personal sanctity and to live their own vocation generously. The Superior General of the Little Sisters of the *Ancianos Desamparados* affirms that: "His writings, which were known to us all, have helped us to increase our love for the Church and for the Pope, and to deepen our knowledge of the doctrine of Jesus Christ." The community of the Discalced Carmelites of the Incarnation (Avila) stress especially the veneration that the Founder of Opus Dei had for priests; this, which is what the Mother St. Theresa wished, was a motive of "great joy and encouragement for us". The nuns of St. Joseph, the first monastery founded by St. Theresa of Avila, affectionately emphasize that Msgr. Escrivá de Balaguer frequently quoted St. Theresa in his preaching, and they point out the esteem in which "he and his spiritual sons have always held the Carmelite order."

One could multiply the testimonies which denote in a simple and spontaneous manner a profound unity of hearts among souls whom God leads along such different paths. Sister Teresa J. García de Samaniego, Superior of the monastery of the Visitation of Our Lady (Oviedo), confirms that her nuns, just as many other enclosed religious, pray for Opus Dei: "Msgr. Josemaría Escrivá knew it and thanked us publicly or through his sons who are priests, who ask us to pray for many of their apostolic works." Sister Teresa expressly refers to a text in *Conversations with Msgr. Escrivá de Balaguer:*

Opus Dei has always enjoyed the admiration and the sympathetic good will of religious of many orders and congregations, especially of enclosed monks and nuns, who pray

for us, write to us often, and make our work known in a thousand ways, because they can appreciate the meaning of our life of contemplatives in the midst of the cares of everyday life.

Sister Teresa concludes: "In our community life we have long experience of meditating on the writings of Msgr. Escrivá de Balaguer. We read his homilies in the refectory and at recreation and we also read them privately so that our mental prayer may be filled with divine inspirations. They lead us to God, they unite us to Jesus Christ, they make us love our Creator more and pray more for all the creatures of the earth. In letting ourselves be led by the hand by this holy Founder, in whom Christ lived in an intense way, many of us have experienced a kind of renewed fervour to live our spirit."

CHAPTER THREE

THE FOUNDATION OF OPUS DEI

1. Madrid, 2 October 1928
2. The Founder of Opus Dei carried on working
3. The sanctification of work
4. Women in Opus Dei, 14 February 1930
5. The Sacerdotal Society of the Holy Cross

1. MADRID, 2 OCTOBER 1928

Don Josemaría began to work in Madrid in the early months of 1927. He did a lot of priestly work, as chaplain to the Patronato de Enfermos of the Damas Apostólicas, giving classes in the Cicuéndez Academy, and preparing his doctorate in law. At the same time he prayed and continued to wait for God's Will to show itself clearly.

The 2nd of October 1928 found him thus. On that date, while he was spending a few days on retreat in a house of the Vincentians in García de Paredes Street in Madrid, Opus Dei came into being.

Msgr. Escrivá de Balaguer never liked to go into the details of that 2 October 1928, because he was convinced that the Work belonged to God, and he did not want to "steal" any of His glory. It was on that date that he learned with crystal clarity that he, then only a twenty-six-year-old priest, virtually unknown, without any human resources, was God's chosen instrument to carry out on earth the divine undertaking of Opus Dei.

In October 1967, the editor of the magazine *Palabra* asked him a leading question: "On several occasions, with reference to the early years of Opus Dei, you have said that all you had was **youth, the grace of God, and a good sense of humour.** Besides, during the twenties, the doctrine of the laity was not as developed as we see it today. Nevertheless, Opus Dei is now a noteworthy factor in the life of the Church. Could you explain to us how, being a young priest, you were able to have sufficient foresight and understanding to carry out this task?"

As on so many other occasions the answer was apparently "evasive":

I never had and I do not have any other aim than that of fulfilling the Will of God. Please do not ask me to go into details about the beginnings of the Work, which the Love of God began to make me suspect back in 1917. They are intimately connected with the story of my soul and belong to my interior life. All I can say is that I acted at every moment with the permission and affectionate blessing of the Bishop of Madrid, who was my very dear friend and in whose diocese Opus Dei was born on 2 October 1928. And later, with the constant approval and encouragement of the Holy See and in each individual case with that of the Ordinaries of the places in which we work.

This attitude reflects a constant reality in the life of the Church: those who have received God's "charisms" have not been very "charismatic". All their efforts are directed towards making others see that their "thing" has the backing of ecclesiastical authority, and that it is of God because it is of the Church and has been approved by the Hierarchy.

The Founder of Opus Dei kept this tactful silence even when among members of the Work; as happened, for instance, in 1968 when he spent 2 October in Pozoalbero (Jerez). Fr. José Luis Múzquiz, who was present on that occasion, recalls that the reasons he gave for saying virtually nothing were:

— first, because **you already know;**
— secondly, because **you will find it all written down when I die;**
— thirdly, because you would think that **I am something when I am only a poor sinner;**
— and the fourth but most important reason is because there have indeed been extraordinary events in the Work, but **"our way" is the sanctification of ordinary things.**

On that 2 October 1928, during his retreat in the house of the Vincentians in García de Paredes Street in Madrid, he had been given a room in a building which is now no longer standing. While he was praying in that room — the facts were recently related in public by Don Alvaro del Portillo — he "saw" Opus Dei and heard the peal of bells of the nearby parish of Our Lady of the Angels, ringing out on their Patron's feast day.

Preaching on 2 October 1962, Msgr. Escrivá de Balaguer said: **From that moment on I never had any** tranquillity **and I began to work, reluctantly, because I did not like the idea of being the founder of anything; but I began to work, to move, to do: to lay the foundations.**

He did so with complete trust in what God wanted, as he himself admitted, gratefully, in 1950: **God's infinite Wisdom has been leading me on, playfully as it were, from the darkness of the first intimations, to the clarity with which I now see every detail of the Work and can well say:** Deus docuisti me a iuventute mea; et usque nunc pronuntiabo mirabilia tua (Ps 70:17), **the Lord has been tutoring me from the beginning of the Work, and I cannot but sing his praises and fight to fulfil his Will, because if I didn't the salvation of my soul would be at stake.**

In 1961 he confirmed this in a letter which is an authentic hymn of thanksgiving to God's mercy: **And to open the way for this divine wish, an event of great theological, pastoral and social importance in the life of the Church, God led me by the hand, quietly, little by little, until** his castle **was built: take that step, he seemed to say, put that here, take that away from here in front and put it over there. That is the way that Our Lord has built his Work, with firm strokes and fine outlines, a work both old and new, as is the Word of Christ.**

This divine game I am talking to you about appears very clearly in the history of our juridical itinerary within the life of the Church. I have not had to calculate, as if I were playing chess; among other things because I have never pretended to guess the other person's moves so as to checkmate him later. What I have had to do is to let myself be led.

Between 1943 and 1950, Opus Dei received all the approvals of the Church. The pontifical documents clearly acknowledge the supernatural character of this mission, for which its Founder continued to consider himself **an inept and deaf instrument.** It was definitively clear, as Cardinal Dell'Aqua would say in April 1970, that in the Church, quite justly, "this Work is considered as a Work of God".

Shortly after the death of Msgr. Escrivá de Balaguer another illustrious prelate, Cardinal Baggio, wrote: "We do not have the necessary perspective to evaluate properly the historical weight and range of the doctrine, in many aspects authentically revolutionary and ahead of its time, and of the incomparably effective pastoral action and influence of this remarkable man of the Church. But it is evident even today that the life, work, and message of Monsignor Escrivá de Balaguer constitute a new and original chapter in the history of christian spirituality, if we consider it, as we should, as a straight path under the guidance of the Holy Spirit."

Cardinal Marcelo González Martín, the Primate of Spain, published some reflections, to which we have already referred in these pages, on the supernatural character of Opus Dei. In his opinion, in order to explain the "success" of the Founder in carrying out his "undertaking" it is not enough to speak of "the personality of the man who achieved it. The secret does not lie there. Since the undertaking is supernatural in character, no matter how much his own talents and qualities may have helped, as an effective instrument helps, the real key is much more intimate and radical. A genius, however persevering and enthusiastic, will be ineffective if he relies simply on his own resources, when the cause is one of living with a love for holiness and of passing on that same love to others. When one relies on oneself alone, activity becomes 'activism', words become shouts or whispers and nothing else; strength of will becomes simply a desire to dominate others. All this is useless for leading others along the path towards a fully christian life. He who tries it will fall at the first hurdle."

What was this supernatural undertaking for which God was calling Don Josemaría Escrivá de Balaguer? The Cardinal Primate of Spain sums it up in a few words: "the association which preaches and promotes sanctification of men in the midst of their life's ordinary work: *for this, which is so simple and so evangelical, had been all but forgotten.*" (The italics are mine.)

After the Second Vatican Council, a large part of the message that the Founder of Opus Dei was spreading since 1928 "sounds" pretty familiar. This is not surprising, because as he said in 1961: the Work is **a novelty, as old as the Gospel, which enables people of all classes and conditions, without any discrimination of race, nation or language, to make that sweet encounter with Jesus Christ in their daily tasks. It is a simple novelty just like the "good news" of the Lord.**

As old as the Gospel, and as new as the Gospel. This is how the Founder often described the spirit of Opus Dei. It is new indeed, because among other things the universal call to sanctity had been forgotten for centuries. It could not have been easy to make it known at the time when the Work was commencing.

Bearing this in mind one can well understand the words with which the Bishop of Pamplona, Msgr. Olaechea, introduced the Founder of Opus Dei in 1937 to the present Bishop of Bilbao, Msgr. Añoveros: "If the Work that this priest proposes is approved by the Church it will mean a real revolution in the lay apostolate."

The proposal was so "novel" that there were some who considered the young priest behind it to be a dreamer and a madman. Many years later, in Brazil, someone asked him about this with a very direct question: "Who called you a madman, and when, and why?" The answer was as follows:

Don't you think it is madness to say that here right where you are you can and should be a saint? That a man who sells ice cream can and should be a saint, and so can a woman who works in the kitchen all day, and a bank manager, and a university lecturer, and a farm labourer, and a porter carrying suitcases on his shoulders . . . ? All are called to sanctity! This has now been included in the last Council, but at that time — in 1928 — it didn't enter into anybody's head. So that . . . it's only natural that they should think I was mad (. . .)

Now it seems obvious, but it was not so then. And if someone wanted to be a saint they would say to him: well, become a . . . fratinho.

Msgr. Escrivá de Balaguer turned then to the Counsellor of Opus Dei in Brazil to ask him if that was what you called a friar in Portuguese . . . *"Fradinho"* was the answer.

No Sir! If God calls him to marry, he should marry, and be a saint: a saintly father of a family. And if not, he need not go to a friary. And if God calls him to be a fradinho, **he should be a** fradinho. **But we are all the same when it comes to answering, each along our own way, the Master's invitation! All called to sanctity! Everyone!**

He expressed himself in similar terms when preaching on 2 October 1962:

I started working and it was not easy: souls slipped through my fingers like eels in water. Besides, the lack of

understanding was savage, because what today is common teaching the world over was not so then. Anyone who says otherwise does not know the truth of the matter.

I had, I repeat, my twenty-six years, God's grace and a good sense of humour, and nothing else. But just as men write with a pen, Our Lord writes with the leg of a table to make it clear that it is He who is doing the writing: that is what is so incredible, so marvellous. All the theological and ascetical doctrine, all the juridical doctrine had to be created. I found before me a break in continuity, a gap of centuries: there was nothing. Humanly speaking, the whole Work was a crazy venture. That is why some people said that I was mad, and that I was a heretic, and so many other things besides.

What he began to teach those students and workers of Madrid was in complete contrast with the general trends of the age, and with the climate of Catholic opinion as well. Don Saturnino de Dios Carrasco, a priest who met the Work in the thirties, testifies that Don Josemaría was aiming at something different from what other associations that arose at that time in Spain had in mind: "He talked about digging deep roots, and embracing everything. It has been no novelty for me to see all that Opus Dei has done these years; I had already heard Don Josemaría say all this. The Father was aiming very high. With the perspective that time gives us, it can be seen that it was all supernatural, divine."

At that time — a little after 1931 — Don Saturnino was really overwhelmed by the boldness of the Founder of Opus Dei. He was "a colossus, very courageous," he says; but he was also "a man of great character, mature for his age; as if he had lived more intensely, more deeply". Don Saturnino loved to hear his apostolic plans, even though "the magnitude of the enterprise was frightening. They were dreams. People didn't think then the way the Father thought. He just had to be a person chosen by God to think and do all that."

Juan Jiménez Vargas, a student who followed the Founder of Opus Dei in the thirties, also believes that the way he spoke about the sanctification of ordinary work could not have occurred to anyone, no matter how great his human qualities: "it had to be a direct supernatural inspiration". Don Josemaría knew the university and its problems as something that he had experienced, but "one detected something that went beyond all that. First because he talked about all types of work and about people of all walks of life: and that the Work did not take anyone out of his place. . . ."

At that time, the great majority of students saw professional work just as a means of carrying out their future plans in life. In the University of Madrid there were also groups of activists who from their very different viewpoints coincided in giving everything a political slant. Among the more intellectual types there were some minorities who rather despised religious practices. Opposing them were groups of committed Catholics who were concerned about the future of religion and were striving to get posts in civil life from which they could serve the Church.

The Founder of Opus Dei was not aiming to solve any immediate problems. His approach to sanctification of work was completely new and original. He used to refer time and again to the early Christians — whether he was explaining the Work or not — and looked on work or study as indispensable elements by which ordinary men could strive to be saints in the middle of the world. Furthermore the effort to sanctify work — whatever it may be — was for him inseparable from the *mandatum novum* of charity: a spirit of service, a capacity for self-sacrifice in order to be a genuine help to others, without any personal selfish motives; and a sense of responsibility in dealing with all human problems.

He went to the root of things: to sanctify work meant, above all else, to convert work into prayer. This reality was so utterly central to his message, that — as Don Alvaro del Portillo pointed out on one occasion — if it had been possible, the Founder would have wanted the Work not even to have a name; until somebody asked him in 1930: "How is that Work of God getting on?" "In a flash it was as clear as daylight that as it must have a name, this was the name: Work of God, Opus Dei, *operatio Dei*, God's task: ordinary professional work, carried out by people who know themselves to be instruments of God; work carried out without abandoning the cares of this world, but work turned into prayer and praise for the Lord — *Opus Dei* — at all the crossroads of the ways of mankind."

Time was needed for the seed to take root and yield its fruit, because the general trend was not in that direction. In 1941, Víctor García Hoz, who used to go to Don Josemaría for Confession, was amazed when he was told one day: **God is calling you to be a contemplative.** He explains: "At that time it was almost incomprehensible for a married man, with two or three children then and expecting to have more (which was indeed what happened) and who had to work to raise a family, to be told that contemplation was something he had to achieve."

The novelty of the spirit of the Work and, above all, the evidently divine vocation of its Founder, was something that was very clear to the first members of the Work and indeed to many others. It is something they came to grasp quite normally, without the least note of sensationalism, and without any concessions to the "extraordinary", because the humble response of the Founder of Opus Dei to an authentically divine calling appeared as clear as daylight. As one of them puts it, within the naturalness and simplicity with which he dealt with them, "it was evident that the Father was the person chosen by God to found the Work, and he had given himself so totally to his concern to make that divine mission a reality, that it had become the most decisive characteristic of his personality".

The supernatural character of the calling and of the response to it, would be recognised in time by thousands of people of good will throughout the world. It was not necessary to be a member of Opus Dei to realise this. It was enough to notice, even if only in general outline, the richness of the fruits being produced in the five continents.

On 5 October 1975, the *Diario de Navarra* published an article written by the Marquis of Lozoya, Don Juan de Contreras y López de Ayala, who is well known and admired in Spain, with half a century of university lecturing behind him. The article was entitled "Universal Spaniards", and he included the Founder of Opus Dei among them: "To create a Work which includes thousands of exemplary priests, and a good number of thousands of lay people, who are outstanding in the most diverse disciplines — men and women of all nations, and races, spread throughout the world, dedicated to the most diverse activities, always for the benefit of the Church or in answer to some human need — is something that goes beyond the natural, and defies human explanation. We detect here the breath of God, overwhelming at first, constant down the centuries and making the gigantic work of 'the founders' possible."

2. THE FOUNDER OF OPUS DEI CARRIED ON WORKING

To carry out Opus Dei it is not necessary to change one's occupation, or do "peculiar" things. That is why, after 2 October 1928, Don Josemaría carried on working at the jobs he had been doing before.

On 17 March 1927 he had obtained permission from the Arch-diocese of Saragossa to go to Madrid for two years, to continue his studies. By the 28th of the following month he was already matriculated in Madrid University to study for a doctorate in law. He did two subjects that year (1927–28), and did the September exams in history of international law and philosophy of law. (Later on he did history of Spanish legal literature, and social politics.)

He lodged at a residence for priests at 3 Larra Street. Some of his fellow residents are still alive. One of them, Msgr. Avelino Gómez Ledo, remembers him going out before breakfast and coming back at lunch-time, normally later than the others. Both he and Don Fidel Gómez Colomo remember that, among other things, he spent some time on his doctoral thesis, which was on the ordination to the priesthood of half-breeds and quadroons in the sixteenth and seventeenth centuries.

However, it was only after the Spanish war that he was able to defend his thesis at the faculty of law in Madrid. He did so on 18 December 1939, and was adjudged *sobresaliente*. This thesis was about the Abbess of the monastery of Las Huelgas. The change was because all his research work on the subject I have just mentioned was lost, together with his very good collection of books, during the civil war. In 1944 he published a book on the Abbess of Las Huelgas. It was based on his doctoral thesis, though completely rewritten. It was reprinted in 1974.

During the academic year 1927–28 he taught Roman law and canon law at the Cicuéndez Academy, which was on the first floor of a house at the junction of San Bernardo Street and Pez Street, opposite the Ministry of Justice. The academy had a good name because the lectures were of university standard, according to Pedro Rocamora. Lectures were given there only in the afternoons, and the pupils who went to them were all taking "external exams", quite often because they were doing other things as well as studying law. This was the case of Julián Cortés Cavanillas, who was studying journalism at the school of *El Debate*.

José Manuel Sanchiz Granero, now a lawyer in Madrid, was a pupil of that academy in 1927–28. He remembers that Don Josemaría's lectures were pleasant and were followed with interest. He was always cheerful. Sometimes, at the end of a lecture, he would stay behind to comment upon some points with Sanchiz. From those conversations, an answer he once gave to someone who said he could not have faith while there were priests who lived a double life, impressed Sanchiz very much. The Founder of Opus Dei had replied that a priest was like a very precious liquid, that could be contained in a very valuable vase, or in an ordinary glass.

José Manuel Sanchiz recalls that one day another priest who lectured at the Cicuéndez Academy told the students about the work that Don Josemaría was doing in the suburbs. This was discussed between lectures, and a group of students did not believe it, because they thought it impossible, given the distinguished air and intellectual stature of their Roman law lecturer. The discussion ended in a bet. Some were assigned to follow him when he finished his classes. They did this for several days, and they found that it was true. He did in fact go out to suburbs such as Vallecas and Tetuán.

Don Josemaría was, in fact, chaplain to the Patronato de Enfermos and he was quietly engaged in an intense apostolic activity in the outskirts of Madrid. Although he was not obliged to do this as chaplain, his priestly zeal drove him to undertake that apostolate with immense enthusiasm and superhuman strength.

The Patronato de Enfermos had been set up by Doña Luz Rodríguez Casanova, the Foundress of the Damas Apostólicas of the Sacred Heart of Jesus who were approved by the Holy See in 1927. Their central house was at 13 Santa Engracia Street, a building opened by King Alfonso XIII on 14 July 1924.

The Damas Apostólicas carried out a number of apostolates, among which were: 1) "The Work of the Preservation of the Faith in Spain" which founded schools in the least cared-for areas (in 1928 they had 61 schools); 2) "The Patronato de Enfermos" for the care of the sick in their own homes, bringing them food, medicine, clothing, and spiritual help: the yearly average of patients looked after by the Damas Apostólicas and the young women who helped them in their work was four thousand; 3) "Charity Dining Rooms" to help the needy; and 4) "After-school Work": night classes and youth associations. The residence for priests in Larra Street, where the Founder of Opus Dei lived, also belonged to the Damas Apostólicas. In 1929 a novitiate for the Damas Apostólicas began in Chamartín de la Rosa.

The spiritual director of these religious was Fr. Rubio S.J., and when he died in 1929, Fr. Valentín Sánchez Ruiz, also a Jesuit, took over. The Founder of Opus Dei was only the chaplain of the church of the Patronato, but he took it upon himself to look for and enthuse diocesan priests who could help in the spiritual care of the sick in the poorest districts of Madrid and of the boys who went to the schools. His efforts were remarkable, says Asunción Muñoz, who now is in Daimiel but was then in the House of Santa Engracia. Don Josemaría took on an immense amount of priestly work, but without interfering in any way in the government of those apostolic activities. Emilia Zabaleta, who used to go to Fr. Rubio for Confession, met Don Josemaría there in 1927. Her sister María Luisa went several times to Don Josemaría when Fr. Rubio was not there. His humility impressed them very much, because when they consulted him on matters concerning their religious congregation, he always answered that it was not he, but the spiritual director who could guide them there.

In the twenties, the hospitals in Madrid were always full, and many of the sick who were poor died in their homes with hardly any medical or spiritual attention. The Damas Apostólicas looked after them with the help of women and girls from Madrid with christian ideals. The work was hard, especially after 1930, for they ran the risk of being insulted and thrown out of the houses or chased from the streets, or having to put up with ugly blasphemies. One of them has not forgotten the fright she got one day in the Ventas district when a group surrounded and intimidated them to scare them off and discourage them from ever returning. On another occasion, in Tetuán, they were dragged through the streets and struck on the head with a cobbler's awl. One of the Damas who tried to protect the others had her hair torn out, leaving her disfigured.

The testimony of Asunción Muñoz, bearing in mind that sort of background, is that "Our chaplain became indispensable (. . .) I was the youngest of the foundation and I had more stamina and could work day or night (. . .) We used to go to the poor homes of these sick people. Often we had to legalise their position, getting them to marry and solving urgent social and moral problems. We had to help them in many ways. Don Josemaría was always available, no matter what the hour, with great dedication and constancy, without any hurry, as one who is fulfilling his vocation, a sacred ministry of love.

"Thus we always knew we could count on the help of our chaplain. He administered the Sacraments, and we did not have to bother the parish at untimely moments. We saw to everything ourselves."

They used to go to the furthest outskirts, which today form part of Madrid, such as Ventas, Pueblo Nuevo, Ciudad Lineal, Tetuán, Almenara and Cuatro Caminos. In 1931 they could get part of the way by tram. But often, from where the line ended, they still had to walk for miles along muddy paths, or cross-country, before reaching the miserable hovels where the sick lived.

On Thursdays he took them Holy Communion in a borrowed car; but, as one of those ladies recalls: "On other days he used to go by tram, walking or whatever way he could manage, even in bad weather, because we attended the sick in both winter and summer." María Luisa Zabaleta stresses that he used to go to all the poorest suburbs, whether to Vallecas or the districts of Lucero or Magín Calvo. Don Josemaría would go everywhere and was always available "with complete self abnegation". Josefina Santos adds the names of other Madrid districts they went to: Paseo de Extremadura, Lavapiés, San Millán, Ribera de Manzanares.

The schools of the Damas Apostólicas were also to be found in those outlying districts. Some of them had a chapel, which might be the only one in a large area with no parish church. Such was the case at Usera. The Damas Apostólicas had difficulty in finding priests ready to say Mass on holidays of obligation, to preach to the children and to talk with them and hear their Confessions. The apostolic zeal of Don Josemaría led him to all these schools. Msgr. Avelino Gómez Ledo says that he was untiring in hearing children's Confessions and teaching them the catechism, at a time of very considerable anticlerical feeling, which meant that in many areas "priests were received not only coldly but with hostility; on some occasions he was even stoned".

The Founder of Opus Dei recalled those days more than once in the last years of his life. On 14 February 1975 he was asked a question in Altoclaro (Venezuela) about children's Confessions. He based his answer on, among other things, his own priestly experience:

I have upon my conscience — and I say it with pride — having dedicated many, many thousands of hours to hearing children's Confessions in the poor districts of Madrid. I would have liked to have gone to hear Confessions in all the saddest and most abandoned slum areas of the whole world. They used to come with runny noses. First you had to clean their noses, before cleaning their poor souls a little. Bring children to God, before the devil gets into them. Believe me, you will do them a lot of good. I speak from experience, from the experience of thousands and thousands of souls, and from my own experience.

In a single year, 1929–30, 4,000 children made their First Communion in the chapel of the Patronato. As there were so many they received Holy Communion on successive days. All the pupils of schools run by the Damas Apostólicas were prepared and confessed by the chaplain of the Patronato, who used to get help, when he could, from the diocesan clergy. He did not exaggerate when he gave the figure of many thousands of hours dedicated to hearing those children's Confessions.

Besides preparing his doctorate in law, teaching at the Cicuéndez Academy, visiting the sick and instructing pupils in the schools of the Damas Apostólicas, Don Josemaría looked after the liturgy at the church of Santa Engracia and cared for the poor who came to eat at the charity dining room there. He used to celebrate Holy Mass in the morning. He led the Holy Rosary and gave Benediction with the Blessed Sacrament. He also attended the poor in the dining room personally: "He was a friend and a holy priest", says Asunción Muñoz, who was very grateful, when she was appointed Novice Mistress, for the visits that the Founder of Opus Dei used to pay them, many Sundays, at their novice house in the Paseo de la Habana in Chamartín: "In spite of his enormous daily activities, Don Josemaría did not seem to be in any hurry. He did everything with peace and simplicity."

There came a moment, however, when it was no longer possible for him to carry on with all these things and carry out all these diverse activities with the necessary minimum of peace of mind and without detriment to his interior life. Besides, as is to be expected, the tasks related to the foundation of the Work were taking up more of his time; and so, in July 1931, he gave up being chaplain to the Damas Apostólicas.

Shortly after that he began to celebrate Mass in the church of the Patronato of Santa Isabel. There was a school there run by nuns of the Assumption and a convent of enclosed Augustinian Recollect nuns, founded by Philip II and Blessed Orozco.

Don Josemaría became chaplain to the enclosed Augustinian nuns of the convent of Santa Isabel (an ancient royal benefice) on 20 September 1931, without any official remuneration, as he stated some time later, on 26 January 1934, when applying to the *Dirección General de Beneficencia* for permission to use the house reserved for the convent's chaplain. His application was successful, the reply being dated 31 January. At the end of the year, the *Gaceta de Madrid* of 13 December 1934 published a decree by which he was appointed rector of the Patronato of Santa Isabel. It was signed by Niceto Alcalá-Zamora, and by the Minister of Works, Health and Social Security, Oriol Anguera de

Sojo, because, according to another decree, dated 17 February 1934, some of the Patronatos of the late Royal House had been transferred to that Ministry. Don Josemaría took over the rectorship officially on 19 December 1934. He had previously obtained permission to accept the post from the Palatine ordinary, the Archbishop of Sion, who held ecclesiastical jurisdiction over the ancient royal benefices, and from the Archbishop of Saragossa, which was Don Josemaría's diocese.

Sister María del Buen Consejo Fernández, an enclosed Augustinian nun in the convent of Santa Isabel, met the Founder of Opus Dei in 1931. She explains that: "The Augustinian Recollect Fathers used to celebrate Holy Mass for the community, but their convent was far away, and as things got worse in the country, especially after the Republic was proclaimed, it was dangerous to walk down the street to come to our convent." One day the Mother Prioress, Sister Vicenta María del Sagrario, called the community together and told them that a priest from Saragossa would be saying Holy Mass for them every day. Don Josemaría had offered himself as chaplain when he heard of the anxious situation in which the Augustinian nuns found themselves, enclosed and without a priest.

Mass was at eight o'clock sharp. Don Josemaría heard Confessions before and after Mass. Whenever necessary he gave Holy Communion to the nuns who were sick. Sister María del Buen Consejo remembers that for two months he had to take Communion every day to a bed-ridden nun.

A group of young women who received spiritual direction from the Founder of Opus Dei used to come for Confession to Santa Isabel. His apostolic work with men was done wherever he could manage: in the street, in a chocolate bar in Alcalá Street called *El Sotanillo*, walking in the Retiro Park, at his own home at 4 Martínez Campos, where he lived with his mother and brother and sister from the end of 1932, or in his visits to hospitals.

God had sent Opus Dei its first members from 1928 on. Naturally all the work of their formation fell upon the shoulders of the Founder, for he was the only one who could teach them the spirit of the Work.

Nevertheless, he always found time — and this was part of the formation that those first members of the Work needed to receive — to spend generously in visiting the most neglected sick in the public hospitals of Madrid.

In the same street of Santa Isabel there was the General Hospital of the Madrid provincial authority, an enormous building which is still standing, although it is now only partly in use and for a different purpose. He used to go there on Sunday afternoons, at least from 1931–32 onwards. A group of young people used to accompany him. They rendered all sorts of services in the hospital, which was full of patients, of the poorest you could find; so much so, that, as there were not enough beds to go round, many of the sick were just huddled up in the corridors. Don Josemaría did a lot of priestly work there, hearing Confessions, taking Holy Communion to the sick, consoling them spiritually and aiding them materially.

His untiring zeal also took him to the King's Hospital, a hospital for infectious diseases. It catered for patients with highly infectious diseases, to prevent the infection spreading. Before this hospital was opened in 1925, that is what tended to happen in the other public hospitals of Madrid, for everybody was crowded together in the crammed conditions then prevailing. Malignant typhus, small-pox and tuberculosis were the three most common infectious diseases. In its first year — 1925 — it took in 637 patients; 1,971 in 1928; 2,666 in 1936. Before the discovery of antibiotics and radiotherapy the mortality rate in the hospital was of the order of 20%. There are no statistics for the different illnesses, but it is believed that at that time the mortality for illnesses such as tuberculosis was almost 100%. In fact the people of Madrid used to call it the "hospital for incurables".

When it opened in 1925 it was cared for by the Daughters of Charity, their Superior being Sister Engracia Echevarría. The budget for Cult and Clergy was abolished soon after the Republic was proclaimed and the King's Hospital was left without a chaplain. It was about then that Don Josemaría went to see Sister Engracia. "He was then a young priest, just thirty, if that, and he told me that I need not worry about not having an official chaplain; that at any time, day or night, and under my responsibility, I should call him depending on the seriousness of the illness of whoever was asking for the Holy Sacraments."

In this work, he was helped a lot by Don José María Somoano Berdasco, a priest from Arriondas in Asturias, who soon came to be, in fact, the chaplain of the hospital. Witnesses stress Fr. Somoano's sturdy piety, his zeal for souls, his courage and his deep loyalty to the Founder of Opus Dei; but he died soon after, suddenly and unexpectedly, in the vigour of his youth. Another priest who helped was Don Lino Bea-Murguía, who, like Fr. Somoano, had asked to join the Work. Fr. Bea-Murguía was later assassinated in Madrid during the war. The truth is that, as Sister Engracia says: "Don Josemaría was the soul of the group of priests who helped at that time": he was a hard worker, and although she thought that he was then working alongside some high dignitary of the Church, he did not stop coming to the hospital and was always available to look after the sick in the King's Hospital, in spite of the fact that it was far from the centre of the city.

Another nun of that community, Sister Isabel Martín testifies that he said Mass for them on Sundays and holydays of obligation. When the weather was fine they used to prepare a portable altar in the garden, in a wide open space where there is now a large statue of the Sacred Heart of Jesus. He used to visit all the wards, for as a priest he could go everywhere, even though a patient might be in strict isolation: "All the necessary precautions were taken, but the fact is that he went."

He also paid regular visits to the Princesa Hospital, a centre run by the *Beneficencia Sanitaria*. It was in San Bernardo Square (now renamed de Ruiz-Giménez Circus). Its capacity was 2,000 patients. They were housed in enormous wards of about 200 or 300 beds each, filled to capacity, for between each bed there was room only for a bedside table and a chair, according to the description given by Dr. Tomás Canales Maeso, who worked there from December 1932 to July 1936. The patients were really poor, and they were nursed free of charge by the *Beneficencia*. Dr. Maeso worked under Dr. Blanc y Fortacín who taught at the faculty of medicine of San Carlos. One day, early in 1933, a young priest was introduced to him by the older doctor as "a great priest, who comes from my home town (Barbastro) and who is not a *trabucaire*". (In those days they used to call the priests who meddled in politics *trabucaires*.)

From then on they met often. Don Josemaría was there practically every morning, going through all the wards, speaking with the patients, hearing their Confessions and bringing Holy Communion to them. "Some days I saw him more than once, so I reckon he must have spent three or four hours there." The doctor adds "Although at that time unfavourable comments were often made about the clergy, one only heard praise for the Father, from both the hospital staff and the patients. They all loved to talk to him, because he was so welcoming. There was something about him which was difficult to define."

It was in those years that the work of Opus Dei was taking shape, firmly rooted in the Cross, with the suffering and the prayers of the poor and of the uncared-for sick of Madrid. The Founder saw the need for a suitable place for the formation of the new vocations and at the same time to continue with the apostolic work he was doing.

In December 1933 he managed to rent a flat at 33 Luchana Street, where many people who were already taking part in the apostolic tasks of Opus Dei would go. He spent a good amount of time there, especially in the evenings. Here again we find that fundamental feature of his personality, which would be with him for the rest of his life: he worked until he was exhausted and then hid his tiredness so as to continue working and helping others.

Don Ricardo Fernández Vallespín remembers noticing this in 1934, in the Luchana flat. "The Father would sometimes come in the afternoon. I cared for him and it hurt me to see him looking so tired, but the Father would quickly change and with immense patience was always ready to speak with whoever wanted to — and we were quite a few! The Father had to do everything!"

Years after, Msgr. Escrivá de Balaguer good-humouredly confided to the members of the Work a story of that period: **Do you know what I used to do — years ago, I was around thirty at the time — when I was so tired that I could hardly sleep? Well, when I got up in the morning I would say to myself: "You can have a little sleep before lunch." Then when I got out into the street, I would add, seeing all the work that awaited me that day: "Josemaría, I have fooled you once again."**

He was firmly convinced that **only the time we spend in the service of God has any value** and so he carried out a vast amount of work, which was never "activism", not even from a purely external point of view, because he managed to work very intensely without appearing to be in any hurry. Referring to the forties, Fr. Jesús Urteaga summarises his own impressions: "It was not very often that I entered his office in Diego de León, in Madrid, to consult or ask him something. But every time I did so I always felt that he was receiving me as if he had been waiting for me, and had nothing else to do. Yet if, on my way out after I had finished, I looked back before closing the door I could always be sure to find him already back at his work, as if no one had interrupted him."

Many years later a Mexican priest, Fr. Jesús Becerra García, who met him in December 1966, made a similar observation: he was "quick in his movements and gestures, never wasting time in going from one activity to the next. But he did so without precipitation, or any lack of gentleness in dealing with others. Furthermore, when he was with people, he never gave the impression of being in a hurry: it was as if he had all the time in the world to attend and listen to them."

Fr. Jesús Urteaga published in the magazine *Mundo Cristiano* a paragraph from a letter which Msgr. Escrivá de Balaguer had written to him from Rome some years earlier: **When you feel overwhelmed because you have too much to do, bear in mind that work — too much work — is an incurable illness for those of us who are children of God in his Opus Dei. And smile, and pass this good spirit on to others.**

To work with a smile, shrugging off tiredness with a bit of humour. The Founder of Opus Dei used to joke in the seventies, saying that he did not wear a watch **because I do not need it: when I finish one thing, I begin another, and that settles it.**

He was like a calm whirlwind. The need to save souls urged him on, and that is why he worked fast, making good use of his time; but he did so without "appearing to be in a hurry", particularly when it came to dealing with souls, which were what really urged him on. That is why he devoted a lot of time to them: because he knew, as he so often repeated, that **souls, like good wine, improve with time.**

If one wished to single out one area where he was immune to impatience, it was spiritual direction and the Sacrament of Penance. It is there that a soul ceases to be anonymous and faces up to its responsibilities before God. He was never short of time to hear Confessions, and even less if it was to hear the Confessions of the sick or of children. After 1931 he also used to go to the Orphanage of Porta Coeli, in García de Paredes Street, to administer the Sacrament of Confession to the boys — little ragamuffins they were — who were looked after there. He continued to go even after his personal apostolate with university students began to absorb a lot of his time.

He was ready to go several times a day to comfort a dying person in any part of Madrid. When Confessions were involved, he would spend hours, if required. Don Ramón Cermeño recalls that when he gave a retreat in 1940 to young priests in the seminary of Avila most of them wanted to go to him for Confession, and he received them with great patience and affection. Encarnación Ortega also adds how impressed she was when Msgr. Escrivá de Balaguer, even though he had a high temperature, got up from his sickbed to sit in the confessional and give absolution even when it was only for one person. She remembers once when she had telephoned his house in Diego de León how soon afterwards he had arrived at the Centre which the Women's Section of Opus Dei had in Jorge Manrique Street.

In the early forties, Professor García Hoz was amazed at the complete availability of the Founder of Opus Dei for those who went to receive spiritual guidance from him. He himself normally went to the residence in Jenner Street, but when it was his wife, Don Josemaría would take the trouble to find a church and a confessional at an appropriate hour: "And this was not just once or twice, but every time my wife wished to see him, which was normally once a week. I remember that he often used confessionals in the church of San José and in the church of Santa Bárbara."

Msgr. Escrivá de Balaguer was able to work a lot, and to work hard, without losing his peace, because he knew how to give importance to what was really important and because he was extraordinarily orderly.

On 11 June 1976, the present President General of Opus Dei, speaking in Aralar University Residence at the University of Navarre to a large group of students, told them a story about this. In the fulfilment of his filial duty, Don Alvaro had always tried to look after the Founder very well. Specifically, whenever they passed through Pamplona, he made arrangements for him to be seen by the doctors. On one occasion, in the course of a general check-up, they took an electroencephalogram and commented: "It is the typical graph of a business man."

Don Alvaro del Portillo added: "And the Father perfected his physical, somatic, constitution and fought a long and intense battle to reach the summit of the virtue of order. In a copybook he wrote around 1932, about his interior struggle, the Father talks about the need to be even more orderly. . . . At that time in his life many unforseen events kept cropping up: looking after the dying in the outskirts of Madrid, catechetical work throughout the city, preparing thousands of children for Confession and First Communion. Besides he spent many hours praying before the Blessed Sacrament, he recited the three parts of the Holy Rosary and read the Breviary calmly and with attention. The Father, who — I'd like to emphasize — was orderly by nature and even by his mental make-up, engaged in a titanic struggle to improve his order and thus be able to reach more souls, without wasting a minute of prayer, of direct conversation with his Father God, which was indispensable in order to live his contemplative life throughout his whole day of tireless work."

The Holy Spirit used this struggle to impress upon his soul two practical consequences. One he wrote down then, in 1932, and included later in *Consideraciones espirituales*. It eventually became point 79 of

The Way: **Virtue without order? Strange virtue!** The second one was subsequently to help many men and women with **unorderly** jobs — such as doctors, or journalists — which are difficult to programme because unforeseen events arise every day. The Founder of Opus Dei always taught them that **each one has to learn how to construct his own order upon that apparent disorder.** This advice summarised a part of his own struggle — when he was the chaplain of Santa Engracia — to be more orderly every day for love of God and of souls, so as to raise his natural orderliness to a supernatural plane, and to prove by deeds that one could not "be" in the big things without "being" in the little ones.

As Don Alvaro del Portillo put it in September 1975, one of the fundamental features of the Founder's spirit "was the marvellous fusion, in so great a heart, between a soul that flew so high and the love for little things, for things which are only noticed by eyes whose pupils have been dilated by love."

His spirit of order, hard work and self-surrender reached heroic degrees in the first residence in Ferraz Street, before the Spanish war. A frequent morning task of his was to scrub floors and make the beds, when the residents had gone to university and could not notice. In July 1975 the Seville daily *ABC* published a letter written by a domestic employee who wished to give thanks publicly to the recently deceased Founder of Opus Dei because she had been fortunate to hear him say marvellous things about her work, words which had helped her to convert it into a work of God: "You have taught me that my work is holy if I do it with perfection; that all jobs have the same value if they are done for God (. . .) Father, I ask myself: How did you know so much about our work if you were a person with so many degrees?"

For work to be God's — *opus Dei* — it had first of all to be work. Msgr. Escrivá de Balaguer did indeed learn to turn all work, even the most humble, into God's work. God so arranged things that he found himself having to do humble tasks, thus engraving upon his soul the universal scope of the calling to sanctify work.

When later, after the Spanish war, the Women's Section of Opus Dei gradually took over the domestic administration of the Centres of the Work, the Founder could assure them that he had personally done a good many of those tasks before they had. He had made beds, cooked meals and scrubbed floors, and was convinced that those jobs were as important as teaching at university, or writing an article for a scholarly magazine.

It seems as if God had wanted there to be nothing "theoretical" about Opus Dei: all that the Founder taught over nearly fifty years had been lived by him previously in one way or another. This was another reason why he was able to demand of members of the Work that they should make the best use of their time, concentrating on pleasing God, not men; that they should avoid any impression of allowing themselves to be waited upon; that they should also learn to rest, that is, to change occupations, employing their time in activities that demanded less effort or a different type of effort from the one they did normally; and finally that they should learn to give their lives entirely, giving themselves to God and to others — without any show — through their ordinary work, which they were to convert into a loving service to God for the good of all souls.

All the conditions were to be found in Msgr. Escrivá de Balaguer for God to use him as an instrument to remind all Christians that, as is stated in the book of Genesis, God made man in order to work; for above all, and from an early age, he worked. He always found time to pray, to celebrate Mass calmly, to preach, to hear Confessions, to do the work of his ministry; to look after the work of directing Opus Dei; to write — he wrote a lot; to re-read periodically textbooks on theology and ecclesiastical subjects; to read works of literature; to keep up to date with the news in the press and on television.

He did not waste time even when such behaviour might have seemed excusable, as for instance during the months he spent in hiding in Madrid during the war. It goes without saying that his first concern then, as always, was the life of the Church and the difficulties and sufferings of so many men.

For some time he took refuge with others in a flat at 29 Sagasta Street, which belonged to the Sainz de los Terreros family. The days seemed endless. They could not go out at all. In those circumstances, apart from making greater demands on himself in his life of piety, he continued to read books of cultural interest, because even in a situation like that he was very clear in his mind that he had to make good use of time.

External conditions changed when he entered the Honduras Legation. The general atmosphere there was one of anxiety, which — according to eye witnesses — gave way to a certain relaxation, and one could excuse and even justify any attempt for seeking a bit of comfort. There were many people there, living in a very confined space, people of widely different ages and temperament who had been generously welcomed by the family who ran the Consulate.

Some aspects of life in that Legation, and of the spirit he wished to instil in the others, have been described in number 697 of *The Way:* **Outside events have placed you in voluntary confinement, worse perhaps, because of its circumstances, than the confinement of a prison. You have suffered an eclipse of your personality.**

On all sides you feel yourself hemmed in: selfishness, curiosity, misunderstanding, people talking behind your back. All right: so what? Have you forgotten your free-will and that power of yours as a "child"? The absence of flowers and leaves (external action) does not exclude the growth and activity of the roots (interior life).

Work: things will change, and you will yield more fruit than before, and sweeter too.

The Founder and the members of Opus Dei who were with him, made out a time-table in order to use those hours of enforced seclusion as best they could. They had fixed times for prayer, for get-togethers, and hours of study and solid intellectual work. Among other things they studied languages, which later on would facilitate the spread of the Work and its apostolates over Europe and America.

This same spirit (an inability to be idle is an **incurable illness** for the children of God in Opus Dei) was also observed in Burgos by those who lived with him there until the end of the war, and by those who came there from the different fronts to spend a few hours with him.

On one of his visits José Luis Múzquiz noticed a bed covered with little piles of filing cards. Two people were classifying them. A similar collection of cards had given rise to the first version of *The Way*, which had been published in Cuenca under the title *Consideraciones espirituales*. Don Josemaría had formed the habit of jotting down in the diary or little notebook which he carried in his cassock pocket things that struck him. He wrote very quickly, in a way that did not interrupt his conversation. Those jottings would later help him to remember the idea he had had, or some turn of phrase that had come up in the conversation. Later, on his own, he would elaborate those ideas.

In the calmer moments of Burgos, he typed out and selected many of those ideas for he wanted to publish them as soon as possible, to help those who were still at the fronts, or in the Navy, with their meditation. As things turned out, the book could not be published until after the war for lack of finance. Don Pedro Casciaro, who spent a lot of time with the Founder of Opus Dei in Burgos, confirms that "he did not spend any hour idle".

One can well understand Don Fidel Gómez Colomo's reply when he met Don Josemaría by chance one day in Rome, in the early fifties. Don Fidel had coincided with him in 1927 in the priests' residence in Larra Street. There were a number of "old" priests living there and three young ones: Don Fidel, Don Josemaría and Don Avelino. They were in charge of repairs in the residence and ensuring that the various jobs pending were carried out. That day in Rome, Don Fidel was walking along towards the Apostolic Datary to take a parcel to Cardinal Tedeschini. A car stopped by and he heard Don Josemaría calling out to him:

Where are you going, Fidel? You look lost. I'll take you by car.

When Don Josemaría later invited him home, Don Fidel declined, saying jokingly: "I have heard that you are still building, and as you make everyone work, I won't go. If I did, you'd soon have me laying bricks."

Fr. Vicente Ballester Domingo, a Salesian, was the private secretary of Don Marcelino Olaechea from 1937 to 1939. Don Marcelino, who loved the Founder of Opus Dei dearly, put him up in the Bishop's House in Pamplona, soon after he had returned to Spain after crossing the Andorra frontier. Don Vincente Ballester summarised those days in three words: "He never stopped. Don Josemaría went from one place to another, in a constant and tireless activity, looking after the members of the Work and many other people who were the object of his pastoral zeal all over Spain, as well as priests for whom he showed special care and affection."

Msgr. Escrivá de Balaguer did not stop until the very moment of his death, on 26 June 1975. He died in the room in which he worked.

3. THE SANCTIFICATION OF WORK

There was a doctor in Cadiz who was always in a bad temper when on duty at his social security surgery. In November 1972 he heard Msgr. Escrivá de Balaguer at Pozoalbero. On the way out he told his wife:

"From now on I am going to look after each one of those patients as if I were their own mother."

There have been thousands of such reactions since October 1928. Men and women all over the world, encouraged by the warmth of the words of the Founder of Opus Dei, have made a firm resolution to sanctify their work. This was the great message that he had come to spread among men, making God's design become alive and real to them.

Josef Ganglberger, a doctor too and a professor at the University of Vienna, wrote in September 1975 that it was thanks to Msgr. Escrivá de Balaguer that he had learned to see work as a means of sanctification: "As he himself said, any human work, however insignificant and humble it may seem, contributes to christianise temporal realities and shows their divine dimension; every type of work is to be taken and inserted into the wonderful work of the Creation and Redemption of the world: work is thus elevated to the order of grace, it is sanctified, it becomes a work of God."

Edwin Zobel, a Swiss, first met some members of Opus Dei in 1949 through his work: "In all of them I admired the same spirit of hard work. They worked hard and conscientiously. It surprised me, an untiring worker all my life, to see how hard those young men worked." It was the example of such persons, who made great personal sacrifices smilingly, that made him change the course of his life.

Juan Sagardoy, a professor of industrial law, asserted in an article that appeared in *Informaciones*, a Madrid daily, that one of the most important innovations introduced by Msgr. Escrivá de Balaguer was his struggle to unite Christianity and ordinary work. Prof. Sagardoy pointed out some possible social consequences to which this spirit would lead: to give a christian meaning to work can liberate and dignify workers in an age such as ours in which all too frequently the opposite obtains and work drains away the best in man.

Alejandro Corniero, the labour relations correspondent of the *Noticiero Universal*, improvised the following lines on Friday 27 June 1975: "This man who died yesterday dedicated his life to help people fulfil their supernatural destiny by being better workers and fairer men. He taught that genuine work means loving one's own professional occupation and carrying it out to the best of one's ability. He taught that the best way of being fair and just is to show the same sort of interest in the performance of all one's duties: because, let us realise, at the root of all injustice there is a denial or limitation of someone else's right and this situation is produced every time that someone who has an obligation towards another person, or towards society in general, does not do his duty. So true is this that if we all fulfilled our duties, we would eradicate injustice: just like that."

A well known Spanish trade unionist, Noel Zapico, thinks that justice requires that recognition be given to "the decisive contribution of Msgr. Escrivá de Balaguer towards us Christians being able to discover the human and supernatural meaning of work".

Many thousands of people throughout the world hold this conviction. They are convinced that it is through the preaching and example of the Founder of Opus Dei that they have learned that the cares of their work and of their family life can be converted into a real service to God and to others. This is confirmed by Juan Muñoz Batanero, a Madrid caretaker: "He has done a lot of good to many people who, like myself, carry out very humdrum jobs and might think that we are really not much use for anything."

It must be made clear, however, that this way of looking at christian living is not confined to a particular historical period. It is by its nature universal, because as long as there are men on earth they will have to work; so that, with and from work, a way of sanctity has been opened up for all men of all times and cultures. It is not necessary to change places to seek sanctity.

To sanctify work requires a respect for the natural order of created things and for legitimate autonomy in temporal matters, because the kingdom of God, far from being a theocratic notion, is a reality in the hearts of all Christians, who give life to the soul of the whole of society (without imposing dogmas or trying to channel everyone in a particular direction) when they strive to make Christ reign in the centre of their everyday lives. The Founder of Opus Dei frequently took the opportunity of explaining that light which God had made him see at the beginning of the Work:

When one day in a quiet church in Madrid, I was feeling that I was ... nothing! — not just very little, because that would still have been something — I thought: "Lord, do you want me to do all this wonderful work?" And I lifted up the Sacred Host, without any distraction, in divine fashion ... and there, in the depth of my soul, I understood with a new and complete sense those words of Scripture: Et ego, si exaltatus fuero a terra, omnia traham ad meipsum (John 12:32). **I understood it perfectly. Our Lord was telling us: "If you place me in the very heart of all human activities, fulfilling your duty each moment, being my witnesses in what seems great and in what seems**

little . . . , then, omnia traham ad meipsum! **My kingdom among you will be a reality!"**

The Founder himself explained this central idea on countless occasions in precise and attractive language. Here are a few paragraphs taken from some of his answers to different journalists which were published in a book entitled *Conversations with Msgr. Escrivá de Balaguer:*

Our Lord gave rise to Opus Dei in 1928 to remind Christians that, as we read in the book of Genesis, God created man to work. We have come to call attention once again to the example of Jesus, who spent thirty years in Nazareth, working as a carpenter. In his hands, a professional occupation, similar to that carried out by millions of men in the world, was turned into a divine task. It became part of our redemption, a way to salvation.

The spirit of Opus Dei reflects the marvellous reality (forgotten for centuries by many Christians) that any honest and worthwhile work can be converted into a divine occupation. In God's service there are no second-class jobs; all of them are important.

To love and serve God there is no need to do anything strange or extraordinary. Christ bids all men without exception to be perfect as his heavenly Father is perfect. Sanctity, for the vast majority of men, implies sanctifying their work, sanctifying themselves in it, and sanctifying others through it. Thus they can encounter God in the course of their daily lives.

The conditions of contemporary society, which places an ever higher value on work, evidently make it easier for the men of our times to understand this aspect of the christian message that the spirit of the Work has recalled. But even more important is the influence of the Holy Spirit. His vivifying action is making our days the witness of a great movement of renewal in all christianity. Reading the decrees of the Second Vatican Council, it is clear that an important part of this renewal has been precisely the revaluation of ordinary work and of the dignity of the christian vocation of life and work in the world.

Since the foundation of the Work in 1928, my teaching has been that sanctity is not reserved for a privileged few. All the ways of the earth, every state in life, every profession, every honest task can be divine. This message has numerous implications which the life of the Work has helped me to grasp with

ever greater depth and clarity. The Work was born small and has grown up normally, little by little, like a living organism, like everything that develops in history.

But its objectives have not changed. Nor will they change, no matter how greatly society may be transformed. Opus Dei's message is that under all circumstances any honest work can be sanctified.

People from all walks of life belong to Opus Dei: doctors, lawyers, engineers, and artists, as well as bricklayers, miners and farm labourers. All professions are represented, from film directors and jet pilots to high-fashion hairdressers. It is perfectly natural for Opus Dei members to be up to date with modern developments and understand the world. Together with their fellow citizens, who are their equals, they are part of the contemporary world and make it modern.

In a long article published by *Avvenire*, the Milan daily, on 26 July 1975, Cardinal Baggio underlined the idea that sanctity was for the man in the street, not the preserve of a privileged few; what at first had seemed heretical to many had become after the Second Vatican Council an irrefutable principle. "But what continues to be revolutionary in the spiritual message of Monsignor Escrivá de Balaguer is the practical manner of directing men and women of every condition in life towards christian sanctity.

"The practical realisation of this truth is based on three new aspects which are characteristic of the spirituality of Opus Dei: (1) The christian laity should not abandon or despise the world, but remain within it, loving and taking part in the life of ordinary men and women. (2) While staying in the world, they should know how to discover the supernatural value of the normal circumstances of their lives, including even the most prosaic and material details. (3) As a consequence, everyday work, the activity which occupies and fills the greatest number of hours of ordinary people, and which characterizes their secular personality, is the first thing that needs to be sanctified and the first instrument for christian apostolate."

Msgr. Escrivá de Balaguer always taught that the laity had to follow the example of the early Christians, the age in which the faithful tried to live up to the requirements of the Gospel by taking part in every honest activity of the society in which they lived, while remaining in the world. Just as the early Christians, both men and women, young and old, patricians, plebeians and slaves, were able to sanctify themselves in their common, everyday life and succeeded in converting the pagan world around them, so today's Christians, if they do not have a vocation to the religious state, are called to sanctify the world from within.

Must I affirm once again — he was heard to say in 1967 — **that the men and women who want to serve Jesus Christ in the Work of God are simply citizens, the same as everyone else, who strive to live their christian vocation to its ultimate consequences with a serious sense of responsibility? Nothing distinguishes my children from their fellow citizens.**

The practical consequences of a true lay spirituality did not escape Msgr. Escrivá de Balaguer:

Light is shed upon many aspects of the world in which you live, when we start from these truths. Think, for example, of your activity as citizens. A man who knows that the world, and not just the church, is the place where he finds Christ, loves that world. He endeavours to become properly trained, intellectually and professionally. He makes up his own mind with complete freedom about the problems of the milieu in which he moves, and makes his own decisions as a consequence. As the decisions of a Christian, they derive from personal reflection which endeavours in all humility to grasp the Will of God in both the unimportant and the important events of his life.

Here, at this point, appears the marked aversion of Msgr. Escrivá de Balaguer to every type of clericalism: **But it would never occur to such a Christian to think or say that he was stepping down from the temple into the world to represent the Church, or that his solutions are "the Catholic solutions" to those problems. That would be completely inadmissible! That would be clericalism, "official Catholicism", or whatever you want to call it. In any case, it means doing violence to the very nature of things.**

This passion for freedom is a rich and fruitful inheritance entrusted by the Founder of Opus Dei to the members of the Work and to all Christians:

You must foster everywhere a genuine lay outlook, **which will lead you to three conclusions:**

> **— be sufficiently honest to shoulder your own personal responsibility;**

— **be sufficiently christian to respect your brothers in the faith, who, in matters of free discussion, propose solutions different from your own;**

— **and be sufficiently catholic so as not to use our Mother the Church, involving her in human factions.**

The christian value of ordinary life is well expressed in the homily he delivered in 1967, on the campus of the University of Navarre: **I often said to the university students and workers who were with me in the thirties** (and Cardinal Baggio observes that this was many years before the pastoral constitution *Gaudium et Spes* of the Second Vatican Council) **that they had to know how to** materialise **their spiritual life. I wanted to keep them from the temptation, so common then and now, of living a kind of double life. On the one hand an interior life, a life of relation with God; and on the other, a separate and distinct professional, social and family life, full of small earthly realities.**

No! we cannot lead a double life. We cannot be like schizophrenics, if we want to be Christians. There is just one life, made of flesh and spirit. And it is this life which has to become, in both soul and body, holy and filled with God. We discover the invisible God in the most visible and material things.

Conscious of the newness of this doctrine, the Founder of Opus Dei insisted:

Authentic Christianity, which professes the resurrection of all flesh, has always quite logically opposed disincarnation, **without fear of being judged materialistic. We can, therefore, rightfully speak of a** christian materialism, **which is boldly opposed to those materialisms which are blind to the spirit.**

Work is thus the raw material that must be sanctified, and at the same time the instrument of one's sanctification and the sanctification of others. This means that the life of a Christian is not made up of "disincarnate" idealisms, but of a specific effort to contribute to the building of a more just society, an effort that dignifies all human activity, from the highest to the most humble and hidden. Msgr. Escrivá de Balaguer often commented on the well known texts of Saint Paul: "All things are yours, you are Christ's and Christ is God's" . . . "In eating, in drinking, do everything as for God's glory."

This doctrine of Holy Scripture, as you know, is to be found in the very nucleus of the spirit of Opus Dei. It leads you

to do your work perfectly, to love God and mankind by putting love into the little things of everyday life, and discovering that "divine something" which is hidden in small details.

In a homily entitled *Towards Holiness* he added: **When faith is alive and throbbing within the soul, one discovers instead that Christians do not step aside from everyday life. And that this great sanctity that God is asking of us is locked up here and now in the little things of each day.**

I like to talk about paths and ways, because we are travellers on our way towards our heavenly home, our fatherland. But remember that although a way may have some particularly difficult stretches, although it may make us ford a river or cross a small but almost impenetrable forest, it is usually smooth, without surprises. The real danger is routine: the thought that God is not present in the things of each and every instant, because they are so simple, so ordinary!

And referring to the members of Opus Dei, who strive to embody this new, yet very simple and natural message that ordinary work is to be sanctified, the Founder of Opus Dei said in his Navarre homily in 1967:

Those who have accompanied this poor sinner, following Christ are: a small percentage of priests, who have previously exercised a secular profession or trade, a large number of secular priests from many dioceses throughout the world (...) and a great multitude made up of men and women of different nations, and tongues, and races, who earn their living with their professional work. The majority of them are married, many others are single. They share with their fellow citizens in the important task of making temporal society more human and more just. And they work, let me repeat, with personal responsibility, shoulder to shoulder with their fellow men, experiencing with them successes and failures in the noble struggle to fulfil their duties and to exercise their social and civil rights. And all this with naturalness, like any other conscientious Christian, without considering themselves special. Blended into the mass of their companions, they try at the same time to detect the flashes of divine splendour which shine through the most common everyday realities.

4. WOMEN IN OPUS DEI, 14 FEBRUARY 1930

"Going through the pages of the Missal, I could not help being disappointed at seeing that all the holy women have been nuns, virgins, martyrs, or at least widows", was the humourous conclusion that Wilhelmine Burkhart, a housewife and music teacher in Vienna, had come to. "It has been a wonderful liberation to think that not only struggles and sufferings but also so many joyful human activities — in my case playing or teaching music — can be turned into a constant prayer. Tens of thousands of people owe this 'way' to Josemaría Escrivá de Balaguer."

Mrs. Burkhart was introduced to the Work by her elder son, who is a member of Opus Dei. She went to Rome to see him on 24 September 1971. It was then that she met Msgr. Escrivá de Balaguer. As her son translated from Spanish into German, she heard words which spoke about serving the Church cheerfully, each one in his own place: **You can convert your art into prayer.**

Today, with the perspective of time, it seems the most natural thing in the world that the spirit which the Founder of Opus Dei saw clearly on 2 October 1928 should be as applicable to women as it is to men. However, at first, the Founder was not thinking about them, as he clearly said to the women members of Opus Dei:

I did not want to found the Men's Section or the Women's Section of Opus Dei. I had never thought of the Women's Section. I assure you with a physical certainty, and I mean physical, that you are daughters of God.

It happened on 14 February 1930. As we know, Msgr. Escrivá de Balaguer did not like to speak about those more intimate moments in which Our Lord had made him know His Will. However, sometimes, following the express indication of the Holy See, or due to the insistence of the members of Opus Dei, he did tell some details so that they should thank God for his mercies towards mankind. Thus, on one occasion he recalled:

So that there could be no doubt that it was He who was carrying out his own Work, Our Lord added external things. I had written: "There will never be women in Opus Dei, no fear!" And a few days later . . . the 14th of February: so that it could be seen that this thing was not mine, but against my inclination and against my will.

I used to go to the house of an old lady of eighty, who came

to me for Confession, to celebrate Mass in the small oratory she had. And it was there, in the Mass, after Communion, that the Women's Section came to the world. When I had finished, I went straight to my confessor who told me: "This is as much God's as all the rest."

The foundation of the Work took place without me; the Women's Section, against my personal opinion; and the Sacerdotal Society of the Holy Cross, when I was seeking it and couldn't find it. It also took place during the Mass. It is not a question of miracles: just the ordinary providence of God. For me that the sun should rise and set every day is as much a miracle as that it should stop. And it is even more of a miracle that it should rise and set every day, according to a law imposed by God, which we men already know.

Thus, following such ordinary procedures, Jesus, Our Lord, the Father, and the Holy Spirit, with the most loving smile of the Mother of God, of the Daughter of God, of the Spouse of God, have made me go forward, in spite of what I am: a poor man, a little donkey that God has wished to take by the hand: Ut iumentum factus sum apud me, et ego semper tecum (Ps 72:23).

The house in which the Founder of Opus Dei celebrated the Holy Mass on 14 February 1930 no longer exists. It was in Alcalá Galiano Street, numbers 1 and 3. The Marchioness of Onteiro, the mother of the Foundress of the Damas Apostólicas, lived there. As she was very old, she had asked her daughter Luz if a priest could say Mass for her in her private oratory. She died on 22 January 1931, and was buried in the family vault in the church of La Concepción, in Madrid.

With the foundation of the Women's Section of Opus Dei, the Lord implanted in Msgr. Escrivá de Balaguer the unshakable conviction that women too shared the mission of christianising the world from within: in the home as well as in any other civil occupation. In time, he would be able to say with full justification to a journalist:

I have spent my life defending the fullness of the christian vocation of the laity, of ordinary men and women who live in the world, and, therefore, I have tried to obtain full theological and legal recognition of their mission in the Church and in the world. (...) It is the task of the millions of christian men and women who fill the earth to bring Christ into all human activities and to announce through their lives the fact that God loves

and wants to save everyone. The best and most important way in which they can participate in the life of the Church, and indeed the way which all others presuppose, is by being truly christian precisely where they are, in the place to which their human vocation has called them.

It is patently clear today, after many years have passed, that it is the same spirit that moves the men and women members of Opus Dei. Their juridical, spiritual and moral unity is as complete as their mutual autonomy is evident. On occasion the Founder has compared the work of each Section to that of two little donkeys pulling the same cart along in the same direction, as two parallel forces which do not mix or interfere with each other.

It could perhaps be thought that Our Lord, in separating the foundation dates of the two Sections of Opus Dei, also wished the Founder to be fully conscious from the very beginning of a reality he would later aptly express as follows:

By God's Will Opus Dei is made up of two different Sections, which are completely separate like two distinct works, one for men and another for women; there is no interference whatsoever, in government, or in financial affairs, or in apostolate, or in fact.

Msgr. Escrivá de Balaguer sometimes gave a supernatural reason for the fact that God brought the Women's Section of the Work into existence sixteen months and twelve days after 2 October 1928:

If I had known in 1928 what was in store for me, I would have died. But God Our Lord treated me as a child. He did not lay the burden on me all at once, but led me onward little by little. A little child is not given four errands at once. First it's given one and then another; and then another, when it has done the previous one. Have you seen a little boy playing with his father? The boy has some wooden blocks, of different shapes and colours.... And his father tells him: "Put this one here, and that one there, and the red one over there." ... And he ends up with a castle!

This is the divine way of doing things, he wrote in 1961, full of gratitude: **first one thing and then another, guiding our steps, using secondary causes, human mediation. See what the Acts of the Apostles tell us when they describe the conversion of Saul. After the Lord has wounded him with his grace, Saul says:** Domine, quid me vis facere? **"Lord, what do you want me to**

do?" And he hears God's answer: surge et ingredere in civitatem et ibi dicetur tibi quid te oporteat facere (Acts 9:6); **"arise, go into the city, and there you will be told what you must do." Do you see? First a grace, then a task; with God selecting the times, ways and circumstances. That is how Our Lord has been making his Work: first one Section, then another, and then — another gift — the priests. And in every aspect of our way, in each battle to be won in this beautiful war of peace, Our Lord has always treated me so: first this, then that. That is why I ask you again to join me in giving thanks for this continuous loving Providence that Our Father God has shown.**

When I consider Our Lord's goodness, I am moved to contrition, for any failure on my part to correspond to such great mercy. And because, along this road, I have made others suffer, through my errors (I know not how to bear injustice without protesting and shedding tears: no matter where it comes from, nor to whom it is done); through my errors, I say, and because God Our Lord needed to prepare me: it seemed as if he was giving one blow on the nail and a hundred on the horse-shoe ... perhaps because other people's pain hurt me more.

From 14 February 1930, Msgr. Escrivá de Balaguer set to work on the Women's Section of Opus Dei. He worked more slowly because — for reasons of prudence and refinement — he could not have the constant and continuous relations that he had with men, with the women who felt attracted by the message of the Work (and this would always be the case: in fact, he never lived in a Centre of the Women's Section).

Besides, at that time, young women (who were the most likely to be able to grasp this new spirit) enjoyed very little freedom. They had to account to their parents for everything they did: where they went, with whom, what they would be doing, when they would be back, etc. Furthermore, in those days the Work had no legal entity. It was passing through the delicate moments of the beginning of gestation.

As we have seen, in 1930 Don Josemaría was the chaplain of the Damas Apostólicas. Many idealistic young women of Madrid helped out in the charity dining rooms, sewing groups, and visits to the sick, run by the Damas Apostólicas; but as far as we can see the Founder never talked about the Work there. Knowing him a little, it is not surprising that he should act thus: first, out of respect for that congregation, for its vocations would normally arise from among those young women; and besides, if they had a religious vocation, they could not have a vocation for the Work that God was asking of him, which involved having a secular job or profession in the middle of society.

This must have been one of the reasons why he gave up working in the Patronato de Enfermos in 1931. As we know, in his job as chaplain he had not restricted himself to the small church of the Damas Apostólicas. His apostolic zeal led him to go daily to the poorest suburbs of Madrid, but he was having to devote more and more time to the Work that God was asking of him. His apostolate with men could be done anywhere: walking along the streets of Madrid, or at home; but in order to give spiritual direction to women he needed a confessional, and preferably in a large public church, such as Santa Isabel. In this church, apart from ministering to the Augustinian Recollect nuns, he heard the Confessions — and indeed had been doing so for some time — of a group of young women, from among whom there came some new members of the Work.

He was in the confessional in the church of Santa Isabel before and after his daily eight o'clock Mass. Some women came to know Opus Dei that way. His devotion as he celebrated the Holy Sacrifice prompted them to go to Confession to him and receive spiritual guidance from him. This was a good opportunity for opening up horizons of sanctity and apostolate. A group developed, made up of very different people: a teacher at the nearby school of the Assumption, a domestic, a nurse, and several girls who were not working yet. They all went for weekly Confession to Santa Isabel. It was only there that they saw the Founder of Opus Dei, for he did not go to the meetings they held from time to time in the house of the two older ones. Nor did he go with them on Sundays to the catechism classes they gave in the district of La Ventilla.

However, he was able to lavish priestly care upon María Ignacia García Escobar and did so with extraordinary zeal. She was one of the first women members of Opus Dei and she died in the King's Hospital, on 13 September 1933, in a very holy way. She had tuberculosis of the intestine and underwent a number of operations, and suffered very much. It is moving to read the copybooks she wrote in that hospital for the incurably sick, in a style that recalls the Spanish classics. She had asked to be admitted to the Work on 9 April 1932. "A new era of Love," she wrote in her diary two days later; but before that date she had already been offering everything up for Don Josemaría's intention: her fever, her multiple aches, and the intense pain, which at times prevented her from writing for weeks on end. María Escobar was well aware that she was doing the Work of God from her hospital bed: "It has to have secure foundations. Let us try to make these foundations out of granite, lest there should happen to us what occurred to the building the Gospel talks about, which was built on sand. First the foundations; the rest will come later."

The sufferings of the sick in that hospital contributed to make the foundations of Opus Dei unshakable. María Ignacia had been praying for the Work since the last months of 1931, when Don José María Somoano Berdasco said to her:

"María, we have to pray a lot for an intention, which is for the good of all mankind. I am asking you to pray for something which is not just for a few days. It is a universal good which requires prayers and sacrifice now, tomorrow and always."

Don José María Somoano encouraged many sick people to offer their sufferings for this intention. They offered their troubles and their very painful operations; or they ate when they had no appetite. María would write: "At night, when my pains do not let me sleep, I spend the time reminding Our Lord many times about his intention."

María's sister Braulia moved to Madrid when María's illness was reaching its end. María "was wonderfully well attended spiritually by the Father. Other girls also went to see her and keep her company: some of them belonged to the Work." Braulia recalls the difficulties one of them encountered in teaching catechism in one of the suburbs of Madrid, for her family was against her going to districts which were so dangerous then. She also remembers another who typed some outlines to help María do her meditation, using spiritual themes that had been developed in the meetings they held.

This group of women was to suffer very much when the Spanish war started in July 1936. They lost contact with the Founder. Furthermore, in the confusion of those dramatic moments, news reached them that he had died. Some never saw him again, convinced he was dead. Others, when the war ended, were helped by Don Josemaría to understand that they did not have a vocation to the Work; not because they were lacking in zeal, but because during those years in which they had been out of touch with him they had turned to ways and modes of behaviour which were proper to the religious life, and which are holy ways for those to whom God gives that vocation but not for those whom he calls to serve him in the world.

In the meantime, the Founder of the Work had recommenced his activity. He looked first of all to the sisters of the young men who were members of the Work or had a great affection for it. It was thus that vocations for the Women's Section arose, even before the Spanish war ended.

When the war was over and Don Josemaría was back in Santa Isabel, they went to him there for Confession. Soon he moved to Jenner Street, where he lived with his mother, sister and brother on a different floor from that of the students' residence.

It was in that house in Jenner that Lola Fisac heard him explain Opus Dei in depth: "I thought it overpowering and beautiful. I was a bit frightened" — because even though the members were very few he was already describing the Work to them as it would be in the future, spread throughout the world, and at that time they had nothing, not even a place where they could meet.

Towards the end of 1940 they hired a small flat in Castelló Street as a centre for apostolate, while they all continued to live with their families. They furnished it as best they could, with furniture brought from their parents' homes. The experiment did not last long: it did not seem prudent for a young priest to be going assiduously to an empty flat to give formation to a group of women who were also young. . . . For this reason, in December of that same year, they left the flat and began to go to Lagasca Street, where it meets Diego de León. Here a new Centre of the Work had been opened. The family of Don Josemaría went to live there in an independent apartment. It was there — completely separate from the men — that he was able to attend them spiritually. Thus the new members of the Women's Section began their formation.

Others would follow shortly. Soon the time came to establish another Centre of the Women's Section of the Work. It commenced in the summer of 1942 in Jorge Manrique Street.

Though the Work was in its beginnings, the apostolic panorama was already well defined. Fr. José Luis Múzquiz remembers how the Founder of Opus Dei in 1943 explained things to the members of the Work who were going to be ordained and would have to look after the spiritual needs of the women of Opus Dei who had to sanctify themselves and to do apostolate in their own profession or job. A few of them would be engaged in the work — which he stressed was a professional job — of looking after and administering the Centres of the Work. The Women's Section, apart from paralleling the apostolates of the Men's Section, would also have some of their own: work with women from rural areas, lending libraries, etc.

The Founder of the Work was enthralled by the tasks that the women members would perform in the future. He prayed, and got others to pray, and he offered mortifications and did penance so that the work would prosper as soon as possible. He put infinite patience into training those women. **Dream and your dreams will fall short,** he would tell them encouragingly. He instilled in them a gigantic faith, because humanly speaking there was hardly anything as yet, but he placed his trust in God alone and was certain that the work would spread throughout the world. He also consoled them when they had to face the inevitable contradictions and misunderstandings: **If you do not find the Cross** — Fr. José Luis Múzquiz remembers him saying once when he blessed one of them who was going on a journey — **it would be a sign that you're off course, for you would not have found Christ.**

From the very first moment, even though it was something practically unheard of at that time, he was concerned about their doctrinal-religious formation. According to Encarnación Ortega, when they were in the Centre in Jorge Manrique Street in 1943: "there were no more than four or five of us in the Work there, and we already had a lecturer from the seminary of Madrid who taught us theology and gregorian chant."

Now, barely thirty years later, many women members of the Work hold doctorates in theology or canon law, and can themselves continue that work of formation.

Many others have reached equivalent standards in the most diverse fields of secular knowledge. As Beatriz Mercedes Briceño-Picón, a Venezuelan journalist, wrote in *El Nacional* (Caracas): "They carry out all the noble jobs and professions on earth, from the simple and endearing work that leads christian love to toil at the land, in a workshop or at home, to the difficult mission of university lecturers or working in top posts in the civil service." It is not surprising to hear that the majority of women in Opus Dei are housewives, who try to make their homes **bright and cheerful** havens of peace, where their children from an early age learn to practise christian virtues and prepare to work seriously in the service of their fellow human beings.

It should be stressed that both men and women share the same spirit and responsibility, and feel an identical human and apostolic

sense of urgency. For Msgr. Escrivá de Balaguer there are no differences whatsoever between them, as far as their personal dignity or condition as children of God is concerned. The special characteristics of
men or women can be properly understood only if one starts on the
basis of their fundamental equality, as is pointed out in the clear and
brilliant answers he gave to the editor of the Madrid magazine *Telva*,
and which were published in *Conversations with Msgr. Escrivá de Balaguer*.
I invite the reader to go, for instance, to number 90 in that book and
read it, but introducing the word "man" every time it says "woman".
He will notice how it does not make any difference, because their
responsibilities as persons and children of God are equal.

It is easy to understand, therefore, his exclamation, in another
passage of that book, at number 14:

**I still remember the surprise and even the criticism with
which some people reacted to the idea of Opus Dei's encouraging women who belong to our Association to seek degrees in
theological studies. Now instead they are tending to imitate us
in this, as in so many other things.**

**Nevertheless I think resistance and misgivings will disap-
pear little by little. Basically it is only a question of understanding the Church, of realising that the Church is not composed
only of clerics and religious, but that the laity also, men and
women, are People of God, and have by divine law a mission
and responsibility of their own.**

5. THE SACERDOTAL SOCIETY OF THE HOLY CROSS

On 13 July 1975, Cardinal Casariego ordained 54 members of
Opus Dei to the priesthood, all of them professional men. Including
them, the number of lay members of the Work who had been called
to the priesthood reached nearly a thousand. The first three, Don
Alvaro del Portillo, Don José María Hernández de Garnica and Don
José Luis Múzquiz, had been ordained by Don Leopoldo Eijo y Garay
in Madrid on 25 June 1944.

This date was an important date and remained impressed in the
heart of the Founder of Opus Dei. He was later to comment many times
that the first ordination of priests had caused him **at the same time
great joy and great sadness:**

I love the lay condition of our Work so much, that it really hurt me to make them clerics; yet, on the other hand, the need for priests was so clear that it had to be pleasing to God Our Lord that those sons of mine should be ordained priests.

The Work needed priests who, together with the training and virtues proper to all good priests, had personal experience and a living knowledge of the spirit of Opus Dei. This would help them to serve the men and women members of the Work effectively and to cooperate in the apostolates of the lay people. Priests were needed because although the lay members do really give effective spiritual help to their equals, nevertheless they inevitably come up against what Msgr. Escrivá de Balaguer graphically called **the sacramental wall.**

In 1945 he wrote: **We need priests with our spirit: priests who are well prepared, cheerful, active and effective; priests who approach life with a sporting spirit and gladly sacrifice themselves for their brethren without feeling that they are victims.**

Recalling the ordination of the first three priests, he was grateful for the sincere congratulations he had received from a great variety of people, and underlined that this was a **new pastoral phenomenon that has arisen within the Work of God: young university graduates, men who could freely choose from among the many prospects that lay open to them in life, who decide to serve all souls — especially those of their brothers and sisters — without receiving stipends, and to work very hard: in fact the hours of each day will not be sufficient for their spiritual task.**

A new pastoral phenomenon had indeed emerged in the life of the Church, but it was also a novelty in Church law, for when someone becomes a priest in Opus Dei his call from God to fulfil his christian vocation perfectly does not change. Although the priesthood is **the greatest thing God can give a soul,** the mind of the Founder of Opus Dei was also that **the priesthood for us is a circumstance, an accident, because, within the Work, the vocation of priests and laity is exactly the same.**

We are all the same in Opus Dei. There is only a practical difference: the priests have a greater obligation than the others of laying their hearts on the ground like a carpet, so that their brothers may tread softly.

This is not the place to analyse the novelty and the rich theological and ascetical consequences of this pastoral phenomenon, which has now spread far and wide. Cardinal Frings summarised it very well, on 27 August 1972, on the occasion of the first solemn Mass of a priest of Opus Dei in Cologne: "It is the will of Jesus Christ, who founded the Church and laid down its rules, that the majority of the holy Sacraments can only be administered by those who have been ordained priests. And that is why this Association too needs priests, who, however, do not as a rule hold office within the Association: that is for the laymen. But when it comes to celebrating Holy Mass or to administering the Sacraments, especially the Sacraments of Penance and the Eucharist, or of giving personal spiritual guidance, priests are required. Priests in Opus Dei play a discreet, unshining role. They therefore have to be conscious from the very beginning, that it is not honours that await them, but a task of service to the lay people who struggle to follow their path in the Church of Christ in order to achieve sanctity. This is the thesis that Msgr. Escrivá de Balaguer has preached for so long and that the Second Vatican Council has made its own."

It is only fair to point out that what today seems normal to thousands and thousands of people all over the world, because they have seen it lived by hundreds of priests of Opus Dei, required much prayer and penance on the Founder's part. In one of his writings of 1956, Msgr. Escrivá de Balaguer told the members of the Work that he had prayed **confidently and eagerly for many years,** for the first priests, **and for those who would later follow in their footsteps: and I prayed so much, that I can now affirm that all the priests of Opus Dei are sons of my prayer.**

He was supernaturally certain that the priests had to come from among the laymen of the Work itself, but he did not know how to solve the serious legal problems that this posed. His years of prayers were listened to:

On 14 February 1943, after having sought and not found the juridical solution, Our Lord wished to give it to me, clearly and precisely. When I had finished celebrating the Holy Mass in a Centre of the Women's Section (...) I was able to speak of the Sacerdotal Society of the Holy Cross.

That Centre was located in a house, which no longer stands, in Jorge Manrique Street in Madrid, where the women of the Work were allowed to have the Blessed Sacrament reserved.

Before 14 February 1943, with the problem as yet unsolved, but with great faith in God's Providence and with years of foresight, he had got a group of members of the Work to begin their priestly studies.

With the approval of the Bishop of Madrid he selected a team of first-class teachers. There were some renowned Dominicans from the *Angelicum* in Rome, who had not been able to go back there because of the World War. Such was the case of Fr. Muñiz, who taught them dogmatic theology, and of Fr. Severino Alvarez, their professor in canon law. The present Archbishop of Seville, Cardinal Bueno Monreal, taught them moral theology. The present Archbishop of the Spanish Forces, Msgr. José López Ortiz, taught them Church history. Fr. Celada, O.P., who had worked for many years in the Biblical Institute of Jerusalem, was their Scripture tutor. Other teachers were the friar Justo Pérez de Urbel, who specialised in liturgy, Don Máximo Yurramendi, later Bishop of Ciudad Rodrigo, Don Joaquín Blázquez, the present Director of the Francisco Suárez Institute of Theology within the *Consejo Superior de Investigaciones Científicas*, Fr. Permuy, C.M., etc.

Many years later, on 25 June 1969, Msgr. Escrivá de Balaguer celebrated in Rome the silver jubilee of the first three priests, and he then recalled:

When these first three were going to be ordained, they studied intensely and they had the best teachers that I could find, because I have always been proud of the scientific preparation my children have had as a basis for their apostolic action. They studied very, very hard . . . I thank you for having given me this holy pride — which in no way offends God — of being able to say that you have had a marvellous ecclesiastical training.

He put a lot of effort into their formation. He made them study without pressing or hurrying them, but at the same time with constancy.

The lectures were given at Diego de León, and examinations were also held there, with an examining board formed by three of the teachers. While it was still necessary they took the exams of the five years of Latin and two years of philosophy at the Conciliar seminary of Madrid.

But their time was not spent exclusively in study. Lectures were combined with work and attending to the apostolic activities. They were really busy, above all Don Alvaro del Portillo, who was already the Secretary General of Opus Dei and helped the Founder in a special way. They had to find time, day or night, to study, and study hard. They were aware that they had to study intensely while being at the same time completely available, for membership in the Work was increasing and so were the apostolic tasks, and Msgr. Escrivá de Balaguer was still the only priest.

As soon as they had finished the lecture courses — having attended the same number of periods as were laid down for a pontifical university — and with only the examinations pending, they would leave Madrid and go to places like El Escorial to concentrate on study and prepare for their final exams.

The Founder of Opus Dei followed their studies very closely. He personally looked after the spiritual, pastoral and apostolic formation of those future priests. Fr. José Luis Múzquiz remembers with gratitude the long walks they had along outlying roads of Madrid, and also, during those periods of preparation for exams (when they stayed at El Escorial or *El Encantiño*, a guesthouse near Torrelodones), the visits he paid them, in the evening, to speak to them or go for a walk, teaching them how best to serve the Church, the Pope, all mankind and the Work, through their future priestly work. "The Father did all this without any fuss, as if it were nothing. But it was an effort added to the burden of work he carried on his shoulders: directing the Work, being the only priest with an unending and exhausting activity: and on top of it all the slander and misunderstanding that he had to put up with."

Years later, in 1956, the Founder referred to the formation of those three priests in the following terms:

When I began to train the first priests of the Work, I exaggerated — if I can put it that way — their philosophical and theological formation, and did so for many reasons: the second reason was to please God; the third because many affectionate eyes were looking to us and I could not let those souls down; the fourth, because there were people who did not like us and were looking for motives to attack us; another is because I have always urged my sons to get the best possible professional formation, and I could not demand less in their religious formation. And the first reason — for I thought I might die at any moment — is because I have to render an account to God of what I have done, and I ardently desire to save my soul.

From then on, without any noise or fuss, this "harvest of priests" has often been repeated. The numbers add up to an extraordinary tally. As Cardinal Casariego said in 1975, "for the first time in the history of the Church, a priest in his lifetime has brought nearly a thousand professional men to the priesthood, all trained in the different branches of knowledge, and proceeding from the five continents". Had he done just this and nothing else, was the comment made at the time by a Seville priest, "he would already have achieved something really admirable".

However, the Sacerdotal Society of the Holy Cross was not, so to speak, complete, until priests who had not belonged to Opus Dei before their ordination could also join. With these diocesan priests, the Founder experienced something similar to what had happened with the ordination of the first members of the Work. The idea was clear enough, but he could not find the legal format for putting it into practice. There was no way open according to the canon law then in force.

From a theological point of view, the vocation to Opus Dei is the same for lay people as for diocesan priests: **the same vocational phenomenon,** as the Founder always said; but he could not see the juridical solution (as happens with so many other problems, which today seem elementary and easy because they have been solved).

He had even made up his mind to leave Opus Dei, to devote himself to a new foundation for diocesan priests: **for love of you, which means for love of Jesus Christ,** he assured a large group of priests, with heartfelt emotion, on 14 November 1972 in La Lloma (Valencia). He informed the directors and directresses of Opus Dei of his decision. They were both sorry, and glad, because they understood the apostolic need. He also told his sister Carmen and his brother Santiago, and asked them not to worry if slanders started all over again: **it's only this.** Before doing this, he had informed the Holy See, which had given its approval.

There were priests who were waiting for the problem to be solved, some of them since they had met the Founder of the Work. They had manifested their wish to form part of Opus Dei there and then. He had to ask them to wait.

At a given moment, however, Our Lord made him know that no new foundation was required, and that there was, therefore, no need for him to abandon the Work.

As he would often explain later, God always does things very well, and as all the members — lay people and priests — share the same vocation, the diocesan priests have also found a legally approved place within Opus Dei. Many years later in 1972, at Islabe (near Bilbao), he confessed to a large group of them:

I am very grateful to Our Lord because you are brothers of your brothers, and that to achieve this it has not been necessary to rend the heart of a father and a mother.

CHAPTER FOUR

A TIME FOR FRIENDS

1. THE FIRST MEMBERS OF OPUS DEI

The history of the beginnings of Opus Dei can be summed up as the history of the friends of its Founder. After 2 October 1928, Don Josemaría, with his new light, carried on life as normal. The new supernatural light now guiding his priesthood led him to seek people who would be ready to share that "madness" that God had proposed to him.

When he went to Madrid in 1927 he left behind most of his friends in Aragon and La Rioja. Some friends of his family lived in Madrid. After 2 October 1928, those friends, together with others he made through his priestly work, and his lecturing at the Cicuéndez Academy and the private classes he gave, were the field where the seed of vocations to Opus Dei would grow.

A case in point was Luis Gordon, one of the first members of Opus Dei. Luis was a relative of the Marchioness of Onteiro, the mother of Doña Luz Rodríguez-Casanova, the Foundress of the Damas Apostólicas. Don Josemaría was the chaplain of their Patronato de Enfermos from 1927 onwards. It was through this family that they met, and in 1931 Luis Gordon was one of the persons on whom the Founder of Opus Dei could rely especially, for he was already an industrial

engineer and had started a malt-house in Ciempozuelos. Luis Gordon is
one of a group, which included the Romeos and other friends, who
from 1931 onwards devoted their Sunday afternoons to visiting the sick
in the General Hospital of Madrid. He is the person referred to in
point 626 of *The Way*:

**Isn't it true, Lord, that you were greatly consoled by the
childlike remark of that man who, when he felt the disconcert-
ing effect of obedience in something unpleasant, whispered to
you: "Jesus, keep me smiling!"?**

The story behind it occurred in that hospital where they used to
go to help the patients in all sorts of ways: cutting their nails, combing
their hair and chatting kindly to them. Msgr. Escrivá de Balaguer
referred to Luis Gordon and to this incident in 1972:

**I remember someone — and I can talk about him because
he has been in Heaven for many years. He was from a well
known family and was one of the first in that period, in the
very early years of Opus Dei. One day he collected a chamber
pot from a tuberculosis patient and it was . . . ! I told him:
"That's the spirit, go and clean it!" Then I felt a bit sorry for
him, because I had seen in his face that it made him sick. I
went after him. On the same floor — it was a general ward —
there was a small room for cleaning those pots, and I saw him
with a marvellous heavenly look, cleaning it with his whole
hand.**

As had happened with other souls of similar supernatural stature,
such as María Ignacia García Escobar and Don José María Somoano,
the Founder of Opus Dei was not able to count on Luis Gordon to
continue with the Work. He died in November 1932.

Through these visits to the General Hospital Don Josemaría met
other people. Some joined the Work, others did not, but all shared his
apostolic zeal. One of the friends he made there was Jenaro Lázaro, the
sculptor. On Sundays, when the visits were over, Jenaro would stay
behind a while talking to Don Josemaría. Those conversations left an
indelible mark: "He was a man of God," Jenaro recalls, "who drew
people towards God. I have often thought since that the Father's
apostolate was based on real friendship, for as soon as one got to know
him, he was a friend for life."

José Manuel Doménech, who now lives in Lérida, also used to
chat with Don Josemaría after his visits to the hospital in Santa Isabel.
He sees as outstanding "the generosity with which he used to spend

time with us — the group of students who went to care for the sick — and also with the patients themselves".

Day by day, untiringly, dedicating the best of his time to prayer, accompanied by the petitions and sufferings of the sick in the hospitals of Madrid, the Founder of Opus Dei carried out his mission: with his friends and with the friends of his friends.

Isidoro Zorzano had been a fellow student of his at school in Logroño. They had hardly seen each other since, although they kept in touch by letter. After 1928, Don Josemaría immediately thought of him, with the idea of speaking to him about the new born Opus Dei. On 24 August 1930 they met in Madrid. Isidoro was working in Malaga as a railway engineer. He had come to Madrid with the idea of speaking to Don Josemaría about his spiritual life. He felt a desire to give himself to God, but he did not know how to proceed, because he also saw his own professional vocation very clearly. Isidoro always considered — until his death in 1943 — that his meeting with the Founder of Opus Dei in 1930 had been providential. God's hand had been behind their unexpected encounter in a Madrid street — Nicasio Gallego Street — which was not one that Don Josemaría normally went along. They talked, and from that day on Isidoro knew he could dedicate himself fully to the service of God in his ordinary life and in his work as an engineer.

Juan Jiménez Vargas met the Founder of Opus Dei at the beginning of 1932, simply as a casual visitor for a few minutes. He was just accompanying a friend of his, Adolfo Gómez, who was going for Confession. Subsequent personal experience taught Juan that Don Josemaría was always asking the young men who went to Confession to him for names of friends who could take part in his apostolate.

The members who joined in those years, when they speak about their vocation, usually say that it was a friend who took them to meet the Father. Don Ricardo Fernández Vallespín was a student at the School of Architecture in Madrid in 1933, and he had just over a year to go to finish his studies. His parents were not very well off and he was helping to pay for his studies by giving private classes to José Romeo. Ever since his Saragossa days the Founder of Opus Dei had been a friend of the Romeo family. He met Ricardo in their house one day when he went to give his class. Ricardo had never thought about vocation. He just wanted to finish his studies as soon as possible and earn a living. At the same time he was concerned about the situation in Spain and thought that something ought to be done about it. Yet he felt attracted by "that priest, who shone through in his speech, which was normal and simple, as someone fully committed to God". He made an appointment to see Don Josemaría. They met a fortnight later, on 29 May, at 4 Martínez Campos. Shortly afterwards Ricardo asked to join the Work.

Msgr. Escrivá de Balaguer was willing to wait; he did not hurry things. In particular, he never exploited friendship. He never turned it into a mere instrument of apostolate. Above all, he was a friend to his friends. God made use of his sincere friendliness to draw the first members towards his Work; but the Founder did not speak about Opus Dei to many of those friends — even to those that came to him for spiritual direction. Often he just asked them to pray for him and for his apostolic work.

Manuel Aznar pointed out in *La Vanguardia Española* of Barcelona, that Don Josemaría never "asked me, or suggested or even hinted in a vague way that I should join the Work. We used to speak about everything, except about that and politics." Aznar introduced his article explaining how they had met. It is once again a story of friendships: "My friendship with the Founder came through the Portillos, who were related to a distinguished friend of mine from Burgos, Luis García Lozano — whom God preserve! — and to the unforgettable Dr. José María Pardo Urdapilleta. I knew three Portillos: a doctor, a captain in the Spanish Legion, and a civil engineer. The name of the last was Alvaro. For many years now he has been a priest, a doctor in canon law and in philosophy, sharp and profound in ecclesiastical matters, the Secretary General of Opus Dei, and from the start an indispensable collaborator of Msgr. Escrivá de Balaguer."

Don Josemaría was if anything even more careful to respect freedom in spiritual direction. He let each person follow his own way. Some young men whom he directed for years were never asked to consider the possibility of joining the Work. Others were guided by him to the priesthood or to the religious life. Many were directed towards matrimony; he helped them see marriage as a vocation, and he told them that in time they could form part of Opus Dei. In the meantime, as was usual with him, he made himself completely available to them, attending to them without any hurry and as if he had nothing else to do.

He practised as a normal thing something which is so characteristic of Opus Dei and which he describes in *The Way* as **the apostolate of friendship and confidence.** A member of the Work, just the same as any other ordinary person, does not do "strange" things in order to find God or to lead others to God. He simply works, and fulfils his professional duties. He is a friend to his friends. He tries to give as good example as he can in his family life. In a word, he devotes himself — without changing his place or state in life — to the same human activities and civil occupations that he would carry out if he were not a member of Opus Dei. That was what the Founder did before 2 October 1928 and what he continued to do afterwards in the light of his new vocation.

2. A CHEERFUL AND OPTIMISTIC FRIEND

"He was very cheerful and understanding, very straightforward and unaffected. He made friends with everyone and everyone loved him. I never heard of anybody who had a personal grudge against him," says the Dominican Fr. Sancho.

This verdict is unanimous: Msgr. Escrivá de Balaguer was a great friend and he had many friends. This was proved to an astonishing degree at the time of his death. It was enough to read the newspapers. Articles, commentaries and memories were published throughout the world, expressing affection for a lost friend. The names of many of those who signed them must by now be familiar to the reader, for they have been quoted in the preceding pages. Here I simply wish to underline the diversity and universality of his friendships.

Alongside the friends of his childhood and of his student days, we find his teachers and his pupils. Then there are journalists and writers, such as Aznar or Cortés Cavanillas. University men, such as Rodríguez-Casado, Albareda or García Hoz; artists and workers, such as Jenaro Lázaro or Gonzalo Larrocha, the errand boy of the DYA residence at 50 Ferraz Street; priests and religious, some of whom were later to render outstanding service to the Church: Vicente Blanco, Sebastián Cirac, José María García Lahiguera, Casimiro Morcillo, Pedro Cantero, José María Bueno Monreal, Marcelino Olaechea, José López Ortiz, and so on.

Viktor E. Frankl, who at seventy is still one of the leading figures in modern psychiatry, met the Founder of Opus Dei in Rome. He and his wife had travelled to Rome for professional reasons, and they were received by Msgr. Escrivá de Balaguer. Prof. Frankl, who is Jewish and works in Vienna, afterwards summarised his impressions:

"If I am to say what it was that fascinated me particularly about his personality, it was above all the refreshing serenity which emanated from him and warmed the whole conversation. Next the unbelievable rhythm with which his thought flows, and finally his amazing capacity for getting into immediate contact with those he is speaking to."

Naturally, the first testimonies of his friendliness come from Barbastro and Logroño. We have seen them in Chapter One. Concepción Pueyo, who met him in Barbastro when she was about twenty-five and he about ten or twelve sums it up nicely: "I remember distinctly that he was a normal boy and mischievous, but very cheerful. His cheerfulness was catching. He passed it on to all of us who were close to him, both family and friends."

José Manuel Doménech de Ibarra still recalls vividly, after many years, his first impressions of Don Josemaría. They first met in 1930 and Doménech still remembers "a young cheerful priest, ever in a good mood". Doménech stresses his youthful appearance, because he had always thought they were the same age and only later found out that the Founder of Opus Dei was in fact seven years older.

Alfredo López met him ten years later, and his recollections, which appeared in the Madrid newspaper *Ya*, are very similar: "When I had the good fortune to approach that priest of God I felt invaded by his inexhaustible affection, which was full of tenderness, kindness, understanding and good humour. I was left with a sensation of spiritual well-being, and a desire to be rid of all selfishness so as to dedicate myself to the service of others."

"When I greeted him for the first time, he was smiling," wrote a Colombian journalist in *El Tiempo* (Bogotá), on 30 June 1975. "And when I saw him for the last time, a few months ago in Caracas, his face continued to show that peace and joy which were the permanent characteristic of his whole life."

It is worth stressing that very different people have reacted in identical fashion. The differences we refer to are not only of temperament, but also with respect to their religious attitude. It is surprising that a Dominican Friar, a Swiss convert, a Camaldolese monk, an Italian journalist, and a student who prides himself on being anti-clerical, all coincide, using practically the same expressions. The Dominican is Fr. Garganta, who met the Founder in the 1940s in Valencia: "Among the human virtues of the Father, what impressed me first of all was his amazing talent for cordiality, from which flowed a talent for understanding, that is marvellous in an apostle."

The Swiss convert is Edwin Zobel. After meeting some members of Opus Dei through his work, he read *The Way* and felt a great desire to meet the person who had been "capable of instilling so great a spirit of love and self-surrender into people of such worth". When he finally visited the Founder in Rome in 1960, he immediately detected "his extraordinarily amiable and cheerful nature, and his capacity for transmitting his spiritual vigour".

Dom Pío María, the Camaldolese monk, informs us that in the forties a comment sometimes heard in the monastery of El Parral, was: " 'Here comes the priest who is always in such a good mood'. . . One felt enormously at ease by his side, because of his amazingly rich human warmth."

The Italian journalist, Cesare Cavalleri, editor of the Milan magazine *Studi Cattolici*, wrote in the July 1975 issue of that publication that it would be for others to sketch the theological profile of Msgr. Escrivá de Balaguer, but he felt it his duty to give a personal and direct testimony: "My testimony is simply this: Msgr. Escrivá de Balaguer was an infinitely lovable priest. . . . It was impossible to come close to him and not to love him."

Finally, Antonio, the anticlerical student, explains how he came to speak with the Founder of Opus Dei in 1953: "The first thing that really struck me when I spoke to Msgr. Escrivá de Balaguer was his directness and frankness. There was a great sense of assurance in all his words and it transferred itself deeply to me. I immediately felt completely at ease talking to him. As our conversation went on I became invaded by a marvellous peace and an enormous serenity that I had not even remotely sought, because I had only come to consult him about my friend's problem." Antonio was half-way through his medical studies and was very much involved in student politics. He was, besides — as he freely admits — "fiercely anticlerical, probably due to a deficient religious formation". A friend of his, and fellow medical student, had imprudently altered the treatment his sick mother was receiving. She died soon afterwards and her death had given him a terrible guilt complex and had led him to have obsessive thoughts of suicide. Antonio had discussed this problem with another friend of his at a political demonstration and this friend talked to him about the Father: "I agreed to see him," Antonio acknowledges, "though I did not have much faith in the advice of priests." He talked to the Father, taking advantage of a trip to Madrid. Given his anticlerical feelings, he cannot explain the extraordinary trust that he found himself placing in the Father: "It was completely unexpected; so much so that I opened up my heart completely to him, telling him all my life. I felt completely at ease, and I sincerely confided in him all my problems, and then those of my friend."

Msgr. Escrivá de Balaguer sowed peace and joy among all those he met because he lived united to God. This also explains his characteristic way — which was both very friendly and very direct — of speaking about both divine and human matters (which in him also became divine). A journalist, Giuseppe Corigliano, in *Il Giorno* of Milan, refers to "his great understanding for all human situations, his great capacity for loving, and that flair and charm that made him so likeable. When you got to know him better you could discern that his great capacity for being so intimate with everybody was a result of his great intimacy with God. He taught, with deeds rather than with words, that whoever has genuine faith is more human, and has a greater capacity for understanding life and the beautiful and just things of this world."

He sowed peace, friendship and joy generously, and it yielded fruit even in the sad moments of his death. Eugenio Montes brought this out in one of his chronicles from Rome in 1975: "Voltairian anticlericalism has slanderously painted the christian faith in dark and foreboding colours, but a sign of beatitude is precisely its cheerfulness. It has been said that one could detect St. Theresa's dimpled smile in her Castilian prose. Florence's St. Philip Neri, arriving in the full tide of the counter-reformation, was a constant bubbling of sparkling phrases. It is likewise with Msgr. Escrivá de Balaguer: just as his face at death banished all gloominess, so his conversation used to transmit a joyful cheerfulness to all. Don Alvaro del Portillo told me that he had once heard him say: **When I die, pray a lot for me, so that I can leap over purgatory as one leaps over the barrier in a bullring.** St. Theresa and St. Philip Neri, I am sure, would have loved that expression."

3. TRUST, LOYALTY AND GRATITUDE

The friendship of the Founder of Opus Dei was so thoroughly human, so full of refinement and cordiality, that it overcame distance or prolonged absence. Juan Antonio Iranzo, a fellow student of his at the University of Saragossa, draws our attention to this. Many years later, also in Saragossa, he went to the First Communion of one of the children of an old friend of his, Juan Antonio Cremades. Afterwards, Iranzo states, "he saw me, and left the children saying: **I have to be with this old colleague of mine. It is a long time since we have seen each other.** And he was with me in a separate room for about twenty minutes. Every time I hinted that people might be waiting for him, he said: **They have me always, but we meet only very seldom.**"

Msgr. Avelino Gómez Ledo, who lived in the priest's residence in Larra Street in Madrid, in 1927, provides us with one of those typical details of good friendship. He celebrated his saint's day on the feast of St. Andrew Avelino, who is not all that well known in Spain: "Msgr. Escrivá was the only one who remembered that day and greeted me affectionately and supernaturally."

It was not just a matter of temperament, or good memory. Msgr. Escrivá de Balaguer was like that, because among other things he knew how to **trust others.** He has transmitted this criterion to those who have a mission of government within the Association he founded. Opus Dei works on the basis of trust. This is so because the Founder always trusted those he was with. It was no mere theory when he advised parents never to give their children the impression that they did not trust them, and that it was preferable to leave oneself open to being deceived sometimes, for **the trust one places in one's children makes them ashamed of having abused that confidence, and they repent; but if they have no freedom, if they see they are not trusted, they will feel moved to deceive always.**

He could give such advice because he himself had already practised it. In fact he trusted the word of a friend or that of a member of Opus Dei more **than the unanimous witness of a hundred notaries,** as he used to affirm so graphically. He always advised parents to become friends of their children and he practised this most profoundly, as the Founder and Father that he was, within the numerous family of Opus Dei. Contemplating this feature of his friendship, it is impossible not to join him in reflecting on the words of Jesus to the apostles at the Last Supper, *vos autem dixi amicos,* "I have called you friends" (John 15: 15). These words sum up the human and divine meaning of the Redemption.

He was often asked which human virtue he liked most or was most important. He used to answer, "sincerity". At the same time, and even more so towards the end, he also frequently praised "loyalty", for how can one be loyal and faithful to God, if one does not relish the beauty of human loyalty, of faithfulness to others?

In matters of friendship, loyalty is inseparable from gratitude. Msgr. Escrivá de Balaguer used to give thanks to God for everything, *etiam ignotis*, also for unknown gifts, those that Our Lord might have given him without his realising.

He also gave thanks to men. It is not surprising that he should be specially grateful to those who helped him in the beginnings of Opus Dei and when the difficulties were great.

Shortly after the Spanish war, he took the first steps to commence the work of Opus Dei in Bilbao. Don Alvaro del Portillo and Don Pedro Casciaro made some trips there and found rather a tense atmosphere. There still floated in the air the consequences of harsh personal attacks on the Founder of Opus Dei, attacks which sought to make people suspicious of the Work. Many closed their doors on him. However, Carito MacMahon de Ibarra, with her usual dignity, trusted him and gave him a welcome in her home. Msgr. Escrivá de Balaguer never forgot it: any occasion was good to show some special affection towards her family. The Marchioness of MacMahon wrote in 1975 that "he was wonderfully grateful and he always remembered with excessive gratitude the little that I and my family did for him at a time when neither he nor the Work were known".

Fr. Garganta, O.P., witnessed the beginnings of the apostolate of Opus Dei in Valencia, before meeting the Founder personally. His first contact with him was via the Provincial of the Philippine Dominicans, Fr. Thomas Tascón, who spent a day in Valencia and told him: "Fr. Escrivá has asked me to give you the following message: **Fr. Garganta, I am very grateful and happy with what you are doing for my boys: a brotherly embrace.**" In summer 1975, Fr. Garganta confirms that "the Father was very grateful for what I did for him and his sons; he went further than I deserved, because he was very generous indeed, and I was only too happy to do it".

His gratitude was not just good manners: a word said and then forgotten. On the contrary, the Founder of Opus Dei continued to be grateful years after the event.

The Moncloa Residence was set up for students in 1943. The Founder of the Work knew the Mother General of the Religious of Domestic Service and he approached her to see if she could find someone who could work in the new residence. In the absence of the Mother General, Mother Carmen Barrasa attended to his request. Recently

Mother Barrasa stated that Msgr. Escrivá de Balaguer never forgot that kindness and that he had gone to the ceremony of beatification of their Foundress in Rome (in 1950) and that, furthermore, he had arranged for the domestics, members of Opus Dei, who were then in Rome, to go as well. That same afternoon, he had gone to their Mother House to congratulate them personally and took them a big box of chocolates to show the high regard in which he held them.

Msgr. José María García Lahiguera also testifies to the gratitude of Msgr. Escrivá de Balaguer, for, while he was the spiritual director of the Major Seminary of Madrid, he had heard the Father's Confession weekly between 1940 and 1944. "In deeds, and in a very refined way, he always showed his gratitude towards me for hearing his Confession during those years."

There are many examples of his gratitude. Reference was made in Chapter Two to a Mass he said in Andorra after passing over the Pyrenees from Barcelona. That Mass deeply impressed Fr. Pujol Tubau who provided him with all he needed to celebrate. When Fr. Pujol noted down his memories of the Founder of Opus Dei, he referred to the way in which he lived friendship with loyalty and gratitude, and he stressed as something worthy of admiration the way in which he had been able to instil this into the members of Opus Dei. "I could hardly have imagined that from that brief encounter in Andorra, which was one of many in that constant flow of refugees, I would have established such permanent and affectionate friendships as I maintain with the members of Opus Dei."

From those days in December 1937, Fr. Pujol and the Founder of the Work kept in touch through the traditional Christmas and birthday greetings. In April 1944, Fr. Pujol went to Saragossa as Archpriest of Andorra on the occasion of the consecration of Ramón Iglesias Navarri as Bishop of Seo de Urgel. At a reception before the ceremony, the good memories and loyal gratitude which Don Josemaría had for him were proved by something the future bishop said when they were introduced. He said that he had heard many good things about him, and that it has been Don Josemaría Escrivá who had said them. Fr. Pujol comments: "It was a surprise to me at the time, to think how Don Josemaría could remember a priest he had known only in such a brief encounter, but I have later realised that such affability was a consequence of a profound sense of friendship."

Msgr. Escrivá de Balaguer felt especially grateful to his teachers. He always showed them his affection and acknowledgement. More than once he publicly praised his former chemistry master. He quoted him as an example of an orderly man who, when he did an experiment in class, as soon as he had finished using a flask or test tube, would clean everything — even the shelves — and leave everything in its place. The Founder of Opus Dei would comment that this example was one of the ways God had used to teach him to take care in doing even the smallest things.

Don Miguel Sancho Izquierdo was one of his tutors in the faculty of law in Saragossa. He was later Rector of that university, which has always had strong links with that of Navarre. In fact, the first two honorary doctorates granted by the University of Navarre, whose Chancellor from the time it received its Charter was Msgr. Escrivá de Balaguer, were conferred on two Rectors of Saragossa, Don Juan Cabrera y Felipe and Don Miguel Sancho Izquierdo. The investiture was held on 28 November 1964. In his speech the Chancellor of the University of Navarre expressed his particular joy in honouring his old master: **I feel proud of having been his pupil in the lecture halls of Saragossa.**

Msgr. Escrivá de Balaguer's gratitude led him to practise justice with remarkable generosity. He felt this especially, and lived up to it, when it came to remunerating those who worked alongside Opus Dei in the apostolic works run by the Work. He always sought to ensure that they were well paid and made every effort to obtain the financial means to do it, even though those apostolic activities are, of their very nature, nearly always run at a loss.

He was a real "Father" and on more than one occasion he said that he admired a healthy "paternalism" because his christian heart found the mere fulfilment of justice cold and insufficient. He never accepted, for example, that the apostolic works promoted by Opus Dei should give free tuition. His idea was that the pupils should pay something — even if it were only the equivalent of their bus fares, he once said very expressively — so that they would be conscious of their "rights" and could claim them if necessary. At the same time he wanted all the rights of the teaching staff and other employees to be clearly recognised, with properly established holidays, so that they too could work with order and efficiency.

To quote one case among hundreds, Encarnación Ortega recalls that, in 1945, the cook of the Moncloa Residence resigned because she was getting on in years and could not cope with the work in the residence. Msgr. Escrivá de Balaguer gave express instruction that she should be very well looked after and that she should be given a generous bonus. His gratitude was such that he never would limit himself to the strict and rigid fulfilment of the duties of justice.

Another manifestation of his sense of friendship, and one which is specially significant in our days, is that he always knew how to find "time" for his friends, to be with them, specially in difficult moments. Don Antonio Rodilla, who was for many years Vicar General of Valencia, rector of the archdiocesan seminary and director of the San Juan de Ribera University Residence in Burjasot, had been a friend of the Founder of Opus Dei as far back as the thirties. In a letter to a priest of the Work he draws a broad picture of the friendly and attentive care that Don Josemaría showed for him and his family: from his words of consolation in painful personal situations, to his being present on the occasion of his mother's funeral.

Some day someone might patiently calculate the hours he invested inviting those many friends of his to a meal, practising — to quote a phrase from *The Way*, 974 — **the hospitality of the Patriarchs of old, together with the fraternal warmth of Bethany.**

Finally, let us say a word about his letters. It will require much patience and research to reconstruct the correspondence of the Founder of Opus Dei. He wrote thousands of letters, as another way of extending the friendship he deeply felt.

He did not stop writing even during the years of the Spanish war, when postal censorship made it dangerous to send letters by mail. Friendship — real affection — discovers a thousand stratagems. It was then that he began to sign his letters **Mariano,** one of the four christian names he received at Baptism. It also reflected his Marian devotion. His letters of the period are full of conventional names and of images taken from family life, as a means of overcoming the censorship which was practised in both zones into which the country was divided between 1936 and 1939. Many have said how happy and grateful they were at the battle front to receive news in this way from the Founder of Opus Dei. It encouraged them to keep those other battles alive: their interior struggle, their apostolic desires, their concern for others, and the rebuilding of their lives. The letters were to help them to carry on that christian sowing of peace once the war was over.

4. A MAN IN LOVE

One of the "secrets" of Msgr. Escrivá de Balaguer was that he was very approachable. With him it was easy to feel understood, protected and moved to love God. His heart overflowed in affection: towards God, towards men, and towards the world. **Passionately loving the world** is the title of the homily he preached in 1967 on the campus of the University of Navarre. As a title it fits him admirably, for it embraces sorrows and joys, bodily and spiritual cares, big things and things that appeared to be trifles.

The prodigious memory of the Founder of Opus Dei is something that has astonished many people. *Ex abundantia enim cordis os loquitur,* Holy Scripture tells us: "It is from the heart's overflow that the mouth speaks" (Matt 12:34). Because he knew how to love, Msgr. Escrivá de Balaguer noticed, and remembered, a hundred little details which seemed of no importance.

There was a typical example of this in Brazil in 1974. Rafael Llano had not seen him for thirteen years. He greeted the Founder of Opus Dei and was greeted in return with the words of an Italian song (*Timida è la bocca tua*) which the Father used to sing to him affectionately years previously in Rome, referring to the by no means small proportions of the mouth of Rafael and his brothers, nearly all of whom belong to the Work. That afternoon the Father added: **I remember one day when there were many people around I saw one of you and I said: "You are so-and-so." And he answered: "How did you recognise me?" "It's your tiny mouth!" Do you remember?**

Rafael said yes, he and all the family liked to be recognised by their mouth, and by the song. When he'd heard the tune that morning he had burst into tears.

The Founder of Opus Dei was so spontaneous, that he often caught even the people who lived with him by surprise, as for instance in Mexico one day in 1970.

In a corner of the main hall of ESDAI Home Economics School which is run by the Women's Section of Opus Dei in Mexico, stood Victoria, a member of the Work, and her aged mother who was hoping to catch a glimpse of the Father as he passed by. When they told Msgr. Escrivá de Balaguer that she was the mother of two daughters who were domestic assistants and two sons who were labourers and that all four were members of the Work, he went towards her to tell her that he had just seen them in Montefalco. Before anyone had time to react, the lady knelt down to express her gratitude and respect and began to bow as if to kiss his feet: **No, no, you musn't do that, my daughter,** and immediately Msgr. Escrivá de Balaguer knelt down as well. **We are just the same, my daughter, we are children of God. The only difference is that I am nothing but a poor sinner, for whom you have to pray a lot.** It all happened so quickly that no one knew what to do. Victoria tried to get her mother to get up. Don Alvaro del Portillo was waiting to help Msgr. Escrivá de Balaguer to get up. There was a minute-long pause. Nobody spoke . . . nobody moved. One could only hear the friendly voice of the Founder of Opus Dei quietly saying things to the elderly mother, who, with her head covered, was crying. As she left, this peasant woman was heard to say between sobs: "Today has been the happiest day of my life."

For Don José Orlandis, Msgr. Escrivá de Balageur was "the most kind, affectionate and loving of men: he truly was the Father. I have never met anyone with his capacity for loving, loving everyone with his arms wide open for all. It seems impossible that one same person could be so much a man of God, and so deeply human."

Orlandis explains, repeating what he had heard the Founder of Opus Dei himself say, that "the secret was simply that he loved God and men with the same heart. He loved the Father, the Son and the Holy Spirit, and Our Lady, with the same heart of flesh with which he had loved his mother, and with which he loved his sons and daughters."

In 1974 they asked him in São Paulo:

"What can we do to make room for everybody in our hearts and not allow our temperament to be too sensitive and get in the way?"

What do you think? Do you think that the human heart is so tiny that there is room to fit just one family and no more? All our family, and we are thousands and thousands of people, of different races, different tongues and from different continents . . . , they all fit. You will see how easy it is. If you do not lose contact with Jesus, Mary and Joseph; if you struggle to have an interior life; if you are a man of prayer; if you work, because if you don't, there is no interior life . . . then your heart expands.

I used to ask myself that question at first (. . .) "Lord, and what will happen when we are many? Because I now love them so much; but what will happen when we are a multitude?" Well now we are very, very many and my heart has become very big: to the measure of the Heart of Christ, where there is room

for all mankind and for a thousand worlds more if they existed. . . .

Msgr. Johannes Pohlschneider, the Bishop of Aachen, wrote in the *Deutsche Tagespost* that on 27 June 1975 he was told over the telephone the completely unexpected news of the death of the Founder and President General of Opus Dei. He was deeply shocked, feeling as if suddenly a bright star had gone out from the firmament of the Church: "What was even more powerful than the strength of his intelligence were the impulses that his heart spread around him. What the Church says about the great apostle of youth, Don Bosco, in the Introit of the Mass on his Feast comes spontaneously to my head: *Dedit illi Deus sapientiam et prudentiam multam nimis, et latitudinem cordis quasi arenam quae est in littore maris.* It was that *latitudo cordis*, that breadth of heart, in which everything and everybody found room, but very specially the love of God and that of his neighbour, which was the essential characteristic of this priest. He loved, he cherished men in the most real sense of that word, and he was concerned for them and cared for them."

Ignorance, misery, hunger for food or culture, sickness, desolation, loneliness . . . all made Msgr. Escrivá de Balaguer suffer. He relived those scenes of the Gospel that describe the mercy of Jesus when faced with the sufferings and needs of men. As he says in one of his homilies: **He feels compassion for the widow of Naim, he weeps at the death of Lazarus, he is concerned for the multitudes that follow him and have nothing to eat, and above all feels compassion for sinners, who wander through the world without knowing the light or the truth.**

This led him to a clear resolution to get to know the Virgin Mary better, because **when we really are children of Mary, we understand Our Lord's attitude and our heart expands and becomes rich in mercy. We then feel the pain of the sufferings, miseries, mistakes, loneliness, anguish, and the sorrow of our fellow men. And we feel an urge to help them in their needs, and to talk to them about God so that they may learn how to behave as his children, and be able to appreciate Mary's motherly favours.**

His concern reached out both to the great crises of humanity, which affect whole multitudes, and also to the little problems that worry those who live close by. He lived and taught from the beginnings of the Work what he would repeat on 1 October 1967, in Tajamar: **The time for giving pennies and old clothes is over. We have to give our heart and our whole life!**

To give oneself to those who are near, to forget oneself completely, was one of the clues to his constant cheerfulness. In his dealings with others he always underlined the positive aspects of people and events. The Prior of the Basilica of *Nuestra Señora de los Desamparados* in Valencia, Don Joaquín Mestre Palacio, comments: "I have never seen him pessimistic, in spite of everything; in spite of all the very many contradictions, difficulties and calumnies he had to put up with. He always went ahead with serenity and charity, clinging to his faith in Jesus Christ."

Some twenty days before his death, on 7 June 1975, while conversing with more than a hundred members of Opus Dei, Msgr. Escrivá de Balaguer's great heart broke forth spontaneously in praise of the **joy of living:**

You are beginning your lives. Some are beginning and others are ending, but we are all the same Life of Christ: and there is so much to be done in the world! Let us ask Our Lord, always, to help us all to be faithful, to keep on working, to live that Life with a capital L which is the only one that is worthwhile: the other is not worthwhile, it escapes like water slipping through your fingers. Instead, this other Life! (. . .)

What do you want me to say? I have always told you: you have been called by God to be holy, we have to be saints, as St. Paul teaches. "Be perfect, as your heavenly Father is perfect," these are the words of Christ.

To be a saint is to be happy, here on earth as well. And you perhaps might ask me: "Father, and you, have you always been happy?" Without telling any lie, I was recalling a few days ago, I am not quite sure where, that my joy has never been complete. Whenever joy has come, one of those that fills the heart, the Lord has also made me feel the bitterness of being on earth, as a spark of Love. . . . However, I have never been unhappy. I cannot recall having been unhappy ever. I realise that I am a great sinner, a sinner who loves Jesus Christ with his whole soul. So, unhappy never; complete happiness, never either. What a muddle I have got into!

Help me to be holy; pray for me that I may be good and faithful. But let it not all stop at words; put it into deeds as well, because one is moved by good example.

Jesús Urteaga writes in the magazine *Mundo Cristiano* that on another occasion, also in Rome, the Founder of Opus Dei had noticed a gesture of annoyance on the face of a student. He asked him what was the matter. When the student answered that he was tired, the Founder told him with a smile: **My son, I have been going against the grain for fifty years.**

It was not easy to notice this for, as he used to teach others, a smile is very often the best mortification. Eleven days before his death, on 15 June 1975, he said in another conversation with a numerous group of members of the Work:

Out of devotion I like to celebrate frequently — when it is liturgically permissible — the Mass of the Blessed Virgin: I think I have mentioned this before. And there is an old prayer, in which the priest asks for health mentis et corporis, **of mind and body, and then the joy of living. How beautiful! There are some who think the joy of living is something pagan, because what they are looking for is the joy of dying, of foolishly committing suicide, doing themselves to death with dung up to their eyebrows. To follow Christ and to seek sanctity is to have the joy of living. Saints are not sad, or melancholic; they have a sense of humour.**

Professor Viktor E. Frankl also noticed that joy of living during his conversation in Rome with the Founder of Opus Dei, and he describes it in precise technical terms: "Msgr. Escrivá evidently lived totally in the present instant, he opened out to it completely, and gave himself entirely to it. In a word, for him the instant possessed all the qualities of the decisive (*Kairos-Qualitäten*)."

His good humour was catching, because it corresponded to a true joy, which stemmed from the peace of his soul in grace and had also roots in suffering: the normal sufferings that necessarily accompany all men's lives on this earth. He had noticed how the fig growers of his native land used to prick the figs, so that they would be sweeter when ripe, and so he cheerfully accepted the annoying things of each day, seeing in them the **pinpricks** with which the Lord would make his day more fruitful and filled with hope.

On 27 June 1975, *El Noticiero* of Saragossa published an article by José María Zaldívar, which reflects the warmth that the Founder of Opus Dei created around him, as if by osmosis. In October 1960 he had gone to Saragossa to receive an honorary doctorate from his old university. José María Zaldívar was sad as he went to the assembly hall of the faculty of medicine where the ceremony was taking place. For several days he had not been able to do his daily radio programme due to the unexpected death of his brother, which had made him very depressed. The mood in the assembly hall was festive. Msgr. Escrivá de Balaguer entered "very much at ease, completely devoid of all human vanity; smiling and familiar. I understood as he trod that academic path, that he — the author of *The Way* — was showing us his own path and his own way of walking along it. Simplicity which, with pure honesty, begets peace; and gentle rigour which can smilingly undergo crucifixion." José María Zaldívar was so moved that at noon that very day he once more "became a voice on the radio, by sinking my sorrows and describing the cheerfulness of that man from Upper Aragon".

Msgr. Escrivá de Balaguer heard this story and wished to greet him. Zaldívar kept the appointment. When he writes fifteen years later he does not publish their dialogue. He only writes about a big embrace, a blessing and a gift: a copy of *The Way* with a dedication written by the Founder of Opus Dei: *Omnia in bonum* (All is to the good). José María Zaldívar concludes: "In my life, as in that of all mortals, it has been my lot to suffer many things that few will know about. . . . But there, as a lesson to me, were the words of Josemaría Escrivá de Balaguer."

His supernatural and human *joie de vivre* appeared in all its strength when he was faced with tremendous suffering, an incurable illness, the slow wasting away of life. On 13 August 1975, the *Diario de Burgos* published an impressive testimony of a man who wished to make public his "Debt to Msgr. Escrivá de Balaguer". That was the title of his article. Manuel Villanueva Vadillo was a young man when the doctor diagnosed that he had progressive paralysis, which was to confine him to a wheelchair, without any hope of ever walking again. In his chair, guided by the Founder of Opus Dei, he learnt the significance of suffering. Little by little he discovered that suffering, if accepted and offered for love of God, made him a co-redeemer with Christ; and he learned the real meaning of those words: **the sick are the treasure of Opus Dei.**

Manuel Villanueva recalls how the Founder of Opus Dei, when he was a young priest, went to the hospitals to find the means to carry out the Work of God: "Those people were sick and forsaken. Some had tuberculosis, an illness that was then incurable. He found his treasure there, among the patients who offered their pain joyfully, and among those who, led by his hand, entered into Christ's eternal presence. I became and am a part of that treasure."

Somebody also published in the press, on the death of Msgr. Escrivá de Balaguer, that his heart had broken from so much loving. More than one recalled the phrase: **to die a bourgeois death, in a good bed, unnoticed ... but to die of love sickness** (*The Way*, 743). Only that the Founder of Opus Dei in his last years preferred to say that you do not die of love, but you live of love. As he did on 7 January 1975 in La Lloma, near Valencia. A few songs had been sung, and among them one called *Si vas para Chile*, that had been sung to him a year previously in Buenos Aires on the eve of his departure for Santiago. It is a gentle, nostalgic song, which speaks of love:

> If you are going to Chile
> traveller, I pray
> remember to tell her,
> that I die of love . . .*

He commented: **Well, all that about dying of love. . . . You die of love. So, set your heart on Our Lord, really love Him! Love his Mother, and St. Joseph, and live with them in Bethlehem, in Nazareth, in Egypt. . . . Really fall in love, and live of love; for one does not die of love, no. Don't come to me with those stories: love gives life. Without love one cannot live. That is why I want you to be in love: because if you are, I have nothing to fear. You will be faithful!**

And the Founder of Opus Dei concluded:

Live of love, my sons, even though you might "lyingly" say that you die of love!

---

* Si vas para Chile, te ruego viajero, le digas a ella, que de amor me muero . . .

CHAPTER FIVE

GOD AND DARING

1. THE BEGINNINGS IN MADRID

On 16 June 1974 Msgr. Escrivá de Balaguer was speaking to thousands of people in the General San Martín congress hall in Buenos Aires. Almost an hour had gone by when an elderly woman took the microphone. She is the grandmother of several members of the Work. At eighty-four and speaking in an unmistakable Argentine accent she nevertheless told the Father that she was from Madrid.

"From Madrid? From Chamberí or where? What street were you born in?"

"In Los Abades."

"Yes of course. I know it. Near Progreso. And the Dos Hermanas is close by. . . . Go on, go on. . . ."

I have condensed this dialogue which I heard along with hundreds of Madrid people from a film taken that day in South America. Hardly any of us knew where Los Abades or Dos Hermanas were. When we looked them up they were indeed near Progreso. Msgr. Escrivá de Balaguer often said jokingly that he was from Madrid, because Opus Dei was born there. He prayed and walked all over Madrid. He noticed a tiled image of Our Lady on the top of a building in Atocha Street and greeted her whenever he passed by. He looked back nostalgically on the *paseo de coches* of the Castellana. How often he must have

walked up and down those streets speaking to young men in the early
years of his apostolate!

Perhaps it was on one of those walks in the early thirties that he
discovered the image of Our Lady of Pilar on the Columbus monument.
This monument to Christopher Columbus is in the Castellana, near the
National Library. The monument's elaborate decoration, flowers in
neo-gothic arcades, mace-bearers, festoons and intricate symbols, almost
hides the little statue of the Madonna and Child on one side of the
base, but it did not escape the alert and loving heart of the Founder
of Opus Dei. It is a stone image and was missed by those who burned
and pillaged churches and made it their business to destroy and profane
sacred images. We know that when the Spanish war started he and
other members of Opus Dei who were still in Madrid went there to
pray and ask the Blessed Virgin for grace and love to make the Work
grow strong.

He knew Madrid better than did many a native of the city.
Though he was on fire with universal desires, he lived with his feet on
the ground and loved the particular spot where God had placed him:
the house where he was born, his family, the Somontano countryside,
the streets of Saragossa or the hidden corners of Madrid. He was not
rootless and with his unmistakable Aragonese accent, which he neither
wished nor needed to hide, he spread his universal message along all
the paths of the earth.

We find in this characteristic trait of his one of the reasons why
he was able to reach men and women of all races and the most diverse
cultures. There is nothing more universal than a true, rich, warm and
sincere personality.

At the same time this spirit flowed from that most nourishing of
sources, the catholicity or universality of the Church.

Both came together to form what God wanted Opus Dei to be: a
way to holiness centred on the sanctification of ordinary work. And
indeed as canon law professor J. M. González del Valle pointed out in
La Voz de Asturias (Oviedo), commenting upon some texts of Msgr.
Escrivá de Balaguer: "Ordinary work is a universal reality, not a
Spanish custom, nor a fashion born in the century we live in. It is not
too much to suppose that men will be working in future centuries. Nor
does it seem right to restrict work to particular sectors of our planet.
And so this way transcends the limits of space and time. It is not only
that the spiritual phenomenon of Opus Dei has spread in fact to the
different regions of the world, but that the spiritual phenomenon is, of

itself and by its very nature, worldwide, both today when there are thousands of members of Opus Dei and in 1928 when it was founded."

Those who were in contact with Don Josemaría in the early days of the Work were clear from the start that Opus Dei had not come to remedy the needs of a particular country or a particular age, but that God wanted a Work for all men and for all ages.

Natividad González was one of these. She met Don Josemaría in late 1933 or early 1934 when she was living at 121 Atocha Street. From there she used to go to the church of Santa Isabel where he celebrated Mass. Natividad noticed that every day there were people waiting to go to Confession to him. One morning she asked a girl if the priest was a good confessor. The girl replied yes, he was a wonderful Father and she would like him. And Natividad began to go to Confession to him.

The Founder of Opus Dei encouraged her to continue with the apostolate she was doing, her catechism lessons to children in outlying parishes, her visits to the poor and the sick. After some time he spoke to her about the spirit of the Work. She remembers vividly: "It was an apostolate which was very broad, embracing people of all kinds. It had as many facets as there are activities among men, because any activity could be converted into a work of apostolate."

When he chatted with people personally in those early days, more than one thought him "mad", a "visionary". Such opinions were understandable enough, if we remember that the Founder of Opus Dei had nothing but "dreams" to show.

He dreamed of the whole world, of men and women of a thousand races and colours. As on that day, between the 20th and 25th of January 1933, when he had given a formation class to a group of young men. Only three turned up, all of them medical students: Vicente Hernando Bocos, José María Valentín-Gamazo and Juan Jiménez Vargas. It took place in the Porta Coeli Orphanage in García de Paredes, a Madrid street that runs parallel to Martínez Campos, near the Iglesia Circus. The building was a home for ragamuffins, **ragamuffins in the kind sense of the word,** Msgr. Escrivá de Balaguer clarified on one occasion, boys who some holy nuns tried to correct and teach how to work. The Founder of Opus Dei used to go there to teach them the catechism and hear their Confessions. He did his work for nothing; so when he asked if he could have the use of a room, the nuns gladly lent him a classroom they had there and also their chapel. After praying and getting others to pray, and offering sacrifice and likewise getting others to do so, he began this new activity. Only three came that day, from among the many who used to go to him for Confession in his mother's house in Martínez Campos.

A picture of Our Lady which he had picked up in the street presided over the class. After 1931 it was not unusual to find bits of torn-up catechisms in the streets and lanes of the outskirts of the city. Religious persecution was in full swing and the teaching of christian doctrine in schools was forbidden. One day at the foot of a tree in the Los Pinos district of Tetuán he found a small print of the Blessed Virgin. It was a page out of a cheap catechism. As a way of atoning for that, Don Josemaría had the picture framed, using a rich piece of tissue some 12″ square as a background. This was the image that presided over the class. Later it hung in the library of the DYA Academy in Luchana Street. Then it was taken to the Ferraz residence and finally it disappeared from there during the Spanish war.

At the end of the class they went to the chapel for Solemn Benediction, which Don Josemaría gave. Juan Jiménez Vargas was impressed by "the way he prayed as he opened the Tabernacle and genuflected, and above all by the way he held the Monstrance in his hands when he gave the blessing".

The Founder of Opus Dei recalled more than once this first eucharistic act in his work with young people. During his trip to Venezuela and Guatemala in 1975 he said:

Only three came. "What a calamity!" you'd have thought. Well, no! I was very optimistic, very happy, and I went to the nuns' oratory. I placed Our Lord in the Monstrance and gave Benediction to those three. It seemed to me that the Lord Jesus, Our God, was blessing three hundred, three hundred thousand, thirty million, three thousand million . . . whites, blacks, yellow races, of all the colours and combinations that human love can produce. And I have fallen short, because after half a century it is a reality. I have fallen short, because Our Lord has been much more generous.

His emotion was understandable when, shortly after reaching Argentina in 1974, he saw for himself the reality which he already knew from his work of government in Opus Dei:

I still can't believe it. Am I really in Buenos Aires, and surrounded by creatures who are in love with Christ and ready for anything?

His emotion was plain to see before that multitude of members of the Work:

I have been here this morning, all morning in fact, contra spem in spem. **Because there was a priest forty-seven years ago, a priest whom I only half know, who is as much a sinner as I, and who was utterly without human means. He had nothing, except his twenty-six years, the grace of God and a good sense of humour. Humanly speaking that doesn't add up to much, does it? But in the Lord's eyes. . . . And now I see you all here; and there are brothers of yours all over the world: of all colours, and races, and tongues.**

2. IN HOSPITALS AND OUTLYING DISTRICTS

José Manuel Doménech de Ibarra writes: "Opus Dei was born in the hospitals and poor districts of Madrid and I, albeit in a tiny way, was a witness to this fact." And Benilde García Escobar, a sister of María Ignacia, that early member of Opus Dei, and of Braulia, to whom we referred briefly in Chapter Three, adds: "Yes, that's perfectly right. That's where my sister met him and joined Opus Dei; and where Braulia and I met him, and we will never cease thanking Our Lord for it."

Benilde notes especially the Founder's zeal in the King's Hospital where her sister was confined. She was not the only one he visited. He cared for all those people who were suffering from tuberculosis, then a much dreaded disease because in most cases there was no cure. "I was impressed by the cheerfulness and serenity of those women, many of them mothers, poor and cut off from their children for fear of infection. No sooner did they see Don Josemaría than they were filled with profound happiness. All they needed to say was: 'Don Josemaría is here.' It said it all."

We have already said something about the Founder of Opus Dei's activity in the Patronato de Enfermos, in the suburbs of Madrid and then in the King's Hospital and the General Hospital in Santa Isabel and the Princesa Hospital in San Bernardo.

What is striking is that he should have sought his wealth precisely in such poor and wretched places. His treasures were the prayers and mortifications of the sick. On St. Joseph's Day in 1975 he opened his heart to members of the Work in Rome:

Time passed by. I went to seek strength in the poorest districts of Madrid. Hours and hours going everywhere, day after day, on foot from one place to another among the shamefully and wretchedly poor, so poor that they had not a thing to their name; among dirty runny-nosed children, but children for all that, which means souls pleasing to God. What indignation I feel in my priestly soul when people say nowadays that children ought not to go to Confession when they are young! It isn't true! They have to make their personal, auricular, secret Confession like everybody else. And what good it does them! How happy they become! I spent many hours in that work. I'm only sorry they weren't more. And in the hospitals and in houses where these sick people were, if those shacks can be called houses. . . . They were sick and forsaken people and some of them had tuberculosis which was then incurable.

More than a hundred people listened to him in silence. He spoke in a quiet voice, as one who opens his heart in God's presence:

So I went to all those places to find the means to do the Work of God. Meanwhile I worked and formed the first ones whom I had by me. There were people of almost every kind among them. There were university students, working-men, small tradesmen, artists. . . .

They were very intense years, in which Opus Dei was growing on the inside almost without our realising it. But I have wanted to tell you — some day they will explain this to you in more detail with documents and papers — that the human strength of the Work has been the sick people in the hospitals of Madrid: the most forsaken ones; those who lived in their houses having lost the last vestige of human hope; the most ignorant in the remotest corners of the city.

On 2 July 1974 in Tabancura School in Santiago de Chile someone asked him to explain why he said that **sick people are the treasure of Opus Dei.** Slowly, as if he savoured those memories, Msgr. Escrivá de Balaguer spoke of a **priest who was twenty-six years of age and had the grace of God, a good sense of humour and nothing else. He had no virtues, no money. And he had to do Opus Dei. . . . And do you know how he managed?** he asked.

In the hospitals. That General Hospital of Madrid, packed with sick and destitute people lying there in the corridors

because there just weren't enough beds. That King's Hospital, full of consumptives at a time when consumption was incurable. . . . Those were the weapons with which to fight and win! That was the treasure with which to pay! And that was the strength with which to go forward! (. . .) And the Lord has taken us all over the world, and we are now in Europe, in Asia, in Africa, in America and in Oceania thanks to the sick, who are a treasure. . . .

A few months later, on 19 February 1975 in Ciudad Vieja (Guatemala), he once again recalled those years when he relied on **all the artillery of many hospitals in Madrid:**

I begged them to offer up their sufferings, their hours in bed, their loneliness (some of them were very lonely): to offer all that to the Lord for the apostolate we were doing with young people.

This was his way of teaching them to discover the joy of suffering, because they were sharing in the Cross of Jesus Christ and were serving a great and divine purpose. The Founder of Opus Dei found in them a real pillar of strength and the conviction that the Lord would carry the Work forward **in spite of men, in spite of myself, who am a poor man.**

From that time on, along with catechism classes in poorer districts, visits to the poor and homeless have been habitual means to develop the apostolate of Opus Dei with young people the world over.

He also spoke about the christian meaning of suffering in Lisbon in November 1972:

You too will meet up with physical pain and be happy with that suffering. You have spoken to me of The Way. **I don't know it by heart but there is a point which says:** Let us bless pain. Love pain. Sanctify pain. . . . Glorify pain! **Do you remember it? I wrote that in a hospital at the bedside of a dying woman to whom I had just administered the Sacrament of Extreme Unction. How I envied her! That woman had had a very good social and economic position in life, and there she was in that wretched hospital bed, alone and dying, with no more company than what I could supply, until she died. And there she was repeating, joyously savouring the words:** Let us bless pain — **and she had every sort of moral and physical pain —** love pain, sanctify pain, glorify pain! **Suffering is a proof that one knows how to love, that one has a heart.**

Braulia, the younger sister of María Ignacia García Escobar, remembers the Founder of Opus Dei in 1931 as "always surrounded by young men who went with him to teach catechism in the slums and shanty towns. You needed a lot of faith to do that then, and a lot of courage too. I can still remember the faces of intense resentment and hatred towards priests and their companions made by the men of those areas."

In 1930 Jenaro Lázaro found that besides working in hospitals the Father was also teaching catechism in a number of places. He cannot recall their exact names, but he does remember that he went often to Vallecas. On 1 October 1967 Msgr. Escrivá de Balaguer returned once more to Vallecas. It had changed a great deal. In the auditorium of Tajamar, an apostolic work run by Opus Dei, its Founder recalled that when he was twenty-five, **I came to these open spaces often, to brush away tears and help those in need, to treat children, the old and the sick with affection, and I received a lot of affection in return . . . and the occasional stone.**

He continued, referring to Tajamar: **Today, for me, this is a dream, a blessed dream, that I relive in so many outskirts of great cities, where we treat people with affection, looking at them straight in the eye, because we are all equal. (. . .) I am a sinner who loves Jesus Christ with all the strength of my soul; I feel very happy, although I have sorrows because sorrow is with us always in this world. I want you to love Jesus Christ, to get to know him, to be happy as I am; and it isn't difficult to attain this relationship. Before God, as men, as creatures, we are all equal.**

(. . .) I have spoken of when I was twenty-five. I had intimations then of what the Lord wanted. Till I was twenty-six I did not know. He wanted this madness, this madness of kindness, of union, of love.

A youthful dream had become a reality. Msgr. Escrivá de Balaguer's priestly heart felt concern for all souls, because before God **we are all equal:** poor creatures needing God's mercy. In those years he suffered greatly because the poor lived and died forsaken in those Madrid slums, with their sordid, subhuman environment which was another factor driving many away from God. He became familiar with many frightening situations, comparable only to those in the hospitals where he worked. He also got the young men around him to accompany him. One of those who went with him to the Hospital of Santa Isabel declares that after spending a Sunday afternoon cutting the hair or nails of the sick and washing their faces or emptying the spitoons, "on going out we almost always vomited".

Juan Jiménez Vargas uses the adjective "repulsive" to describe the manner in which many, sometimes through indolence, lived in that area of Tetuán where they used to go to teach catechism. He himself was from a middle-class family, a student of medicine, and not easily shocked. He relates that shortly after that christian formation class in the Porta Coeli Orphanage they began to give catechism classes in the Tetuán district, which was one of the worst districts in Madrid. There he discovered that the Founder of the Work had a lot of experience in dealing with children. He knew how to get them to understand Catholic doctrine and helped them prepare for Confession.

He carried out an intense apostolic activity with persons of all walks of life. He encouraged students to do apostolate especially with their fellow students, but without forgetting that there was room for everyone, including workers, in Opus Dei. Dr. Jiménez Vargas remembers well a bank clerk, Dorado by name, who understood the Work well. He died at the beginning of the War.

Braulia García Escobar also keeps in her memory the image of the house in Martínez Campos where Msgr. Escrivá de Balaguer lived. Young men of all sorts were constantly in and out of there: "There were many students but also many workers."

Vicente Hernando Bocos thinks he met Don Josemaría in the *Casa del Estudiante* either in 1929 or 1930. Then military service, his intense political activity, prison from 1932 and finally exile in 1935 severed their relations. At the beginning Don Josemaría was living in a residence for priests at 3 Larra Street and "he had started off his apostolate with a group of manual workers, clerks and white collar workers, in addition to dealing with us university students".

In 1940, according to an article which appeared in the *Hoja del Lunes* written by Pedro Gómez Aparicio about the history of the early years of the School of Journalism, Msgr. Escrivá de Balaguer "was a young Aragonese priest already enjoying a certain popularity among the student world and working population in Madrid to which he devoted himself with special interest".

This wide open apostolate of the Founder of Opus Dei is summarised in an expression he repeated constantly over the years: **out of a hundred souls we are interested in a hundred.** His priestly heart refused to discriminate. It was necessary to reach everyone because, as he repeated a thousand times, expounding the doctrine of St. Paul, **each soul is worth all the blood of Jesus Christ.**

In his years in Madrid he also dreamed of reaching the rural areas. In 1935 he wrote some notes about the apostolic work which members of Opus Dei would carry out in the countryside. Years later Joaquín Herreros Robles, President of the National Coordinating Committee of the EFA (Family Schools for Agricultural workers in Spain) was profoundly moved to note the sorrow of the Founder of Opus Dei for the precarious living conditions in which many rural families suffered in many countries.

This idea of human and professional development together with christian formation in rural life was cherished by Msgr. Escrivá de Balaguer from his earliest years, and would blossom out in time into many activities: some of them are apostolic works directly undertaken by Opus Dei, like Montefalco in Morelos, Mexico; others are personal initiatives of members of the Work and their friends, which come as a fruit of their apostolic enthusiasm and of their zeal to serve mankind. The EFA schools were in fact a personal response on the part of Joaquín Herreros and other members of Opus Dei to an express wish of the Founder. By 1976 there were thirty-six such schools in Spain, inspired by a multitude of enthusiastic and generous people who want to fulfil the aims of the EFA: to give christian formation and foster human, cultural and professional development in rural districts.

Joaquín Herreros visited the Founder of Opus Dei in Rome in February 1966 and told him of his hopes, experience and plans. "He was very moved and encouraged us to carry them out soon. But he asked us above all to pray very much for all that beautiful work which we could foresee and for which, he added in a very affectionate tone, he had for many years been praying with great confidence in Our Lord."

Six years later he was in Pozoalbero (Jerez) and he was invited to visit one of the schools in the south of Spain. He did not think it was a good idea, because as he used to say he only had one **saucepan** and he did not want to single anyone out. **I would like them all to come here to Pozoalbero,** he explained, **because they all have sufficient formation to grasp everything, like everyone else.** The President of the EFA commented afterwards: "I was very moved by the Father's great tact and sensitivity and the way he understood that had he made a special visit to the EFA on that occasion in which get-togethers were being organised in Pozoalbero for people of every class and condition, it could have been interpreted as a way of condescending to the agricultural workers."

Work was carried out with peasants with the same spirit of **looking at them face to face, for we are all equal.** In those days of 1972 in Pozoalbero, Msgr. Escrivá de Balaguer was not speaking idly when he said to Anastasio and Pedro who were working in the garden:

What a fine show of plants and flowers you've got here. . . . Now, tell me: whose work is worth more, yours or that of a government minister?

They were silent. He at once continued:

It depends on the love of God you put into it. If you put more Love in than a minister does, then your work is worth more.

Two years previously, he had been in Montefalco in Mexico. According to Santiago Vázquez Alvarez, a peasant of that land, he had spoken a lot about the equality of the children of God, of the need of more human and hygienic houses, of study and professional formation, of lifting up those who are below without "bringing down" those above. The people of Morelos know a lot about having to struggle for a better life. Ruins from the time of the revolution are still in evidence in the hacienda of Montefalco. All over the Amilpas Valley there are men who knew and fought alongside Emiliano Zapata and are still poor. Santiago Vázquez was amazed at the kindness of the Founder of Opus Dei and at his concern for the material and spiritual well-being of the peoples of that land. He thinks that from Heaven "he will help us still more, interceding before God Our Lord, for us to continue to make his dreams come true".

3. AN ACT OF DARING: THE DYA ACADEMY

Pedro Rocamora met Msgr. Escrivá de Balaguer around 1928 and, although Rocamora did not join Opus Dei, he felt right from the start a deep respect and affection for that young priest, Don Josemaría, who trusted him as a true friend and who, shortly after the birth of the Work, talked to him about his "foundational" ideas. These struck Rocamora as being too ambitious: "He expressed them with such simplicity and he was so convinced they would succeed that I was just amazed." Though he admired Don Josemaría, he "could not hide a certain scepticism regarding such projects. They seemed too big, beautiful indeed, but almost impossible to achieve."

Even those who had faith in — as well as friendship for – the Founder of Opus Dei felt a sense of vertigo when he spoke to them about the future, because his "dreams" had no human foundation whatsoever. This same impression of vertigo — produced by Don Josemaría's faith and confidence in God — is, as we saw, what remains in the memories of the members of the Women's Section of the Work when they recall how he talked about the tasks their Section would undertake in the future. He always insisted that the most important thing would be the personal apostolate of each member, which was something impossible to gauge or measure; but the zeal they put into their personal apostolate would give rise in its turn to the most varied initiatives: farming schools for country girls, centres for the professional training of women, halls of residence for college students, activities in the field of fashion. . . . When those few women expressed their amazement, the Founder of Opus Dei urged them to see that the only thing they needed was to trust in God: the Lord wanted all this to come about and so it would be God who would push his Work ahead.

It should be pointed out that, from the very beginning, Don Josemaría had in his mind and nurtured in his heart many activities that would not become reality till years later. These projects included, as we have just seen, the apostolic works that Opus Dei would promote. They would be both professional and secular in content, and totally orientated towards carrying out a christian service on behalf of society. That is to say, they would be tasks of an exclusively apostolic stamp.

The members of the Work have not forgotten the horizons that the Founder opened up to them, back in the thirties, when it was all beginning. Juan Jiménez Vargas remembers receiving a clear and detailed explanation in 1933 of what these apostolic tasks of Opus Dei would be in the field of education. They were to set up, among other things, private centres of education, whose spirit would be thoroughly christian, but they would never be called "Catholic". These centres would always be few, the fruit of the initiative of some members of the Work, just some of those working professionally in the field of education, because many members would prefer, following their own free choice, to continue working in official centres. In turn these professionals would never be many compared to the total members of Opus Dei. Professor Jiménez Vargas stresses that "when, nearly twenty years later, I was told about the plans for the University of Navarre, I was not in the least surprised because the ideas went back a long time". He adds, "those ideas were the same as I had heard from him in 1933".

Don Josemaría knew how to combine the universality that God wanted for his Work in the future with a sober concentration on the present moment. Thus he began, with the few means at his disposal, what was to be the first apostolic undertaking of Opus Dei. It had all the characteristics that these activities would have later on all over the world. It was the DYA Academy, which began working in 1933 in a flat at 33 Luchana Street, at the corner of Juan de Austria Street.

Until then, the Founder of Opus Dei, as may be easily deduced from the preceding pages, had carried out his apostolic work in all kinds of places as best he could. Julian Cortés Cavanillas, the journalist, remembers his walks with Don Josemaría down Recoletos Street, and the times they drank chocolate and ate buttered toast or doughnuts in *El Sotanillo*, a quiet place very near the Puerta de Alcalá, coming up from Correos. It was still there in the fifties, when it had the air of a historical relic, even retaining the lettering of the façade — *chocolatería* — although it no longer had much to do with what was actually drunk there. Inside it looked the same as when those students sat around a table in 1931, listening to Don Josemaría. From Alcalá Street, a few steps led down to a longish sort of corridor partitioned into sections that were almost independent of one another, with tables and chairs. Surprisingly, even in the fifties, and in spite of the heavy street traffic, it continued to be a quiet refuge, an ideal place for the traditional Madrid *tertulia*, when friends would get together for lively conversation. There, because of the lack of material means, the Founder of Opus Dei was quietly preparing the work which would soon widen its scope in Luchana Street.

The DYA Academy was a cultural and educational centre. There were classes of professional orientation, and various lectures were organised, some of them on doctrinal themes, as for example the courses on apologetics given by Fr. Vicente Blanco. Classes of spiritual and apostolic formation were also held there for the members of the Work and for those young men who, although not members, also took part in the work and came to chat with Don Josemaría about their personal problems.

Although the establishment was relatively small, it was very difficult to keep it going, because they were so short of money. The initials of the Academy — DYA — fitted the classes that were given there: *Derecho y Arquitectura* (Law and Architecture). "But deep down," says

Pedro Rocamora, "they were the abbreviation of a motto which Don Josemaría had talked to me about in 1928: *Dios y Audacia* (God and Daring). To the frivolous or for those with bad will, the motto might have appeared scandalous. What Don Josemaría intended was that each young man should place his trust in God and, seeking to make himself Our Lord's ally and friend, set forth to do good throughout the world with apostolic daring. I emphasize this because contemporary malice has tried to discover human motives behind this daring. Nothing was further from the Father's mind. He meant daring to be an apostle, daring in self-sacrifice, daring to do good, daring to help the suffering, those in pain and the needy, daring to give advice even if unwelcome and to wrest a friend from the clutches of sin. This was the daring that Don Josemaría preached."

On one of his last visits to Madrid, the Founder of Opus Dei one day passed by Luchana Street. He recalled the occasion in Rome, on St. Joseph's Day in 1975, three months before his unexpected death:

We passed in front of the building a short time back and how my heart pounded. . . . How much suffering! How much contradiction! How much gossip! What whopping lies! . . .

Referring to his family's generosity in helping him to set up the house, he recalled a spirited commentary made by his brother Santiago, then scarcely in his teens:

Each day, when I was leaving my mother's house, my brother Santiago would come up and put his hands in my pockets and ask me, "what are you taking to your nest?"

His daring sprang from his conviction that his vocation was from God. He counted on God, through the intercession of St. Joseph (soon he was also relying on St. Nicholas of Bari) to solve the economic problems of the academy, since in this respect things were going very badly. A priest friend of his, Don Saturnino de Dios Carrasco, also asked people he knew if they would like to contribute to DYA. Among the people he asked were the Ruiz Ballesteros family, where he was chaplain and tutor. "Don Josemaría aimed to include all sectors of society in his apostolate. He was not afraid of the university of those years. Rather he was trying to counteract the negative work of some university professors, offering good doctrinal formation to the boys who attended the DYA Academy with classes in religion and by other means of christian formation."

One of these means were spiritual retreats, which he gave in the Redemptorist church, which was nearby in Manuel Silvela Street. A letter dated 26 April 1934 and sent by the Founder of Opus Dei to Don Francisco Morán, then Vicar General of the diocese of Madrid, still exists. Among other things he speaks of the next day of recollection, which was due to take place on the first Sunday in May, and he tells him that, **with God's help, I hope that it will be fruitful, because the university students who have attended the previous days of recollection have responded very well.**

I'm convinced that Our Lord is blessing the young men who are running the academy, where we find so many opportunities for our priestly **apostolate among intellectuals and where, as well, I can fulfil the clear will of God for me, which is to "pass unnoticed and disappear".**

I ask you, Father Vicar, to remember this group of boys in the Holy Mass: they deserve it (. . .).

In this same letter he informs the Vicar General of Madrid that his *Consideraciones espirituales* are about to be published: **For reasons of economy, with the approval of the Rt. Rev. Bishop of Cuenca, a little pamphlet is being printed — there will be others to follow — at the Imprenta Moderna, formerly the Imprenta del Seminario, of that city (Cuenca). They are notes that I use to help me with the spiritual direction and formation of young people and which until now were duplicated.**

He adds, **I must tell you straight away that I make no claims for them. They have no importance and they are being published anonymously. Indeed, they are only useful for certain souls, who really** want: **1) to have an interior life; and 2) to excel in their professional work, because this is a serious obligation.**

The Founder of Opus Dei did not count on money to carry out the Work on earth. From the very beginning, both ends and means were very clear and supernatural. As he summed up in Rome in March 1975:

And then, God led us along the paths of our interior life . . . along specific ones. What was I seeking? Cor Mariae Dulcissimum, iter para tutum! **I went to seek strength in the Mother of God, like a young son, following the paths of childhood. I turned to St. Joseph, my Father and my Lord. I wanted to see him powerful, very powerful indeed, chief of that great divine clan, whom God Himself obeyed:** erat subditus illis! **I turned with simplicity to the saints for their intercession, in a Latin which was awkward but pious:** Sancte Nicolaë, curam domus age! **And I had**

devotion to the Holy Guardian Angels, because it was a 2nd of October when those bells rang out . . . the bells of Our Lady of the Angels, a Madrid parish, close to Cuatro Caminos. . . . I turned to the Holy Angels with confidence, like a little child, without realising that God was leading me along paths of spiritual childhood. But you don't have to imitate me. Long live freedom!

What can a creature do if he has to carry out a mission and has neither means, nor age, nor knowledge, nor virtues, nor anything? He goes to his mother and his father, he turns to those who can do something, he asks help from his friends . . . this is what I did in the spiritual life. . . . And of course to the accompaniment of the strokes of the discipline.

The Founder of Opus Dei concluded:

I'm telling you a little of what my prayer has been this morning, and it's to fill myself with shame and with gratitude, and with more love. All that has been done up till now is a lot, but it is little: in Europe, in Asia, in Africa, in America and in Oceania. It is all the work of Jesus, Our Lord. It has all been done by Our Father in Heaven.

4. "LET EACH WAYFARER MAKE HIS OWN WAY"

The task of carrying out Opus Dei overwhelmed its Founder: he felt himself to be an **inept and deaf** instrument, lacking in any human means; but, with unlimited generosity, he gave his all to carry out the mission that God had given him. It is important also to notice that bearing the burden of his specific calling in no way made him lose sight of the needs of the whole Church.

Msgr. Escrivá de Balaguer's image bears no resemblance to that of a "specialised apostle". He felt as his own the cares of all those working for the Church. He drew many souls to a life of prayer, both in the street and in the cloister. He worked on behalf of priests and religious. He loved the Hierarchy and proved his love with deeds. His life was totally committed to the service of the entire Church.

This deeply impressed Natividad González, one of those girls who used to go to Confession to him in the church of Santa Isabel. He often spoke to her about loving the Church and the Pope with deeds, about obeying all their commands. He explained to her that the Work was and always would be very Roman, that it gloried and would always glory in its love for the Church, Holy, One, Catholic, Apostolic and Roman.

Asunción Muñoz, a Dama Apostólica and a very close witness of what the Founder of Opus Dei was doing between 1927 and 1931, relates that "he understood our spirit very well, even though afterwards he founded Opus Dei, which had a very different manner of seeking sanctity. Having known him, I find this easy to understand, for he welcomed everything that was good, and great, and holy. . . . He had a truly universal spirit. He loved everything that was for the Glory of God. And that is why he came to know us very well and helped us a very great deal and had great affection for us."

From 1933 onwards, as we know, he pursued his apostolic work with young people in a more organised way: circles, meditations and retreats, acts of eucharistic devotion, and so on. From the beginning, when he explained these activities to those who came to them, he always told them that there was no question of setting up an association: **there are already plenty of very good associations,** he used to repeat. All he was doing was offering certain means of formation, some classes of christian doctrine which, both theoretically and in fact, were compatible with belonging to, or continuing to belong to, any of the associations that were then in existence. His attitude was not a matter of "tactics", but a direct consequence of his spirit which was open, universal, catholic. He rejoiced — as he was to rejoice all through his life — on seeing the zeal of others.

In 1935 Fr. Sancho, O.P., returned to Spain from Manila. At that time, he had a special interest in the apostolate with young people. He came to know the Teresians, and Miss Segovia. She spoke to him one day about Don Josemaría. Fr. Sancho bears witness to the affection with which the Founder of Opus Dei helped this Institute and how he blessed God for any apostolate that he heard about: "He was never exclusive. He had a very open spirit and an untiring zeal for all souls."

After the Spanish war, Fr. Sancho was once again able to experience this spirit at close quarters. A number of apostolic groups were making their appearance about that time. Some were promoted by secular priests, others by religious who began working with the laity. Fr. Sancho has not forgotten the joy with which Msgr. Escrivá de Balaguer welcomed these initiatives. "He always used to say, 'the more people there are serving God, the better'."

As has been said so often, the Founder of Opus Dei was called to be a "pioneer of lay spirituality", but such was the power of his word and his writings, so rich was the doctrine impressed upon his soul by the Holy Spirit, that, in practice, he has done enormous good not only to thousands of people in all walks of life, who were to discover God in the midst of their most ordinary cares, but also to the religious, who have consecrated their lives to God apart from the world and follow paths that could not be more different from those of Opus Dei.

Faithfulness to Christ has manifested itself both in the past and nowadays in a notable variety of personal and institutional situations, which demonstrate the *catholic*, universal character of the Church, without there needing to exist any ties or connections between these institutions. Over and above the differences, we always find a radical common denominator: the Gospel message. Msgr. Escrivá de Balaguer always stressed the decisive point that normal lay people, to be holy in the world, need to learn how to live a *contemplative* life, how to have presence of God in the ordinary circumstances of their everyday lives.

The contemplative spirit is the common thread which goes a long way towards explaining how the Founder of Opus Dei was able to understand so well the vocations of other persons, which often had very different characteristics. A professed brother in the Charterhouse of Aula Dei (Saragossa), Hugo María Quesada, testifies how from May 1942 he received weekly spiritual direction from Don Josemaría until he entered the Charterhouse of Miraflores. Don Josemaría helped him little by little to have presence of God, to see prayer as a simple and friendly dialogue with God, to be mortified not only in special circumstances, but as part and parcel of his ordinary life. . . . In short, he helped him to mature his vocation, so that his entry into the Charterhouse would not be the fruit of passing enthusiasm. Finally he said to him, **Off you go, the Holy Spirit is leading you that way.** Brother Hugo María remembers that advice with gratitude and he keeps a dedicated copy of *The Way*, which "continues to do me good in my life as a Carthusian".

From her monastery in Valencia, Sister María Rosa Pérez, a Poor Clare, affirms that the writings of Msgr. Escrivá de Balaguer, "which are full of deep spiritual content, have been a powerful help in the different stages of my life, both when I was a lay person and now in my consecrated life. They all reflect the greatness of his soul, his deep faith and extraordinary confidence in God."

In her letter dated 21 August 1975, Sister María Jesús Rodríguez

Cuervo, Abbess of the Cistercian Monastery of Our Lady of the Angels in Oviedo, recognises that the works of the Founder of Opus Dei help her to live her contemplative vocation and to be faithful to the Rule of St. Benedict.

Sister Teresa J. García de Samaniego, the Superior of the monastery of the Visitation of Our Lady, also in Oviedo, says something similar. There they read and meditate upon the writings of the Founder of Opus Dei. Some of the nuns in the monastery affirm that they owe much of their vocation to him. All of them regard his homilies as a leaven of supernatural life, of faith and hope, of serenity and joy. For one of the sisters of the monastery, who has been blind for many years, the braille edition of *The Way* is a mainstay for her prayer and her life of piety. Sister Teresa concludes, "the spirituality of this Founder is universal. It is the spirituality of a man of God".

The Founder of Opus Dei had a breadth of vision that was all-embracing. Moved by the Love of God, he wanted all the glory to be for Him and for His Church. This is why whenever he saw any flame of apostolic service being lit, his attitude was one of decided support, insofar as it was in his power to help. At the very least, he responded with gladness and prayer, as he wrote in *The Way*:

Rejoice, when you see others working in good apostolic activities. And ask God to grant them abundant grace and that they may respond to that grace (*The Way*, 965).

He was delighted that there were many ways in the Church:

There need to be many; so that each soul can find its own in that wonderful variety (*The Way*, 964).

Since he had suffered the pain of being misunderstood by a few who had succumbed to that temptation of envy, which appears even among the first disciples of Christ, he fostered right from the start among those who worked alongside him a spirit of concentrating on their own tasks, without mortifying in any way other people who were also working for God:

You show bad spirit if it hurts you to see others work for Christ without regard for what you are doing. Remember this passage in St. Mark: "Master, we saw a man who is not one of us casting out devils in your name; and because he was not one of us we tried to stop him." But Jesus said, "You must not stop him: no one who works a miracle in my name is likely to speak evil of me. Anyone who is not against us is for us" (*The Way*, 966).

Shortly after the Spanish war, he preached a retreat for students in Burjasot, near Valencia. The building had been some sort of republican barracks. There were still graffiti on the walls, although many had been removed. He asked the students to leave one which ran: *Cada caminante siga su camino* (Let each wayfarer make his own way). It could almost be a motto for the open spirit which characterised his apostolic work.

Throughout his life he had many occasions of confirming, with deeds, that he had incorporated this evangelical spirit into his conduct. One example is cited by the Bishop of Ciudad Real. Briefly, Msgr. Juan Hervás began a great movement of christian renewal and lay apostolate, the well-known *Cursillos de Cristiandad*, which expanded rapidly; but, as often happens, a terrible storm was unleashed against him. Some time about 1957, he went to unburden himself to his friend Don Josemaría, whom he had met before 1936, when Don Juan, only recently ordained, was devoting his priestly work to Catholic Action, then in its beginnings.

Times had changed, but they talked as easily and cordially as before. "His words", Msgr. Hervás wrote in 1975, "were brief and to the point and they brought me great comfort at a time when things were certainly difficult for the *Cursillos de Cristiandad*. And I also remember how insistently he emphasized — I felt that he was pouring his own soul out to me — that we should love those who do not understand us and pray for those who judge without wanting to find out; that we should be attentive to the voice of the Church and not to street rumours, and that we should keep our hearts free from bitterness and resentment.

"In this providential and unexpected way that man of God, which is what he undoubtedly was, intervened to encourage an undertaking that was not his own and poured out charity and understanding on a method of spirituality and lay apostolate which was following paths different from his own."

Rejoice, when you see others working in good apostolic activities (. . .). Then, you, on your way: convince yourself that it's the only way for you.

Thus ends point 965 of *The Way*, which we have just quoted. It implies that each should concentrate on his own task, with its particular spirit, and should venerate and understand others, without interfering in their affairs or making superfluous plans for coordination.

Nevertheless, when it was necessary, the Founder of Opus Dei worked — or set others to work — on behalf of organisations or apostolic movements that follow principles or methods different from those of the Work.

This happened, for example, with regard to Spanish Catholic Action, after the War. When the Bishop of Madrid asked him in 1949 for a priest of Opus Dei, whom he could appoint as counsellor of the University Youth Section of the Madrid Catholic Action, Msgr. Escrivá de Balaguer gave the Bishop several names from which to choose. This must have been quite a sacrifice because there were still very few priests of Opus Dei and its own apostolic needs were great; but what concerns us here is that when the Founder told Fr. Urteaga that he was going to receive this diocesan appointment he explained to him with absolute clarity his firm desire that he should work **following Catholic Action's own spirit.**

He always gave identical advice to people of Catholic Action who came to him for spiritual guidance. Alfredo López, who was president of the Spanish Catholic Action in 1953, gave public witness of this in 1964 in the Madrid newspaper *ABC*. Another friend, Manolo Aparici, "the unforgettable president and counsellor of Young Catholic Action", had introduced him to Don Josemaría in 1939. Alfredo López's public testimony of gratitude ends thus: "Over the years we were together I very often heard these words from the lips of the Founder of Opus Dei: **Love Catholic Action very much!** I did love it and I served it and I continue to love it, it is true. But at the same time the memory of these words of his disturbs me, because if I had carried out the duties that flowed from my position of responsibility as Msgr. Escrivá de Balaguer wanted me to carry them out, my contribution to Catholic Action would have had a perfection which at times it lacked."

Alfredo López had occasion to experience at close quarters the warmth of the Founder of Opus Dei, whose heart was "wide open to all that is noble and pure in life". He grasped that there was a single interest in Don Josemaría's life, the search for holiness, "because he is a man who truly loves Jesus Christ and is committed to filling the world with that love". Among the members of his own family, Alfredo López also found that for Don Josemaría all paths led to God: "He had a sure understanding of the lay vocation and great love for his own vocation as a diocesan priest. But he also understood and loved a vocation very different from his own — that of the religious — and was able to detect its signs in the souls that he dealt with, when God wanted them away from the world. He blessed and confirmed one of my daughters in this

vocation. She had read *The Way* so often that she knew much of it off
by heart. She is now a religious of the Assumption."

As the former bishop of Santander reflected in the Bilbao newspaper *La Gaceta del Norte*, "Msgr. Escrivá was a man of ideas that were
both universal and particular. He lived the Gospel, 'the letter of the
Gospel' and its spirit. He loved the Church, as the work of Christ; he
loved it as an institution, making no distinction of epochs; he loved the
Church of Paul VI as he loved that of John XXIII, and received with
the same veneration the teachings of the Vatican Councils, both Second
and First, as those of the Council of Trent. This ecclesial spirit shines
through in all his writings, in *The Way*, a sure path of spirituality, as
well as and especially in his *Homilies*, where he develops extensively the
idea of the constant presence of Christ in His Church, and of the Church
in the world, projecting the truth of the Gospel over all human
experience."

5. "THE RACE OF THE CHILDREN OF GOD"

Geographically Opus Dei was born in Spain, but as its Founder
declared on 15 April 1967 to *Time* correspondent Peter Forbath, **from
the first moment, the Work was universal,** Catholic. **It was not
born to solve the concrete problems facing Europe in the
twenties.** However, he added to the same journalist, **the Work was
born very small. It was only a young priest's desire to do what
God asked of him.**

Msgr. Escrivá de Balaguer began by continually encouraging the
young men he was forming to study languages: **to extend this Work
of ours to other countries,** he would often say to them. Studying
languages was a way of making better use of time, above all during the
summer holidays. Besides, their knowledge of languages would help
them improve their own professional work. Above all, this recommenda-
tion expressed his keenness to spread Opus Dei throughout the world.

Early in 1935, the Founder was already preparing to start work
in France, specifically in Paris. But, with the outbreak of the civil war
in Spain and then the Second World War, it was necessary to postpone
this expansion.

Even during the various phases of the religious persecution which
took place in Madrid from 18 July 1936 onwards, Don Josemaría never

wavered in this ambition. With his boundless confidence in God, from his various hiding places in the city, he got those close to him to continue studying foreign languages.

He did the same in Burgos, where he stayed from the beginning of 1938 to April 1939. He continued to dream about going to new countries. Burgos is the Castilian city mentioned in point 811 of *The Way*:

Do you remember? Night was falling as you and I began our prayer. From close by came the murmur of water. And, through the stillness of the city, we also seemed to hear voices from many lands crying to us in anguish that they do not yet know Christ.

Unashamedly you kissed your Crucifix and asked him to make you an apostle of apostles.

No sooner had the war in Spain ended than the World War broke out. Until 1945 the activities of Opus Dei had to be centred almost exclusively in the Iberian Peninsula. From 1940 work commenced in Portugal, and journeys were made to other countries. When hostilities ended, a beginning was made in England, Ireland, France, Italy, U.S.A. and Mexico. From 1949 and 1950 onwards members of Opus Dei went to Germany, Holland, Switzerland, Argentina, Canada, Venezuela and the remaining countries of Europe and America. At the same time the apostolate of the Association was spreading to other continents: Northern Africa, Japan, Kenya, and other East African countries, Australia, the Philippines, Nigeria, and so on.

The intimate happiness of gratitude to God came naturally to Msgr. Escrivá de Balaguer. As he said in 1966 to the journalist Jacques Guillemé-Brûlon, of *Le Figaro*.

Opus Dei feels as much at home in England as in Kenya, in Nigeria as in Japan, in the United States as in Austria, in Ireland as in Mexico or Argentina. In each place it is the same theological and pastoral phenomenon which takes root in the souls of the people of that country. It is not anchored in one particular culture nor in one specific historical period.

We might also think of the sorrow occasioned him by the difficulties he had to face in Spain, and about which he confided briefly to Peter Forbath in 1967:

In very few places have we had fewer facilities than in Spain. I don't like to say so, because I naturally love my country deeply, but it is in Spain that we have had the greatest diffi-

culties in making the Work take root. No sooner had it been born, than it met with the opposition of all the enemies of personal freedom and of people who were so attached to traditional ideas that they could not understand the life of Opus Dei members, ordinary Christians who strive to live their christian vocation fully without leaving the world.

Furthermore, Msgr. Escrivá de Balaguer continued:

In the course of its international expansion, Opus Dei's spirit has been very well received in all countries. Our difficulties have in large part been the result of falsehoods originating in Spain. They were invented by members of certain well-defined sectors of Spanish society.

On this occasion, at the end of the interview, Msgr. Escrivá de Balaguer forestalled any misunderstanding or misconception by saying: **Don't think I don't love my country;** but his christian patriotism never clouded over his vision of limitless horizons. As may be read in *The Way*:

To be "Catholic" means to love your country and to be second to none in that love. And at the same time, to hold as your own the noble aspirations of other lands. So many glories of France are glories of mine! And in the same way, much that makes Germans proud, and the peoples of Italy and of England . . . , and Americans and Asians and Africans, is a source of pride to me also.

Catholic: big heart, broad mind (*The Way*, 525).

Moved by this clearsightedness — a spirit that came from God — he started the Roman College of the Holy Cross as soon as he could. It was to be a centre of formation in the heart of Christianity, where people of Opus Dei from all over the world could live together while studying in the various athenaeums and universities of Rome. There the members' worldwide aspirations would increase, so that later on they might act as instruments of unity, spread all over the world.

The Founder of Opus Dei was fired with zeal for the salvation of all souls. The fire that Christ had come to spread on earth, so that it might blaze in men's hearts, made geographical or political frontiers seem unimportant to him. With his universal outlook, he would discover apostolic possibilities that remained unnoticed by others, as happened in Brazil in 1974. The thousands of Brazilians who listened to him were not expecting the vast apostolic panorama he opened up for them.

Their first surprise was when Msgr. Escrivá de Balaguer, two days after arriving in Brazil, began to tell them that their country was a continent, not a nation. He had been struck by the mixture of races and peoples, who knew how to live together and to love one another. He saw their spiritual and apostolic possibilities reaching out across the world.

At different moments during his stay in that country he would exclaim, **Brazil! The first thing I have found here is a mother: big, beautiful, fruitful and gentle, opening her arms to all, without distinction of language, race or nation, and who calls them all her children.**

As an example of Brazil's fertility, he was told the story about a place where they had put up some goalposts and these began sprouting branches. . . . Everyone knows that Brazil has endless sources of wealth which are yet to be exploited. Seeing this panorama, the Founder of Opus Dei urged the Brazilians, telling them:

There is a lot, a lot to be done here. There are many good souls in Brazil. And you bear in your hearts the fire of God, the fire that Jesus Christ came to spread on earth. But you must also set other hearts on fire! You have the attraction and goodness, and the human and supernatural capacity to do it (. . .) So, get moving! Multiply yourselves and do many good things in this land which is so fruitful.

He was not blind to problems. He was conscious of the vast social differences that exist in that land, as in the rest of the world, but he preferred to emphasise the positive side, because only christian charity, Love, can change people and eradicate injustice.

In this country, he said, warming to his theme, **you find it natural to open your arms to everyone and you receive them with love and affection. I should like this to be turned into a supernatural endeavour, a great undertaking to draw all souls to the knowledge of God; I should like you to be united, to do good not only in this nation, but also, from this great country, to the whole world. You can! And you should! And since the Lord has given you the means, he will also help you to want to get working.**

He said the same again on the feast of Pentecost, when addressing several thousands of people. Slowly, pronouncing the words carefully, as if he were afraid that the language barrier might make it harder for him to be understood:

You must do supernaturally **what you do** naturally; **and afterwards, you must carry this eagerness for charity, for fraternity, for understanding, for love, for christian spirit, to all the peoples of the earth.** I see the Brazilian people as a great missionary people, now and in the future, a great people of God, and I see you yourselves proclaiming the wonders of the Lord all over the earth.

Those who were there say they find it difficult to describe the impression that his words made on them, because these words meant a complete about-turn. Brazil had always been thought of as a mission country, and now Msgr. Escrivá de Balaguer was portraying it as a great missionary people, with the duty of carrying to other countries the supernatural riches of the Faith.

To a member of the Work who is a *nissei*, a Japanese born in Brazil, he confided:

When I see your little face, I remember your country. I love you Japanese very much. Yours is a great and noble country, of men of science and of culture, who thirst for truth and for God, and who are in the darkness of paganism.

And I think of Africa. Here there are so many black people, whose ancestors were brought here unjustly from Africa. . . . How wonderful it would be to have many vocations in this country from people of African descent and who would like to return to Africa! Here, with your great sense of nationhood, you can carry out much more easily the command to "Go forth," ut eatis!

Ut eatis! **not just to the great Brazilian continent.** Ut eatis! **to Japan;** ut eatis! **to Africa, which is a continent awaiting us with open arms.**

The Founder of Opus Dei dreamed of these men, who had reached Brazil by force of historical circumstances, returning of their own free will to their countries of origin to carry the love of Christ there.

During his stay in Brazil, he answered many specific questions and opened up great horizons of apostolate. He encouraged the members of the Work to set themselves each day more demanding goals within Brazil and thence throughout the world:

In Brazil we Catholics have much to do, because there are people here lacking the most basic necessities: without religious instruction — there are so many unbaptized — and also so many lacking the basic elements of culture. We have to lift

them up so that there is no one without a job, so that there is not a single old person who is worried because he is uncared for; so that no sick person is left forsaken; so that there is no one who hungers and thirsts for justice and is unable to quench his thirst.

From this marvellous platform — he went on, looking into the distance, with his hand extended, they were to go out to meet the spiritual needs of the East, where people are very well received, but even better "if the face helps", as they say in São Paulo:

Then if we truly love Japan, for example, and China — with its traditions dating back thousands of years, its imposing culture, its art and grace and history — we should want there to be Japanese and Chinese people, formed here, and in the Philippines, and in Peru, and in other places, who will freely want to return to their ancestors' countries of origin, to bring them the good news of Christ.

With the peoples of Africa, many Europeans — not all, but many — committed a terrible evil, which was to bring them here by force and in slavery. This was a crime against humanity! A real crime! We must make amends. In this respect, Opus Dei can do a lot, and Brazil can do a lot. . . . So then, if there are many vocations (. . .) and they go over there ready to carry Christ, they will be much better received. From Brazil. . . .

Does that mean everyone? No. But some, yes. They will also go from other countries. They are so happy to go! There are sons of mine in the Philippines — where the Lord is consoling my poor priestly heart by sending many vocations, abundant vocations and such good ones — that when they see my hunger to extend the kingdom of Christ, they say to me, "Don't worry, with faces like ours, we can go anywhere."

Msgr. Escrivá de Balaguer left a written record of this constant "refrain" of his in the deed of consecration of the oratory of the central offices of Opus Dei in Brazil. From the time when Pius XII granted him the faculty to consecrate altars, he always followed the custom of depositing a deed beneath the altar-stone in which he expressed his petition during the ceremony. The document said briefly that, **while I was making this consecration I prayed intensely to God, Three in One, through the intercession of Blessed Mary ever Virgin, and of St. Joseph, Our Father and Lord, to make his children in this Brazilian Region and myself good and faithful**

**and always ready to spread the Kingdom of Christ Our Lord
to all this immense nation and also to others, even to the most
distant lands.**

On the feast of Pentecost, 2 June 1974, thousands of people
gathered together in the Assembly Hall of the Mauá Palace in São
Paulo. **I can see here,** observed Msgr. Escrivá de Balaguer, **people of
every country and of very language who are listening to the
voice of Christ.** In truth, with such an audience, the first Pentecost
seemed extraordinarily near, that day when the Apostles **began to
speak of the** magnalia Dei, **the wonderful works of God, and
each heard them in his own language.** This time as well people of
many races were listening intently to the doctrine of Christ: black
people and yellow people, copper coloured and mulattoes, and whites
of the most diverse tones and shades. In each soul, these words were to
resound with a different echo. The miracle of tongues was again repeating itself in the depths of people's hearts.

In that place, the great heart of the Founder of Opus Dei saw but
one race: **the race of the children of God.**

CHAPTER SIX

THE MARK OF DIVINE FILIATION

1. THE DIVINE "CRAZINESS" OF THE CHILDREN OF GOD

It all became possible because the Founder of Opus Dei placed an unlimited and childlike trust in God his Father. This is the only explanation for his faith in what was for so many, himself included, a crazy enterprise. Ricardo Fernández Vallespín says that when, towards the end of 1933, the Founder of Opus Dei explained to them what God wanted Opus Dei to be in the future, it seemed sheer madness! A young priest, with no material means, was urging them to place the whole world at the feet of Christ. "And we who were no longer children — Isidoro Zorzano was the Father's age — did not doubt for a minute that all that he said would come true, because God wanted it so."

It was about that time that Don Josemaría asked a priest friend what he thought of his project of starting a students' residence in Ferraz Street. The good priest told him it "would be like going up in an aeroplane and then jumping out without a parachute".

Many people thought Don Josemaría's plans unreasonable. He must have been told this often. In 1934 he wrote in *Consideraciones espirituales*:

That — your ideal, your vocation — is madness. And the others — your friends, your brothers — are crazy. Have you never heard that cry deep down inside?

Answer, firmly, that you thank God for the honour of being one of those "lunatics".

Forty years later in São Paulo, a youngster called Gilberto asked him what he had meant by those words. Msgr. Escrivá de Balaguer began to reply and then, suddenly, he turned to Gilberto:

Have you ever seen a crazy person?

Gilberto was taken by surprise. He shook his head.

No? Have you never seen anyone who was mad? Look at me!

Gilberto and all the others who were there laughed. Msgr. Escrivá de Balaguer went on:

Many years ago they said I was mad. They were right. I have never said I was not. I am crazy, but with the love of God! And I would like you to have the same complaint.

That the Founder of Opus Dei knew what it means to be "madly" in love is confirmed in the many references he makes to the subject in his writings. In *The Way* he speaks of a **crazy** person, kissing the recently-consecrated sacred vessels:

Crazy! Yes, I saw you in the Bishop's chapel — alone, so you thought — as you left a kiss on each newly-consecrated chalice and paten: so that He might find them there, when he came for the first time to those eucharistic vessels (*The Way*, 438).

He described apostolic zeal, love for all souls, as a **divine craziness,** with three clear symptoms: **hunger to know the Master; constant concern for souls; perseverance that nothing can shake** (*The Way*, 934). In another passage, referring to the tactics to be used in the battles of the interior struggle and in apostolic action, he asks: **Is there any greater folly than to scatter the golden wheat on the ground to let it rot? Without that generous folly there would be no harvest** (*The Way*, 834); because when all is said and done the ones who are really out of their minds are those who do not want to savour God's love towards men: **Don't you long to shout to those young men and women moving around you: Fools, leave those wordly things that shackle the heart and very often degrade it ... leave all that and come with us in search of Love?** (*The Way*, 790).

The Founder of Opus Dei was "sane" enough to undertake this sequence of *impossibles* which Our Lord was asking of him by relying on the hard fact that he was a son of God. This gave him unshakable faith and hope. As he said of himself, it did not matter to him to be nothing, to be worth nothing, to have nothing, if God was his Father. Little did he mind if he lacked the wherewithal to start some new apostolic activity, nor was he put off by real or imaginary difficulties in the environment.

Ismael Sánchez Bella was the first Rector of the University of Navarre. He summarises the beginnings of that Centre referring to "the disproportion between the means we had in 1951 and the job Msgr. Escrivǎ de Balaguer had entrusted us with"; but the disproportion "was bridged by his faith, which was that of a man of God". Edwin Zobel corroborates this: "I am a witness of what Opus Dei has been able to do in my country and with my countrymen. I would never have believed or imagined it. I remember the Father's faith. It was so impressive when he told us how eagerly he awaited the apostolic fruit which would ripen in Switzerland by the grace of God." His faith "overcame all obstacles".

Don Josemaría relied above all on the will of God, but not in a "quietist" way. His utter acceptance of God's will led him to stress first the need of prayer, mortification and work done for God. He was still begging for prayers right up to his death, as he had done since the twenties. He was convinced that this was the most important way to move souls. He asked everyone. He asked his friends and the young people he was dealing with. He asked priests and religious, and also the sick people he looked after.

There are countless witnesses of this. Sister Cecilia Agut, a Poor Clare, met the Founder of Opus Dei in 1935 when he went to Valencia. He visited her convent and asked the nuns to pray to Our Lord for him. "I was most impressed with the faith and the extraordinary trust in God reflected in his words. His supernatural outlook and purity of intention were such that ever since he spoke to us we have never omitted to pray to Our Lord for Opus Dei and its Founder."

Don Casimiro Morcillo, when he was Archbishop of Madrid, remembered perfectly well, nearly forty years after the event, how the Founder of Opus Dei had asked him to pray for a special intention of his — such was the intensity of his words. It happened in 1929 and at the time they were unacquainted. Don Josemaría used to cross paths with him at six o'clock in the morning in Eloy Gonzalo Street. One day he stopped him and said:

Are you going to say Mass? Would you pray for an intention of mine?

Don Casimiro was amazed but he promised to pray and so he did. Afterwards they became firm friends and Don Casimiro always fondly remembered their first conversation.

This was not an isolated case. That young priest did the same with other people whom he did not know at all. More than once in the street, when he saw an honest-looking person going by, he would ask them to pray for an intention of his which was to give great glory to God. At the time the Work was still in gestation. Later they would realise they had been praying for Opus Dei.

José María González Barredo used to go to Mass at the Patronato de Enfermos in Santa Engracia Street. He tells how one day Don Josemaría, who was hearing Confessions there, came up to him to ask him to pray for a special intention of his. The priest's tone impressed him so much that although he left Madrid for a time, he continued praying to God each day without fail for an intention he knew nothing about, coming from a priest he had never met before.

Msgr. Escrivá de Balaguer was consistent with what he had written when he was less than thirty and which he published later in 1934 as one of the *Consideraciones espirituales*: **Next to the prayer of priests and of consecrated virgins, the prayer most pleasing to God is the prayer of children and that of the sick.** Thus he sought the strength he needed to carry on, among the sick and the most forsaken children of Madrid.

Thousands retain a vivid impression of him going about his **apostolic excursions** around the world, with his outstretched arm and open hand:

That's how I ask, like a beggar by the wayside. I ask you to pray for me — as if you were giving me alms — that the Father may be good and faithful.

Contrary to what one might think at first sight, his insistence came from a childlike trust in God, who is close by, who, as he always taught, is not only far above where the stars are shining, but is also continually by our side — or rather in us — as a Father who dearly loves his children. Prayer was the consequence of this closeness. It was a son's way of showing affection for his father whom he likes to have near, so as to learn from his gestures and rejoice in his riches.

So he continued until his death. In a Requiem Mass celebrated in Madrid, the Counsellor of Opus Dei in Spain, Don Florencio Sánchez Bella, recalled a conversation they had had together during the Father's last stay in Spain in May 1975: "He spoke to me of his death, I knew that ever since he was a young priest he had meditated daily on the subject, and he asked me to pray for his soul. He was aware that God could call him and anybody else at any time and he asked me once more, affectionately but insistently, that the moment we heard of his death we should all pray for him very much. He was begging again for an alms of prayer, so that the Lord would have mercy on him."

His attitude to death was the same as his attitude to life. He prayed with a child's trust, but at the same time tenaciously and perseveringly, as he had so often pointed out to the members of the Work:

The only answer is perseverance! Pray! Pray! Pray! Do you not see what I do? I try to put this spirit into practice. When I want something, I get all my children to pray; I tell them to offer their Communions, the Rosary, so many mortifications and so many aspirations, thousands of them! And God Our Lord will give us all the means we need to be more effective and extend His Kingdom throughout the world, if we persevere with personal perseverance.

2. "NOT AFRAID TO DIE"

Everything is to the good, when you love God. *Omnia in bonum!* There you have a quick synthesis of what St. Paul wrote: "God makes all things work together for the good for those who love him" (Rom 8:28). It is an aspiration, a thought addressed to God, in which Msgr. Escrivá de Balaguer found the peace and trust which belong to those who know they are children of God, and from it he drew the assurance he took with him wherever he went.

At a time when life in Spain was fraught with danger, after the burning of the convents in 1931, he offered his services as chaplain to the convent of the Augustinian Recollects of Santa Isabel. Sister María del Buen Consejo, a religious in that community, saw him always as "an exemplary priest who was very devout, with a great spirit of recollection, which he made compatible with naturalness and cheerfulness". She has a vivid recollection of "his way of laughing which made the atmosphere peaceful by making light of things".

It was also then that he tended the sick in the King's Hospital. Sister Isabel Martín belonged to the community of the Daughters of Charity who worked in that hospital for infectious diseases. She has not forgotten the joy he radiated around him: "we used to long for him to come, at that time of uncertainty and imminent persecution". The atmosphere in which the nuns had to work was not at all pleasant. Officially they were not even allowed to have a chaplain. According to Sister Isabel, "priests at that time had to be very brave to exercise their ministry, but Don Josemaría Escrivá was not afraid of anyone or anything. He had the necessary supernatural Faith and human courage for it."

When the Spanish war broke out, his cheerfulness stood out in a remarkable way in contrast to the tremendous difficulties he had to face. We have already mentioned some details about this period of his life, and there will be more in the next Chapter. Here we simply wish to record that even during this time he abandoned himself — as always — in God's hands.

At the beginning of the war, in July 1936, Don Ricardo Fernández Vallespín was in Valencia. He had just arrived to settle some details about renting a house which was going to be a students' residence. Then communications between Madrid and Valencia broke down. However, he found out that on 20 July a fierce battle had occurred in Madrid at the Montaña Barracks which were just opposite the Opus Dei residence at 16 Ferraz Street: "The formation we had received had prepared us to face that terrible situation without discouragement. We were convinced that the Work would survive the storm, but we were human and couldn't help suffering at the thought of the dangers the Father and the others were facing in Madrid." Ricardo was unable to get back to Madrid till April 1937. At that time the Founder of the Work had taken refuge in a flat which was under the diplomatic protection of Honduras. Ricardo went to see hin, accompanied by Isidoro Zorzano. Two things impressed him especially: how thin the Father was, and how with his habitual good spirits he kept encouraging the others to persevere above all else in the fulfilment of the norms of piety which he had recommended to the members of Opus Dei. In the midst of all these difficulties he had not lost his bearings and he continued directing souls towards God.

It was a constant attitude in his life, which can be summarised in an idea he used often to propose for meditation:

Never worry, even though the ground is shaking beneath your feet. The only serious thing is infidelity, breaking your union with God.

"I have had the good fortune," declares Don Antonio Rodilla, "of conversing with him for considerable periods of time and on many occasions, and I can't remember one conversation that wasn't a continuous act of faith." His cheerful hope was "paradoxically buoyed up by the sorrow of feeling himself a sinner". This attitude of Don Josemaría reminded Don Antonio of the reaction of euphoria when a person escapes alive from a near-fatal accident. Sorrow, wherever it came from, drove Don Josemaría to pray, and in prayer his peace and joy were reaffirmed. The Founder of the Work was a "champion" of faith.

There were plenty of sorrows in the seventy-three years of his life. Only rarely did he refer to them, as when he addressed some women members of the Work in Rome on 28 March 1950, which was his Silver Jubilee as a priest:

It's been a completely happy day, not a common thing on the more important dates in my life when Our Lord has always wanted to send me some mishap.

As if to make light of what he had just said, he added with a smile:

Even on my First Communion day, when the barber was combing my hair he burnt me with his tweezers. It wasn't anything much, but for a child of that age it was enough.

Msgr. Escrivá de Balaguer experienced a lot of suffering, because he did not sidestep it when it came. Sometimes, however, although his shoulders were broad, the weight of his mission to serve the whole Church and souls weighed him down till he felt "crippled" under the burden. In June 1974 he described a picture over a door leading to the oratory of the Holy Family in the central offices of the Work in Rome:

It was painted by a fourth- or fifth-rank artist called Del Arco, more or less about the time of Velazquez. It depicts Christ crowned with thorns and overwhelmed, really crushed! I too have seen myself overwhelmed so often in the evening, tired and exhausted. It consoles me very much to think of that image of Christ Jesus, just as he is in that picture. He who is all beauty, strength, wisdom . . . yet there — tied to the Pillar — he was like that. So if things get you down and you feel overwhelmed, remember Jesus. Jesus, backbroken. Jesus who is hungry. Jesus who is thirsty. Jesus who is tired. Jesus who weeps. Jesus who knows how to be a friend to his friends. . . . And, above all, Jesus with Mary and Joseph: that's the ultimate. Go there! Go there! Learn! And then things will go well.

It is not difficult to imagine how warmly he spoke in those moments, wishing to bring souls to picture Our Lord in each one of those instants of his life on earth. He sought to impress upon people that to follow in Jesus' footsteps is, and will be, the way to solve all problems and difficulties. The Founder of Opus Dei was speaking from his own experience when he added:

Don't be misled. If we rely exclusively on human means we will fail every time. But with supernatural means, we will always find a way forward. There will always be difficulties; there have to be. Because ... unfortunately we are not yet in Heaven: we are on earth, and we have defects.

He expressed himself with the realism of one who knows the key to finding joy in sorrow: to know one is a son of God and live accordingly. **The roots of joy take the form of a cross,** he taught. For many years he used to write on the first page of his *Ordo* (the liturgical calendar that priests use to know what Mass they can or ought to say, and what parts of the Divine Office they have to read) a very expressive ejaculation: *in laetitia, nulla dies sine cruce!* (With joy, no day without the Cross!)

He had written in *The Way*, 217: **I want you to be happy on earth. And you will not be happy if you don't lose that fear of suffering. For, as long as we are "wayfarers", it is precisely in suffering that our happiness lies.** He himself was happy in the midst of countless physical and spiritual afflictions. Other people were not quick to spot them, because he never lost his sense of humour and because he practised what he preached: that often a smile is the best mortification. It is especially difficult to smile when one is backbroken. It is very likely that he learned this ascetical idea, that a smile is the best mortification, from his father Don José whom he had never seen sad, although Our Lord had treated him in the same way as Job.

Let those who do not know they are children of God be sad. In the life of a Christian sadness, fear and complaints are out of place, because a Christian's **treasures** are precisely: **hunger, thirst, heat, cold, pain, dishonour, poverty, loneliness, betrayal, slander, prison ...** (*The Way*, 194). Many learned from him not to be afraid of anything or anybody, not even of God because, as he insisted, God is our Father who loves us more than all the mothers and fathers in the world put together. In this way he was able to strengthen hundreds of sick people with christian fortitude, helping them to die in a holy way with the joy of those who know by faith that to die is to go to meet their Father God. Speaking about his years at the King's Hospital, Sister Isabel Martín describes "how the young consumptive girls even recovered their natural good spirits, although they knew they were going to die. But they accepted death without making it a tragedy, with naturalness and hope. They even took care of their personal appearance so as not to make the people around them sad, and to go to meet God with joy."

The Founder of Opus Dei showed by example that those who decide to follow in the footsteps of Jesus Christ **are not afraid of life and not afraid of death,** because those who truly live as children of God cannot fear death. Not long ago, opening his heart to some members of the Work in Rome, he said:

I was very young when I wrote that Jesus will not be my Judge or yours: he will be Jesus, a God who forgives, and now I repeat the same words with relish.

There was an Italian song in the fifties that he liked a lot because it made him think of going to Heaven:

> Open the windows and let in the sun,
> It's springtime, it's springtime.
> Open the windows and let in the sun,
> It's springtime, the festival of Love.*

Many times he was heard to say that: **once I have received Extreme Unction — if the Lord has mercy on me — I'd like them to sing that song to me. It will prepare me to go to meet God. It helps me to pray.**

There was a period in the fifties, in Rome, when his diabetes got worse. In 1974 he described how he had reacted to this:

I got them to fix a bell in my room within arm's reach. I said: "I can at least ring, and when you hear the din you can come and give me Extreme Unction." Once that bell starts ringing they have to go a long way to stop it.

When night-time came I would think: "Lord, I don't know if I will be alive by morning; I thank you for the life you have given me and I am happy to die in your arms. I trust in your mercy." In the morning when I awoke my first thought was the same.

His condition was serious as was indicated by the weekly analyses which yielded identical results, in spite of a strict diet and high doses

---

*Aprite le finestre al nuovo sole, è primavera, è primavera. Aprite le finestre al nuovo sole, è primavera, è festa dell'Amor.

of insulin. On 27 April 1954, a little before one o'clock in the afternoon, he was with Don Alvaro del Portillo. He had just received a delayed-action insulin injection at the correct time and he felt well. Suddenly, shortly after the injection, he suffered an anaphilactic shock. Just before losing consciousness he exclaimed to Don Alvaro: **Absolution, absolution.**

It all happened so quickly. There had been no warning symptoms which could have suggested such a serious turn of events and Don Alvaro del Portillo did not understand what he was saying. "What solution?" he asked. Msgr. Escrivá de Balaguer, as if to urge him on, replied with the opening words of absolution: *Ego te absolvo....* Seconds later he fell unconscious.

Don Alvaro del Portillo tried to revive him. He asked for some sugar, thinking that this could be a hypoglucemic coma, and he tried to make him swallow some, but without success as his jaw had stiffened. Meanwhile Msgr. Escrivá de Balaguer's face had taken on such a colour that although Don Alvaro called the doctor he thought there was nothing a doctor could do.

God willed that the Father should come back to himself after fifteen minutes, before the doctor arrived. That afternoon, when he recovered his eyesight, which he had lost for several hours, he called for the three women members of the Work who had learned from Don Alvaro about his state and who were still alarmed. He wanted them to stop worrying. To set their minds at rest, he started working at a job where he needed their help.

Those persons have never forgotten this lesson of calm abandonment in the hands of God.

It is worth noting that, from that day onwards, Msgr. Escrivá de Balaguer never again suffered from diabetes, an illness which medical opinion regards as irreversible.

3. "NOT AFRAID TO LIVE"

It would be misleading to think that the Founder of Opus Dei only had recourse to divine filiation in difficult moments. On the contrary, being and knowing that he was a son of God was so real to him that it penetrated his whole life. He wrote in *Consideraciones espirituales*: **We've got to be filled, to be imbued with the idea that God is our Father, and very much our Father, who is both**

near us and in Heaven. He always insisted on the need to think often, every day, about this great reality, because to know that one is a son of God is not only consoling: it also prompts one to live a better life. This is also reflected in another of these spiritual considerations of 1934:

Children. . . . How they seek to behave worthily in the presence of their parents.

And the children of Kings, in the presence of their father the King, how they seek to uphold the royal dignity!

And you? Don't you realise that you are always in the presence of the Great King, God, your Father?

Msgr. Escrivá de Balaguer directed these teachings to everyone, and of course to members of Opus Dei as well. On 24 May 1974 he said to them in São Paulo:

Our Lord wants us to be in the world and to love the world but without being worldly. Our Lord wants us to remain in this world — which is now all topsy-turvy and where the clamour of lust and disobedience and purposeless rebellion can be heard — so that we may teach people to live with joy. People are unhappy. They make a lot of noise, they sing and dance and shout, but they are weeping quietly. Deep down in their hearts there is nothing but tears. They are not happy, they are miserable. And Our Lord wants you and me to be happy.

For practically everybody there, it was the first time they had been with the Founder of Opus Dei, and perhaps they were taken by surprise by his ability to summarise in a few words, as he did then, the story of a well-lived vocation:

We shall be happy if we fight and conquer. Each one of us has his own experience, as I have mine. Each one of us knows that he will have his share of battles every day.

He ended on an optimistic note:

I know you are all determined to fight. I know that none of you is a coward, that you are all brave and that you are not afraid . . . because, as we have said before, a son of God cannot be afraid. When we know that God is our Father our self-surrender becomes serene and our interior struggle confident. This sense of divine filiation, though it is a general characteristic of the christian life, nevertheless took on a special and intense significance in the life of the Founder of Opus Dei at a particular moment in 1931:

They were difficult times, from a human point of view, but even so I was quite sure of the impossible — this impossibility which you can now see as an accomplished reality. I felt God acting within me with overriding force, filling my heart and bringing to my lips this tender invocation: Abba! Pater! **I was out in the street, in a tram: being out in the street is no hindrance for our contemplative dialogue; for us, the hustle and bustle of the world is a place for prayer.**

This happened one very sunny day, in a tram he had taken in Atocha (Madrid). It was a new light which illuminated from a different angle what he had seen clearly on 2 October 1928. The Christian can and should be a saint in the midst of and through the ordinary things of his life (his profession, his family and friends) without needing to leave his place.

The Founder of Opus Dei referred to this when he taught **those university students and workers who were with me in the thirties that they had to** materialise **their spiritual life. I wanted to keep them from the temptation, so common then and now, of living a kind of double life. On the one hand, an interior life, a life of relation with God; and on the other a separate and distinct professional, social and family life, full of small earthly realities.**

No! We cannot lead a double life. We cannot be like schizophrenics, if we want to be Christians. There is just one life, made of flesh and spirit. And it is this life which has to become, in both soul and body, holy and filled with God. We discover the invisible God in the most visible and material things.

There is no other way. Either we learn to find Our Lord in ordinary, everyday life, or else we shall never find him.

Don Ricardo Fernández Vallespín recalls a practical instance of how the Founder of Opus Dei "materialised" the spiritual life. Before asking to join the Work, Ricardo had made a promise, which he had not yet fulfilled, to go from Madrid to the shrine of Sonsoles (at Avila). Don Josemaría told him that although he could dispense Ricardo from this promise, they would fulfil it and he would accompany Ricardo and they would do the pilgrimage in a different way from what Ricardo had originally planned.

So one day in the spring of 1934 they went from Madrid to Avila by train. José María González Barredo and Manuel Sainz de los Terreros went along with them. From Avila they took the road to

Sonsoles saying five mysteries of the Rosary. In the shrine they said another five, and they said the remaining five on the way back. It was a bumpy, dusty road although traffic could go along it. There is a moment when the shrine can be glimpsed in the distance, but then a little hill hides it from view until once the hill is crossed it can be seen once more. A few days later the Founder of Opus Dei pointed out in a meditation that the same thing applies in the interior life. There are times when the goal is hidden from view, and life becomes an uphill struggle; but, he told them, if they were faithful and docile they would be rewarded and, having crossed the hill, they would see their goal once more. Then they would have peace and happiness.

Don Josemaría told Natividad González the story of John the milkman, which took place in the church of the Patronato of Santa Isabel. John used to take his milk churns round the town on a hand-cart. Don Josemaría as he sat in the confessional each day kept hearing, always at the same time, a noise that interrupted the early morning silence. At last, one day, he went out to see what was going on, and he found a milkman with his milk churns at the church door. The man entered for a moment and said: "Jesus, here's John the milkman." The Founder of Opus Dei spent the rest of the day repeating this aspiration:

Lord, here is this wretch, this wretched priest who doesn't know how to love you like John the milkman. He was very moved by this simple man's beautiful way of praying. He learned from him, and used the story of John the milkman to help people to learn to approach prayer with the milkman's naturalness and trust.

Don Avelino Gómez Ledo was similarly impressed when years after their stay in the residence of Larra Street, he came across the Founder of Opus Dei in Madrid quite by chance. It was near Cibeles Square where the Bank of Spain is. He did not doubt for a moment that it was the Father, wrapped in his cloak, as if using its very folds to help him to be recollected. He was walking down the pavement of that Madrid street, praying, united to God.

Don Josémaría gave spiritual guidance to many souls, teaching them to acquire a deep interior life. He demanded a lot of them, but he also led them along straightforward ordinary ways, without doing odd or complicated things. All his life and preaching, all the spirit of Opus Dei, abounded with this kind but nonetheless demanding tone which was a consequence of his filial conversation with God. Here, as a token sample, are some considerations from *The Way* which have helped thousands of men and women set out upon a life of prayer:

You say you don't know how to pray? Put yourself in the presence of God, and once you have said, "Lord, I don't know how to pray!" rest assured that you have begun to do so (*The Way*, 90).

You write: "To pray is to talk with God. But about what?" About what? About him, about yourself; joys, sorrows, successes and failures, noble ambitions, daily worries, weaknesses! And acts of thanksgiving and petitions: and Love and reparation.

In a word: to get to know him and to get to know yourself: "to get acquainted!" (*The Way*, 91).

If people told him they were "cold" and could not "feel anything", that going to Mass, praying, offering their work to God and spending time in prayer in this state seemed "like play-acting", Msgr. Escrivá de Balaguer put to them the simple but delightful story of the juggler in the Canticles of King Alfonso who, moved by a desire to love God more, entered a monastery.

Day after day the juggler searched his soul for something worthwhile with which to honour the Blessed Virgin like the other friars did with their studies, their voices or their handicrafts, but our friar was illiterate, and had no skills. Then one day a thought crossed his mind which made him smile. When in the world he had earned his living, albeit poorly, with tricks and skills he had acquired as a child: he could juggle, doing somersaults and catching the balls without letting a single one fall. Children laughed and were amused. The friar hardly thought he could earn Heaven with what he was earning his living with before; but now he did not really want to earn anything. He just wanted to honour Our Lady . . . so at night-time he would tiptoe out of his cell and present himself before the sympathetic and motherly gaze of the Blessed Virgin. There he performed his somersaults and all sorts of sleights of hand; until one day the Superior caught him at it; but he said nothing, and the juggler-monk continued his prayer in his own fashion.

In a homily given on 5 April 1964, Msgr. Escrivá de Balaguer said:

It's no secret that over the years people have come to me and have told me with real sorrow: "Father, I don't know what's wrong, but I find myself tired and cold. My piety used to be so clear and strong, but now it feels like a farce. . . ." Well,

for those who are going through that phase, and for all of you, I answer: A farce? That's a marvellous thing! The Lord is playing with us as a father does with his children.

(. . .) Don't lose your peace: for you the moment has arrived to play out a human comedy before a divine spectator. Persevere, for the Father, the Son, and the Holy Spirit are contemplating your acting: do it all for love of God, to please him, although you find it hard.

How beautiful it is to be a clown for God! How beautiful to act out that role for Love, with sacrifice, seeking no personal satisfaction, but just to please Our Father God who is playing with us! Turn to Our Lord with confidence and say to him: "I don't feel like doing this at all, but I will offer it up for You." And then get on with the job, even though you think it is a farce. Blessed farce! I assure you it isn't hypocrisy, because hypocrites need a public for their pantomimes. Whereas the spectators of our play, let me repeat, are the Father, the Son and the Holy Spirit, the Most Holy Virgin, St. Joseph and all the Angels and Saints in Heaven.

"God's clown": so the poet Jose Ramón de Dolarea described Msgr. Escrivá de Balaguer in *El Tiempo*, a newspaper of the city of Piura (Peru), on 14 July 1975, because he took the part of **God's clown** in front of thousands of persons in the seventies, as for instance in Barcelona on 25 November 1972.

The gymnasium of the Brafa Sports School had been turned into an auditorium. About 4,000 people were there that afternoon, all of them young. Questions flowed in quick succession. One youngster from the back of the hall spoke about getting "as soft as cream cheese", instead of being tough to be able to respond generously to God when he demands sacrifice.

In his reply the Founder of Opus Dei referred to the sports and physical exercise they do in Brafa. Passing on to the recently held Olympic Games, he went on to tell them that he had been in the north of Italy just a couple of miles or so from the Swiss border and had seen some of the sports on television. He began to describe, and re-enact, the adventures and misadventures of a pole-vaulter. First the athlete measured the distance; then he concentrated; then he relaxed his muscles; finally he jumped, and then retraced his steps, crestfallen. Then followed another attempt and another failure; until in the end he succeeded. Msgr. Escrivá de Balaguer all this time was imitating the gestures and the facial expressions of the athletes we have seen so often. The people followed all this with great amusement and were absorbed by his "performance". **Forgive me,** he said, **if I play the part of Our Lord's juggler,** because, **in the end they succeeded! Well, with the grace of God, which is the best pole, the only pole a Christian has, we can jump over anything. And we get tougher, and we do the marvels that these boys here are doing.**

It would not be easy to conceive a more natural, amusing and at the same time demanding manner of urging young people — with his **gift of tongues** — towards the interior struggle. This picture of the pole-vaulter is a good example of the sporting approach to the ascetical struggle which is so characteristic of the spirit of Opus Dei; that **smiling asceticism** which is second nature to Msgr. Escrivá de Balaguer and to any genuine son of God.

He was proposing a way of striving to fulfil God's will which in effect was an about-turn to the conventional approach to the interior struggle. For years, centuries even, many writers of ascetical works and directors of souls had ordinarily insisted too much on the "negative" aspects of Christianity. They insisted too much on the fulfilment of one's duty pure and simple, for fear of the divine retribution which all sin carries with it. Consequently people tended to forget, in practice, that the Christian is a son of God and that a son owes his father piety, reverence, affection and even "fear": but filial fear, Msgr. Escrivá de Balaguer explained, a sense of sorrow at the thought of displeasing one's father — not "fear" in the literal and usual meaning of the word.

It is easy to see that the first people to gather around the Founder of Opus Dei found great interior peace and calm with which to face up to the battles they would have to undertake in the middle of the world, their work and their homes, in his insistence on the **cheerfulness of the children of God.** Divine filiation brought with it a new meaning to prayer and the life of piety, to sacrifice and serving others, to fraternity and apostolate, to troubles and sorrows, victories and defeats, to the past and the future.

In a very special way it demonstrated the feasibility of sanctifying oneself in ordinary life without leaving the world and also without being afraid of the "world", because Jesus had prayed to his Father: "I do not ask you to take them out of the world, but to keep them from evil" (John 17: 15). The Christian should see the world as God's creation. The world has come to us from the hands of Our Father and he passes it on to his children as an inheritance (cf. Psalm 2: 8). The world, then, is good, except, as the Founder of the Work pointed out, where we men have made it bad with our sins.

Looking at things in this way, it is easy to see why the apostolic outlook of Msgr. Escrivá de Balaguer was always positive and never negative. His realism and awareness of evil in the world did not lead him to pessimism. Because he trusted in God, he was not afraid of anything or anyone. A man who is not afraid does not see "enemies". Hence he was wont to repeat frequently that Opus Dei is not **anti-anything** nor **anti-anyone.** All its apostolate can be summarised in the graphic phrase, **to smother evil in an abundance of good.**

Over the years, persons, who though not members of the Work regarded it with affection, from time to time saw it misguidedly as a possible solution "against" one movement or another, to which they attributed the misfortunes of the Church or religion in general. These could be freemasonry or communism, the *Institución Libre de Enseñanza* (in the case of the Spanish higher education during the first third of the twentieth century) or the secularism of other countries; but this was to misunderstand the spirit of the Founder of Opus Dei. By 1934 he had already written in the first of his *Consideraciones espirituales*:

Don't let your life be barren. Be useful. Make yourself felt. Shine forth with the torch of your faith and your love.

With your apostolic life, wipe out the trail of filth and slime left by the corrupt sowers of hatred. And set aflame all the ways of the earth with the fire of Christ that you bear in your heart.

Forty years later he repeated the same idea in different words:

Don't be afraid of the paganised world, because Our Lord has chosen us to be leaven, salt and light in this world. Don't be worried. The world won't harm you unless you want it to. No enemy of our soul can do anything if we don't consent. And we won't consent, with the grace of God and the protection of our Mother in Heaven.

Have piety and pray. Once I was worried by the situation in a particular country and I said: "My God, what is going to happen there?" The atmosphere there was really very bad. And then one of the Directors came and told me: "Father, don't worry, we are praying a lot.". . . Be prayerful and don't be afraid of the paganised world. We'll rid the world of paganism, with our prayer.

But one must not think only of the risks of a "hostile environment". Very often, what makes christian life difficult are not great "enemies" from without, but simply the pressure of time: being overwhelmed with work, too much to do, or feeling unable to cope. There are moments when one can get nervous and lose that supernatural outlook which ought to guide everything one does, even the most human things.

This lack of calm robs us of our presence of God and can destroy our perspective in such a way that one reaches the conclusion that it is meaningless to leave some very urgent job in order to devote a few minutes exclusively to prayer or some act of piety. Then we not only waste an opportunity to sanctify our efforts, but in practice we are diminishing the very efficacy of our work and we even end up wasting time.

Since the Founder of Opus Dei knew so much about urgency in work, he never let an opportunity pass him by. If, in the case of parents, their most important work is their dedication to their own children, he concluded that for a son of God his life of piety, his conversation with his Father, was always his most important work and could never be put off.

He made this very clear in that well-known homily of 8 October 1967, given on the campus of the University of Navarre:

I assure you, my sons, that when a Christian carries out with love the most insignificant everyday action, that action overflows with the transcendence of God. That is why I have told you repeatedly, and hammered away once and again on the idea, that the christian vocation consists in making heroic verse out of the prose of each day. Heaven and earth seem to merge, my sons, on the horizon. But where they really meet is in your hearts, when you sanctify your everyday lives. . . .

4. SUPERNATURAL PRUDENCE

Take no notice. Madness has always been the term that "prudent" people apply to God's works.
Forward! Without fear! (*The Way*, 479).

Nevertheless, daring is not imprudence, nor is it recklessness (cf. *The Way*, 401). The Founder of Opus Dei learned to leave all his worries in God's hands:

Children have nothing of their own, everything belongs to their parents ... and your Father always knows best how to manage your affairs. His confidence in God, however, did not lead him to shrug off his personal responsibility. On the contrary, precisely because he trusted God he felt he could not despise any human means. There was nothing in him of the doctrinally-empty "charismatic" or the irresponsible "visionary". He would say in jest that **he was neither a prophet nor the son of a prophet,** but he repeated the Prophet's words *electi mei non laborabunt frustra* (Isaiah 65: 23): the work of the sons of God will always bear fruit.

We must bear in mind Msgr. Escrivá de Balaguer's prudence if we wish to get a deep understanding of how he lived his filial relation with God, which was the source of his joy and peace, his serenity and daring. This at the same time was the foundation on which his efforts and exhausting days of work rested.

In Chapter Three I referred to an important expression of the Founder's supernatural prudence, the fact that he did not wish to be a founder of anything. He did everything he could to find out if what God was asking of him already existed. He always acted with the permission and blessing of the Bishop of Madrid. When the time was ripe he worked to get Opus Dei approved and, once he saw clearly it was the Will of God, he spared himself no effort to carry it out.

Together with that there is a long list of lesser aspects of Msgr. Escrivá de Balaguer's prudence which are aptly summarised in his family motto, **Alma, calma.**

He was never indecisive, but he knew how to wait — although he found this hard to do, with his lively temperament. Once, soon after his arrival in Rome, he was heard to say: **I have learned to wait, which is no mean achievement.**

He put thought into his decisions. He never improvised or acted hastily, and he taught those who held positions of responsibility within Opus Dei to do the same. He often warned against the danger of rushing with a typical expression of his: **urgent things can wait; very urgent things must wait. . . .** Here was a practical way of distinguishing between what was important and what was urgent. What cannot and must not wait is what is truly important, even though apparently it is not urgent.

He was never in a hurry with people. **Souls, like good wine, improve with time.** He knew how to wait also when there was a case of pressing need, yet for one reason or another there was hardly anything he could do about it.

The plants lay hidden under the snow. And the farmer, the owner of the land, observed with satisfaction: "Now they are growing on the inside."

I thought of you: of your forced inactivity. . . .

Tell me : are you too growing "on the inside"? (*The Way*, 294).

His prudence in letting time pass — **calma** — was compatible with the courage and impatient speed — **alma** — with which he launched out as soon as he recognised clearly what God wanted, how he wanted it, and that he wanted it now. In Cardinal Tedeschini's opinion Msgr. Escrivá de Balaguer was, of all the people he had met, the one most concerned to discover God's plans and to put them into effect immediately. He knew how to wait, but when the moment came to decide or to act, he did not allow himself a moment's delay. He gave the impression of having no inertia.

The women members of Opus Dei noticed this in the early years of their work. They were few and they were full of apostolic zeal and anxious to grow and multiply, but they had little experience as yet. **Calma! Calma!** (Steady! Steady!), he would often say to them; but, a few years later, when the time was ripe, he urged them on with a very different expression: **Hurry! At God's pace!**

If his daring was not imprudence, his prudence was never cowardice. In *The Way* he wrote about something which he had suffered in his own flesh: **I don't like your euphemistic habit of calling cowardice prudence.**

Sister Engracia Echevarría, the Superior of the community which looked after the King's Hospital, stresses his prudence and courage during the difficult years between 1931 and 1936. The Founder of Opus Dei faced the problems produced by the anticlericalism of the time with a serene but energetic attitude: "It was already apparent that he had a talent for governing." She was impressed by the serenity of a man so young. He was "already very sensible, serious and courageous at a time when courage and prudence were necessary to overcome so much opposition."

The nuns of Santa Isabel also remember him as a dignified and prudent priest. Two separate religious communities were housed in that ancient Royal Patronato: the convent of the Augustinian Recollects and the College of the Assumption. Before he was appointed rector of the Patronato — in 1934 — Don Josemaría was chaplain only to the Augustinians, although both communities shared the chapel for liturgical acts. "His exquisite prudence," according to Sister Aránzazu Minteguiaga, a religious of the Assumption in Pamplona, "fostered the harmonious relationships which were a continual help at a time when religious persecution and destruction were rife."

He stuck to the facts. His prudence and his sense of justice helped him **to learn how to listen.** He expressed this principle with a graphic phrase which many people including several not of Opus Dei remember: **listen to each bell and, where possible, get to know who the bell-ringer is.**

He also lacked "inertia" in his judgments or decisions. When the facts changed, he changed his opinion cheerfully. He did not go about with preconceived plans of what had to be done. He preferred things to emerge from life, experience or custom. Nor did he stick rigidly to past experience. If new factors arose which required things to be seen differently, he readily and humbly changed his approach.

An important expression of his supernatural prudence is permanently incorporated in the specific manner in which Opus Dei is run, which is **collegially.** The Founder was a man of authority. Fr. Garganta, O.P., says: "He was a man who knew how to persuade and make others reflect; but when he commanded, that was that. He was a man of outstanding prudence in governing." This very reason explains his abhorrence of tyranny and personal government. Collegiality was established very soon — **not without special providence of God,** he would say — at all levels of government in Opus Dei: central, regional and local. Decisions are not given by one person; several individuals are involved in coming to them. He was often to remark, in interviews with journalists and elsewhere, that, as President within the General Council of Opus Dei, he only had one vote. Things have always been run this way, from the central organisms of the Association down to the last local centre to be set up.

Msgr. Escrivá de Balaguer kept his feet on the ground. He was a "realist", because he knew with supernatural certainty that God was bent on fulfilling this "madness" He had entrusted to him. The Work was of God and Heaven would see it was done. His "dreams" were not unreal — quite the contrary: there is nothing more real than fulfilling an imperative command from Christ, and nothing more prudent than such madness.

CHAPTER SEVEN

THE HOURS OF HOPE

1. WAR TIME IN SPAIN

The Madrid battle-front, June 1938. From the military observation post in upper Carabanchel, the Founder of Opus Dei used the
artillery range-finding telescope to look at 16 Ferraz Street. The house
which had cost him so much difficulty and effort to get going, lay in
ruins.

It meant starting again from scratch. The war had undone the
material achievement of several years, but he continued to trust and
hope. In Vitoria, in or about 1938, Msgr. Beitia was an eye witness of
the "cheerfulness" of the Founder of Opus Dei when faced with the
ruin of his efforts: **If it's for his glory, Our Lord will build it up
again.**

It was very much a time for hope.

With the triumph of the Popular Front in the elections of February
1936, the already confused situation of Spanish public life deteriorated.
Religious persecution intensified. In many places in Spain churches
were once again burned and sacked. There were mass demonstrations,
shootings, reprisals, a break-down in law and order, a build-up of
events that foreshadowed the civil war.

Don Josemaría realised things were serious. He made constant
acts of reparation for the attacks upon religion, but he did not lose his
calm, nor did he allow himself to be carried away by the alarm of the

pessimists. He managed to a great extent to prevent the country's uneasy atmosphere from interrupting his apostolic work. The Ferraz residence kept on running and the activities of spiritual formation went on regularly.

The Founder of Opus Dei realised that he was a son of God, a son of Our Lady, **the Mother of God and our Mother,** as he so often called her. This, as we have just seen, was the foundation of his whole life:

I had an image of Our Lady which the communists stole from me during the Spanish War. I called it the Virgin of the kisses. I never went in or out of that first residence of ours without first going to the Director's room, where the image was, and kissing it. I don't think I ever did it mechanically. It was a human kiss, the kiss of a son who is afraid. . . . But I have said so often that I am not afraid of anyone or of anything, so we'd better not say afraid. It was the kiss of a son who was worried that he was too young and who went to seek in Our Lady all the tenderness of her affection. I went to seek all the fortitude I needed in God through the Blessed Virgin.

Former residents of 50 Ferraz still recall his infectious courage, which made them immune to the prevailing atmosphere of defeatism and enabled them to carry on their apostolic work as if there were nothing amiss.

The Founder of Opus Dei lived through those times with special intensity. He kept reminding all the members of the Work that they had a duty to be well informed. They had to be immersed in reality, for they were normal citizens, and they should try to ensure that their own calm attitude was not misunderstood by others, and that it did not lead to any type of isolationism or escapism. He also made use of those circumstances to give formation to those around him. He taught them to trust above all in the Will of God. He made them realise that, no matter how serious the situation got, they could not go in for an uncontrolled activism which might make them forget that prayer and the supernatural means were much the most important things. He warned them against the risk of pride and self-love in politics. Also, without giving it too much importance, he gave them practical lessons in prudence.

In the early months of 1936, despite the growing social and political upheaval, he was still determined to find a larger house because there was so much apostolic work that the residence at 50 Ferraz had become too small. At the same time he kept looking for the financial resources needed to finance this expansion. He worked in the present. What he wanted was a large family house. Because of the political situation, houses of this kind were being put up for sale at moderate prices because there was hardly any demand for them. With the help of the young people who lived in or visited the residence, the whole of Madrid was searched, though his preferences were for the Argüelles district, probably because it was close to San Bernado and to the new University buildings beyond Moncloa.

In the end they found a house in Ferraz Street itself, at number 16. It belong to the Count Real who was living in France at the time. An agreement was reached with the administrator and arrangements were made to take the building over on 1 July 1936.

At the same time he was planning a new residence for students in Valencia. Francisco Botella, who had been born in Alcoy, was to go at the end of the academic year, with the job of looking for a house which could be used in the following year. As soon as he found something suitable he was to get in touch with Madrid so that Ricardo Fernández Vallespín could go to Valencia to sign the contract, if the choice was suitable. The plan was that Fernández Vallespín would be the director of this centre and would be helped by Francisco Botella, who would continue studying for his science degree there. Isidoro Zorzano for his part would take over in Madrid as Director of DYA, as the Ferraz residence and academy was still called, after resigning from his job as chief engineer in the locomotive works of the Andalusian Railways in Malaga. In effect, at the end of June or beginning of July, Isidoro did travel to Madrid, where he was to remain for good.

The political situation became tense. Many families brought forward their holidays, because people on both sides now knew that a coup d'état was inevitable. Rumours ran like wildfire. The atmosphere was highly charged.

13 July proved to be a critical day. Calvo Sotelo, the leader of the conservative opposition in the legislature, was assassinated. Unrest spread, and the general feeling was that "it was only a matter of hours". The Founder of Opus Dei, however, continued unperturbed, putting into practice the plans for expansion as if nothing had happened. The then Director of Ferraz affirms: "People thought he was crazy."

Hope led him to live **today, now.** He speeded up the transfer to 16 Ferraz Street; one of the reasons for this was that he did not want to pay rent any longer than necessary for 50 Ferraz Street. All the furniture was taken to 16 Ferraz. The house needed a minimum of repair work to put it in order. As there was no money, everyone lent a hand and little by little the future residence took shape.

This new Centre was situated in front of the Montaña Barracks, which was to be the nerve centre of the uprising in Madrid. From the balcony of one of the windows of the centre, on Sunday 19 July, they could see the people involved in the uprising gathering in the barracks. In the early afternoon, the streets that led to the barracks were blocked by guards and militiamen who asked all passers-by to show their papers. At about 8 p.m. the students who lived with their families left the residence. Don Josemaría requested them with fatherly care to telephone back so that he might know that they were safely home. The attack began during the night. Bullets penetrated the residence and embedded themselves in the walls and ceilings. Next morning, as the militiamen, elated by their victory, were taking over the Montaña Barracks, Don Josemaría, together with the few who had spent the night there, abandoned Ferraz. They got him to put on a boiler suit, one of the ones that had been used in the cleaning up of the house. Even though it did not fit him well, there were no other lay clothes for him. They passed through the excited masses of people coming to celebrate the triumph and managed to get to his mother's house in Doctor Cárceles Street (nowadays re-named Rey Francisco Street).

The Montaña Barracks had fallen. The situation became confused and terror spread over Madrid. It was known that many people had been shot by firing squad. By 21 July there were so many corpses in the public mortuary that they began to pile them up at the entrance. It was obvious that all precautions had to be taken.

Don Josemaría had to remain in his mother's house, without being able to go out, because the fact that he was a priest was commonly known in the district. Just as for any other priest in Madrid at the time, his only alternatives were to hide or leave himself open to assassination by any street patrol. Even in hiding he ran the risk of frequent house searches.

The civil war had broken out just as he could count on a basis of well trained people, with whom he could have undertaken his plans for immediate expansion, which included enlarging the Madrid residence, starting one in Valencia and beginning the work in France. Instead everything was collapsing. As a Father, he suffered greatly because, due to the break-down in communications, he knew nothing about how many of the members of Opus Dei who were out of Madrid were getting on. To crown it all he could not say Holy Mass, or pray by the Tabernacle.

A long nightmare began. He had to go from one hiding place to another, in constant difficulty and danger. Don Josemaría never thought of himself, but of souls, of the Church, of the Work and each one of its members, of his mother and sister and brother. Those at his side felt the strength of his unshakable faith in the supernatural character of the Work, and his hope-filled fortitude in the way he faced all sorts of problems. His constant supernatural reactions, the way he ceaselessly repeated a brief aspiration *fiat!*, which expressed his abandonment in God's hands, was something that deeply impressed those who were with him during those months. They soon became convinced that whatever course things might take, everything would be for the good, *omnia in bonum!*

A point in *The Way* reflects in good measure these interior dispositions of Don Josemaría, although I am not certain that he wrote it in those early days of the war: **War! "War," you tell me, "has a supernatural end that the world is unaware of: war has been for us. . . ."**

War is the greatest obstacle to the easy way. But in the end we will have to love it, as the religious should love his disciplines. (*The Way*, 311.)

His optimism was always tempered with a degree of sober objectivity. When many thought that the war would not last long and that the end was imminent, he pointed out to those around him that it might not be so and that they should foresee a much longer wait than people imagined. Afterwards, some saw in this type of statement, which did not correspond to the generally known facts, an inspiration that in some ways could not be explained by natural causes. Jiménez Vargas comments: "Without doubting that the high success rate of his surmises during his life indicated a genuine divine inspiration, in this specific case (as on other occasions as, for example, when we crossed the Pyrenees) I think that what one would have to emphasize above all is the fact of genuine personal virtue. He had such prudence in the face of events that, in the midst of his very heavy worries, he was able to have his feet more firmly on the ground than anyone and to be more objective when the time came for action."

The people of the Work were convinced that nothing would happen to the Founder, because he had to carry out Opus Dei. Nevertheless, they did everything possible to ensure his safety.

He stayed at his mother's flat until someone gave a warning that there were suspicions that people were hiding in different flats in the building. He left, and indeed shortly afterwards the house was searched. This happened on or about 9 August 1936.

They were days and months of tremendous confusion. There were abundant outrages and abuses. Many crimes were committed. Among the victims there was a high percentage of priests and religious. In his careful and well documented *Historia de la persecución religiosa en España*, Antonio Montero, now Auxiliary Bishop of Seville, gives the following frightening figures. During the entire war 4,184 secular priests (13% of the total), 2,365 religious (23%) and 283 nuns met their death.

It is easy to understand, therefore, that when in the early days of the war some people received the false news of the death of the Founder of Opus Dei, they accepted it; more so because, as happened in some of the cases, the information came with all kinds of detail.

Until the end of August 1936 he was in the house of a friend in 29 Sagasta Street. He spent September in a flat in Serrano Street. It belonged to some Argentine friends of Don Alvaro del Portillo. On 1 October he had to abandon this hiding place and he spent several days on the run, sleeping where and as he could. Shortly afterwards, he succeeded in finding a new hiding place, by passing himself off as mentally sick. The psychiatric sanatorium of Ciudad Lineal, at 492 Arturo Soria Street, was run by Dr. Suils, an acquaintance of Don Josemaría from his Logroño days. His stay in the lunatic asylum, which was under the official control of the UGT trade union, was especially harsh. Among other things his rheumatism got worse there. He spent nearly two weeks without being able to move. It got so bad that he needed someone to feed him.

At that time the Madrid front had stabilised. It now looked very much as if the war was going to last a long while. It became urgent to find a more normal and safe place of refuge. After various attempts to get him into an embassy, there arose the possibility of the Honduras Legation. (Strictly speaking it was only the house of the Consul, but it was officially recognised and protected.) He arrived there in March 1937.

He had suffered so much and had been eating so little that he was incredibly thin to the point of being unrecognisable. While he was at this "Legation", between March and August 1937, one day his mother visited him. She was waiting for him in the hall, near the door of the flat. When he appeared, emaciated and pale and dressed in lay clothes,

Doña Dolores did not recognise him until she heard his voice: **How wonderful to see you, Mummy!**

At the Legation the panorama of Don Josemaría's life changed. At last he was able to celebrate Holy Mass, and besides, he had the company of several members of the Work. A few months later he began to go out into the street, thanks to a document from the Consul of Honduras accrediting him as an employee of the Legation. Then, on 1 September, he went to live in an attic at 73 Ayala Street and he carried on an intense apostolic activity in Madrid. He gave spiritual direction; he said Holy Mass and took Holy Communion to people; he gave meditations.

It was in these circumstances that Thomas Alvira met him, as he related in an article in September 1975: "I remember in detail the first time I spoke with Msgr. Escrivá de Balaguer. It was early one evening in July 1937, in Madrid." He was impressed by "the strong personality of that young priest; by the supernatural outlook which permeated everything he said; by his optimism and joy, which were not easy to have at such a difficult time and were only comprehensible when one saw they were based on a deep faith".

Thomas Alvira was very surprised to be invited one day to attend a retreat with a few other people. His surprise was justified, because at that time priests were persecuted in Madrid, and no churches were open. That is why that retreat, which lasted three days, took place in different houses. Each person arrived separately. They would have a meditation and then they left, one by one again, so as not to be together for very long. They carried on meditating in the streets and saying the Rosary, etc. Then they would have the next meditation in another house. One of these houses belonged to José María Albareda and was in Menéndez Pelayo Street. Another was Thomas Alvira's. It was at 28 General Pardiñas Street, on the first floor.

Towards the end of the summer of 1937 the number of assassinations in Madrid diminished somewhat, but it was still impossible for a priest to live there openly. Even though in those circumstances the presence of the Founder in the city was very necessary, it became clear that he should leave Madrid and cross over to the other zone of Spain. It was a very difficult decision to take. He found it very hard to leave the city and abandon his mother and his sister, Carmen and Santiago, his brother, and the majority of the members of Opus Dei in Madrid. Nevertheless he overcame his doubts and, helped by the insistence of everyone, his mother included, he decided to leave. Once the problem of documents had been solved, he left for Valencia. It was October.

In Valencia he found Francisco Botella and Pedro Casciaro. They had been told that he might arrive at any moment. Pedro Casciaro used to go each evening to the Botellas' house. One day he entered a small room there and he saw Juan Jiménez Vargas with another person, a "very thin gentleman in a grey suit. Hardly had he seen me when he greeted me saying: **Pedro, how wonderful to see you again!**" The Founder's looks had altered so much in the previous fifteen months that Pedro Casciaro only recognised him by his voice: just as happened with his own mother, Doña Dolores, as we have already seen. Pedro Casciaro writes: "He had lost more than ninety pounds. Until then I had always seen him in a cassock, with very short hair and a large tonsure which he used to cover with a black skull-cap, and with round thin-rimmed glasses. Now his cheeks were sunken and his broad forehead was more prominent. His eyes were more penetrating; his hair relatively long and combed with a parting on one side; his glasses were oval-shaped and had a heavier rim. I noticed especially a detail in itself insignificant but, who knows why, it was very significant for me: the knot in his tie was very neatly made. The only thing which hadn't changed at all was the tone of his voice."

From Valencia he proceeded to Barcelona by overnight train. A tense period of waiting began in Barcelona because it turned out to be more difficult than had appeared in Madrid to connect up with the people who smuggled refugees out of Spain. Once again he was beset with doubts as to the wisdom of what he was doing, but he ended up convinced it was God's Will.

They left Barcelona at last on 19 November in a bus headed for Seo de Urgel. After difficult days they succeeded in crossing the border into Andorra on 2 December 1937 and proceeded to Sant Juliá. It was the end of a nightmare which had begun in October 1937. The Founder of Opus Dei had suffered a great deal. On top of the constant worry for those who remained behind in Madrid or were at the battlefronts, he was in such a state of physical exhaustion that he was on the verge of collapse from the very first night of the trek. Nevertheless, all who were with him agree that it was he who constantly kept their spirits high, spreading peace and joy about him. Juan Jiménez Vargas asserts that it was not till then that he really came to understand what was meant by **the happiness of knowing that one is a son of God.** Shortly afterwards Juan made a brief note summarising their experi-

ences during those three months. It was to give rise to point 659 of
The Way:

**The cheerfulness you should have is not the kind we might
call physiological good spirits — the happiness of a healthy
animal. You must seek something more: the supernatural
happiness that comes from the abandonment of everything and
the abandonment of yourself into the loving arms of our Father
God.**

With such cheerfulness, the Founder of Opus Dei set out once
more. He passed through Lourdes before going back to Spain. He
crossed the frontier at Irún. In Pamplona his good friend Don Marcelino Olaechea found him a room in the bishop's house. Shortly afterwards he went to Burgos where the Bishop of Madrid was living.
From Burgos it would be easier for him to re-establish contact with a
number of people he had known before the war and who were now
dispersed all over the country.

His difficulties, however, did not end there. Most of those who had
accompanied him across the Pyrenees were conscripted into the army.
Fortunately many others came to Burgos whenever they got leave from
their units. From Burgos Don Josemaría carried out a very extensive
letter apostolate. He also travelled as often as he was needed, whether
it was to attend to someone in difficulties, or preach a retreat, or visit
a bishop, or to solve some problem which had arisen. Thomas Alvira,
who crossed the Pyrenees with him, still has a letter Don Josemaría
wrote to him from Burgos dated 4 February 1938:

May Jesus keep you well.

**Dear Thomas, How I would like to be with you. In the
meantime, please help us with your prayers and your work.**

**I am trotting all over the place: I am just back from
Vitoria and Bilbao. Before that I was in Palencia, Valladolid,
Salamanca and Avila. I am just recovering from a cold I
caught in the North. Next I will be off to León and Astorga.**

**Tommy, when can you get away so that we can have a
chat?**

Many would write to Burgos asking where the Father would be on
such and such a date when they were due for leave. He was not always
able to give them a precise answer. Sometimes he had to say: "in a
railway carriage, or in some charabanc travelling down these roads,
or . . . at the front."

In Burgos, people were the first concern of the Founder of Opus

Dei. He wanted to renew contact with those who had attended apostolic activities before the war, and help them keep their interior life and apostolic zeal alive. He also wanted to make new friends. His desire to reach as many as possible by correspondence led to the appearance of a kind of collective letter: through it everyone could be told how the others were getting on. It was not a new idea, since as far back as the summer of 1934, Don Josemaría had arranged to have these family letters written. They were full of supernatural outlook and also good humour. Some of these typewritten hectographed sheets survive today. Letters received in the DYA Academy during the summer were summarised, so that the others could know their authors' whereabouts and summer activities: their sporting and cultural activities, their studies, the languages they were learning, their efforts to help out doctors in rural areas, their apostolic ventures, etc. At the same time the letters were a way of encouraging all to persevere in their life of piety and to keep alive their desire to transmit their christian ideals to others, so that in the coming academic year they could go "ahead with **God and daring!**"

We find the same tone in the *Noticias* from Burgos, though now interspersed with anecdotes relating to the war. Grateful acknowledgement is made of letters arriving from the battlefronts or from the ships of the Navy, letters with "the same zeal, common concerns and an identical supernatural and cheerful optimism". They also gave news of those who had passed through Burgos to spend a while with the Founder of the Work.

There were lots of picturesque details and amusing jokes in the letters. There was a constant insistence on the need to keep studying (languages especially) despite the inherent difficulties of the situation: "a willing heart gets more done than perfect conditions." From Burgos requests went out for grammars, dictionaries and texts to be translated. There are references to a library that was being built up and to books arriving, some even from abroad. With this in mind, they had written to academic centres in several countries. In a letter dated 1938 we read: "Do you know that we are asking for books — in several languages — because we want to read them? It may seem obvious, but it's not always the case when people ask for books."

The newsletter, brief and rudimentary though it was, came out monthly, at times with a "forgive the brevity of these pages, but paper is so scarce". Sometimes there was also news that someone had died on the battlefield: "Another friend in heaven!" There was news too of those who were still in the other part of Spain: "the faith and endurance with which they keep working is an example to us all."

The letter was well seasoned with supernatural references which came in very naturally. In one issue we find a phrase which sums up very well the spirit of those times: "Books, languages, study: instruments for your work. But do not forget that the supernatural character of our undertaking requires PRAYER, SACRIFICE AND FREQUENT RECEPTION OF THE SACRAMENTS."

Such was the Founder's apostolic zeal that he asked everyone to help him locate all who were still missing. He wanted to find out what their definite (or most likely) home addresses would be when the war was over. He was constantly encouraging each one to do apostolate: **among all those generous young men you know, don't you think there might be at least one who could understand us?**

For those working by Don Josemaría's side, horizons opened wide, for he was not thinking only of Spain. One of the writers in the newsletter points out: "To plan for the Spain of tomorrow is little. As one writes these family letters, one begins to feel the world is small."

Nevertheless, he did not lose sight of the immediate goal, which was to get back to Madrid. The Founder of Opus Dei was making all the preparations he could, in material things as well. Together with the books, he was collecting all the necessary things to set up a new oratory: a Tabernacle, candlesticks. . . . He ordered albs and vestments from the family of Vicente Rodríguez Casado who lived in Burgos. Others were asked to design and make a chalice. This desire also found its way into a newsletter: "The sacred vessels, vestments and other liturgical items are being made for our oratory, with that anonymous spirit which characterized artists' workshops in ancient times. You can be sure that God (and you as well) will be pleased with them because of the spirit with which they are being made, because of the genuineness of the material that is being used, and because of the care being taken that they all match together perfectly." Many of these liturgical items were stored in the bishop's house in Avila. The bishop had offered to look after them until the moment came for the return to Madrid.

Don Josemaría stayed at the Hotel Sabadell, at 32 Merced Street. In late 1938 or early 1939 he was to move to an even more modest house at 9 Concepción Street, third floor on the left. He kept on making trips whenever necessary, sometimes simply to visit a wounded man.

That was the way he got the opportunity to visit the Madrid front. On 7 June 1938 Ricardo Fernández Vallespín was working in a bomb disposal unit when a faulty hand grenade exploded close by him and injured him. He managed to send a telegram to the Father from the field hospital. Don Josemaría went to see him as soon as he could and spent the night at the artillery command post on the heights of Carabanchel. An officer took him to the observation post in what had once been the Carabanchel Automobile School. From there he observed through the telescope the remains of 16 Ferraz Street. As he gazed at the ruins, he began to laugh. The officer asked him why he was laughing. His faith in God's providence undaunted, he replied: **because I have just seen what little remains of my home.** God will put it all right, he thought, although he said nothing. Naturally, the officer was disconcerted and did not understand a thing.

The tragic parenthesis of the war, which had opened for Opus Dei with these ruins, was soon to close. The months spent in Burgos were now behind like a foundation-laying period in which contact with many was renewed and and the future prepared. It was a period of hope, prayer and intense mortification on the part of the Founder of Opus Dei.

So keen was he to return that he reached Madrid at the same time as the first relief column. Ricardo Fernández Vallespín, who was with him when he made his first visit to the remains of Ferraz, comments: "When we got home, we found the house destroyed. It was worse than we had thought." The building had been damaged during the assault on the Montaña Barracks. Later it had been requisitioned by the militia. Finally, as the Madrid front approached the city, it was destroyed by shellfire.

For a while he went back to where he had been living before the war, in the lodgings of the rector of the Royal Patronato of Santa Isabel. From there he carried on his apostolic work and once again began to look for a suitable place to set up a students' residence. He wanted to open it before October 1939. He did so by renting some flats in Jenner Street near the Castellana. All told, they were approximately the same size as the original residence at 50 Ferraz Street.

Once again, the Founder of Opus Dei began without material means, trusting in the clear conviction that God was determined to see His Work done. Angel Galíndez who was a resident both in Ferraz and later in Jenner, was to admit in 1975 in an article in *El Correo Español* of Bilbao: "during what is now nearly forty years I have often reflected on the Father's personality which is so rich and unfathomable, and so daring and apostolic. . . . Indeed, I have often thought of his immense faith and irrepressible courage and apostolic zeal, which made it possible for that small residence to be transformed into the gigantic Work we now see."

His unshakable hope made everything possible. Manuel Aznar stressed this point in the Barcelona *La Vanguardia Española*: "I can't think what charismatic gift he must have had, but he boosted hope, broadened horizons, overcame pessimism and communicated his conviction that the future was bright. He calmed fretful minds, shone light where there was doubt, saw himself above all else as a priest of God, and as such felt able to preach and demand a living perseverance in the faith, a burning charity, and also a luminous hope. I imagine he must have meditated a lot on Saint Paul, for he was without doubt a man who instilled hope."

The Founder himself was to write in 1940:

The Work is developing thanks to prayer: thanks to my prayer — and to my miseries — which in God's eyes is the force that brings about what is required to fulfil his Will; and to the prayer of so many souls — priests and laymen, young and old, healthy and sick — to whom I have had recourse in the full assurance that Our Lord will listen to them, asking them to pray for a specific intention which, at first, was known to me alone. And together with prayer, there is the mortification and work of those who live at my side: these have been our only yet powerful weapons for this struggle.

This is the way — now and in the future — to make the Work take shape and grow, in all environments: in the hospitals and in the university; through catechizing the most needy quarters; in the homes and meeting-places of ordinary men and women; among the poor, the rich and people of every sort, so as to make the message which God has entrusted to us reach every single person.

This is its mission and the Work has plunged wholeheartedly into fulfilling it, generously and honestly, without human subterfuges or patronage, without — to give an example for what it is worth — having recourse to a constant chasing after the sunniest climes, or the richest and prettiest flower: the sun is within us and the work is done — as it must be done — out in the open street and it is open to everyone.

In these early years I am filled with deep gratitude towards God. And at the same time, my sons, I think of how far we still

have to go till we have sown this catholic and universal seed which Opus Dei has come to scatter over all nations, to the whole world and in all spheres of human activity.

That is why I carry on relying on prayer, mortification, professional work and the happiness of you all, whilst I constantly renew my confidence in God: universi, qui sustinent te, non confundentur (Ps 24: 3), **none of those who place their trust in God will be disappointed.**

2. THE LEGAL ITINERARY OF OPUS DEI

You are right. "The peak," you told me, "dominates the country for miles around, and yet there is not a single plain to be seen: just one mountain after another. At times the landscape seems to level out, but then the mist rises and reveals another range that had been hidden."

So it is, so it must be with the horizon of your apostolate: the world has to be crossed. But there are no ways made for you. You yourselves will make them through the mountains with the impact of your feet (*The Way*, 928).

It is likely that when the author of *The Way* wrote these words he was envisaging the vast apostolic panorama which with the passing years was to unfold the world over before the members of the Work. There would be no lack of difficulties. The Spanish war had ended. Now the time was coming to open a path for Opus Dei in the field of canon law.

The Work was unlike any of the other organisations that existed in the Church. Its members neither wished to be nor could be religious, who seek holiness by separating themselves from the world, by retreating to the desert or by serving souls actively in schools, hospitals and the like. The fully apostolic vocation which God wanted for Opus Dei also distinguishes it from the simple confraternities or pious unions which are recognised by the Code of Canon Law.

The one model there was, though quite precise in its theological outline, had never yet been defined in legal terms: it was that of the *early Christians*. As the Founder was to declare to Peter Forbath, a correspondent of *Time*: **the easiest way to understand Opus Dei is to consider the life of the early Christians. They lived**

their christian vocation seriously, seeking earnestly the holiness to which they had been called by their Baptism. Externally they did nothing to distinguish themselves from their fellow citizens. The members of Opus Dei are ordinary people. They work like everyone else and live in the midst of the world just as they did before they joined. There is nothing false or artificial about their behaviour. They live like any other christian citizen who wants to respond fully to the demands of his faith, because that is what they are.

There was no outlet in canon law for an association which proposed the way of living of the early Christians. Besides, the Founder, with his keen legal mind, realised that laws follow upon life and not the other way round. The ways would be opened by the impact of their footsteps. The ascetical and apostolic phenomenon had to precede the legal framework.

Nevertheless Don Josemaría, who sought to be a faithful son of the Church and knew that no work is fruitful if it cuts itself off from the ecclesiastical Hierarchy, did everything — as he said on countless occasions — **with the approval and the affectionate blessing of his Lordship the Bishop of Madrid whom I loved so well and in whose city Opus Dei was born on 2 October 1928. And later on, always with the agreement and encouragement of the Holy See, and, in each case, with that of the Bishops of the places where we work.**

This is also confirmed by the Salesian Fr. Vicente Ballester Domingo, who was private secretary to Don Marcelino Olaechea, the Bishop of Pamplona, who offered Don Josemaría hospitality in his episcopal palace in 1937. Many bishops passed through there and Don Josemaría spoke to them about Opus Dei. Fr. Ballester testifies that "he always sought the goodwill of the Hierarchy even though at that time it was not easy to understand what Opus Dei was".

The sense of urgency that permeated his efforts to save souls vanished when it came to the problem of finding a proper legal outlet for the Work. Here there was no hurry. He trusted in God's will. At the same time he was very succinct when speaking about Opus Dei, precisely because it did not yet have any legal status within the Church. Fr. Sancho, O.P., remembers an explanation Don Josemaría gave for this enforced reserve: the Work was still being formed in the womb, like a child as yet "unborn". Later, when the Holy See gave its *decretum laudis*, the Founder of Opus Dei told Fr. Sancho that thanks be

to God they could henceforth speak about Opus Dei without reserva-
tion, because it was now something public and the Church had given
it motherly praise. Fr. Sancho commented: "I saw there a clear
expression of Josemaría's deep love for the Church, in submitting to the
decisions of its supreme authority."

However in the years immediately after the war this conscientious
behaviour of his gave rise to suspicion and slander. "Some said he was
a saint and others a heretic," recalls Dr. Eladio de la Concha, now a
paediatric surgeon in Gijón. "It was a matter of trusting him, though
whoever knew him could not but trust him." The Founder of Opus
Dei placed absolute trust in the Providence of God, his Father; a trust
which was echoed in the members of the Work and their friends, who
placed all their confidence in a priest who was seeking, above all else,
to fulfil God's Will. The members of Opus Dei and the ever-increasing
numbers of people who took part in its apostolates, were certain that
the Work was "God's work". They knew the bishops were encouraging
Don Josemaría, and they were confident that the legal problems would
be solved one day.

When some people stepped up their attacks against Opus Dei and
its Founder, the Bishop of Madrid took things into his own hands and
gave the Work an approval in writing, with the aim of mitigating
the campaign of slander. Such a measure could not be considered
definitive for it did nothing to solve the legal problems posed by the
Association; but it might help to dampen the campaign. So on 19 March
1941 Don Leopoldo Eijo y Garay approved Opus Dei as a Pious Union.
Its Founder received the news at 14 Diego de León. He recalled the
event in the very same place some thirty years later: he had gone to
the oratory with his mother and a few members of the Work who
**were at home, because there was no one else: they were all
working, for our job is to work. I went to my mother and told
her: "Look, the Bishop has just rung and he tells me, against
my will, because I did not want any approval, that the decree
has been drawn up. Let's give thanks." We knelt down on the
altar step and gave thanks to God.**

He went on waiting. The slander did not die down. The way the
apostolate was going — it was now spreading to new cities, Valencia,
Barcelona, Saragossa, Valladolid, Seville — made it necessary to find
a juridical solution which was more satisfactory than that of a simple
Pious Union. Besides, a group of members of Opus Dei had begun their
studies with a view to being ordained to the priesthood: it was in-

dispensable too to solve the points of law which their ordination would pose.

Years later, on a feast of the Motherhood of Our Lady, the Founder was to say to a group of members: **My sons, I have on occasions considered and asked you to consider the fact that each step in the legal itinerary of the Work has been taken under the protection of the Mother of God. In celebrating her Divine Motherhood today I recall — and cannot but recall — that the first time the Holy See blessed the Work was on this feast day, so many years ago.**

He referred also to something Don Alvaro del Portillo, who was at his side, had once said to him: **"Father, you will be glad, for tomorrow is Our Lady of Pilar." And I replied: "One feast or another, all the feasts of the Blessed Virgin move me; I think they are splendid. But if we must choose, I prefer today's, the Motherhood." I didn't know at that time that the Mother of God had interceded on behalf of this Work of God and that the first approval had been granted.**

Many reasons combined to make it necessary to have Papal approval. In February 1946 Don Alvaro del Portillo was sent to Rome to place before the Vatican the relevant documents on the Work, which had been prepared by the Founder. Not long afterwards Don Alvaro wrote to him saying that he would have to come to Rome himself to try to make some headway because, humanly speaking, progress seemed impossible.

Just then, the Father's diabetes, which he had had for some years, had got worse. He was having several injections daily. The Roman summer was unlikely to do his illness any good. His doctor not only advised against the journey but declared that were it to take place he refused to share any responsibility for the outcome — but the Founder of Opus Dei did not hesitate. He saw clearly that Our Lord wanted him to go to Rome, regardless of the sacrifice involved. He brought together those who then made up the General Council of the Association and told them what he had decided. The members of the Council, having considered the matter in God's presence, agreed unanimously to the Founder's plans.

Calling to mind this decisive moment in his own life story and in the history of Opus Dei, he wrote in 1961:

To the world and to the Church, the Work seemed a novelty. And the juridical solution I was looking for, an im-

possibility. But (. . .) I couldn't wait for things to become pos-
**sible. A distinguished member of the Roman Curia told us:
"You have come a century too soon." Nevertheless we had to
try the impossible. I was being urged by the thousands of
souls who were committing themselves to God in his Work,
with that fullness of dedication which we have, to carry out
the apostolate in the midst of the world.**

He was accompanied on that trip to Rome by Don José Orlandis
who spoke Italian. Orlandis explains: "To go from Madrid to Rome
in the immediate post-war period was almost an adventure, and in
any event, a long and tiring journey, by land and sea, which took
almost five days. There were no air services as yet and since the
Pyrenees frontier with France was closed for political reasons, the only
link between Spain and Italy was by a mail boat which sailed each
week from Barcelona to Genoa."

They left Madrid by car on Wednesday, 19 June 1946, in the early
afternoon. They stopped in Saragossa and Barcelona. Msgr. Escrivá
de Balaguer was praying especially to the Virgin Mary for her protection in the momentous matter that was taking him to Rome. On
Thursday 20th, in the morning, he went to the Basilica of Our Lady
of Pilar and, following his custom, he went up with the ordinary pilgrims, unrecognised, to kiss the Pillar of the Virgin. Later, when they
approached Igualada, he visited Montserrat to pray before the Black
Madonna, the Patron of Catalonia. The next day he placed himself in
a special way in the hands of the Mother of God who, under the title
of Our Lady of Ransom, is the Patron of the city of Barcelona, from
which port he was to embark for Italy. He went in the morning to the
Basilica of La Merced and prayed to Our Lady with great confidence,
asking for her help and her mercy in this most important stage in the
journey towards Opus Dei's approval by the highest authority in the
Church.

Years later, in 1961, Msgr. Escrivá de Balaguer related that he
had made that trip to Rome, **with my heart set on my Mother, the
most Holy Virgin, and with a burning faith in God Our Lord,
whom I invoked full of trust, saying to him:** Ecce nos reliquimus
omnia, et secuti sumus te: quid ergo erit nobis? (Matt 19:27). **"What
will become of us, my Father?" We had abandoned everything: honour — with so much slander upon us — our
whole life, each one of us in his own place doing what Our Lord
was asking of us. God listened, and in those years in Rome,**

he wrote another marvellous chapter in the history of the Work.

On that morning of 21 June 1946 he had celebrated Holy Mass in the oratory of the Centre of Opus Dei in Barcelona where he had spent the night: a flat at 444 Muntaner Street. Before Mass, he directed the meditation of the members of the Work present there. His words were full of faith and those who heard him have never forgotten what was said on that occasion. He took for his meditation, as he spoke aloud, that passage in St. Matthew's Gospel where Peter says to Jesus that they have abandoned all things to follow him. Enkindled by these words of Scripture a deep sense of faith arose in his heart and impelled him to speak to Our Lord directly and say, full of filial daring:

Lord! Can you have allowed me in good faith to deceive so many souls? When all I have done has been for your glory and knowing that it is your Will! Is it possible that the Holy See can say that we have come a century too soon ...? Ecce nos reliquimus omnia, et secuti sumus te (Matt 19:27).

He concluded the meditation with an act of confident and total self-surrender to the loving Providence of God, for whom all things are possible, even those which men call impossible.

That same afternoon he embarked on the vessel which was to take him to Italy, the J.J. Sister, a little steamer of the *Compañia Transmediterránea*, some 1,500 tons in weight and fifty years of age. A furious storm, which was unusual for the Mediterranean and even more so in the month of June, buffeted the boat for nearly twenty seemingly endless hours. The Founder of Opus Dei, ill as he already was, suffered much in this his first sea voyage.

It was nearly midnight on Saturday 22nd when the J.J. Sister reached the port of Genoa, several hours late due to the gale. Don Alvaro del Portillo and Don Salvador Canals were waiting for them. On the following day, Sunday 23rd, after he had celebrated his first Mass on Italian soil, he went by car from Genoa to Rome.

The Founder wrote in 1961: **What did I want? A place for the Work within the law of the Church, in accordance with the nature of our vocation and the demands imposed by the expansion of our apostolates; a full approval from the Magisterium for our supernatural way, including a clear and explicit description of our spiritual character. The growth of the Work, the multitude of vocations of people of every class and walk of life, all this which was a blessing from God urged me to try to**

obtain — from the Holy See — full juridical approval for the way which Our Lord had opened up.

Earlier, in the same document, he had referred to the motive for his first trip to Rome:

We were not intended to be a group that turns in on itself, to seek personal sanctity and then to sanctify others from the collective shelter of an institution. Our Lord wanted us where we were — nel bel mezzo della strada, **as I like to say in Italian — in the situation, condition and job which each one of us has in the world.**

And it was there **that he gave us the mission of sanctifying others, of drawing them to Christ, through the witness, doctrine, friendship and example of a clean life. This apostolic mission urged us to seek sanctity:** out there, **where we were, each in his own profession and job. This job, when raised by grace to the supernatural order and carried out with human perfection, became a specific way of sanctification. My sons, I could not accept the religious state for us, because it differs in its asceticism, its means and its specific aims, from the asceticism, means and aims which God, in his providence, wanted for his Work.**

The Founder of Opus Dei cast the burden of his cares upon the Lord and He sustained him (cf. Ps 54: 23). Relying with full assurance on the fact of his divine calling, and guided by God's hand, he was able to open the way. Our Lord listens to those who have confident recourse to him, with no weapons other than abandonment into his powerful arms, and no support other than confidence in his Most Holy Mother. Msgr. Escrivá de Balaguer recognised this when he wrote in 1950:

Despite my many weaknesses — perhaps, precisely because of them, so that it should be seen that the Work was his — Our Lord has deigned to give this poor sinner the inspiration of Opus Dei and in fact, from 1917 to 1928 and ever since, I have had the impression that he has treated me as we read in Scripture, et delectabar per singulos dies ludens coram eo, omni tempore ludens in orbe terrarum: et deliciae meae esse cum filiis hominum (Prov 8: 30 and 31): **God's Wisdom played as with a child, before the Lord each day, all over the world's orb; because God delights to be with the children of men.**

His infinite Wisdom has been guiding me, as if playing with me, from the obscurity of the first intimations, to the

clarity with which I now see every detail of the Work and can truly say: Deus docuisti me a iuventute mea; et usque nunc pronuntiabo mirabilia tua (Ps 70: 17), **the Lord has been instructing me from the beginning of the Work and I cannot but sing his marvels.**

Our Lord, with his unfathomable wisdom, guided the footsteps of the Founder of Opus Dei. He filled him with faith and confidence to attempt the impossible, so as to show once again that *ecce non est abbreviata manus Domini:* **God's arm, his power, has not grown weaker!** (*The Way*, 586).

Msgr. Escrivá de Balaguer returned to Madrid on 31 August 1946 with an "approval of aims", a document which the Holy See had not issued for over a century. He spent the summer in Madrid and Molinoviejo (Segovia). On 21 October he was back in Barcelona to thank Our Lady of Ransom. He was once again on his way to Rome. Not long after, on 24 February 1947, the Work was to receive the *Decretum laudis* from the Holy See, and on 16 June 1950, the definitive approval.

When Enrico Zuppi and Antonio Fugardi, Editor and Deputy Editor respectively of *L'Osservatore della Domenica*, asked Msgr. Excrivá de Balaguer in 1968 if he was satisfied with the past forty years of activity of Opus Dei, and whether the recent social changes or the advent of the Second Vatican Council would warrant any changes in the structure of Opus Dei, the Founder replied:

Satisfied? I cannot but be satisfied, when I see that, despite my own wretchedness, Our Lord has built up so many wonderful things around this Work of God. The life of a man who lives by faith will always be the story of the mercies of God. At some moments the story may perhaps be difficult to read, because everything can seem useless and even a failure. But at other times Our Lord lets one see how the fruit abounds and then it is natural for one's soul to break out in thanksgiving.

Indeed, one of my greatest joys was to see the Second Vatican Council so clearly proclaim the divine vocation of the laity. Without any boasting, I would say that as far as our spirit is concerned the Council has not meant an invitation to change but, on the contrary, has confirmed what, with the grace of God, we have been living and teaching for so many years. The principal characteristic of Opus Dei is not a set of techniques or methods of apostolate, nor any specific structure, but a spirit which moves one to sanctify one's ordinary work.

As I have repeated on so many occasions, we all have personal shortcomings and miseries. And all of us should seriously examine ourselves in God's presence and check to see how our life measures up to Our Lord's demands. But we should not forget the most important thing: Si scires donum Dei! . . . "If only you knew the gift of God!" (John 4: 10) as Jesus said to the Samaritan woman. And St Pauls adds: "We carry this treasure in earthenware jars, to show that the abundance of the power is God's and not ours" (2 Cor 4: 7).

Humility, christian self-examination, begins with recognising God's gift. It is something quite distinct from shrugging one's shoulders at the way things are going. And it has nothing to do with a sense of futility or discouragement in the face of history. In one's personal life, and sometimes also in the life of associations or institutions, there may be things which have to change, perhaps a lot of things. But the attitude with which a Christian should face these problems should be above all one of amazement at the greatness of the works of God, compared with the littleness of man.

3. "PETER'S BOAT CANNOT SINK"

Shortly before celebrating his Golden Jubilee as a priest, on 28 March 1975, Msgr. Escrivá de Balaguer spoke to a group of members of Opus Dei in the following terms:

When I became a priest, the Church of God looked as firm as a rock, without a single crack in it. Its external appearance was a clear expression of its unity: a block of marvellous strength. Now, if we look at it with merely human eyes, it looks like a building in ruins, a crumbling heap of sand, which people kick, toss about, destroy. . . . The Pope has said on occasions that it is destroying itself. Hard, terrible words! But this cannot happen because Jesus has promised that the Holy Spirit will assist it always, to the end of time.

What are we to do? We are to pray. We must pray. I am sure that my daughters and my sons, many thousands of people all over the world, will pray especially for the intentions of my Mass when I celebrate my priestly Golden Jubilee. They will be the same intentions as always: the Church, the Pope, the Work. I always use those three brush strokes, even though from day to day there may be alterations of colour, varying intensity, shades blending from one colour to the next. But the common denominator of my petitions to Our Lord is always the same: the Church, the Pope and Opus Dei.

Msgr. Escrivá de Balaguer always had hope in the Church, **in spite of everything.** Once he confided to a Cardinal that often as he was reciting the Creed when he came to affirm his faith in the divinity of the Church, *One, Holy, Catholic and Apostolic,* he would add: **in spite of everything.** When the Cardinal asked him what he meant by that, he answered: **in spite of your sins and mine.**

He was firmly convinced that it is the Holy Spirit who governs the Church. Hence his contagious optimism when the Boat of Peter was seen to be buffeted by apparently insuperable difficulties.

He was always utterly faithful to the Magisterium, to all the Magisterium of the Church, and to the constant and unified character of its teachings. That is why he was not happy with the arbitrary, and at times misplaced, usage of the term "postconciliar", which meant forgetting — he commented more than once — that **we have been in a postconciliar era since some thirty years after the death of Our Lord Jesus Christ: since the Council of Jerusalem where with that awesome authority, with that human and divine daring, the Apostles said:** Visum est Spiritui Sancto et nobis, **"it appears to the Holy Spirit and to us. . . ."**

He followed the progress of the Second Vatican Council very closely, first and above all with his prayer for the fruits of the Council. Long before the opening session, he asked all the members of Opus Dei to entrust the work of the Council to the Holy Spirit's protection. He said that each should offer up to God what he wished but he insisted that they should pray a lot and daily.

Everyone soon came to know the affection and love for the Church with which he followed from the very beginning the work of the bishops, the Curia and the council experts. Among his main concerns one soon showed itself to be the most important: his great love for the Roman Pontiff.

When the Editor of *Palabra* magazine addressed a series of questions to him in 1967, he thought fit to ask first what significance Msgr. Escrivá de Balaguer gave to the word *aggiornamento*, which at the time was very much in vogue when referring to the Church. Msgr. Escrivá

de Balaguer's reply sums up his whole basic attitude and his hope
regarding the Church's mission:

Faithfulness. Aggiornamento, **as I see it, means above all**
faithfulness. **A husband, a soldier, an administrator, who faithfully fulfils at each moment, in each new circumstance of his
life, the duties of love and justice which he once took on, will
always be just that much better a husband, soldier or administrator. It is difficult to keep this keen sense of loyalty
constantly active, as it is always difficult to apply a principle
to the changing realities of the contingent world. But it is the
best defence against ageing of the spirit, hardening of the heart
and stiffening of the mind.**

**The same applies to the lives of institutions, and in a very
special way to the life of the Church which does not follow a
precarious human plan but a God-given design. The world's
redemption and salvation are the fruit of Jesus Christ's loving
filial faithfulness to the will of the heavenly Father who sent
him, and of our faithfulness to him. Therefore** aggiornamento
**in the Church, today, as in any other period, is fundamentally
a joyful reaffirmation of the People of God's faithfulness to the
mission received, to the Gospel.**

**This faithfulness should be alive and active in every cir-
cumstance of men's lives. It therefore requires opportune
doctrinal developments in the exposition of the riches of the**
depositum fidei, **as can clearly be seen in the two thousand years
of the Church's history and recently in the Second Vatican
Council. It may also require suitable changes and reforms to
improve, in their human and perfectible element, the organi-
sational structures and the missionary and apostolic methods
of the Church. But it would be, to say the least, superficial to
think that** aggiornamento **consists primarily in** change, **or that
all change produces** aggiornamento. **One need only consider that
there are people who seek changes which go outside and against
the Council's doctrine and would put the progressive movement of the People of God back several centuries in history,
back at least to feudal times.**

Hope and prudence were two virtues which Msgr. Escrivá de
Balaguer practised especially intensely from the sixties onwards, as a
way of expressing his loyalty to the Church. At the end of the interview just mentioned, he emphasised christian optimism, **the joyful**

**certainty that the Holy Spirit will draw fruit from the doctrine
with which he has enriched the spouse of Christ;** for this doctrinal wealth of the Council had set the entire Church — the entire
priestly People of God — **on a new supremely hopeful track of
renewed fidelity to the divine plan of salvation which has been
entrusted to it.**

Nevertheless this hope-filled optimism was inseparable from sound
judgment, since the times were still problematic. Many theological
conclusions had **immediate and direct applications in the pastoral,
ascetic and disciplinary fields, which touch very deeply the
internal and external life of the Church: liturgy, organisa-
tional structures of the Hierarchy, apostolic forms, Magisterium, dialogue with the world, ecumenism. Therefore at the
same time this theology touches very deeply the christian life
and the very conscience of the faithful.**

Hence he stressed the need for **prudence on the part of those
who study and govern because, now especially, immense harm
could result from a lack of cool-headedness and consideration
in the study of these problems.**

This is not the proper place to go into the difficult and painful
situation in which the Church has found itself in recent times. Here it
is more our concern to point out that Msgr. Escrivá de Balaguer never
lost his cheerfulness, his serenity, his faith and hope that God would
put everything right. Nor did he lose his prudence when as "good
shepherd" of the widespread family of Opus Dei he had to make
decisions for the spiritual welfare of its members. He was aware of the
complexity of the problem, which often made it **a difficult task to
discern what is positive and good, what are real contributions
towards the development of theological science and genuine
desires for a christian life and apostolic zeal, from what
constitutes a grave attack upon faith and morals.**

With genuine and wise pastoral vigilance, which at times he had
to exercise in a heroic manner, he fostered in these years the formation
of the men and women of Opus Dei, **in the common doctrine of
the Church** — in libertatem gloriae filiorum Dei — **without having
our own school in matters which the Magisterium of the Church
leaves to the free discussion of men:** fortes in fide, **with purity of
intention, with openness and vigilance, avoiding extremes and
laziness of any kind. And without being cowed by passing
fashions and moods: because our love for the Church, for the**

Work and for souls will lead us to sift out the good and leave aside the rest, and sometimes to go against the current, out of loyalty to Jesus Christ and his doctrine.

Resting on these solid supports, Msgr. Escrivá de Balaguer's pastoral work shone out with the twin characteristics already mentioned: optimism and prudence. He kept to his place and he led the Association with a vitality and assurance which set souls alight, instilled courage and marked out a sure path that was rich in supernatural fruitfulness.

His tireless teaching, in private conversations or with thousands of people, was a great comfort to souls. He moved men's hearts, confirmed their faith and opened up apostolic horizons. As Prof. Kummer, of the University of Vienna, who was with him in February 1968, writes: "a profound love for the Church and the Pope came through in all he said, and it was this which gave his conversation its true tone. I was very impressed because, despite the seriousness of what he had to say, he communicated an optimism that was contagious. His attitude, given his knowledge of the situation, could only be explained by his deep union with God. When I left I felt strengthened in the faith and moved to be more generous in the apostolate."

Fr. Juan Ordóñez Márquez wrote in a Seville newspaper the day after Msgr. Escrivá de Balaguer died that he had possibly been "the man to whom Vatican II had little or nothing new to say, because he had already long previously been treading its paths".

The Cardinal Primate of Spain, Msgr. González Martín, was to point out something similar a few weeks later: "Long before the Second Vatican Council he had worked, as no one else, to bring out the laity, to bring them out genuinely and profoundly, not in those ridiculous and sad caricatures which have abounded so and still parade up and down in these post-conciliar years; and the same in the field of ecumenism, and in that of dialogue with the modern world, and in the effective recognition of a healthy autonomy for temporal matters.

"Precisely because of that, now, when so many are frenziedly turning this way and that, not knowing where they are going, because their frivolity deprives them of light, he knew how to remain firm and upright upon the rock of faithfulness without ever becoming an empty futurologist who, thinking he is glimpsing the future, allows the present to fall to pieces before his very eyes. Because he knew how to be a genuine progressive, he was also — and could not but be — a courageous and stalwart conservative, belonging to the line of the martyrs and

PETER'S BOAT CANNOT SINK

confessors of the faith, or simply to the spiritual lineage of those who, imitating Mary, know how to conserve in their hearts as poor men of the kingdom what they must conserve for ever if they are to remain faithful."

The fact is that the Founder of Opus Dei was not taken in by superficiality. He always refused to accept that it could be right, or even possible, to catalogue or simplify people into categories like "integrists against progressives". As he pointed out in 1967 to the Editor of *Palabra*:

This division is at times taken to great extremes and perpetuated as if theologians, and the faithful in general, were destined always to be circling these opposite poles. As far as I can see, it seems to derive ultimately from the belief that progress in the doctrine and in the life of the People of God is the result of a perpetual dialectical tension. I on the other hand prefer to believe, wholeheartedly, in the action of the Holy Spirit, who breathes where he will and upon whom he will.

Some years later, in early 1974, the Founder of Opus Dei was with Cardinal König, the President of the Pontifical Secretariat for Non-Believers. In an article which appeared on 9 November 1975 in the *Corriere della Sera* (Milan) Card. König referred to that conversation, emphasising the "great spiritual authority" of Msgr. Escrivá de Balaguer, "his serenity, his disarming frankness and his organising talents. These qualities were combined with a warm understanding of the concerns and the joys of others, and an ardent zeal for the things of God".

About the same time, the President of the Secretariat for Non-Christians, Cardinal Pignedoli wrote in *Il Veltro, Rivista della Civiltà Italiana*: "He bore the sufferings of the Church and rejoiced with her rejoicing. He felt deep sorrow at the present abandonment of so many souls, and with that in mind he prayed and worked, day after day, with renewed zeal, and would ask for the prayers of others. He would stretch out his hand 'like a beggar of God imploring the alms of prayer'. He incessantly reminded people that this troubled time, in which the devil once again sifts the Church of Christ like wheat (cf. Luke 22:31), is the hour for prayer and reparation. The more the onslaught rages and the greater the unfaithfulness, the more he must seek intimacy with God through prayer and penance.

"But his faith did not allow him to be sad, or much less, discouraged. He offered his suffering, his whole life, for the Church and the Pope, while he continued working happily, sowing peace and joy, full of optimism, giving assurance and consolation to all around him."

"A life for the Church" was the title chosen by the Milan monthly *Studi Cattolici* for its article on the death of Msgr. Escrivá de Balaguer. The title sought to summarise that love for the Church which gave meaning to the life of the Founder of Opus Dei, a love which grew with a steady crescendo right to the end of his days. As Don Alvaro del Portillo wrote on 29 June 1975, referring to the morning of 26 June: "We found it hard to convince ourselves that he had died. For us, indeed, his death has come quite unexpectedly; for the Father, we may be sure, it was something which had been ripening — I am not afraid to say — more in his soul than in his body, because he offered his life for the Church more frequently each day." Don Alvaro del Portillo, now President General of Opus Dei, went on to say: "For some time now, the Father, with growing intensity as time passed, had been offering Our Lord his life and — he usually added — **a thousand lives were I to have them** for the Holy Church and for the Pope, whoever he may be. This offering was the daily intention of his Mass. A constant fervour in his soul, it revealed the sorrow of his heart and expressed the watchfulness of his life."

Those who have lived close to Msgr. Escrivá de Balaguer in these last few years know of his nights of prayerful vigil when overwhelmed by *sorrowful* events in the life of the Church, *he could not rest* at the thought of souls who might be losing eternal life. They were years (days and nights) of continuous prayer and tireless work and permanent and loving reparation. It was a long period, in which he forgot himself, his reputation and his honour in order to serve only the Church, with genuine service, thinking only of souls and the glory of God. Throughout that time he sustained the members of Opus Dei like a genuine "good shepherd". Impossible though it may seem, the effort he put into his prayer, his mortification and his apostolic work increased day by day, both in the apparent calm of Rome and in the months spent preaching over half the world. In these stormy hours, he shored up people's supernatural hope in the Church:

The seas are a little rough. . . . They will grow calm again, don't worry. Even when Jesus was with them in the boat, the boat seemed to be sinking. Peter's boat cannot sink!

"And so he carried on," Don Alvaro del Portillo was to recall, "down to the very last day, to the last hours he spent on earth." On 26 June 1975, less than two hours before his death, the Founder of

Opus Dei was urging souls — in this case the students of the *Istituto Internazionale di Pedagogia* in Castelgandolfo — to grow in interior life, **so as to be close to God and his Blessed Mother, our Mother, and to St. Joseph, our Father and Lord, and to our Guardian Angels, so as to help this Holy Church, our Mother, who is in such great need and is having such a hard time in the world at present. We must have a great love for the Church and for the Pope, whoever he may be. Ask Our Lord that our service to his Church and to the Holy Father may be fruitful.**

CHAPTER EIGHT

THE FREEDOM OF THE CHILDREN OF GOD

1. THE OPPOSITION OF THE GOOD

It was mid-afternoon when the Founder of Opus Dei reached 14 Diego de León. Two or three students were sitting on the bench in the large hall, at the foot of the staircase which leads to the visitors' area in that house. He greeted them and stayed with them a while, chatting with them about their studies. Meanwhile, other students were arriving back from lectures. They tried to detain him, telling him some news of the work of the apostolate. Someone began to tell the story of a friend who some time back had taken part in a demonstration in which there were also some protests against Opus Dei. . . . Before the young man could finish the story, the Founder of Opus Dei interrupted him and said something like: **Good for him. He was within his rights. If that was what he thought, he had a duty to act that way.**

At that moment Luis Calle arrived to hear how afterwards the student in question had come to know the Association properly and had asked to join the Work. Luis realised they were actually speaking about him, and said without hesitation: "It was me, Father."

Msgr. Escrivá de Balaguer smiled and greeted him warmly. Then, looking at him affectionately, he spoke about perseverance, while making the sign of the Cross on his forehead.

This anecdote tells us something of the very great love which the Founder of Opus Dei always had for freedom. It was one of the reasons why he always sought to understand others and to find excuses for them, even when they did not understand him or when they insulted the Work. He never sought to defend if the attacks were directed against himself, but if they referred to Opus Dei, he always found a way of pointing the truth out very clearly, forgiving the people involved but without conceding their errors, just as a good son would never allow others to ill-treat his parents.

This manner of behaviour explains why he felt so affectionately towards the nineteenth century Romantics. During Easter in 1974 he spoke a bit about them to university students from all over the world:

They had all that romantic enthusiasm. They sacrificed themselves and fought to achieve the democracy they dreamed of and personal freedom with personal responsibility.

That is the way to love freedom: with personal responsibility. (. . .) I sometimes think, he said jokingly, **that I am the last Romantic, because I love the personal freedom of everyone, of non-Catholics too. . . . I love the freedom of others, yours, and that of the person who is walking down the street at this very moment, because if I did not love his freedom I could not defend my own. But this is not the main reason. The main reason is that Christ died on the Cross to give us freedom, so that we should end up** in libertatem gloriae filiorum Dei.

I was present on the first occasion, in the hall of Diego de León on 12 April 1972, but it could easily have taken place thirty years previously, for it was there in Diego de León that the Founder of Opus Dei, who had tasted the unpleasantness of opposition as far back as 1929, suffered from 1940 onwards serious and harsh calumnies, which Our Lord helped him to bear cheerfully with supernatural outlook and also with a great respect for the freedom of others.

He had already experienced the bitterness of misunderstanding in the early years of the foundation. In 1932, with his eyes on the future, he wrote:

Be understanding, then, even though at times there are those who do not wish to understand. Your love for souls should lead you to love all men, to seek excuses for them, to forgive. Yours should be a love that makes up for all the deficiencies of human weakness; it should be a marvellous

charity: veritatem facientes in caritate (Eph 4: 15), **following the truth of the Gospel with charity.**

Realise that charity consists not so much in giving as in understanding. I will not hide from you that I am learning in my own flesh how hard it goes with one not to be understood. I have always tried to make myself understood. But there are some who are determined not to understand me. This is another reason why I wish to understand everyone; and you in turn must always make an effort to understand others.

I have tried to write the next few pages with a spirit of understanding and of love for the truth; and so, though I must necessarily refer to terrible mistakes and errors committed by persons of flesh and blood, I mention no names, mainly out of loyalty to the person who suffered them in his own soul. The Founder of Opus Dei not only understood and forgave right away; but also forbade the members of Opus Dei to speak, even amongst themselves, about these happenings, so as never to give even the slightest occasion to possible faults against charity. He told them, besides, that if people who did not belong to the Association brought the matter up in their conversations, they should simply tell the truth, say that they forgave, and then forget and carry on working without giving any further importance to gossip and hearsay, however insidious it might be.

This was not just a passing counsel. The Founder of Opus Dei always inculcated this clear way of practising charity. Before he had to suffer in his own flesh both petty gossip and grave slanders, he had been prepared by his rich interior life to pass over such things, bearing them with sorrow, in silence and without a murmur. His dispositions had been reflected some time previously when he drew up some points of *The Way*, which was published in 1939:

Tongues have been wagging and you have suffered rebuffs that hurt you all the more because you were not expecting them.

Your supernatural reaction should be to pardon, — and even to ask pardon — and to take advantage of the experience to detach yourself from creatures (*The Way*, 689).

When you meet with suffering, contempt, the Cross, your thought should be: what is this compared with what I deserve? (*The Way*, 690).

I myself met the Founder of Opus Dei on 8 September 1960, in Aralar University Residence in Pamplona. Some hundred or so students were there. Someone asked him when the history of the Work would be written and when we would be able to know all that had taken place before its definitive approval by the Holy See. He answered with a metaphor that spoke of thorns and roses. The idea registered deeply in me. At times, a person cutting roses gets hurt by the thorns; but the beauty and perfume of the flower makes him forget the pain.

Many years later this image has come back to me on reading texts of Msgr. Escrivá de Balaguer about the spirit of the members of the Work who **do not harbour in their hearts any sentiments other than those of love, understanding and supernatural forgiveness.** Nevertheless, though he knew this, the Founder insisted on not speaking about those moments in the history of the Work, lest certain events might provoke, especially among the younger ones, **a not very measured reaction — pure, but full of youthful impulsiveness — which might unjustly be interpreted as aggressive or unchristian.**

God saw fit to use people who were convinced that they were fighting a good cause to make the Founder of Opus Dei share even more closely in the Cross of Christ — it was He above all who underwent persecution and slander from "good people". In any case, Our Lord would find ways of writing straight even along crooked lines.

On 16 June 1974 in Buenos Aires, a mother spoke to the Founder of Opus Dei about the vocation of her children which some people did not understand. Msgr. Escrivá de Balaguer answered with a question: what would become of a painting if it was all light and there were no shadows? **There would be no picture! So it is fitting that some should not understand. Besides, when they do come to understand, they feel very ashamed and they become saints.**

He had had personal experience of this since 1929. Misunderstandings at that time could be identified one by one, because the Work was scarcely known, but all shared an identical root, a radical lack of understanding of the central message of Opus Dei which consists in bringing holiness into the heart of ordinary life. As we have seen, many thought this message "madness". Others simply clung to established ways of thinking which are relevant for those who have a different vocation. Hence if a young person showed signs of wanting to be more committed in his christian life, they argued that there was no other way for him but to enter a seminary or a novitiate. They could not conceive that he could also continue "in the world", battling for sanctity without changing his situation at work or in his family.

It was after 1939 that the difficulties became really great, especially in Madrid and Barcelona. At first the Founder of Opus Dei did not want to believe that he was faced with a real and tenacious campaign, but the evidence mounted up in such a way that he simply had to yield to it.

They went as far as troubling the consciences of the parents of the members of the Work. Sometimes it was through the confessional. At other times, they would make a special visit to the families concerned. As a significant example of the novelty of the message of the Founder of Opus Dei, we have the story which Don Amadeo de Fuenmayor told to a journalist the day Msgr. Escrivá de Balaguer died: "Perhaps because today it is exactly one year since my mother died, I have remembered something she told me in 1941. . . . She told me that she had recently received a visit from someone to warn her that her son was in danger of damnation. When I asked her if the visitor had explained the reasons for such a terrifying warning, she said she'd been told that we, the members of Opus Dei, were suffering from hallucinations, because we were being led to believe that we could be saints in the middle of the world."

The visitor who had never previously met Amadeo's mother, had gone to see her in Barcelona when she made a trip there from her home in Valencia. He also told her that she could and should dissuade her son from following the way he had embarked on, and that she should not be put off by the objection, which Amadeo would probably make, that he was already "of age". He also warned her against Don Antonio Rodilla, the Vicar General of the diocese of Valencia, because he "was one of their lot". So there was no way out. She could not go to the Archbishop — Msgr. Melo y Alcalde — because he was very old.

Amadeo de Fuenmayor concluded: "I need hardly say that my mother suffered terribly. She fell ill and was confined to bed for several days. In the end, with the help of Don Antonio Rodilla to whom she turned for advice, everything was clarified. Her distress turned to great happiness because she knew her son had found a way to sanctity in the world."

Many parents wept. They were being told, in practice, that their sons were in something "heretical" and that they were on the road to perdition — and all this because those people did not understand the significance of the preaching of the Founder of Opus Dei on the universal call to holiness. Many years later Cardinal Bueno Monreal, the Archbishop of Seville, spoke about those times to the students of the

Guadaira University Residence. He defined Opus Dei for them as a new spiritual phenomenon in the life of the Church. "This very novelty," we read in a press cutting from a Seville newspaper of the time, "was what provoked years ago the misunderstanding of some people who didn't understand its lay spirituality which is eminently apostolic and supernatural."

Don Antonio Rodilla himself comments: "He was persecuted, falsely accused and publicly slandered. I myself had to undo lies before prelates and national Counsellors of the Catholic Action movement. The persecution was fierce and persistent. I didn't hear slanders or accusations about his private life, but I did hear them about his apostolic activities, whose aims were considered erroneous, and also about his orthodoxy. In the novitiate of a goodly congregation of nuns he was portrayed as the antichrist, and it was said and repeated in many religious establishments that this was a new heresy. (. . .) A story would be built up by mixing true and verifiable facts with others that were invented and damaging. Once the damage had been done, the flames would be fanned, inducing total blindness and then the story spread like a forest fire not only among people who were resentful and ever-ready to bite, but also among those people who were most sensitive about injustice. Both evil and good people united against the innocent slandered person: for them, Don Josemaría and his Work were a secret, clandestine and heretical organisation."

One of these items of gossip centred on the residence in Jenner Street. The story went around Madrid that its oratory was full of "cabalistic signs". The simple fact was that on the centre of the frieze above the altar was written a verse from a liturgical hymn: *Congregavit nos in unum Christi amor*, and on the sides a phrase from the Acts of the Apostles: *Erant autem perseverantes in doctrina Apostolorum, in communicatione fractionis panis, et orationibus* (Acts 3: 42). The words were separated by eucharistic and liturgical symbols: loaves, an ear of corn, the vine, a lamp, a dove, the cross. . . . These were the cabalistic signs.

Another popular story was that of the "elliptical" oratory in the house in Diego de León. The Dominican Fr. Severino Alvarez, dean of the faculty of canon law in the Angelicum in Rome, said in 1950 that some time previously they had received in the Holy Office a denunciation against Opus Dei; among the things it mentioned was that there was an oratory in a Centre in Madrid which was "elliptical". The Master General of the Dominicans, taking occasion of the fact that Fr. Severino was going to Spain, asked him to find out personally what might be wrong with the oratory in question. Fr. Severino went to Diego de León and examined everything in detail. He reported, half indignant and half laughing, what could be wrong with an oratory which was set up in a room which was somewhat like an ellipse in shape and was the best and largest room in that house which had formerly belonged to the López Puigcerver family.

All witnesses agree that the Founder of Opus Dei's reaction to these happenings was always supernatural. He offered his Mass for those who slandered him and he encouraged the members of Opus Dei to offer tough mortifications for them, including corporal ones. Not a single uncharitable word — Fr. José Luis Múzquiz writes — escaped his lips: it was genuinely heroic because he suffered a lot; and because on top of his very intense apostolic work, he had to carry the weight of the opposition of the good.

In 1941, this opposition became especially acute in Barcelona. Quite a number of young men frequented the *Palau*, a little flat in Balmes Street, near Aragón Street. It was rented by Alfonso Balcells who, although he had not asked to join Opus Dei, offered to help because he was the only one who had finished his degree.

Although in those days there were probably not more than half a dozen people in Barcelona who had asked to join Opus Dei, all of whom were students still, a big rumpus was raised against the Work. On one occasion, Fr. Pascual Galindo, a friend of the Founder, went to Barcelona and stayed in the *Palau*. On the following day he said Mass in a college of nuns which stood on the corner of Diagonal Street and the Rambla de Cataluña. Some of the students from the *Palau* accompanied him and went to Mass and to Communion. The Mother Superior and some other nuns present were very edified by the piety of those young students and they invited them to stay to breakfast with Fr. Galindo. In the middle of breakfast Fr. Pascual said to the Mother Superior: "These are the heretics for whose conversion you asked me to offer the Mass." One of the students recalls: "The poor nun almost fainted. They had made her believe we were a vast legion of real heretics and she found that we were a few perfectly ordinary students who went devoutly to Mass and Holy Communion."

In the university they were branded publicly as heretics and declared to be "odd", but their behaviour was perfectly normal, without a word of complaint or resentment. They followed the Founder's advice and example. They kept silent and worked. They smiled and forgave. They saw it all as something providential which God would turn to good account. Rafael Termes, who was then the director of the *Palau*, made the Founder very happy when he wrote to him from Barcelona saying that he need not worry about them, because not a single uncharitable word had escaped their lips.

Though the *Palau* did not have an oratory, it did have a wooden cross, like that plain wooden cross without the image of the Crucified which was described in 1934 in *Consideraciones espirituales*:

When you see a poor wooden Cross, alone, uncared for, and of no value . . . and without its Crucified, don't forget that that Cross is your Cross: the Cross of each day, the hidden Cross, without splendour or consolation . . . , the Cross which is awaiting the Crucified it lacks: and that the Crucified must be you.

The story was spread around Barcelona that they used to crucify themselves on this poor cross and that some students were performing "blood rites" in Balmes Street.

Don Josemaría was deeply hurt by this absurd story, but he prudently substituted the cross by another tiny one: **That way,** he jokingly commented, **they won't be able to say that we are crucifying ourselves because there just isn't room.**

Friar José López Ortiz corroborates that the Founder of Opus Dei was very hurt by these and other attacks and falsehoods, though "it wasn't for himself that he suffered, but for Our Lord, for the Church, for the Work and for souls. He was not concerned about his own honour (even with so much slander against him), nor about his prestige, or reputation or anything: his humility was quite exemplary."

Things got to such a point that he could not go to Barcelona for fear of being imprisoned. Nevertheless, he did go there by plane from Madrid, returning the same day so as not to have to put up at any hotel. His ticket was made out to Josemaría E. de Balaguer so as not to arouse police suspicions, because he was then better known as Fr. Escrivá. It was Msgr. Cicognani, the Apostolic Nuncio, who gave him this advice.

The civil governor of Barcelona at the time was Correa Veglison. Years later, Dr. Balcells spoke to him of that trip. Correa said: "I'm glad that I didn't know then that Msgr. Escrivá had come to Barcelona. They were saying such things about him that I would certainly have sent the police to the airport to arrest him."

At that time, the monastery of Montserrat was one of the foremost centres of spirituality in Spain. Fortunately, when this campaign was unleashed, the Abbot-Coadjutor of Montserrat, Dom Aurelio M. Escarré, wrote to the Bishop of Madrid for information about Opus Dei. Don Leopoldo Eijo y Garay said in his reply to Abbot Escarré on 24 May 1941: "I know about the storm that has been raised against Opus Dei in Barcelona. It's easy to see that the evil enemy has been stung. But the sad thing is that it is people who are very much given to God who are instrumental in this evil. It is obvious that they are acting *putantes obsequium se praestare Deo.*" Don Leopoldo added that he knew everything about Opus Dei, because "since it was founded in 1928 it has been so much in the hands of the Church that the diocesan Ordinary (that is either my Vicar General or myself) has known and, where necessary, has directed all the steps it has taken: so that everything about it from its first whimpers at birth until its present cries of pain has echoed in our ears, and . . . in our heart. Believe me, most reverend Father Abbot, the *Opus* is truly *Dei*, from its first conception through all its steps and trials."

In this letter the Bishop of Madrid described at length the priestly virtues of the Founder of Opus Dei, not forgetting to mention his profound docility to his Bishop, and he rebutted specifically the slanders alleging that the Work is "secret": "The 'secret association', so called by its denigrators, was born with the blessing of the diocesan authorities and it has not taken a single step of any importance without asking for and obtaining our approval." The discreet reserve — which was never a secret — inculcated by Dr. Escrivá is simply "an antidote against boasting, the defence of a humility which he desires to be not only individual but collective. (. . .) *Opus Dei* deserves nothing but praise," Don Leopoldo ends, "but we who love it do not want it to be praised, nor proclaimed from the house-tops," because its only desire is "to work quietly and humbly, with internal cheerfulness and an apostolic enthusiasm which will not lose its savour precisely because it does not overflow into ostentation".

This letter was important because many families found support and consolation in Montserrat and they were able to set their minds at rest. The rector of the seminary of Barcelona, Fr. Vicente Lores, who on 11 July 1941 sent Bishop Díaz Gómara, then Apostolic Administrator of Barcelona, a long report on Opus Dei, sent with it a copy of the letter. For him it was "definitive": "Once one reads the letter all doubts are dispelled, even in the most exigent minds."

Meanwhile in Madrid the calumny alleging that the members of Opus Dei were "masons" was reaching its climax. Though the charge was absurd, those who pressed it went so far as to denounce the Founder to the "Tribunal for the Repression of Freemasonry".

Opus Dei was accused of being a "Jewish branch of the Masons", or "a Jewish sect in league with the Masons". General Saliquet who was president of the Tribunal put an end to this saga. He was told that the members of Opus Dei were ordinary citizens and Christians who were in no way different from their fellow men; and that they were clean-living people, and honest and hard working and that they led chaste lives. . . . At this point he interrupted: "Are they really chaste?" They answered: "Yes". He replied: "In that case there's nothing to worry about. If they are chaste they aren't masons. I've never met a chaste mason." With that he closed the case.

Nevertheless all this had made the Founder of Opus Dei suffer and Fr. Sancho, O.P., recalls how one day, after giving a class in 14 Diego de León, he went up to Don Josemaría's study which was beside the oratory. He found him very sad. Don Josemaría explained to him that they had been denounced as "masons" and pointed out that the only motive he could think of was the naturalness of the members of Opus Dei who were ordinary faithful just as any other and did not proclaim to the four winds the fact of their personal dedication to God in Opus Dei, which was then in a state of legal gestation within the Church.

Fr. Sancho consoled him as best he could. He realised what serious consequences such an accusation could have at that particular moment in Spain. He adds: "What stood out on that day, in which the Father was so sorrow-stricken after a whole night of suffering and prayer, was his supernatural outlook. He always took everything to God. And he offered up his sufferings to the Lord calmly and cheerfully."

Don Antonio Rodilla adds: "It would not have been a real test if he had not felt the pain and shame of scratches and bites, blows and spittle. It hurt and it's possible that it drew tears from his eyes and shook him; but never for a moment did he slacken in his loving embrace of the Cross, nor in his love for his persecutors."

In the midst of all these trials, he had the encouragement and the consolation of the faithfulness of the members of the Work. Many other people too had the loyalty and supernatural sense to stand by him. As Fr. Sancho certifies: "thank God the bishops to a man were on his side; he was especially loved and blessed by the Bishop of Madrid, Don Leopoldo Eijo y Garay."

It is only fair to emphasise with Fr. Sancho the firm and clear attitude which Don Leopoldo Eijo y Garay took up at all times. He always spoke in terms similar to those he used in his letter of May 1941 to Abbot Escarré.

Msgr. Castán, then Auxiliary Bishop of Tarragona, was told by Don Leopoldo that a deputation was sent to him one day to accuse and denounce Opus Dei and to ask him to intervene against the Association and its Founder. Don Leopoldo let them state their case and then he replied firmly that when he had approved the Work he had acted with full deliberation and in full possession of all the facts of the case. Msgr. Castán remembers the very words which the Bishop of Madrid used on that occasion: "This creature was born in my very hands."

Fr. Carlos Calaf tells a similar anecdote which was told him by Don Leopoldo himself. He places it in 1940. On the day of the Corpus Christi procession one of the pall bearers walking beside the bishop was a young man who had said something unfortunate about Opus Dei. "The Patriarch said to me: 'Even though I was carrying the Blessed Sacrament in my hands, I turned to him and said: look, by all that is most holy in the world and most precious to me, which is Jesus in the Blessed Sacrament, don't attack, don't say anything to discredit this Work which I treasure as the apple of my eye.' "

Years later, the Founder of Opus Dei was to recall: **A long, long time ago when I was living in Lagasca, one night when I was in bed and beginning to fall asleep — when I slept, I slept very well, I have never lost sleep over the slanders, persecutions and falsehoods of those times — the telephone rang. I took it and heard "Josemaría. . . ." It was Don Leopoldo, then Bishop of Madrid. There was a special warmth in his voice. On many other occasions he had called me at that hour, because he used to go to bed late, in the early hours of the morning, and say Mass at eleven a.m.**

"What is it?" I asked. And he told me: Ecce Satanas expetivit vos ut cribraret sicut triticum (Luke 22:31). **"He will shake you and sift you, as corn is sifted in the threshing." And then he added: "I pray so much for you. . . .** Et tu . . . confirma filios tuos! **You, confirm your sons." And he rang off. Wonderful, wasn't it?**

Quite a few people just could not make head or tail of the Patriarch. He was considered to be a rather traditional bishop who had a preference for "a rural clergy, neatly classified according to seniority". How then could he be giving "decisive protection to an experiment like Opus Dei which was just the opposite"? This is how Fr. Federico

Sopeña puts it in his book *Defence of a Generation*. Fr. Sopeña also refers to an incident which seems to have been pretty widely known in the forties. One day, the Patriarch before giving Communion to a well known layman, said to him pointedly: "Whoever criticizes Opus Dei, criticizes the Patriarch."

On 25 June 1944 Don Leopoldo Eijo y Garay conferred the Sacrament of Holy Orders upon the first three priests of Opus Dei. That day he went to have lunch in 14 Diego de León and was chatting afterwards with a good number of members of the Work who had come from other cities for the ordination. He confided to them that there had been a time when he had been afraid they might react violently or uncharitably to the continual campaign of slander, but that his mind had been set at rest one day when Don Alvaro del Portillo told him, as he glanced at the crucifix:

"No! We forgive them and besides we are grateful to them for it all. Why should a patient complain about the scalpel, and especially if it is made of platinum?"

Don Alvaro had learned from the Founder to forgive and to see all that as coming from God who wanted to purify him and Opus Dei. "How much he owes his persecutors!" Don Antonio Rodilla exclaims: they drove him to pray, to be humble and mortified, to practise the most heroic charity, and to form the members of Opus Dei supernaturally.

He taught them, with his example and word, to forgive those unseeing detractors at once and without hesitation. When anyone brought news to him of a new falsehood, which often happened several times in one day, his first reaction was to invite them to say an Our Father or a Hail Mary for the person who had slandered him. In referring to them or their behaviour he always used a significant expression which epitomised his supernatural reaction: it was **the opposition of the good,** who were acting *putantes obsequium se praestare Deo*, believing that they were rendering a service to God.

Fr. Sancho confirms: "Never did I seem him react with malice. He wasn't that kind of man. He was understanding, forgiving and quick to forget. He always reacted supernaturally and with great gentleness."

Friar José López Ortiz emphasises the same idea: "He suffered a lot because he had a broad open spirit and a magnanimous heart."

Many years later, in Buenos Aires, Msgr. Escrivá de Balaguer alluded in passing to those terrible moments in the forties:

Always use the plus sign, which stands for the Cross and for addition. In that way you will attract, not repel. And if you're insulted? More than I was, I rather doubt it: . . . like a tattered rag! There was a moment one night when I had to go to the Tabernacle there in Diego de León and say: "Lord," and I found it hard, I found it hard because I am very proud, and I wept big tears . . . "Lord, if you don't need my honour, what do I need it for?"

The Founder of Opus Dei, who also had a great human sensitivity, could not but feel the weight of so much filth heaped upon himself. He forgave, and helped others to forgive, right away; but those who were close to him cannot forget that in 1940 and 1941 there were days so heavy that in the evening he literally could not keep on his feet, because his body just could not take any more. He was exhausted, not so much by his constant rhythm of work — he seemed to have strength to spare to push forward the work of Opus Dei all over Spain: he was the motor of the apostolate, urging on the members of the Work and constantly making trips to cities all over the country — but because he was deeply grieved at the possible offence given to God by these attacks, and at the confusion they spread in so many souls. He did not think of himself, and that is why he was happy and cheerful, with his usual smile and good humour.

On 27 June 1975, straight after the news of Msgr. Escrivá de Balaguer's death, *La Vanguardia Española* of Barcelona printed the impressions of Alfonso Balcells Gorina, who was an exceptionally close witness of the difficult times in that city: "When in the early forties there was misunderstanding and slander in Barcelona, he taught us how to love freedom and how to respect the freedom of everyone, and he wished that in the oratory of the Monterols University Residence there should be placed the inscription *Veritas liberabit vos*. Years before our war, he saw to it that in the first students' residence in Madrid, as was to happen afterwards in so many others, there should be placed in a visible spot the text of the *Mandatum novum:* 'love one another . . .', so that it should remain firmly engraved in the minds of all that the spirit of that house and of Opus Dei is based on love."

During all the abuse and suffering, the Founder of Opus Dei never lost his happiness. He bore everything with understanding and affection, never once complaining, and savouring in his prayer the silence of the Son of God before Herod: *Jesus autem tacebat.*

Don Miguel Sancho Izquierdo, who taught him natural law in the

University of Saragossa, was always very impressed by this silent attitude of Msgr. Escrivá de Balaguer, noting that whereas he never defended his own honour, he always came out in defence of the Church and the Vicar of Christ if anyone should offend their good name.

They were difficult years, the Founder wrote for the members of Opus Dei in 1961, **because they made their slanders reach the very highest places in the Church, sowing distrust and suspicion against the Work. For myself, I (...) kept quiet and prayed. But it is natural — now that many of the people who tried to do so much harm, thinking perhaps** obsequium se praestare Deo (John 16:2) **that they were doing an act of service to God, now that many of them have passed away, while others opening their eyes have changed their opinion — that I should at least tell you that those contradictions existed.**

Nevertheless, even then, he did not want the members who had not lived through those pages of the history of Opus Dei to know the details, to avoid even the slightest **feeling of resentment or unkindness for those who voluntarily or involuntarily may have been the cause of some of the sufferings which we have had to undergo.**

Right down to the end of his days on earth his example was that of of a great-hearted person, who forgave unreservedly:

In the Holy Mass I remember to pray not only for my sons and daughters, for my parents and brothers, for the parents and brothers of my children, but also for those who are still living and want to trouble us, and for those who have slandered us and have already gone to render accounts with Our Lord. I say: "Lord, I forgive them so that you may forgive them and so that you may forgive our sins. I offer you suffrages for their souls; the same suffrages as I offer you for my children, and for my parents, and for the parents of my children. The same for all!"

Our Lord is pleased, and I too find great peace. I advise you to do likewise: never ever wish anyone evil. To bear a grudge can lead only to unhappiness and how can we who are children of God be unhappy? We must learn to forgive.

And then if someone tells you that that is heroism you just laugh. It's a wonderful thing. Does not God forgive us when we offend him? How then can we refuse to forgive?

Despite this generous attitude — which has its measure of christian elegance and a fine sense of humour — the Founder of Opus Dei felt very keenly the grave opposition, which is barely touched upon here.

Perhaps his feelings might be understood a little better by those who saw on television the film of what took place in the Coliseo Theatre in Buenos Aires on 23 June 1974. A widow began telling him about her only son, a priest, and Msgr. Escrivá de Balaguer was following her words with a broad welcoming smile. His happy expression, however, gave way to grave concern when that mother — her face lined by deep sorrow — started telling him, amidst sobs, that her son was beginning to falter in his vocation.

His great impassioned heart which identified so easily with the sufferings of others, suffered indescribably in the forties because he saw that the tremendous injustices he was undergoing offended God, confused many people and poisoned the souls of those who committed them. The Founder of Opus Dei who knew how to love said nothing, forgave and prayed, giving no importance to his heroism: **If someone tells you it's heroic, you just laugh. . . .**

Here we find another trait of his personality. He drew attention away from himself and centred it upon God, thus showing the genuineness of his christian humility. Evidently, to offer the same suffrages for those who have loved us as for those who have done us harm is unexpected, disproportionate, heroic; but someone who behaves that way because he is really trying to put the Gospel into practice thinks it is little, a trifle, because his faithful soul never ceases to compare that effort with the divine Sacrifice that Christ offered on Calvary.

Jesus Christ dies on the Cross to redeem the whole of mankind. His love, which wins for us the freedom of the glory of the children of God, unquestionably demands that we should forgive always and in everything, even though humanly we may find it hard and difficult to understand and practise: the Christian can do all things with the grace of God. The open arms of Jesus upon the Cross — opened with the gesture of a high priest, an expression much loved by the Founder of Opus Dei, who felt the Cross so close to him during the **opposition of the good** — helped Msgr. Escrivá de Balaguer to carry gracefully the tremendous weight of that opposition, which in reality was very painful, exhausting and difficult to understand, even when the years had passed.

2. WITHOUT FREEDOM ONE CANNOT LOVE GOD

"Besides his human warmth, his zeal and supernatural outlook, one of the things that moved me most in my conversations with Msgr. Escrivá de Balaguer was his love of freedom." So wrote Msgr. Onclin, the dean of the Louvain faculty of canon law in *La Libre Belgique*, a few days after the death of the Founder of Opus Dei. Msgr. Onclin comments on this spirit of freedom, noting that "he never mentioned that word without coupling it with another word: responsibility". He also quoted another key idea, so often reiterated by Msgr. Escrivá de Balaguer: **without freedom one cannot love God.**

In Spain's history, Aragon has always been a land of freedom. Even before England's Magna Carta the tradition of *habeas corpus* existed there. The *Justicia Mayor* of Aragon wrote glorious and tragic pages in Spanish history, but it was not so much an earthly tradition which gave Msgr. Escrivá de Balaguer his feeling and love for freedom, which was indeed a feature of his family home. His love of freedom had deeper roots. It had christian origins. It proceeded from his meditation upon the Cross, following in St. Paul's footsteps. Creatures have been freed "from the tyranny of corruption to share in the glorious freedom of God's sons" (Rom 8: 21). God is our Father. God is also a Spirit and "where the Lord's Spirit is there is freedom" (2 Cor 3: 17). Without freedom, one cannot love God, because Christians have been "called to freedom" (Gal 5: 13).

A Colombian journalist Javier Abad Gómez wrote on 30 June 1975 in *El Tiempo* of Bogotá: "What most impressed me was his love of freedom. There was nothing fanatical about him. He had an enormous respect for the conscience of each individual person. And he found room in his great heart not only for those who thought as he did, but also for those who thought or behaved differently. Many people are surely recalling it now, men of letters and workers, intellectuals and farmers, people belonging to the most diverse religions and holding the most contradictory ideological viewpoints."

His love of freedom was not a passing fancy. He felt within himself, with all the strength of his being, the profound and uniquely liberating character of Christ's redeeming Cross. He would sum up his feelings in a very clear, vivid and true phrase: **each soul is worth all the blood of Christ.** On 22 October 1972, in the auditorium of the Tajamar Institute in Madrid, a woman spoke to him of the anguish of certain parents when confronted by children claiming freedom and independence from family ties in a violent and insolent way. Msgr. Escrivá de Balaguer gave her some general advice but at the same time recommended her to get advice for each individual case:

In order to give you the right advice I would need more facts; I like to make suits to measure. I love souls very much. Each soul is worth all the blood of Christ. Empti enim estis pretio magno, **are St Paul's words** (1 Cor 6: 20). **You, and each one of us, he says, have been bought at a great price, the price of all the blood of Jesus Christ. That is why I cannot hand out a standard reply. I would like to make out a separate prescription for each one of your children; not even one for all of them together. Consult each case, and you will discover how much power you mothers have with God when you pray. With your prayers you will help your children over their difficulties and this little storm will pass.**

As previously in Spain and Portugal, so too after going to Rome in 1946, he kept up an intense personal apostolate. In Rome, even though his motto was to **pass unnoticed and disappear,** he immediately began receiving people who came from all over the world to ask his advice, to tell him their sorrows or joys. He bestowed on all of them the balm of charity, the light of doctrine and the impulse of his priestly words.

His **apostolic travels** began in 1948 and they covered most of Europe. New apostolates arose through his foresight, guidance and, at times, his direct personal involvement. Besides, at the same time as Opus Dei was developing in other continents under his kindly watchful eye, he had begun from the end of the forties to receive groups, which grew more numerous as time went by, made up of men or women from the most diverse countries.

In the final years of his life, Msgr. Escrivá de Balaguer felt the need to open out his work of catechesis to even larger groups of people. To do this, he started travelling all over Europe. Later this work took him also to many nations in America. People of very different professions, walks of life, races and tongues, came to listen to his words. Large halls, gymnasiums, esplanades and theatres were needed to accommodate his listeners. Even when the meetings were for larger groups they were still warm and friendly. There was spontaneity in the questions and answers; and an almost confidential tone, such as one would expect to find only in a family, and a very deep respect for the intimacy of each person. A well known figure in Spanish intellectual and university circles, Enrique Gutiérrez Ríos, sums it up in the Madrid newspaper *ABC*: "Even though he might be speaking before a large crowd, his attention was always for the individual there before him who is unique and irreplaceable. He used to say that in spiritual matters each person requires specific, individual attention, and that souls cannot be treated *en masse!*"

The Founder of Opus Dei suffered if he saw people applying a mass-production approach to human relationships. He loved those words of Scripture which say: *Redemi te, et vocavi te nomine tuo; meus es tu.* Our Lord has elected each one of us, calling us by our name. *Meus es tu:* you are mine. Our reply must also be a personal one: *Ecce ego quia vocasti me*, here I am answering your call. He rejected the trend towards **anonymity,** especially in our dealings with God. As Giuseppe Molteni wrote in *L'Osservatore Romano,* all his apostolate consisted in bringing Christians face to face with Christ: **It is Christ** who is passing by! **Christ who continues passing by, through the streets and squares of the world, by means of his disciples, the Christians.** Msgr. Escrivá de Balaguer's preaching could be summed up as a permanent invitation to his listeners to meet God personally: in the Sacraments, in prayer, in ordinary life. It should be a life of faith, a life of prayer — and through a loving reading of the Gospel, seeing oneself present there as a protagonist like any other, playing one's full part in every scene and shunning anonymity.

More than once he asked people to reflect on the case of the **brave** youth who dared to throw a stone at a marvellous stained glass window of a Cathedral — a splendid jewel which, he would add, **belongs to everyone** —, but then will not admit: "I did it!" He hides anonymously in the crowd, for he is a coward. . . . The example was applied to the cowardice of the person who does not dare to go out individually **to encounter God in his daily work, without doing anything odd, without wagging his tongue, without voicing words, but seeking God the Father, the Son and the Holy Spirit in the centre of one's soul, in the depths of one's heart, because He is there if we do not cast him out** (Tajamar, 1 October 1967).

His awareness of the dignity and freedom of the individual had many practical consequences.

No sacrifice was too great to help a single soul. He would get up from bed — with a temperature of 100°F. and more — to hear a Confession; or travel hundreds of miles, as he did in the late thirties, to go from Burgos to Andalusia in the trains of that period and without enough money for a meal or even to finish his journey; he would preach, even if just one person came. This has always been the custom in Opus Dei, but it was the Founder who set the standard. For example, in July 1935, he began a weekly class of formation for just one person: Alvaro del Portillo. Later, at the end of the month, a second person, José María Hernández de Garnica, joined the class. It was a practical demonstration of the priceless value of each soul.

His apostolic zeal always went hand in hand with freedom, which he fostered at every opportunity. Because he detested anonymity, he encouraged personal effort and stressed that everyone had to find his own personal way to God. He was no friend of straitjackets, nor of standard recipes. He never sought to regulate the interior life. The idea was to allow the Holy Spirit to do his work within each soul. He insisted again and again that Christ, perfect God and perfect Man, was the only model. He carefully avoided proposing any other models for imitation, and especially if people showed signs of wanting to imitate him. He emphasised this once again on the feast of St. Joseph in 1975. We have already quoted the text, but it is worth while reflecting upon it once more, from this view point of freedom. The Founder of Opus Dei recalled the difficulties of the beginnings:

What was I seeking? Cor Mariae Dulcissimum, iter para tutum! **I went to seek strength in the Mother of God, like a young son, following the paths of childhood. I turned to St. Joseph, my Father and my Lord. I wanted to see him powerful, very powerful indeed, the chief of that great divine clan, whom God himself obeyed:** erat subditus illis! **I turned with simplicity to the saints for their intercession, in a Latin which was awkward but pious:** Sancte Nicolaë, curam domus age! **And I had devotion to the Holy Guardian Angels, because it was on a 2nd of October when those bells rang out ... the bells of Our Lady of the Angels, a Madrid parish, close to Cuatro Caminos. ... I turned to the Holy Angels with confidence, like a little child, without realising that God was leading me along paths of spiritual childhood. But you don't have to imitate me. Long live freedom!**

Among the men of our times he spread the christian virtues and devotions of old: Christ, Mary and Joseph — he liked to call the Holy Family the **trinity on earth** and spoke of it as a short cut to the Blessed Trinity — the Pope ... Holy Mass, prayer, mortification, work ... Confession and the Holy Eucharist. ... He loved to recite the prayers of the early Christians, the same ones that will be used by Christians in centuries to come; but he never imposed devotions. He distinguished extremely carefully between what has been laid down by the Church, and what it merely recommends or praises. When he gave a piece of personal advice, he always made a point of stating clearly that it was just that, advice which could be followed or not, but which was in no way binding in conscience. Juridical precision and theological exactness joined hands to defend the freedom of consciences.

He was delighted to hear of souls being natural and spontaneous with God. He would have liked all men and women to speak with Him from the heart, using the same words that lovers do. Someone asked him in May 1974 how to offer things to God when one feels tired. He answered:

Tell Our Lord about it, quite naturally, as you would tell your mother, as you are telling me now face to face. . . .

There is no reason why anyone should feel shy within a family:

So if you wouldn't feel shy about telling it to your mother on earth, tell it to your Mother in Heaven: "Mother! I am finding it very hard to lift my heart up to your Son, to offer him all the work of the day. . . ." That is prayer! Say it to him the way you please. You can say the usual vocal prayers we Christians say, which are marvellous. But besides that, you pray: you are a contemplative soul, as those of Opus Dei are; and you speak without voicing the words, while you are in the street, or eating, smiling at someone, or studying. . . . Tell the Mother of God what you have been asking me; and you will already be offering your day.

A few weeks later, he came back again to the need for giving one's heart a free rein in the interior life of the soul. He was asked:

"What can we do, Father, when sometimes our hearts get a little hardened and do not respond to the things of God?"

That's the normal state of affairs; so much so that often we show too little understanding for people who are very sensitive. We think they are being hysterical, and often it's not so. When I was a young priest I felt annoyed when I saw old women sighing in a corner of the Church, and — I repeat it to my shame — I used to think: "We shall have to burn all those pious books, they are full of tears. . . ." And now I would not burn a single one of them. Instead I would burn these things that don't have a single sigh in them, nor any affection. Is this clear?

You see, my son, I have been working for forty-seven years in Opus Dei. And a good few years before that I felt the intimations of God's love. He wanted something and I did not know what it was. I am not going to go into details, which many of you here know perfectly well. Normally I have to go against the grain. Here at this moment I am very pleased to be with you. I thank Our Lord for giving me this joy, which is not a sentimental joy, but true love and affection. Yet, my son, my heart feels as hard as stone. But men's hearts when they are hard are of bronze, and when bronze is brought near the fire it melts into tears. Some day you will cry. Don't worry. You will cry and that day you will be even more a man. Don't think that men like us don't cry.

One of the reasons, apart from humility, why Msgr. Escrivá de Balaguer liked **hidden and silent** sacrifice offered to God was his love of freedom. There is no reason why others should notice a personal mortification, either in big things or in things apparently small.

Don Jesús Urteaga tells a story which, though brief, illustrates well how the Founder of Opus Dei wanted God to be served freely. It took place around 1957. Urteaga was in the Roman College of the Holy Cross. At that time he smoked too much. One day the Father mentioned to him: **Jesús, you smoke a lot;** but as he was saying this he gave him a packet of the cigarettes Urteaga usually smoked. . . .

Another anecdote also refers to smoking. It was Don Alvaro del Portillo who told it just after being elected President General of Opus Dei: "When we first three priests of the Work were ordained, none of us smoked. Neither did the Father, for when he entered the seminary he had given his pipes and tobacco to the porter. Then the Father said to me: 'I don't smoke; nor does any of you three either. Alvaro, you will have to take up smoking, because if not the others might think there's something wrong with smoking and I don't want them to feel they are not free to smoke if they want to.' "

This stress on freedom comes out especially clearly in the vocation and self-surrender of the members of Opus Dei. José María Casciaro, the present dean of the faculty of theology of the University of Navarre, has described with considerable precision and detail the steps leading up to his decision to dedicate himself to God in Opus Dei. It is a typical example of what happened in many similar cases.

He was in the sixth year of *Bachillerato* in Barcelona and had gone home to Torrevieja in Alicante for the Christmas vacation. His brother

Pedro, who was already in the Work, turned up one day and spoke to José María about his possible vocation. He suggested that José María might like to think it over calmly in the presence of God. They agreed they would have another talk later on when Pedro went to Barcelona. José María made up his mind he had a vocation and said so to his brother in April 1940, but he was asked to wait, because the Founder of Opus Dei was expected in Barcelona and "had indicated that, as my brother Pedro was a good deal older than I (he is eight and a half years older), it was important to ensure that I enjoyed complete freedom before taking such a step and that I wasn't being influenced in any way by my elder brother".

It was not till 12 May in the afternoon in the Urbis Hotel that José María Casciaro at last met the Founder of Opus Dei. During the conversation, he was asked several times — in a tone that struck José María as serious, emphatic, even severe — whether he might not have been influenced by his brother, instead of acting freely and after having considered his decision in the presence of God. As José María's answers were always that he was acting freely, the Founder in the end told him that from then on he could consider himself as belonging to the Work. Recalling that conversation José María declares: "Later, when I heard him say, as he so often did, that the entry door is narrow and the exit is wide open, I used to remember that episode on 12 May 1940 and understood deeply the exact meaning of his words."

This love for freedom is very much in line with the supernatural character of Opus Dei and with the external characteristics of the members' dedication. They are ordinary citizens, exactly the same as any other, who live at home and with their families and work in the middle of the world. They go as and where they please, spontaneously and naturally. They either live their vocation freely (for the love of God) or not at all. External control of any kind would destroy its true nature. The same is true of it as with human love, that it can only be conditioned by its own affection.

Everyone who asks to join Opus Dei does so free from every form of coercion. Furthermore, he has to work so as to be financially self-sufficient and maintain the apostolates. This fact, which avoids any **idle rich** tendencies, is also a guarantee of freedom. If someone wants to leave the Association, he can do so easily. If he perseveres, it is for supernatural and not human motives.

It would, however, be a mistake to confuse freedom with indifference. The Founder of Opus Dei wanted everyone to persevere in his vocation and did everything he could to ensure this. He formed the members and prayed for them. If they were going through difficult moments, he intensified his care for them. More than once he found occasion to have a **chance meeting** with someone who was wavering, as Our Lord had done with the disillusioned disciples on the road to Emmaus. Whenever necessary he would leave everything and go in search of the lost sheep.

Antonio Ivars comments on these two facets (the fact that he was both demanding and understanding) which reflect an identical spirit of love: "In some way I think that he mirrored the behaviour of Christ as no one else did. He was affectionate and gentle with children, or public sinners; but demanding and at times seemingly irate with the pharisees and indeed with his own apostles. Don Josemaría's motherly tenderness combined harmoniously with his fortitude. He could understand the greatest miseries, welcome the greatest sinner with deep affection, and seriously reprimand one of his sons because he had omitted some tiny detail."

Finally, to complete this brief review, we shall refer to his attitude towards those who were not Catholics.

He was not just making a "nice speech" when he declared that he was ready to lay down his life a hundred times to defend the freedom of a single conscience. He had to engage in a hard-fought **filial tussle** before getting the Holy See to approve something previously unheard of in the history of Catholic associations: that people without the Catholic faith could be Cooperators of Opus Dei.

In 1966 he told Jacques Guillemé-Brûlon of *Le Figaro* what he had once said to Pope John XXIII, influenced by his kindly and fatherly manner: **"Holy Father, in our Work all men, Catholics or not, have always found a welcome. It is not from Your Holiness that I learned ecumenism." And Pope John chuckled knowingly, because he was aware that since 1950, the Holy See had authorised Opus Dei to receive in the Association as Cooperators people who are not Catholics or even Christians.**

A little earlier, the same journalist had asked him about the "position of the Work" as regards the Second Vatican Council Declaration on religious freedom. His answer was very clear:

With respect to religious freedom, from its foundation Opus Dei has never practised discrimination of any kind. It works and lives with everyone because it sees in each person a soul which must be respected and loved. These are not mere

words. Our Work is the first Catholic organisation which, with the authorisation of the Holy See, admits non-Catholics, whether Christian or not, as Cooperators. I have always defended the freedom of individual consciences. I do not understand violence; I do not consider it a proper way either to persuade or to win over. Error is overcome by prayer, by God's grace, and by study; never by force; always with charity. From the first moment this is the spirit we have lived. You can understand, then, how the Council's teaching on the subject could only make me happy.

Msgr. Escrivá de Balaguer was always very loyal in his dealings with souls. He defended the freedom of their consciences, but without hiding his own full adherence to the Catholic faith (which, of course, includes the defence of that freedom). I think it is worth giving a summary of a conversation that took place between him and a married couple in Brazil in 1974, in front of a large gathering:

"We are an ecumenical family, my wife is a Methodist. . . ."

"God bless her. Is she here?"

She was, seated just in front of her husband.

"Tell her I love her very much."

"We are very united on the religious education of our children. . . ."

"Very good!"

"Two have already made their First Communion. . . ."

"Good!"

"They are now beginning to do a little bit of spiritual reading before going to bed, the eldest goes to Mass each day with his father."

"Good!"

"I would like you to say a few words to my wife."

"My daughter, I'll tell you this: that you have a wonderful husband and that I love you very much in the Lord. I love all souls. But a mother who gives freedom to her children, who also is concerned that they should be brought up in this marvellous faith, who sees them going up to receive the Holy Sacrament of the Eucharist joyfully. . . . I admire a mother like that. I admire you! I love you very much! Pray for me. And for the time being that's enough. But tomorrow in the Mass, I am going to remember you very much. There, I'm no longer myself. You do not need to believe it, as yet. I will ask Our Lord to grant you my faith, because — and don't get angry with me — yours is not the true one. I would lay down my life a hundred

times to defend the freedom of your conscience; so, we would be great friends if I lived here. But, of course, I fully believe that I am in possession of the true faith; if not, I wouldn't go about dressed in this 'umbrella'. (He was referring to his cassock.)

Pray for me! There is no one like your husband to defend your faith. And no one like your husband or like me, to ask Our Lord to send you much light and a great clarity of ideas. And thank you because you are very generous and very good."

Over the years, situations like this have happened hundreds of times. When the apostolic work of Opus Dei was beginning in Geneva, they got to know the son of a Calvinist minister. He became very enthusiastic about the Work and especially about *The Way*, which he distributed among his friends in different translations: French, English, German, Italian. Some time later he wrote to a member of Opus Dei he had met in Switzerland, sending him Christmas greetings. He talked effusively about his visit to Msgr. Escrivá de Balaguer in Rome. The Founder had received him very kindly — as he always received every-one — and had not failed to tell him that it is the Catholics who are in possession of the truth. Msgr. Escrivá de Balaguer had no need to hide his faith — quite the contrary — to get people who were not Catholics to respond with affection and gratitude to his affection and loyalty.

At an open-air gathering in Altoclaro, a conference centre near Caracas, some five thousand people listened to his teachings in 1975. A young man got up, with a big thick beard which enhanced his jovial air.

"Father, I am Jewish. . . ."

The Founder of Opus Dei interjected:

I love the Jews very much because I love Jesus Christ — I am madly in love with him — and he is Jewish. I do not say was, but is: Iesus Christus, heri et hodie, ipse et in saecula. Jesus Christ goes on living, and he is Jewish like yourself. The second love of my life is Jewish too, she is Holy Mary, the Mother of Jesus Christ. So I look upon you with affection. Go on. . . .

That man with a wide open smile won a warm round of applause when he replied:

"I think my question has already been answered."

3. NO DOGMAS IN TEMPORAL MATTERS

Raffaello Cortesini, who is a professor of experimental surgery at the University of Rome, described Msgr. Escrivá de Balaguer in *Il Popolo* as "A man who loved freedom".

The Founder of Opus Dei loved freedom in the interior life. He could not understand how anybody could give himself to God and serve him under constraint. He was ready to give a hundred lives if he had them to defend the freedom of consciences. He respected, he understood, he forgave and he loved those who did not understand him or had slandered him; and so it was natural that he should also defend freedom in strictly human matters such as work, social action, education or politics.

In a previous section we have seen the inconsistency of those rumours that were spread about in the forties. Equally false were the rumours that began to circulate in the fifties about an alleged political attitude of the Association. The first official note of the Secretariat of Opus Dei was issued in 1957, making it clear that the Work had nothing to do with the temporal activities of its members in public life. Though the facts speak for themselves, some people refused to accept the evidence. Perhaps they could not, because of a mistaken clerical outlook which they were accustomed to use in their assessment of spiritual and temporal affairs. They could not grasp that it is perfectly compatible to be completely honest with God and, at the same time, completely honest with men, by meeting one's civic responsibilities. They seemed incapable of understanding that supernatural life is a spur and a stimulus towards human solidarity, but that it does not lead to "confessionalism" of any kind, because as a rule there is no single Catholic solution to human problems. The problem is that, as the Italian journalist Cesare Cavalleri put it in *Il Corriere della Sera* (Milan), "clericalism dies hard".

In the fifties and sixties, the atmosphere was relatively favourable for making the appropriate distinction between religion and politics. The spirit of Opus Dei — if one might say so — went with the current. What is surprising, and worth stressing, is the Founder's faithfulness to that spirit during the thirties and forties when to speak about freedom and pluralism among Catholics went very much against the current.

Evidently there can be exceptional circumstances in the lives of nations in which the Catholic Hierarchy may — and should — speak in very definite terms, and then *each individual Catholic* has the responsibility to follow the advice of his Bishop, but it is a right, an obligation, which the Hierarchy alone and no one else may claim.

At the beginning of the thirties strong pressure was exerted in Spain to unite Catholics in public life as a way of defending the rights of the Church. Many came to believe that they were duty-bound to follow such a course of action, even though the bishops had not made any collective pronouncement to that effect. (Such a pronouncement was only made later, after the outbreak of the war.)

In that context, the Founder of Opus Dei's defence of the rightful freedom of Christians did not seem at all *profitable in the short term*. José Antonio Palacios sums up his experience of 1932 saying that Don Josemaría's way of focusing things "was not in any way attractive, in principle, to people like us. We were young and we viewed the situation in Spain as a big religious problem. With the growing menace of religious persecution, we could conceive no other solution than a political one. That is why we were fully committed to total action and we were seeking a violent solution to the whole problem."

Don Josemaría was in no hurry; nor was he afraid of the future. He would have nothing to do with tactics for the attaining of human objectives, however noble the intentions might be. He preferred to trust in the divine effectiveness of Christ's message, which includes loving the personal liberty of all Christians. Why impose dogmas in matters of opinion? He defended the risk of freedom. It was also because of this, and not only due to his priestly zeal, that he went to visit a prison to see some young friends of his, who had been jailed after the failure of the uprising of 10 August 1932. José Antonio Palacios recalls his visits to the Modelo Prison, which was at the far end of Princesa Street, where the Air Ministry now stands: "He never wavered when it came to looking after people, no matter how great the risk. He visited the prison frequently, even though his visits to the detainees made him a marked man, especially being a priest."

During these visits he gave priestly advice to his friends, either individually or as a group. From the other side of the bars of the long gallery where visitors were allowed to speak with political prisoners, he spoke about spiritual matters. He fostered the prisoners' devotion to Our Lady, their divine filiation, their love for the Church and the Pope. He encouraged them to receive the Sacraments frequently. He also encouraged them to use their time well while in prison and to bring a supernatural motive into their study and their work.

José Antonio Palacios recalls an amusing and characteristic episode that occurred during his twelve months in prison. After the rebellion of Casas Viejas, a number of anarchists who had been involved in it were rounded up and sent to the same Modelo Prison. When the weather was fine, the inmates were taken to the different prison yards to do some exercise. Some of them played football. Palacios was very surprised when he realised that these anarchists were being brought down to the same yard as he and his companions used. On one of Don Josemaría's visits to the prison, he asked him for advice on how they should deal with those men whose outlook was so opposed to religion. The Founder of Opus Dei told him that he had a splendid opportunity of treating them with affection and to try to make them realise their errors in religious matters. He said, more or less: "You must realise that they probably did not have christian parents as you have, nor were they brought up in an environment like yours. What would you and I be like if we had been in their situation?"

Don Josemaría encouraged them to make their faith tell by living and playing sports with the anarchists like the best of friends. He helped them to get a deeper awareness of Christ's teaching: they should love those men as themselves. He also gave them a piece of very practical advice: the teams should be mixed; they should have anarchists on both sides.

Palacios and his friends decided to follow his advice and a few days later joined the anarchists for their first football match. Palacios still remembers how he played goalkeeper and had two anarchist full backs: "I have never played such a gentlemanly and non-violent game of football," he commented. "Traditionalists and anarchists together! What a combination!"

Although I cannot say for sure that he formed part of this group, José Manuel Doménech de Ibarra was also imprisoned on 10 August 1932. He tells of Don Josemaría's concern for his interior life while completely disregarding any political considerations. It was either on August 11th or 12th that a prison officer gave José Manuel a parcel through the small peep hole of his cell door. The parcel contained a "Little Office of Our Lady", with the following dedication: *Beata Mater et intacta Virgo, gloriosa Regina Mundi, intercede pro hispanis ad Dominum.*

For José M. Doménech, with much affection.
Madrid, August, 1932

The Founder of Opus Dei must have gone to a lot of trouble to get the parcel to him, because it was not easy to send things to the prisoners in solitary confinement, and even less to get a prison officer to take it. José Manuel Doménech writes: "It made a deep impression when I realised the Father's affection and his concern for my interior life. He was aware that I knew and recited the Little Office, and he did not want me to abandon my devotions in those moments of anxiety and tribulation. I was naturally very grateful and recited those prayers with piety during those days." This story is all the more remarkable if one bears in mind that the Little Office was not one of the devotions that the Founder of Opus Dei recommended.

Another who was taken prisoner in August 1932 was Vicente Hernando Bocos. In those times of hard political struggle, he acknowledges that he advocated the use of violence. He did not let himself be convinced by Don Josemaría, who encouraged him to defend his policies with constancy and tenacity, but without hurting anyone. He stuck to his own policy of "hitting out regardless". The advice the Father gave was priestly, not political. Vicente Hernando expressly states: "Don Josemaría never discriminated against anyone on account of his political or social opinions. He respected personal freedom in all matters."

These incidents show that for the Founder of Opus Dei respect for political freedom did not mean "indifference" or lack of concern. He felt social problems keenly — like any other conscientious citizen would — but he believed it was not his mission to solve them. In this, as in everything else, he taught the doctrines of the Church clearly and was precise in pointing out doctrinal error. In this way he helped the souls of those who tackled, whether successfully or not, these problems (which were essentially civil matters) and he formed their consciences well, so that each individual would be able to sanctify himself through his efforts to make society more humane and just.

The following words, spoken in 1967 on the campus of the University of Navarre, are a brief summary of his preaching since 1928:

A man who knows that the world, and not just the church, is the place where he finds Christ, loves that world. He endeavours to become properly trained, intellectually and professionally. He makes up his own mind with complete freedom about the problems of the environment in which he moves, and he takes his own decisions in consequence. As the decisions of a Christian, they derive from personal reflection, which endeavours in all humility to grasp the will of God in both the unimportant and the important events of his life.

José Luis Múzquiz first heard of Opus Dei in 1934, through an acquaintance of his called Laureano who used to help Don Josemaría in the Porta Coeli Orphanage. Laureano arranged an appointment at the residence at 50 Ferraz Street, towards the end of 1934 or in January 1935. José Luis went along with "a certain curiosity to know what this foundation Laureano had talked to me about was, and wondering what that priest would think about the current political situation, the different parties and political figures who were prominent at the time", because, he adds, it was normal in that turbulent pre-war era for priests to express their political opinions. Much to his surprise however, Don Josemaría talked to him from the very beginning in a supernatural, priestly and apostolic tone. In spite of that José Luis Múzquiz asked him what he thought of a well known political leader for whom he then had a certain admiration. The Founder of Opus Dei immediately answered that no one there was ever asked about his politics and that people of all tendencies came to the residence. He added: **Yesterday the President and Secretary of the Basque National Students' Association were here.** To clarify the point further, he added with a smile: **On the other hand you will be asked many other "awkward" questions. You will be asked if you pray, if you make good use of your time, if you keep your parents happy, if you study, because for a student studying is a serious obligation.**

What Don Ricardo Fernández Vallespín remembers of his first personal conversation with Don Josemaría on 29 May 1933 is very similar: "He talked to me about things of the soul, not about political problems. He gave me advice. He encouraged me to be better." Some time later Fernández Vallespín asked to join the Work: "With infinite patience, he helped us enter upon the spiritual life. He never spoke to us about politics, but he said a lot about our duty to be saints in the middle of the world."

Public life in Spain was becoming more and more complicated. According to a well known historian, "politics got socialised" during the Second Republic, for the first time in Spanish history. The whole country talked and lived politics. Nevertheless Don Josemaría went against the prevailing trend and remained faithful to his priestly vocation: he talked only about God. His attitude offered such a contrast that it became a differentiating factor. The Founder of Opus Dei stood out as a priest who was not *trabucaire*, that is, he did not get involved in politics. As we have already seen, this was how he was introduced to Dr. Canales Maeso in the Princesa Hospital early in 1933.

In June 1975, in the Valencia daily *Las Provincias*, Aurelio Mota related his journey to Madrid with some university students from Valencia in the year 1935–36. They were worried about the way things were going in Spain and wanted to consult Don Josemaría, on account of his profound knowledge of the student world and his reputation for prudence and discretion.

Although the problems they put to him were a mixture of political and religious affairs, Aurelio Mota emphasises that Don Josemaría carefully "distinguished the respective fields and clarified that his mission was purely spiritual, and that as a priest he had nothing to say about political matters". He certainly indicated what points in the ideologies of some groups were contrary to the Church's doctrine, but to do so was to speak about religion, not about politics. He repeatedly said that "he was interested in souls, and that other matters were up to the laymen".

Even at the risk of being repetitive, I feel it is worth insisting on this point. He was not indifferent, but he was very determined to avoid **bad clericalism** at all costs. For that reason, the Founder of Opus Dei restricted himself to forming the consciences of Christians to help them become more aware of their responsibilities before God and men, and then act on their own account and not as the *longa manus* (the long arm) of the ecclesiastical Hierarchy or of some priest.

He explained all this very clearly once again when, many years later, he was answering questions in Buenos Aires:

"What can I do to make our friends understand that the most important thing is to get to know God, to be aware of God, and that they shouldn't worry so much about other things . . . such as politics. . . . ?"

Well, you can't tell them not to be concerned about politics. Because some people, precisely because they love God, do make politics their concern: but not me! That's not my subject, but it's my view that there should be people involved in it who are very honest: some leaning to the right, others to the left, others leaning that way, and none of them is wrong, they are all men of good will. I would not tell them to leave politics. What I can and should advise is that they shouldn't make personal attacks. Let them defend their programme without offending anybody personally; and this refers both to present-

day personalities and to those who belong to the immediate past. If not, there will never be any decent person in a country who is prepared to make the sacrifice necessary to be a leader. For he will think: "If afterwards this fails, they will not only take it out on me, but also on my children and on my family and on everybody else." And there follows one persecution after another. It becomes a madhouse!

So certainly, let good men be concerned with politics if they want to. I know I am not answering your question exactly, because you have just quoted that as an example. But you have given me an opportunity of reminding you that there should be no hatred. We should be concerned about the things of this world. You and I can turn our hand to anything, except what is intrinsically evil. So, with all that is good or indifferent, there's no reason why we shouldn't do as King Midas did: turn everything into gold. Is that clear?

That same day another person who worked for television wanted an answer to some doubts he had about how to use the mass media in an apostolic way.

My son, there are many specialists in that matter. So don't ask me professional things. You know much more than I do about them. I can talk to you about your apostolic zeal, about your desire to pass on to other souls the Love you have for Christ. But as to the specific way ... you are the experts, why should I get involved in that? I don't like it. We priests should not talk about professional matters, which we probably don't understand, and in any case, it's not our job.

I can advise you to have more concern and a greater hunger for souls; and I will insist that you spend more time in prayer, that you make many acts of Love and of atonement; and that you be very good at your job. But as to the way you go about your work, that's your business. What would you say if I started now, here, to deal with sociology or politics ... ? You would have to feel sorry for me. You would think: "The Father has gone mad. He is not speaking to us about God."

Don Alvaro del Portillo came up to him — it was nearly twelve o'clock — and before praying the Angelus, Msgr. Escrivá de Balaguer added:

Don Alvaro has asked me to repeat that this is the only thing I can tell you, because each one of you should make up

his own mind on temporal matters. There's no need for you to think the same as the others do. Many diverse opinions can be good, noble and self-sacrificing solutions, and they all deserve respect. There are no dogmas in temporal affairs: only in religion.

Those were the clear unequivocal principles that he always pro-claimed, quite independently from the events that took place in his life time. At the end of his life he was teaching the same ideas he had taught in 1930 and 1940.

As is well known, Spain in 1939 witnessed the consolidation of a changed attitude towards the Church on the part of the civil authorities and this was reflected in many speeches and public displays, but the Founder of Opus Dei who had kept quietly in his place years before, did not change his position because the wind was now blowing in a different direction.

The meditation he gave in the student residence of Jenner on the last Sunday of October 1939, the Feast of Christ the King, deeply impressed one of those present on account of the priestly way in which, after referring to the noble and patriotic aspirations of the people, he passed on immediately to speak of a much greater Kingdom, the Kingdom of Christ, which has no end. The question he put to each one of those present went very deep: **If Christ is to reign in the world, he must first reign in your heart. Does he really? Is your heart for Jesus Christ?**

This spirit was not only in his preaching. Everything about that students' residence spoke of freedom. Vicente Mortes arrived in Madrid in the early days of September 1940. He was looking for accommoda-tion and was going to study civil engineering. He had been told in Valencia about the residence by Fr. Eladio España, the rector of Corpus Christi College, who gave spiritual guidance to many young people. Vicente Mortes went along to Jenner with his father. They greeted the priest who welcomed them. He looked strong and approachable. They sat down and Vicente's father began to speak. He said that Vicente was his only son and it would be his first time living away from home. Vicente had been a good pupil at the Piarist School in Valencia and he was afraid that his son might "lose his way" in the big city. He therefore wanted to leave him in a place where there would be no danger; where his comings and goings would be controlled; where, in other words, he would be carefully supervised. . . .

Don Josemaría interrupted and explained that in this residence nobody supervised anybody else. They simply tried to help everyone to be good Christians and good citizens, free men who would know how to make up their now minds and bear the responsibility of their own actions. . . .

At first Vicente's father was quite put out, but they went on chatting and he began to understand that the priest was right: vigilance was of no use if a personal sense of responsibility was lacking.

The clear message of the Founder of Opus Dei was sometimes misunderstood at first by people who, though very good, were not able to grasp its novelty and *originality* and tried to fit it into old moulds. Such was the case, for instance, of Don Manuel García Morente. One day when Víctor García Hoz had gone to Diego de León to see Don Josemaría he was asked to wait a little, because there was another visitor with him. It was Don Manuel García Morente, professor of philosophy in Madrid University. He had at one time drifted away from religion, but had later returned and had become a priest. Don Manuel García Morente wanted to find out about Opus Dei and had been talking to its Founder. To summarise his impressions, Morente said: "So Opus Dei is like a Catholic *Institución Libre de Enseñanza.*" When Don Josemaría received Víctor García Hoz, he remarked in passing that it was a pity that a man as good and clever as Don Manuel could only conceive the Work in the framework of a political-educational institution.

García Morente got to know and love the Work well, after a series of conversations; but some people who were not so good or so clever, and who perhaps had not bothered to speak to anyone about Opus Dei, would repeat over the years that the Work was a sort of *anti-Institución Libre de Enseñanza*. They did not realise that this approach was radically opposed to the positive spirit of Opus Dei. The Work was never anti-anything or anti-anybody. Furthermore, a fundamental fact was missing: the Founder's careful and effective respect for the freedom of action of the members in political, social or cultural matters.

Nobody who had the university at heart could be unaware of the influence wielded by this Institute in the twenties and thirties. The Founder of Opus Dei, who dealt with many students and around that time, knew the situation well and, according to Dr. Jiménez Vargas, he referred to it occasionally in the 1932–33 period, but he always left it very clear that the solution to the issues in question was the responsibility of those who were involved in university education. His attitude was so transparent that "no person in good faith who had heard him say something about this matter could ever have thought that the Work had arisen in opposition to the *Institución Libre de Enseñanza*".

In the thirties and forties, when the members of Opus Dei were young, the Founder's careful respect for their professional freedom had necessarily to be heroic, for they would frequently discuss subjects in which he was very well informed: for instance, university, legal, artistic or historical matters. However, he always preferred to run the **risk of freedom.**

This same spirit is also found in the way the apostolic works undertaken by Opus Dei are run. It is a well known fact that these activities have a supernatural purpose; but they are organised and directed with a **lay mentality,** that is to say, by people for whom that task is their own professional work. That is why these works are not confessional or denominational; nor do they follow a fixed pattern. They arise from the social needs of a region, the circumstances of a particular area, or from the opportunities offered in each case by the relevant civil legislation.

The Founder of Opus Dei gave plenty of criteria for these apo-stolates by word and in writing. Such indications referred both to the basic principles (which ensured their apostolic character) and also to specific aspects of their organisation or practical viability, for he felt the urge to transmit all his experience, even down to the smallest details, so that others might use it with personal responsibility. The principles underlying the running of Opus Dei — decentralisation, collegiality, autonomy — made it possible for decisions to be taken as often as possible at the local level. Thus apostolic works arose in many parts of the world as the result of the same christian inspiration, but carried out in the most varied ways and by very different people.

Shortly after 1950, when the work of Opus Dei was beginning in the United States, a project was started in Boston to increase apostolic work at university level in that famous university city (the home of Harvard University and M.I.T.). This initiative aroused interest among many people who were not of Opus Dei, but who were ready to help. A Patrons' Committee was set up to channel their assistance and pro-mote further aid. It was made up of people of the most varied political tendencies, such as the Republican Governor of the State of Massa-chusetts, Mr. Volpe; Mr. Fitzgerald, one of the leaders of the Demo-cratic Party in Boston; and Mr. Richardson, a Republican, who was Vice-Governor of the State and not a Catholic.

The same appreciation for the open spirit of Opus Dei was seen in

London, when Netherhall House was planning its new buildings as a means of extending its work with overseas students. The president of the Netherhall Development Committee was Bernard Audley, who was not a Catholic, and among its members there were people of the most varied and indeed opposite tendencies. One day, some of the members of the committee were meeting in a private room of the Houses of Parliament in Westminster. When they were studying the different ways of helping Netherhall, a division bell rang. Among those present there were some Members of Parliament, from both the Conservative and Labour parties, who were on the Netherhall committee. One of them instinctively got up, but another suggested: "Let's carry on with Netherhall House, we are paired and our absence will not affect the result of the voting"; and they continued with the Residence project.

With the personal initiatives of members of the Work, the Founder of Opus Dei respected and fostered freedom with all the more reason. Joaquín Herreros Robles, the President of EFA (Family Schools for Agricultural workers in Spain) was speaking with Msgr. Escrivá de Balaguer one morning in November 1972 at Pozoalbero (Jerez) and at a given moment of their conversation the Father said, more or less:

With your personal work, my son, and with your personal responsibility, you are going to carry out a considerable work of christian training in the countryside, which will also have an important professional, social and even political character. But don't let it ever be a one-party approach!

Joaquín Herreros attempted to explain that the EFA schools would never dream of getting affiliated or forming part of a political party: they were something totally different. But before he could continue the Founder of Opus Dei said quite firmly:

No my son, if you think differently, there is no need to explain. . . .

Joaquín Herreros, agreeing, said nothing in reply. "I guessed that the Father understood perfectly well what I was going to say and if he did not permit me to speak, it was only to show me how fully he respected my freedom."

The Founder of Opus Dei practised this high regard for freedom to a heroic degree. He did so both in easy and in difficult times. It must have been particularly difficult — only a brief sketch has been attempted here — during the turbulent times prior to the war in Spain, and the years immediately after it. In both those periods it was generally taken for granted that certain political attitudes were linked to the cause of religion. To disagree with this could appear to imply that one did not love the Gospel and was not a faithful son of the Church. (This tendency has appeared again with a vengeance in the seventies — it is proposed at times in harsh and uncompromising terms — and has led to further misunderstandings about the spirit of Opus Dei. Some people cannot bring themselves to understand that the defence of freedom does not imply indifference towards human problems, or lack of unity among Catholics, but that it stems from faithfulness both to the principle of autonomy in the temporal order and to the message of Christ.)

The proclamation of pluralism among Catholics in the first years of Opus Dei was for many an unintelligible novelty, because they had been brought up to think just the opposite. The Second Vatican Council would later declare unequivocally the traditional doctrine of the Church which seemed to have been forgotten. In the Constitution *Gaudium et Spes*, no. 43, we read: "No one is allowed to appropriate the authority of the Church for his opinion." Nevertheless, even today, this doctrine which already belongs to the common heritage of the Church has not percolated through completely to the practical level.

One can understand the surprise of Msgr. Escrivá de Balaguer and his "indignation" when someone from the Vatican Curia congratulated him in 1957 on the appointment of a member of Opus Dei, Alberto Ullastres, as a Minister in the Spanish Government: **What do I care if he is a minister or a road sweeper? What I care about is that he should sanctify himself in his work.**

In 1964 he was asked in the Gayarre Theatre in Pamplona:

"What stand do the members of Opus Dei take in public life?"

Msgr. Escrivá de Balaguer explained once more the freedom that exists in the Work, **always within Catholic doctrine;** but he began his answer with an instant retort: **Whatever they want.** The packed theatre gave him a resounding ovation.

CHAPTER NINE

THE FATHER OF A LARGE AND POOR FAMILY

1. Like a grain of mustard seed
2. A very poor person
3. The sacrifice of Abel

1. LIKE A GRAIN OF MUSTARD SEED

"More than sixty thousand people called him Father" was the title in *Il Giorno* of Milan on 26 July 1975 of Giuseppe Corigliano's article on Msgr. Escrivá de Balaguer who had died a month previously in Rome. A surprising phenomenon had taken place in the Church: at the death of a Founder his Work had spread to the five continents.

I have already mentioned in Chapter Five the worldwide vision which the Founder of Opus Dei had from the very beginning and how as early as 1935 he had set his heart on commencing apostolic work in Paris. The war in Spain and then the world war inevitably delayed expansion to other countries. When World War II ended the Founder had to devote special effort to securing legal recognition for the Work. The central offices of the Association which had been in Madrid were moved to Rome. From there in a short space of time apostolic work began in many countries.

It is not my purpose here to give a detailed account of the world-wide expansion of Opus Dei. I will simply point to some significant moments. What I wish to emphasise is the spirit with which Msgr. Escrivá set about spreading his apostolic zeal.

The first trips to Portugal had been made in 1940, although strictly speaking it was not until 1945 that the Association began stable work in that country. Something similar happened in Italy. In 1942 José Orlandis and Salvador Canals went to study in Rome. The real development, however, began in 1946 when Don Alvaro del Portillo was appointed Counsellor. Soon afterwards, the Founder of Opus Dei took up residence in Rome. That same year work started in England, and in 1947 in France and in Ireland. The plan for 1949 was to start apostolic work in one American country. In the end it began in two, Mexico and the United States. In 1950 work started in Argentina and Chile.

In those years part of the central government of Opus Dei — the General Council in the Men's Section and the Central Advisory in the Women's Section — was already in Rome and gradually the necessary buildings were prepared. At first the same buildings also housed the Roman College of the Holy Cross (1948) and the Roman College of Holy Mary (1953) which from Rome gave a boost to the activities of formation of the members of both Sections of Opus Dei, with a view to the requirements of worldwide development.

Necessarily almost all the people who started the Work of the Association in so many countries came from Spain. 1951 marked the first arrivals in Venezuela and in Colombia. 1953, in Peru, Germany and Guatemala. 1954 in Ecuador. Shortly before then, in 1952, Ismael Sánchez Bella returned to Spain from Argentina to set up the future University of Navarre.

From Rome Msgr. Escrivá de Balaguer followed the progress of Opus Dei all over the world with unlimited confidence in God. From 1946 onwards he had made periodic trips to Spain and Portugal and had also visited many cities in Italy and other European countries, as part of the **prehistory** of the apostolic work there. In 1955 he undertook another long trip through much of Europe to encourage those who were already working in several countries and to lay the foundations for the future work in others. He passed through Germany, France, Switzerland, Holland, Belgium and Austria. In Austria, he brought a new aspiration into his interior life. He began praying to Our Lady, *Sancta Maria, Stella Orientis, filios tuos adiuva!* after having said Mass at the altar of Hl. Marie Pötsch in the Cathedral of Vienna, on 3 December of that year.

After the final Papal approval in 1950, the Association held a General Congress in the Molinoviejo Conference Centre in Spain. In 1956 another such congress was held in Einsiedeln, Switzerland. The Work continued to grow. In that very year, 1956, it went to Uruguay;

in 1957, to Brazil and Austria, and apostolic activity began in Yauyos, Peru, whose Prelature *Nullius* had been entrusted to Opus Dei by the Holy See. Work began soon afterwards in Africa (Kenya) in 1958, and in Asia (Japan) in 1959. Then there was Australia in 1963 and the Philippines in 1964.

This expansion often brought to the mind and heart of the Founder of Opus Dei the Gospel parable of the grain of mustard seed, that small seed which grows up into a tree where the birds of heaven may come and settle:

I alone know how we have started. In human terms we had nothing. Nothing but the grace of God. But once again the parable has been fulfilled; and we should fill ourselves with gratitude to God Our Lord.

The little seed which God had sown on 2 October 1928 had germinated. The newly-born plant had overcome many obstacles. On more than one occasion, humbly forgetting himself, the Founder of Opus Dei was to say that the Work had been built upon the holy lives of the first members: **With their constant smile, with prayer, with work, with silence: that is how Opus Dei has been built up. Opus Dei which has also experienced its silent but marvellous cross and resurrection.**

The bush grew into a big tree, because God strengthened its roots and spread its branches. It was to him that Msgr. Escrivá de Balaguer gave thanks for the fact that in Opus Dei, **as in a new Pentecost, one hears diverse tongues, which manifest the Spirit of God and the catholicity of our spirit.**

And what of the means?, he asked himself in 1934 in *Consideraciones espirituales*. The answer came unequivocally: **They are the same as those of Peter and of Paul, of Dominic and Francis, of Ignatius and Xavier: the Cross and the Gospel. Don't they satisfy you?** The only requirement to spread the Kingdom of God is to trust fully in God's omnipotence and to live a life of faith and hope and love: "Take nothing with you to use on your journey, staff, or wallet, or bread, or money. You are not to have more than one coat apiece" (Luke 9: 3). On one occasion Jesus sends his disciples out just like that, with nothing, so that they may realise clearly that success is not due to them. Thus it was clear that neither conversions, nor miracles, nor people's acceptance of the doctrine they preach, are due to their personal qualities.

Opus Dei too began without human means, placing all its reliance upon supernatural means: **because in these early days,** the Founder wrote in 1941, **just as the Lord sent out his disciples, I too send my sons to begin new works of apostolate: I send them out as poor as the first disciples were, with a blessing which the Lord gives them from heaven and which I give them here on earth.**

So it was to continue for a good many years. When Fr. José Luis Múzquiz and Salvador Martínez Ferigle went to the United States in 1949 they took with them the blessing of the Founder and a picture of the Blessed Virgin which had been in one of the houses in which he lived in Burgos: **I can give you nothing else, my sons.**

It might be fairer to think that for the Founder of Opus Dei, more important than not having material means — he had been used to that since 1928 — was having to do without the close cooperation of people who were mature in the spirit of the Work. From 1950 onwards those who might have been his direct collaborators were sent to one country or another. Indeed Msgr. Escrivá de Balaguer could comment justly that he was left **all alone:** but it was worth while. The Founder of Opus Dei was convinced that such generous sowing of the seed all over the world would give much glory to God. Don Alvaro del Portillo, the person who had been closest to him since 1939, would continue at his side in Rome, where he had lived since 1946, as Procurator General and first Regional Counsellor of Italy.

In those years, when the needs of expansion meant the departure from Spain of members of Opus Dei of unquestionable talent and distinguished professional qualifications (it would not be right to quote names) one of those who stayed behind, and has since died, commented at the time: "we who are left are like the cast-offs." If Florentino Pérez-Embid, the author of these words, a professor of history, a brilliant and prolific writer who was very well known in the public life of Spain, could consider himself a "cast-off", the human and spiritual qualities of those whom the Founder sent all over the world must indeed have been considerable.

Many were very young, but they had matured in the crucible of the **opposition of the good** to which I have referred in the previous Chapter. Msgr. Escrivá de Balaguer was to underline the fact in a letter to the members of Opus Dei: **Where I come from they pierce the unripe figs, which thus get filled with sweetness and ripen sooner. God Our Lord, wishing to make us more fruitful, has blessed us with the Cross.**

In 1971 he emphasised the same idea: **Do you know why the Work has developed so much? Because they have treated it like a sack of corn; it's been beaten and battered about. But the seeds are so small that they haven't broken. On the contrary, they've been scattered to the four winds; they've landed wherever there have been hearts hungry and ready for the truth. And now we have so many vocations and we are a very large family, and there are millions of souls who admire and love the Work because they see in it a sign of God's presence among men, and recognise the inexhaustible riches of his mercy.**

Difficulties have had the effect of producing **what happens when obstacles are put in the way of the workings of God. Birds and insects, with their voraciousness, whilst causing damage to plants, also perform a very fruitful task. They carry the seed far away, stuck to their legs. In this way God made us arrive in places which we might otherwise not have reached so soon — through suffering defamation. The seed is never lost.**

The supernatural magnanimity of Msgr. Escrivá de Balaguer went hand in hand with his human temperament; but his awareness of the broad apostolic objectives was not the result of his character but of his complete assurance that God was helping him:

The Work has been poor from the start and will always be so, because Our Lord will never cease to ask us for more apostolic work, for more initiatives, for more expenditure of money and of people. We will never have enough money to spread the Work as fast as God wants us to. They are calling us from so many places, and through lack of financial resources we cannot go immediately! (...) But I take this opportunity to thank God Our Lord, because the Work will always be poor: it will always need more than it has, if it is to fulfil its apostolic purpose, no matter how abundant our means may appear to others.

He was never daunted by financial difficulties, neither in the early days when he started that first Academy in Luchana Street in Madrid nor, later on, when the apostolic undertakings fostered by Opus Dei had spread all over the world. His only motivation was the glory of God and therefore he did not sit back when he had one instrument for the apostolate. He was immediately thinking of another one, that might be a new way to spread the message of the Gospel. He illustrated this, half jokingly, in December 1973:

Do you remember how some days ago we were saying that there will always be privation and real poverty in the Work? And I was telling you that there will always be Centres where the people humanly speaking are having a rough time. Well, the day before yesterday, I received a letter from a son of mine who is in a big country, where he is a university professor. He has told me very cheerfully that they already have a house, in a central part of the city. It's a nice house, but they haven't got a stick of furniture, not even a bed. He was telling me they are camping inside the house, they eat where they can, and they are really happy.

He was specially glad to hear that they were praying and working and doing a lot of apostolate in the midst of financial difficulties. Since the same thing was happening in many places, he pointed out: **it's good that it should happen.**

A decisive chapter in this human and divine adventure of Opus Dei is taken up by the Roman College of the Holy Cross. It is worth going into, because it shows how the Founder worked to spread the Work all over the world.

The Roman College was set up on 29 June 1948. It began in the Parioli district in Rome, in an old building which had been the Hungarian Legation to the Holy See. Obtaining that house was a real act of daring, because there was no money. **They want payment in Swiss francs,** Msgr. Escrivá de Balaguer commented at the time. **Since we haven't got a penny, what does it matter to Our Lord? He can as easily get us Swiss francs as Italian lire!** Then some people turned up who were ready to buy the house and finance the necessary building, not only for the Roman College — a centre of formation for members of Opus Dei from all over the world — but also for the central offices of the Work.

Don Alvaro del Portillo was directly concerned with the financial side of all this and he did it all despite being ill and running a high temperature. Msgr. Escrivá de Balaguer used to say jokingly, that the best way to nurse Don Alvaro back to health would be to apply a **hot poultice** of several thousand dollars.

The privations experienced by the Founder of Opus Dei and those about him were constant. The students of the College went to the universities and athenaeums of Rome on foot because they could not afford the bus fare, and as there was no money to buy even the cheapest Italian cigarettes many gave up smoking. Years later when the discomfort was still there, but the toughest moments had passed, Msgr. Escrivá de Balaguer encouraged them:

Accept these extraordinary circumstances as a sacrifice that you can offer to Our Lord and don't forget that there were times when we were much more uncomfortable than you are now. The difficulties you may find now are nothing compared with those we have lived with for many years. (...) When we began there were times when we ate only once a day, and that only when it was possible.

There was not even a proper place to sleep here. We had just one bed, which was used by whoever was sick. The rest of us just lay down where we could, down there, in the porter's lodge which has since been pulled down. For a good number of years, I used to go in and out of scaffolding at night to sleep in a room as best I could. We have never been well off.

Here is a story which reflects the shortage of money. A Lambretta was bought in 1951 to do many and varied jobs related to the building works. It was used so much that soon it needed to be replaced. The mother of one of the students gave the money, but that money had to be used instead to pay some suppliers and the old Lambretta kept on going through the streets of Rome for another four years.

Despite the pressures and the fact that people were needed everywhere to develop the apostolates, **we were always trying,** the Founder of Opus Dei pointed out, **to bring more people to the Roman College, as many as possible, because it was necessary: for the glory of God, for the service of the Church, of souls and of the Work, and so that (...) you could learn to love other countries, to see the good things and also the defects which exist in other countries, as they exist in our own. It was also necessary in order to enable people to acquire the good spirit of the Work.**

At the same time the students of the Roman College were studying in the Pontifical Universities to obtain the degrees stipulated by the Founder. The first doctoral thesis was that of Don Alvaro del Portillo. Over the years hundreds of doctoral theses came to be written by the students of the Roman College of the Holy Cross: in theology, canon law and philosophy.

Hand in hand with academic work went manual work. The buildings needed decoration and maintenance. As well as attending classes and doing research, the students of the Roman College spent many hours painting and carrying sacks of cement. They were encouraged always by Msgr. Escrivá de Balaguer who, as one of them recalls: "corrects little details and he notices what we often overlook. He speaks to us and leaves us deeply impressed by his words, which are always timely and affectionate."

It is understandable that the Founder of Opus Dei could say of these walls that **they seem to be stone but really they are made of love.** In the midst of misunderstanding, of financial difficulties and countless discomforts which he bore cheerfully, Msgr. Escrivá de Balaguer did not neglect magnanimity which he practised even when material means were lacking. He wanted to leave to those who came after him an instrument which, both technically and aesthetically, would be suitable and lasting. The architecture of the building was rooted in the traditional values of Roman architecture so that from the very first moment it would blend into its traditional surroundings and would not run the risk of becoming old-fashioned or ridiculous within a few years of completion. At the same time the Founder of Opus Dei and Don Alvaro del Portillo used every opportunity to obtain at very low prices from builders' yards, second-hand stores and the like, countless objects which served admirably for the decoration of these buildings: furniture, old stones, ancient Roman fragments, capitals, mouldings, busts, little sculptures, pictures, candlesticks, lamps, carpets, chests and so on.

Msgr. Escrivá de Balaguer often looked round the works and the builders soon got used to seeing *Monsignore* going up and down the scaffolding and ladders. As soon as a particular area was completed, the students of the Roman College immediately went in to finish it down to the smallest details and to give everything a thorough cleaning. It was this care in finishing things off — a task carried out especially by the members of the Women's Section of Opus Dei who were looking after the domestic administration — which made it possible for those buildings, in which hundreds of people were to live, never to lose their family character, that welcoming and cheerful environment which is proper to the spirit of Opus Dei.

The story of the building of the Roman College enshrines countless practical lessons for the members of the Work. These lessons were not missed by those who visited the house and, as Cardinal Baggio observed, visitors noticed that this building had nothing in common with conventional ecclesiastical establishments. It was a building which fitted in naturally with the others of the Parioli district. Everything was clean and cared for. That style ("I was not expecting it at all", the

Cardinal admits) was part of the lay spirituality of Opus Dei. It was a real novelty and was to give rise to misunderstandings. The Founder of Opus Dei was often obliged to point out — as he had done so often in the past — that there was a radical difference between poverty and dirt.

Something similar happened when he wanted to bless the **last stone** of that house. Everyone knew that he liked to see a job finished, and that he preferred last stones to first stones. The moment came, on 9 January 1960, and he went to find the appropriate prayer in the Roman Ritual but he could not find any prayers for such an occasion. **So,** he decided, **we are going to do something else. I will begin by making the sign of the Cross, we'll pray a** Te Deum **and then a prayer of thanksgiving, and finally the blessing** signo crucis; **and that's it.**

So by 1960, the dream that the Founder of Opus Dei had been cherishing since the end of the forties had come true:

From here, from the Roman College, hundreds — thousands — of priests and laymen will go out to further the Work where it is already being carried out; and they will start it in many other countries that are awaiting us; and they will set up Centres of formation for men of all nations and races to serve the Church.

Nevertheless, the principal purpose of those buildings was to serve as the central offices of the Work. No sooner were they complete, than the Founder of Opus Dei was planning to embark on a new adventure: the building of the definitive Roman College in another part of Rome. He said it would be **the last folly** of his life:

Everywhere in the world we have begun to set up instruments to work with, without any money. I have done it myself previously on many occasions. But I had made a resolution many years ago not to do it again. Nevertheless, realising that it is desirable for the good of the Church and the good of the Work in its service to the Church and to souls, that many of my sons should pass through Rome, we have started building with just a few lire. I did not want to repeat this folly, but we are at it again.

Such behaviour gave rise to differing reactions. There were some, including ecclesiastics, who did not understand. Some were scandalised, as if Opus Dei were the first institution in the history of the Church to have used noble human means to further its apostolic aims.

No one can be surprised, the Founder had written in 1954, **that Opus Dei should need material means for its work. Since it carries out its supernatural task of sanctification among men and for men, it must use a minimum of material means just as all other associations without exception have done, no matter what kind of association they may be: artistic, sporting, cultural, religious, etc.**

He had foreseen the problem when he commented in 1941: **Naturally, the more the Work spreads, the greater will be our need of material means, means which we shall always try to sanctify. There is no one on earth, however noble his aims, who gets things done without using human means.**

Jesus Christ himself used material things to fulfil his divine mission, things such as the possessions of the poor people who followed him, a few loaves and fishes, a bit of clay, etc. They lent him a small donkey for his entry into Jerusalem; he borrowed a room to celebrate his last Paschal feast on earth. . . .

It is the life of Christ that the Founder of Opus Dei wished to imitate. To get his apostolic projects under way he counted on the work of the members of Opus Dei, but he also relied on the help of many other people who saw that these apostolates deserved their support, because they were for the benefit of mankind.

In 1950, when the Association was growing and the financial difficulties caused by this expansion were multiple, he stressed that neither Opus Dei nor its members **need money, because each one works at his professional task and more than earns his keep. But as regards our corporate works, the more we are helped the better we can serve souls.**

This financial cooperation has always been channelled in a normal secular way. The apostolic works of Opus Dei are Centres set up by ordinary citizens, who use them to carry out, freely, their own professional activities. So they are not "Catholic" works, still less "ecclesiastical" works, though in them the doctrine of the Church is followed faithfully. They are set up and run with a **lay mentality,** in accordance with the laws of each country, without privilege of any kind, financial or otherwise. They solve their own problems and are answerable to the appropriate legal entities established in each country, as for instance, to the proprietors of the buildings or installations, if these have been leased or rented.

This lay character of the apostolic undertakings of Opus Dei (which are not confessional nor ecclesiastic) also explains why co-operators who are not Catholics also lend a hand, as was mentioned in Chapter Eight. Experience shows that they also derive great spiritual benefit, as the Founder was quick to explain: **When we ask these people to contribute financially or with their professional work to serve the apostolic undertakings we run — undertakings which are also always humanly useful — we are bringing them into the very heart of our activity and are giving them an opportunity to be an arm of God to carry out his Work among men.**

One day in 1972 an American was telling Msgr. Escrivá de Balaguer in Rome that they had been given a flat in San Francisco, so that christian formation classes would be organised there. The Founder of Opus Dei reaffirmed:

We could not do a thing without the help of so many wonderful people. There are some who have such a marvellous supernatural outlook when they help in the things of God that they set just one condition to their generous cooperation: that it should not be known that they have given even a cent. Sometimes they are people whom I do not know.

He often quoted the Gospel passage of the widow's mite, as he gratefully reflected on the help Opus Dei received from people of very modest means:

Perhaps their constant effort is more disinterested and liberal than all the others put together. Certainly they are not giving from what they have to spare, because they haven't anything to spare. I am certain that, on seeing such gifts, Our Lord's eyes will light up once more with divine affection.

On another occasion he described the great variety of ways of helping the apostolic activities of the Association:

Your own generous conduct has been my teacher: from that aristocrat both by birth and in spirit, who handed over her own mansion in times of slander and persecution, down to the most humble peasants, the parents of a young servant girl, who sell their donkey and cheerfully send the money; from that good friend in South America who, in agreement with his family, has taken on one of our apostolic works as a partner in his business — a partner who does not share in the losses —, down to little children (...) who send the money they have received as a present on their First Communion Day; from the

person who sends furniture to set up house, to the person who pays all the expenses of the poor car which is indispensable for the work of apostolate.

Nothing is sufficient, however, when it is a question not only of keeping up what has already been started, but also of opening up new apostolic horizons to reach more souls. Therefore, the members' sense of responsibility leads them to work many hours each day, feeling what they have learned from the Founder: **the urgent needs, economic as well, of this supernatural family to which we belong.** No one feels exempt from this duty which is inseparable from his own vocation:

The fully secular character of our dedication to God in the world means that professional work is also the ordinary means of getting the necessary money to sustain ourselves and the apostolic works of Opus Dei.

Msgr. Escrivá de Balaguer trusted in supernatural means: everything, he knew, depends on God. At the same time, he did not neglect any licit human source, especially work, because, as he explained, **we cannot tempt God, demanding that he do miracles when we can and should use our noble, honest professional work to obtain the financial resources we need.**

So it was prayer, work and the help of many people, which made it possible to build up this great mosaic of apostolic initiatives throughout the world. Zeal to draw more people towards God is a guarantee of detachment from material goods: **We will always be poor. We will never have sufficient financial means to cover all our needs, because, thanks to God, however hard we work, the apostolates will always grow faster and this will always be the case.**

The Founder compared the Work to a large and poor family. Each one of the members was to feel in his very flesh the financial pressures of a large family which never quite gets out of difficulties and yet is not deterred from doing what it should, for the benefit of souls. He began to invoke St. Nichólas of Bari's aid in solving money problems back in the thirties when he was carrying out his priestly ministry in the Patronato of Santa Isabel:

I was going to celebrate Mass and I had some tremendous financial problems. As St. Nicholas is the saint for financial difficulties, and the saint for marrying the unmarriable, I said to him: "If you get me out of this one, I will appoint you Inter-

cessor!" But before going up to the altar I repented and added: "And even if you don't, I'll appoint you just the same."

He was telling this on Palm Sunday in 1968, and someone ventured to ask him if that particular problem had been solved. Msgr. Escrivá de Balaguer went on.

Where would you and I be, if it hadn't been! Living in a tent or an old tin shack. But I am not looking for miraculous things. The first thing I ask is that we work, and that we earn our keep with our work and, when we can't make ends meet, we ask Our Lord to help us to manage. I am not a charismatic. We have to use the human means, and at the same time the supernatural ones; they always go hand in hand.

That was how the DYA Academy went ahead and then the first residences for university students and, later on, the hundreds of apostolic undertakings set up by Opus Dei, all of them seeking to provide a christian service to society and to be instruments to co-redeem with Christ.

2. A VERY POOR PERSON

The Founder of Opus Dei always saw the lack of material means as a special sign of God's love. On one occasion he was giving a meditation to a group of members of the Work and he brought to their consideration the Gospel passage of the rich young man:

"Sell what thou hast and give it to the poor. . . ." You see, my sons: detachment is of capital importance. You and I have not behaved like that poor young man: his ille auditis contristatus est, quia dives erat valde (Luke 18:23) "he, hearing all this was saddened because he was very rich". We have all of us left whatever we had, and have done so gladly, in order to follow Our Lord freely. It's all the same whether it was much or little, because we have abandoned it all with the same thoroughness: what we had and what people who have a marvellous youthfulness like yourselves might have had. We've done so cheerfully, my sons. We do not want anything for ourselves. Say so, each one of you, to Our Lord: "My God, for your love I give you everything. I want nothing for myself. It is all for you."

He referred afterwards in that meditation to the answer Jesus

Christ gave to the disciples of John the Baptist: "Go and tell John what your eyes have witnessed: how the blind see, and the lame walk, the lepers are made clean and the deaf hear, the dead are raised to life and the poor have the Gospel preached to them" (Matt 11:4–5).

My sons you have heard what Our Lord is saying to us: his words move me deeply. So, we've to love detachment, we've to love it with our whole heart: because when the spirit of poverty begins to falter it is a sign that the whole interior life is going badly.

The Founder's detachment was real and effective, and he practised it down to the last consequences, but always with naturalness, and making light of it, because, as he taught: **Ours is a poverty which doesn't proclaim "I am poor": we savour it cheerfully. Our Lord makes it a joy to have nothing, to be unable to stretch our arm any further than our sleeve. We are to be poor and smiling. Our situation should pass unnoticed, both in health and in sickness.**

Nevertheless the lack of means was so real that, in spite of everything, it was noticed by those who were closest to him. It was always wrapped in a pleasing external form, which is what one would expect of someone who is carrying out his apostolic work among his equals, his fellow men, and who realises that detachment from material things is not the same as wretchedness, or dirt, or meanness.

It was a lesson he had learned in good measure at home. Opus Dei had not yet been born when already God was shaping its spirit in the one who was to be its Founder. One characteristic of this spirit is the lay mentality which throws light on how to practise all the christian virtues.

The Founder of Opus Dei spent his whole life lacking even the most necessary things and detached from everything. He did so with the greatest naturalness and without any ostentation. Vicente Hernando Bocos went one day to visit him at the residence in Larra Street in Madrid, because Don Josemaría had a heavy cold. His room was very plain. It had "a poor table, with some prayer books". Nevertheless, "Don Josemaría dressed elegantly, cleanly and correctly. His appearance was pleasant." This went hand in hand with his behaviour. "The impression I got was of a priest who enjoyed life; he was always in a good mood and very straightforward. I remember that there was already some slander against him at that time and that we stamped it out with determination."

In those days, when he devoted so many hours to the Patronato de Enfermos, the Founder of Opus Dei suffered a great deal seeing day after day the wretched conditions in which the poor of Madrid lived and died, but it did not make him forget that christian detachment goes beyond a pure lack of means. He stressed this in 1972 when he answered a question put to him in the IESE Business School in Barcelona:

The simple fact of dealing with or having money does not not mean that one is attached to riches. I will give you an example. I knew a pauper who used to go to an eating place run by a charitable organisation. He did not even have the card which was given to the needy. He came to receive a little of the left-overs. It was a difficult time for one who had a christian heart, seeing those people suffering real hunger. Each would bring his own bowl to eat from. His was broken. But then he would take out a pewter spoon, which he kept deep down in his pocket, and would look at it with satisfaction. The others had no spoon and clearly he was thinking: "This is mine, this is mine." And with that spoon he ate the chick peas and soup that he was given. Then he would take another look at his spoon, a passionate look like that of a miser contemplating his jewels, lick it a couple of times and put it away again. He was rich!

I also remember the case of a person whom I loved dearly and who is undoubtedly in heaven. She was a member of the Spanish nobility. Even though she is dead, I will mention only her christian name, because it is a name she shares with many: she was called Mary. Her home was full of splendid furniture. She had many servants, and a fine collection of silver ... everything you would expect to find in a noble mansion. Yet she, poor thing, spent less on herself than on the least of her servants. She gave everything away. I am a witness of her generosity.

Opus Dei would not have developed without the generosity of many souls. Of course, its Founder never confused trusting in God with an irresponsible "providentialism". In the difficult years of the DYA Academy, when he was planning to open a residence for students, he saw to it that detailed calculations were made of all possible expenses and sources of income. No doubt Isidoro Zorzano, when he came from Malaga to Madrid, gave some help in this financial planning, but it was Don Josemaría — surrounded as he was by the poor and the sick — who had to go about getting help from the people he knew in Madrid. What is certain is that he was not prepared to delay apostolic work because there was no money: it would come eventually.

Financial difficulties did not haunt him. He was scarcely managing with the Luchana flat, and he was already thinking of starting the student residence of Ferraz which began after the summer of 1934. He was able to provide a minimum of furniture and to buy the kitchenware with money from the sale of the family property in Fonz, Huesca. The bed linen was obtained on credit from Almacenes Simeón in Madrid. The director of the residence recalls that during that first year 1934–35 there was never enough money at the end of the month to pay the rent, nor the butchers, nor the grocery bills. Fortunately, Don Javier Bordiu who owned the house was always patient. It was Don Josemaría himself who went to see him about it each month.

During that year which was so full of financial pressures, the apostolate grew apace. The Founder of Opus Dei used **visits to the poor** as a way of forming the young students who came to Ferraz. Collections were made among the students who attended classes of christian formation. The money collected was taken by the students themselves on their visits to poor people. So to the pleasantness of their youthful company and conversation, they were able to add a little money and something to eat, as a little surprise. It was also a way of helping the students to become spiritually mature. Some of them had no notion whatsoever of the misery in which so many people in Madrid then lived.

These visits to the sick and needy are an inseparable part of Opus Dei's apostolic work all over the world. They have a deeply human and charitable purpose: to take a little cheer and tenderness to people who often have scarcely ever heard a loving word, nor received a friendly look, nor the brotherly gesture of christian help.

In 1942 the Founder of Opus Dei lamented: **Charity has been so disfigured and some of its external aspects so satirised that some people have come to consider certain works, which are proper to the christian spirit, as archaic. That is why I want you to understand well, and to get others to understand, the deep supernatural and human significance of these means when they are practised as we have done from the beginning.**

The purpose of such visits, then as now, is not to solve a social problem. They aim to bring young people to their neighbour who is in need, so that they may see **Jesus Christ in the poor, in the sick, in the infirm, in the lonely, in the sufferer, in the child.** That way they learn that **a great battle has to be waged against poverty, against ignorance, against disease, against suffering.** The Founder of Opus Dei saw clearly that **this contact with poverty or with human weakness is an occasion which Our Lord likes to make use of to enkindle in a soul desires of generosity and divine adventures. At the same time, it makes young people sensitive so that they may always harbour in their hearts a deep desire of justice and charity.**

At the same time, he rebelled against deformations of this virtue: **it is not fair that manifestations of genuine christian charity should be discarded, because some people have turned them into an ostentatious or frivolous gesture, or into a sedative for their feelings of remorse.**

This work was to be done even in the most developed countries, because there would always be sectors of the population who were neglected by the others:

I dare to say, he added with conviction in 1942, **that when social circumstances seem to have taken away misery, poverty or pain, precisely then the perceptiveness of christian charity becomes more urgent, this charity which discovers intuitively where there is a need for consolation in the midst of apparent general well-being.**

Nowadays most governments try to alleviate basic needs and bring about social progress, through welfare agencies or social security. Nevertheless, Msgr. Escrivá de Balaguer warned: **the fact that there are social schemes devised by governments to tackle the wide-spread suffering and need in our society (so that it is now possible to achieve humanitarian results which could hardly have been dreamed of in former times) will never be able to replace — because such social remedies are of a different order — the effective human and supernatural tenderness which comes from immediate, personal contact with one's neighbour: with that poor person who dwells nearby, with someone else who is living out his pain in a vast hospital; or with those other people, who could perhaps be rich, who need a few minutes of affectionate conversation, the warmth of christian friendship, to alleviate their loneliness, a spiritual shelter where they can heal their doubts and scepticism.**

Let us return to 1934 and to the Ferraz Residence. The house was beginning to look quite attractive. Good taste, ingenuity and long hours of manual work had made up for the lack of money. Soon it was the homely and welcoming place the Founder wanted it to be: **The houses of Opus Dei are welcoming and clean, never luxurious, even though we like them to have that minimum of well-being which is necessary to serve God, to practise the christian virtues, to be in a position to work and to enable the human personality to develop with dignity and without ostentation. Our houses have the simplicity of the home in Nazareth, which was the setting for the hidden life of Jesus, and the warmth that was both human and divine of that home in Bethany, which the Lord sanctified when he went there to seek genuine friendship, intimacy and understanding.**

When Pedro Casciaro went to 50 Ferraz Street for the first time he was immediately impressed by the entrance hall: "It was not a cold and unkempt place, but the hall of a middle to lower middle class family; it was in good taste and, above all, it was very clean."

Don Josemaría worked in a little room which had no other light than that of a window which opened onto an interior patio. It had just two pieces of furniture: a divan, which he seldom used because he slept in the rectory of the Patronato of Santa Isabel, and a wardrobe where the liturgical vestments were kept. His love of detachment led him to use the shoes which had been thrown out by residents, though he polished them carefully so that they would not seem old. Of his cassock he used to say, jokingly, that it had more embroidery than a Manila shawl. Nevertheless it was always neatly pressed and clean.

Then the Spanish war came. Needless to say, it was for them, as for many others, a time of privation and real hunger.

Sister Ascensión Quiroga, who was Capuchin Tertiary, met Don Josemaría in Madrid during the war. She managed to escape and, in 1938 together with other nuns, she belonged to the community which, through the initiative of Msgr. Lauzurica, the Bishop of Vitoria, looked after the priests. The bishop begged the Founder of Opus Dei to preach a retreat to the community. They found the talks and meditations impressive: "the best retreat I have ever done — and I've had a long life — was the one given us by Don Josemaría in 1938."

She also remembers how he practised the most complete detachment from material things: "He only had one cassock. Once he gave it to us to be mended. It was all in shreds. We tried to repair it as best we could and quickly, because he was in his room waiting for us to finish. His underclothes were so worn that there was no way of getting a needle into them to repair them, and so Mother Juana decided to buy him two new sets."

She adds: "He bore these privations cheerfully. He had a great sense of humour, though with us his priestly gravity was more in evidence. But when he was with Bishop Lauzurica, you could hear them laughing heartily together." A little further on in her testimony she quotes her elder sister, Juana Quiroga, also a nun, who did the same retreat: "She remembers especially clearly Don Josemaría's total unconcern for himself. He just never thought of himself. He was interested only in his sanctity and that of others." Sister Ascensión, who shared the cleaning of his room with Sister Elvira, says that she never saw so much order or care in things: "One cannot simply say that he was orderly; he was *very orderly indeed*."

"I am certain," she continues, "that often he did not sleep or, at least so it seemed to us, he did not sleep on the bed. In fact the sheets were uncreased and, even though he left the bed open as if he had used it, we realised that if he had slept at all it was not on the bed. We think that he used the hard floor. Besides, many nights we would find him kneeling at the foot of the Tabernacle, praying for hours on end. Sister Elvira remembers that his breakfast each day consisted of a splash of milky coffee." Sister Regina affirms that the Founder of Opus Dei "never had anything. His personal belongings when he travelled consisted of an inkpot filled with holy water, and his razor".

The same spirit, which is compatible with external dignity, appeared also when the residence in Jenner Street began in 1939. Marciano Fernández López, who lived there, gives the following account: "The Father's appearance just as the decoration and atmosphere of the Residence, all reflected his ideals. They were simple, elegant, clean and tasteful, producing a very agreeable impression."

The residence was small and the little space it had was really well used. Many people remember the room beside the hall, which served as an extension for the oratory, as a dispensary, and as the secretary's office. It also contained Isidoro Zorzano's bed.

In January 1975, Msgr. Escrivá de Balaguer spent a few days in La Lloma, near Valencia. There, surrounded by members of the Work, he recalled the first house he had had in Valencia:

There were two rooms and a passage way. And one of the

rooms was chock-a-block with copies of the first edition of The Way.

Who would have thought that with the passing of years thousands of copies would be sold in more than thirty languages!

The fact is that we could not live there: there just wasn't room.

He spoke to them of the only time in his life when he had fallen ill during Mass. Don Antonio Rodilla had been given a chalice and some vestments as a present and he wanted Don Josemaría to be the first to use them. He got as far as the Gospel and could go no further. Federico Suárez who was serving his Mass at the altar of the Trinity in the Cathedral of Valencia, managed to get him to the sacristy.

Then they took me home. We used to sleep on an iron bedstead and some wooden planks, as was the custom then in the barracks. The only thing we had in the way of bedclothes were some curtains which were in a poor state. So here too we lived in poverty as we have done all over the world. There is never a moment in Opus Dei in which very real poverty is not being lived by someone. . . . Not to worry: he is in Opus Dei, and he is happy.

Don Alvaro del Portillo was in the get-together and the Father said to him smilingly:

Alvaro, we are in rice country! What splendid rice you and I used to make for ourselves and one or two others! We ate nothing else: there in the fire-place we used to put a few cups of rice and water. And it was fine, wasn't it?

"Excellent, especially when you are hungry, which is the best kind of seasoning."

And we did not tell anyone. . . .

In Valencia, they still have a heavy beige trench coat which José Manuel Casas Torres used to wear during the war, and which he took with him to that flat in Samaniego Street. Later they took the coat with them to 16 Samaniego Street, which was a bitterly cold building in winter time. On his trips to Valencia, the Founder of Opus Dei used to wear the coat to keep out the cold whilst he was giving a circle, or looking after the work. Others like Don Amadeo de Fuenmayor, Don Justo Martí, Don Pedro Casciaro, or Don Federico Suárez did the same, when they had to spend hours on end at the desk in the director's room.

Msgr. Escrivá de Balaguer always taught that one should choose the worst for oneself, and put this criterion into practice himself, for example, when he went to live in 14 Diego de León, in the early forties.

The building was an old French-style mansion. Living conditions were very poor. Its outside appearance might have given some people a different impression, especially if they compared it with religious buildings, because it did not look at all like a convent. The residents managed little by little and with considerable effort to make the rooms on the first two floors of the building look quite presentable. These rooms were the visitors' area. The Founder of Opus Dei received his visitors in a room on the first floor which was tastefully furnished. There was wood panelling, a three piece suite in upholstered leather, a solid table of classical design and good curtains, but the rest of the house was very poor and the worst room was his own. He had chosen a bedroom which was freezing in winter and like an oven in summer. It was on the third floor.

Eventually, members of the Work managed to change this state of affairs, by making use of his absence once when he was preaching a retreat out of town. They then took his things to a better room on the second floor.

This was a larger room and it is kept today as it was then. It still has the poor iron bedstead in which he slept. From time to time they suggested getting him a better and larger bed, but he always refused. He used this bed for the last time in May 1975, a month before his death. On one side there is an old writing desk, which he always referred to as the "pianola", because in fact it looks like an old family pianola. Among the items of decoration there is a little donkey, a photograph of the ordination of the first three priests of the Work, a globe and a picture of St. Peter by an unknown artist. The painter had tried putting a cock beside the Apostle but it had turned out a rather odd bird. From Rome, in February 1948, Msgr. Escrivá de Balaguer wrote in a P.S. to a letter: **How I would like to see St. Peter's partridge in my room turned into a cock! The Apostle could do with a bit of a face-lift too. . . .**

Don Manuel Martínez Martínez visited him one day in Diego de León. He was accompanying Msgr. Ballester, then Bishop of León. He later wrote: "I was amazed at the austerity in which those men lived. One of them was, I think, a town clerk, another a civil engineer, in other words people of a certain standing, which made it all the more surprising. When I came away I said to myself: not even a Capuchin lives as austerely as these do." When they were leaving, the Founder of the Work asked them to say nothing of what they had seen. It was obvious to Fr. Martínez that "he did not want people to know the austerity practised there, so that no one could comment on it".

Don Vicente Pazos, who is now Counsellor of Opus Dei in Peru, noticed on the occasion when they changed the Founder's room, that his clothes and personal effects were a bare minimum. The Founder of Opus Dei did not like such facts to be noised abroad, but he knew how to teach the members of Opus Dei all the practical consequences which detachment from material things should have in their lives: both in ordinary circumstances and in extraordinary ones, as for example in those early years in Rome, during which, as he recalled: **many have been hungry with me; not just one day or two, but for long stretches. There were times when we did not put the heating on because we did not have a penny.**

They did not even have beds to sleep on: **Often I lay down by the street door. It was one of the most distinguished places, but there was a very cold draught, and a lot of damp came through the cracks in the walls. . . .**

Those who lived there often heard him emphasise the value of such a lack of material well-being: **I have it written most clearly on my heart. It has a decisive influence on the life of self-surrender and on the effectiveness or otherwise of our apostolate. Blessed poverty! Love it!**

He expected the members of Opus Dei to be full of supernatural outlook. They should thus **live in the world with realism, but also as pilgrims who are on their way to their eternal home and, therefore, they must fill themselves with a desire to be totally detached from the things they use. They must work with a right intention, without desiring personal gain. They must learn to love the discomfort, privation and poverty that come their way, as something coming from the hands of God. They must strive to help personally, with their work, to remedy the material and spiritual indigence of so many souls, while abandoning their cares in the Lord.**

The Founder of Opus Dei lived a spirit of detachment with such sensitivity that it descended even to apparently insignificant details. There was a time in the thirties when he noticed that he was getting "attached" to the holy pictures which he was using as bookmarks in his breviary. He did not want to have as his own even something like that, which was worth so little. Years later he told how he had reacted:

I got rid of the pictures and used some slips of paper instead. On seeing the blank slips I decided to write on them: Ure igne Sancti Spiritus! . . . **I used them for many years, and each time I looked at them it was like asking the Holy Spirit: "Enkindle me! Make me a burning coal!"**

In a glass case in one of the rooms in the central residence of the Association, among various decorative gifts and family mementoes, is to be seen an ordinary porcelain cup with a large triangular chip on the edge. Msgr. Escrivá de Balaguer asked for it to be put there. The first time he saw it was in Paris, one morning in 1955. He had just said Holy Mass in a Centre of Opus Dei, for a group of members in the early years of the apostolate there. Breakfast was no problem as the Father always took a cup of milky coffee without sugar and a slice of bread. There was a problem though when it came to the crockery. Even though there were very few people in the house, there were not enough cups to go round. They had to use a cup that was chipped and broken; so they tried to make it less obvious by distributing the napkins cleverly. To their dismay the Father went to sit precisely where that cup had been laid. He was delighted at what he found and insisted on drinking his coffee out of that cup. He was happy with the "wealth," of these members of the Work, lecturers, doctors, engineers. . . . After the meal he put on a plastic apron and helped with the washing up, as he had done in the times of the Ferraz Residence:

Looking back on these twenty-six years, he had said in the spring of that year, 1955, **I have often found myself with absolutely nothing, utterly destitute and with the future looking completely closed and empty. We were short of even the bare essentials. But, how happy we were! For we were seeking the kingdom of God and his justice, and so we knew that the rest was there for the asking. My sons should do what they can not to go short, but they should be cheerful if at times things are lacking!**

There is more to the spirit of poverty for the average Christian than merely being detached from things. He must also learn to use the goods of the world properly, in the service of others. Poverty does not only mean avoiding creating needs for oneself, or just bearing joyfully the lack of basic essentials. A Christian must also practise solidarity with his fellow men. He must prove his detachment by using his time as best he can, for the benefit of others. Time is a gift from God which does not belong to the individual, who will often be short of time. He must therefore really make the best use of the time he has, not getting worried or rushing around, but using time with genuine human and supernatural effectiveness.

This spirit also leads one to care for the things one uses, so that they give good and lasting service to God and souls. The Founder of Opus Dei pointed out many specific details which help to "materialise" this spirit: repairing what gets damaged; using stops to avoid damage to doors, windows and walls; switching on the necessary lights but no more; hanging a painting on two hooks instead of one, so that it is firmly fixed and doesn't scratch the paintwork; and so on.

I suffer, he once confided to a group of members of the Work, **when I see a number of people passing by a picture that is hanging crooked and no one stops to put it straight. It makes me suffer likewise to see everyone leave a room and forget to put each thing back in its place. Things are there to be used. If they get worn out or break through usage, well and good. But not because they have not been properly cared for. We have to look after things with a manly care. It is a question of doing things as a person in love does them.**

He used to give an unequivocal example to explain how this human and divine way of detachment from material things was to be practised even in the tiniest details: he spoke of seeing oneself as the father or mother of a large and poor family. Many members of the Work have heard him say **when you, wherever you are, have a doubt in this matter and don't have someone to consult, don't forget the clear criterion I have given you: we are parents of a large and poor family. You will see how you come up with the right answer.**

Love for sobriety can only thrive if the interior life is alive and throbbing. It is not a matter of rules, economics, or penny-pinching, for, as we are seeing in the life of Msgr. Escrivá de Balaguer, poverty cannot be separated from magnanimity, which leads a man to embark without human resources upon the apostolic undertakings which God wants. Caring for little things is not a narrowing of one's horizons, but just the opposite: it expresses the large-heartedness of one who loves so much that he notices details which escape the attention of the person who is not in love.

Besides, the attentiveness of love goes hand in hand with what we have referred to as the lay outlook. Ordinary people, which is what the members of Opus Dei are, live ordinary lives and use ordinary means like everyone else. If they are to be of service to others in their work, they have to stretch themselves to the limit. This they do both in big things (such as using the fruit of their labours to remedy poverty, by setting up new enterprises for the common good) and in little ones (for instance, making use of left-overs from meals, or writing on paper that has already been used on one side). On this last point, Msgr. Escrivá de Balaguer used to say, jokingly, that when he was gone the members of the Work would find that the only part of the paper he used which was not written on was the edge. Yet, he was never known to send a letter which was not perfectly written in every respect.

He taught by his own example how to practise the detachment which God wanted for Opus Dei. In 1968 he said in an interview with the editor of *Telva* magazine:

Those who do not love and practise the virtue of poverty do not have Christ's spirit. This holds true for everyone. For the hermit who retires to the desert; and for the ordinary Christian who lives among his fellow men, whether he enjoys the use of this world's resources or is short of many of them.

But, he added later on, **poverty is not a state of miserable want; and it has nothing to do with dirtiness;** besides, **poverty is not simply renunciation,** especially when it is to be practised by Christians who are living in the middle of the world and have to give **an explicit testimony of love for the world and of solidarity with our fellow men.** One must therefore learn how to live poverty, so that it is not **reduced to an ideal about which much is written but which no one seriously puts into practice.** Specifically:

Every ordinary Christian has to reconcile two aspects in his life that can at first sight seem contradictory. There is on the one hand true poverty **which is obvious and tangible and made up of specific things. This poverty should be an expression of faith in God and a sign that the heart is not satisfied with created things and aspires to the Creator; that it wants to be filled with love of God so as to be able to give this same love to everyone. On the other hand an ordinary Christian is and wants to be** just one more among his fellow men, **sharing their way of life, their joys and happiness; working with them, loving the world and all the good things that exist in it; using all created things**

to solve the problems of human life and to establish a spiritual and material environment which will foster personal and social development.

The Founder of Opus Dei went on to say that rather than laying down fixed rules, he was suggesting guidelines, because **to achieve a synthesis between these two aspects is to a great extent a personal matter. It requires interior life, which will help us to assess in every circumstance what God is asking of us.**

These guidelines are to be found in numbers 110 and 111 of the well-known book *Conversations with Msgr. Escrivá de Balaguer*. They contain insights which give much food for thought and which clearly derive from what he had himself already practised. They point to interesting practical consequences, some of which are especially significant for our times in which many people seem to be dominated by a consumer mentality.

The Founder of Opus Dei wanted the members of the Work to dress correctly, elegantly even, each in accordance with their position and personal circumstances. He liked to see people properly dressed, with clean shoes and nicely ironed clothes:

I remember meeting a man who liked to dress expensively. He spent a vast amount on clothes, but when he got home he used to throw them all over the place in a most untidy way. He justified his behaviour by saying: "I don't belong to the clothes. The clothes belong to me." (...) Things should be used, certainly, but we must realise we have no right to misuse them. We must make them last, because really they are not ours. They are a means to achieve our sanctity and to do our apostolate.

He always tried to be properly dressed for each occasion. There was a time when he wore a skull-cap to make up for his youthful appearance: **Grant me, Lord, eighty years of graveness!** was a prayer he repeated often. Later, by way of emphasising the secularity of Opus Dei, he would sometimes wear the crimson-lined cassock and the other distinctive marks of his status as a Domestic Prelate. Years later he confessed that he found this harder to do than wearing a cilice.

The cassock he normally wore in 1963 had seen eighteen years' service. It was old, but it was very clean and decent. Every button was in place. He would sew them on himself if they were coming loose. It was a practical lesson for the members of the Work.

He felt very happy inside his much-mended cassock, but on the rare occasions that it was necessary he would wear his Prelate's robes or the **trappings,** as he called them, of a University Chancellor, which he was.

It is with exactly the same spirit, which teaches that detachment from earthly goods and symbols of honour can never be an excuse for not fulfilling one's duties, that in 1968, thinking of his family, he exercised his right of calling out of abeyance the title of Marquis of Peralta, which had been conferred in 1718 upon one of his direct ancestors, Don Tomás de Peralta, Secretary of State for War and Justice in the Kingdom of Naples.

This decision, which some have assessed very superficially, took some heroism and is a rich lesson in human and christian behaviour, which some day will have to be studied in detail. For the purpose of this present work it is sufficient to note that Msgr. Escrivá de Balaguer was well aware of the criticism which his petition would arouse; but he was morally certain that he was the only member of his family who was entitled to start the legal proceedings to call the title out of abeyance and thus restore it to the family patrimony.

As always the Founder of Opus Dei did what his conscience told him. He did so after consulting some of the Cardinals of the Roman Curia, most noted for their wisdom, and with the Vatican Secretariat of State. It was, as I have said, a heroic act because he knew that his action would make him the target of gossip and ill-intentioned comment. He did not let this stop him. Four years later he handed on the title, which in fact he had never used, to his younger brother Santiago.

The Cardinal Primate of Toledo wrote an article in the Madrid newspaper *ABC*, referring to "the bright splendour of a poor heart, not one established down here on earth, but rather detached, open to all men, overflowing with confidence in God in the midst of the hardest trials. That is the true poverty of the Gospel, even though the person who practises it undertakes to mobilise all imaginable resources in the service of God and men. Perhaps there we have the secret that explains something of his life".

Msgr. Escrivá de Balaguer lived and died with the strictest detachment from earthly goods. One day, shortly before God called him from this life, he was saying to the students of the Roman College of the Holy Cross that, speaking earlier that morning with the members of the General Council of the Association, he had told them:

Today I have realised that I am still a very poor person. Not only because I am wearing my old cassock, since I could

put on another better one that I have, but because I cannot do what a person of my age in any more or less civilized country is allowed to do. There are workers at my age who have already retired and can quietly enjoy their retirement. If one night they have not slept well (which is what happened to me last night, and so I have had occasion to pray more), they can stay in bed a little longer next morning. But here I am with you, and I am much better off than if I had stayed in bed. But I have realised that in fact I am still today, after half a century of priesthood, a very poor person.

3. THE SACRIFICE OF ABEL

On 31 March 1935 the Founder of Opus Dei reserved the Blessed Sacrament for the first time in a Tabernacle of a Centre of Opus Dei, in the students' residence at 50 Ferraz Street. When he rented the house, the first thing he did was to choose the best room for the oratory. It was a relatively large room, to which there was access from the main hall. It also gave on to a large and quiet patio. At first all they had was a table and a long bench, which had been donated by someone. The bench was repaired and divided into two smaller ones by a carpenter. A crucifix and two candlesticks were placed on the table. There were also one or two kneelers.

Little by little during the year 1934–35 all the necessary items were obtained. An altar with a plain frontal was made. In front of it would hang a wooden frame covered with cloth of the liturgical colour of the day. The first vestments were of white damask. The chasuble was gothic-shaped, of generous proportions. Chasubles were ordinarily only of Roman style at that time, but Don Josemaría received permission to use gothic-type chasubles. The wall behind the altar was covered with dark olive green drapery, the width of the altar. The drapery reached up to the ceiling and continued as a kind of baldachin over the altar, for the law says that there should be a baldachin when there are living rooms above an oratory. He planned to place a statue of Our Lady over the altar. It was to be made by Jenaro Lázaro, the sculptor. In the meantime, he put a picture of Emmaus depicting the scene when the disciples recognise Jesus in the breaking of the Bread.

Whilst the oratory was being set up, Don Josemaría personally requested from the Bishop's House in Madrid permission to reserve the Blessed Sacrament. The parish priest of San Marcos certified that everything was in conformity with canon law. The first Tabernacle, which was made of gilded wood, was lent by some nuns who were not using it in their convent.

The Founder of Opus Dei was looking forward to having Our Lord present in that first residence. 19 March, the feast of St. Joseph, was the date he had fixed to inaugurate the oratory; but this was not to be, because several items were still missing: candlesticks, cruets, a lectern, a bell, a communion plate. . . . Providentially, one of those days, the doorman of the building came up with a parcel which contained everything they were short of. The director of the residence, Ricardo Fernández Vallespín, asked who had left the parcel, but the donor had gone without leaving his name. Finally, on 31 March, Don Josemaría said Holy Mass in Ferraz.

The story was to repeat itself hundreds of times, all over the world. Even though there might be no money, the best they had was always reserved for the oratory. A house might be virtually unfurnished with people sleeping on the floor if necessary, as it often was, but the first thing was the oratory and it had to be properly set up. No liturgical ceremonies were allowed to take place until the oratory was perfectly ready, with absolutely everything that was necessary. The Founder of Opus Dei would not allow exceptions. He was always very demanding in all that had to do with the worship of God, as Sister Isabel Martín, who looked after the chapel in the King's Hospital in the thirties, remembers with affection. Don Antonio Rodilla says that Don Josemaría reminded him of St. John of Ribera "who saw the Sacrament of the Altar as the high point of God's love for men, and whose heart burnt with unrealisable desires — witness his tears — to answer the *Tibi post haec, fili mi, ultra quid faciam* (After this, what more can I do for you, my son?) of Jesus in the Eucharist, with another *ultra quid faciam* (What more can I do?) of his generosity toward the Blessed Sacrament."

Don Saturnino Escudero who held a Benefice in the Cathedral of León met Don Josemaría in 1940 or 1941. The Founder of Opus Dei commissioned him to make an inscription on green velvet with gold edges, bearing the words *Ubi caritas et amor, Deus ibi est* (Where charity and love are, there is God). It was for an oratory. Don Saturnino liked the motto very much: "It was very appropriate, especially in those

post-war years when there was still a lot of discord, hatred and rancour."
From the conversations they had, he remembered very clearly that Don
Josemaría "wanted to dignify sacred art. He had no time for imitation
stone made of decorated cardboard, which was so common then, nor
for the cheap statues of the time. He preferred what was sober, simple,
genuine and dignified. He did not think it right to haggle in matters of
worship. We had to give God the very best we had. He liked sober and
proper oratories, which helped the faithful to get close to God."

Another person who made his acquaintance in those days was
Don Abundio García Román, who was very impressed by his insistence that the Holy Mass was the **centre and root of the interior
life:** "It was not common to hear a person like that in the forties in
Spain; and even less common was the care and affection he had for
the Sacred Liturgy." Don Abundio was impressed by his unhurried
way of saying the Mass, and how all present took part, dialoguing the
Mass. "It is worth while stressing this now, because I think he was a
precursor of the indications which the Second Vatican Council gave
regarding the participation of the faithful in the divine worship."

Thousands of people all over the world have derived great benefit
and spiritual strength from celebrating the liturgy in this way, which
is briefly summed up in the following considerations from *The Way*:

**Don't buy those "mass-produced" statues. I prefer a rough
wrought-iron figure of Christ to those coloured plaster Cruci-
fixes that look as if they were made of sugar candy** (*The Way*,
542).

**You saw me celebrate the Holy Mass on a plain altar-table
and stone, without a reredos. Both Crucifix and candlesticks
were large and solid, with wax-candles of graded height,
sloping up towards the Cross. The frontal, of the liturgical
colour of the day. A sweeping chasuble. The chalice, rich,
simple in line, with a broad cup. No electric light, nor did we
miss it.**

**And you found it difficult to leave the oratory: you felt at
home there. Do you see how we are led to God, brought closer
to him, by the severity of the liturgy?** (*The Way*, 543).

A few pages earlier we read:

**That woman in the house of Simon the leper in Bethany,
who annoints the Master's head with precious ointment, re-
minds us of our duty to be generous in the worship of God.**

All beauty, richness and majesty seem little to me.

And against those who attack the richness of sacred vessels, of vestments and altars, stands the praise given by Jesus: opus enim bonum operata est in me — **"she has acted well towards me"** (*The Way*, 527).

That was how he did things throughout his fifty years as a priest. I have referred more than once to the Jenner Residence in Madrid. Money was scarce and times were hard. The war in Spain had just ended and the world war had just begun. Almost all the furniture in the house was made up of old bits and pieces, carefully repaired by the members of the Work and their friends. The little money there was went into the oratory, so that it might have a certain degree of dignity. The altar was made of wood, with a thin fascia of ebony on the frontal. The Tabernacle, also of wood, was lined inside with gold tissue. The six candlesticks, with a cross-shaped base, were skilfully made from ordinary iron tubing, as was the ceiling lamp. Only the crucifix was bought new. The walls were covered in pleated hessian and there was a frieze near the ceiling with an inscription from the Acts of the Apostles. This was also home-made. First of all the words were traced on the wood, then they were carefully hollowed out with a chisel and painted red. The whole, set off against the light backcloth and chestnut coloured wood, was cheerful and attractive, though extremely simple. These inscriptions, so lovingly made, are still kept in a Centre in Villaviciosa de Odón, near Madrid. They recall the cheerful and uncomplaining poverty which was experienced then, and ever since.

The story repeated itself with the oratory of 14 Diego de León. The Founder of Opus Dei chose the best room of the house for the oratory. In setting it up, faith and good taste made up for the shortage of resources. It was easy to be recollected with Our Lord there. This oratory is intimately connected with decisive moments in the history of Opus Dei. It is kept now practically as it was then, even though with the passing years it has been enriched little by little, following precise indications from the Founder himself, so as to have it as he would have liked to have set it up in 1941, if he had had the means to do so.

He wanted to express his great love for Our Lord through the richness of the objects of worship. People in love have always given each other precious things (it is not simply a matter of cost) as a measure of their love: **Lovers do not give each other gifts of iron or sacks of cement. They give precious things, the very best they have. When they do something different, so will we.**

Richness in worship also expresses the spirit of adoration of God, who is sovereign Lord of life. He should be offered "the sacrifice of Abel", the very best we have. It was this that the Founder of Opus Dei taught:

Read the Scriptures. Go to the Old Testament and you will see how God Our Lord describes point by point the way the Tabernacle is to be decorated, how the sacred vessels are to be made, how the priests are to dress, especially the High Priest, even down to his undergarments! Everything had to be of gold or other precious metals, and fine carefully fashioned fabrics.

(. . .) And the Temple of Solomon was only the promise of what was to come. Jesus Christ was not there really and truly present, as he is on our altars and in our Tabernacles. The priesthood of the Old Law was but a shadow of the true priesthood instituted by Christ. Nevertheless, the Holy Spirit said: Nolite tangere Christos meos! **"Do not ill-treat my Christs, do not profane holy things." It is the voice of the Lord defending his majesty! Because his priesthood transforms the one who receives it into another Christ:** alter Christus, ipse Christus, **and it turns everything which is used for the renewal of the Holy Sacrifice of the Mass into something sacred.**

In June 1946 the first Tabernacle of Opus Dei in Rome was set up in a flat in Piazza Città Leonina. As always, the oratory occupied the most spacious room in the flat. The Tabernacle was a poor one; it was made of wood, and Msgr. Escrivá de Balaguer had it decorated as well as possible. Shortly afterwards the building which was to be the central residence of Opus Dei was obtained; and there more worthy oratories and tabernacles were built.

He pointed this out in 1957 when he blessed the oratory of the General Council of the Association and consecrated its altar, at a time when Opus Dei was **in full development, spreading itself the world over with marvellous poverty.** Special care had been put into that oratory, because it was to be the meeting point where all the members of the Work, married or single, widowed or priests, were present in spirit; men and women who **have given themselves to Our Lord with their whole heart, with their whole mind and their whole strength, in generous fulfilment of the divine command.** The Founder added: **We have made this Tabernacle for Jesus. It is the richest we could make.**

This manner of behaviour always caused surprise. Once, in 1973, a jeweller in Rome refused to take apart a brooch made up of diamonds mounted on platinum:

"What you are asking me to do is a crime. Do you realise what you are doing? This piece of jewellery is over a hundred years old."

When, however, the jeweller was told what the diamonds were to be used for, he set to work and refused to charge.

Similar stories have happened in many places. The jewels and precious materials used to make up the sacred vessels and vestments usually come from generous people who understand and appreciate what it means to be generous with God, and are prepared to give up family heirlooms to honour Jesus, thus making reparation for the insensitivity or irreverence with which some people treat objects of worship:

It is a pity, my sons, to see how centuries-old treasures are cast aside. Not so much for what they are worth in themselves, but because it impoverishes the liturgy. A loss in splendour, in tenderness, in sacrifice. We must teach people that it is not right to take a sacred vessel and put it to a profane use; it is indecent to turn a confessional into a telephone box or a bird cage. Who would dream of turning a tabernacle into a cocktail cabinet or a waste paper basket? It is diabolically absurd. Even from an artistic point of view it shows very poor taste. Each liturgical object has been made for a definite purpose, and we have to try to ensure that they continue to fulfil that purpose. And, if possible, enriching them, filling them with love.

He never tired of repeating these ideas, sometimes before thousands of people, as on that Sunday morning in the Coliseo Theatre in Buenos Aires, in June 1974. He had hardly started speaking when a gentleman from that land, with a smile on his lips and a somewhat mischievous gesture, intervened:

"When a very close friend of mine was ordained to the priesthood I gave him a present of a gold chalice. Some friends of mine who are Catholics told me my present was socially irrelevant; others that I was lacking in social conscience. It also happens — please don't laugh — that we have a very fine dog at home which costs us quite a lot to feed. None of my friends has told me that I haven't got a social conscience because I keep the dog. I would like you to tell me what you think about the present of the chalice and the dog."

The people who filled the theatre were very amused by the question. They became serious, and then laughed once more when they heard the reply:

As a rule I celebrate Mass with a brass chalice. I would love to use a gold chalice daily and I would think it was little enough. God bless you, because you have given that little bit of your affection to Our Lord. You did well! All you have to do is to read what Our Lord laid down in the Old Testament, and how everything had to be made of gold. Everything had to be of gold! Now, in their opinion, anything is good enough for Our Lord and nothing is good enough for themselves. Some people have become egocentric, wretched, thinking only of themselves. To Our Lord, they offer the sacrifice of Cain. History is repeating itself. A good son sacrifices the very best he has, gold, whatever he can give, what is precious to him. The others would want to offer mud, wretchedness.

As for the dog, remember St. Francis of Assisi. That will console you, and you can carry on being affectionate to your dog. Why should we treat animals badly? If you have a good heart for an animal, I know you have even more heart for your neighbour. Let every needy person find in you an open heart and a generous hand. God bless you.

It was not the first time that Msgr. Escrivá de Balaguer had referred to that brass chalice. On other occasions he had commented: **I celebrate Mass each day and have done for many years with a chalice which cost me three hundred pesetas. It is a bit like I am; people see it and say: "It's made of gold. . . ." But it's all show. When you dismantle it, you find witten on the inside in big letters the simple statement: "brass".**

All the charm of this chalice stems from the hands that fashioned it and coated it in a very fine layer of gold. Nevertheless, the craftsman was honest enough to admit clearly that he had made it from base metal. He wrote the fact in a hidden, but accessible place. He did his work so well that at first sight no one, not even an expert, would doubt the richness of the sacred vessel. It was necessary to take it to pieces and look inside to discover the truth. Only the cup was of silver, following the rules of the liturgy. It was all a lesson in sincerity, in naturalness, in love for what is genuine and authentic, which in addition moved the Founder of Opus Dei to make an act of humility: **When I raise the chalice in the Holy Mass after the Consecration, I see in that**

chalice a reflection of my poor life: the struggles, the victories and the defeats. The victories are his, Christ's; the defeats are mine.

With confidence such as this in God, defeats can never be an occasion for being disheartened or sad. When one seeks strength in the arms of God Our Father, one begins to understand the lesson of this chalice which **does not want to deceive anyone with its golden appearance, because it shouts aloud, saying: "Brass!"** — and a resolution flows naturally:

Be very sincere, my children. Do not hide your wretchedness when receiving spiritual direction. Only thus will your lives shine like jewels and your hearts will truly become thrones for God, who will triumph in your weakness.

The Founder of Opus Dei had a lover's heart and he needed to show his love just as every lover does. As he often repeated, he did not have one heart for loving people and a different heart for loving God. That is why, for example, in Rome, when there was not even money for essentials, there was always a freshly picked rose for the image of Our Lady in the room where he worked for many hours each day. It was a way of showing externally the love he had in his heart. Richness in the things of worship — as we see clearly in the anecdotes we have recalled here — was the outpouring of a genuine and tender affection of a lover to whom everything seemed little for the Person he loved: **How little a life is to offer to God!** (*The Way*, 420).

It was his constant teaching. To devote the best things to worship was a specific way of showing real detachment from earthly things, of accepting wholeheartedly God's dominion over created things and of expressing a spirit of adoration and piety. He deeply appreciated and was very grateful for the efforts which people of Opus Dei made all over the world to practise this refinement of love:

Our Lord is very glad to see that you treat him lovingly, caring affectionately and tenderly for the things of worship, which is where we strive to devote the best our blessed poverty can gather together. And Jesus must be glad also to see each one of you entering into intimate personal dialogue with him. May God bless you!

EPILOGUE

1975: "LIKE A FALTERING CHILD"

When night falls and I examine myself and do my sums and check what they add up to, do you know what the answer is? It is, pauper servus et humilis!

These were the terms in which the Founder of Opus Dei spoke of himself and his listeners could not but be moved by the real and deep humility with which he uttered them. Before Our Lord, he saw himself a poor and worthless servant, who wanted to be **good and faithful.** Each night, before going to bed, he prostrated himself on the ground and recited Psalm 50 in which is found the verse he so often repeated as an aspiration: *Cor contritum et humiliatum, Deus, non despicies!* (Thou, O God, will never disdain and humble a contrite heart).

On Sunday 26 May 1974 he celebrated Holy Mass in the oratory of a Centre of Opus Dei in São Paulo. After Mass he expressed his thanksgiving out loud. In a quiet voice he said:

It would be well for each one of us to invoke his Guardian Angel, asking him to be a witness to this constant miracle, this union, this communion, this identification of a poor sinner — which is what each one of us is, especially myself, who am a wretch — with his God.

Knowing who he is, we greet him, bowing our heads to the ground in adoration. Serviam! We want to serve you. Let us ask him to pardon our miseries, and our sins, and let us feel sorry too for the sins of the whole world. Supra dorsum meum fabricaverunt peccatores: let us feel the weight of this burden of iniquity, of all the wretchedness there is in the world, especially in these last few years. Let us yearn not only to beg pardon, but in some way to make up for all this, to make reparation!

Let us confess our nothingness: Lord, I can do nothing. I am worth nothing! I know nothing! I have nothing! I am nothing! But you are everything. I am your son, and your brother. And I can take on your infinite merits, and the merits of your Mother and those of the Patriarch St. Joseph, my Father and Lord, the virtues of the Saints, the gold of my children, the tiny lights that shine in the nightfall of my life through your infinite mercy and my little correspondence. All this I offer to you, with my miseries and my nothingness, so that you may place yourself on top of these miseries and so stand higher.

I turn to St. Joseph. We have said we would treat him well, we promised as much to Our Lady. I go to St. Joseph, who is my Father and Lord. With him, I go to his beloved Spouse, the Virgin Mother, who is my Mother also. With Mary and Joseph I approach Jesus — I have him now in my heart — and I tell him: I believe, I believe! Adauge nobis fidem, spem, caritatem! Increase our faith, hope and love. Because we must live by Love, and You alone can give us these virtues.

Then, knowing that he listens to us and loves us, knowing that we are Christ — because he in some way takes us to himself — it gives us joy to praise him thus: glory be to the Father, glory be to the Son, glory be to the Holy Spirit. From this blessed earth, so full of good things, so full of souls who love him and of souls who do not know him, for whom Christ is as yet an unknown figure or a myth. My God! Can this be so? Twenty centuries have gone by — twenty centuries! — and the Redemption is still taking place.

A few days later, Msgr. Escrivá de Balaguer was speaking with a group of older members of the Work in Brazil. He reminded them of their grave responsibility as **cofounders** of Opus Dei:

When I was young I did not dare to say it. But for some

years now I have been saying it. I am a poor sinner who loves Jesus Christ; a poor sinner. But look: I have known a whole host of very important persons. . . . But Founders of Opus Dei, there is just one; very much a sinner, but just one. A Father to you all? Yes. There will be others, better than me; the next one, and those who come after him. You will have to love him and cherish him much more than me. First, because God wants it that way; and also, because he will deserve it.

But Our Lord will ask you to render an account for having been close to me. Not because I am good, but because He — he didn't find anything worse — chose me so that it could be seen that it is He who has done the Work. You and I — I will say it to you, as I usually do, in a way which makes it easy to understand — when we write, we use a pen. Our Lord however writes with a table leg and he writes marvellously, so that it can be seen that it is his doing, not the table leg's. And now that I am making it quite plain that I am nothing but a poor instrument — ut iumentum factus sum apud te, like a little donkey before God, a little donkey pulling the cart — well, in spite of everything, I insist: Our Lord will ask you to account for having been close to the Founder. So you have foundational grace and, whilst I live, you are cofounders. You must really put your shoulders to the task, cheerfully and enthusiastically. And even when you do not feel enthusiastic, just the same.

"Father, have you often felt enthusiastic?" At this moment it is as if God was giving me enthusiasm: I look at you. . . . I love you so much, my sons! I know it pleases Our Lord that I should love you so much, because my love for you is so pure. But for the greater part of these forty-seven years, I have worked without enthusiasm, because the work had to be done; because God wanted it done and it was my duty to be his instrument: a bad one, but an instrument. I had to allow God to work and so I could not abandon the task. I couldn't step aside and say: "I don't feel like it." Nor can you. You must be constant, you must concern yourselves for your brothers and give your lives for them.

Ut iumentum. . . . The Founder of Opus Dei liked donkeys very much, for that is how he saw himself before God, like a little donkey.

A priest from Avila, Canon Mariano Taberna, described in *El Diario de Avila* something he remembered from a walk he had taken

EPILOGUE

many years ago with Msgr. Escrivá de Balaguer: "He took out a little notebook and he showed me a motto he had written there: *Ut iumentum factus sum apud Te, Domine.* . . . **Don't you think,** he told me, **that it is a good motto for a founder? The way I translate it is: Lord, if on occasions I am like a mule and I don't want to go where you want me, hit me hard Lord, until I learn. . . ."**

He had taken as his life's motto, **to pass unnoticed and disappear.** He put his whole trust in God. He did not consider himself indispensable for anything, not even to set the Work on its way. More than once, as far back at least as 1936, he would ask members of the Work individually:

If I were to die, would you continue the Work?

Some remember him putting the question to them on 1 October 1940. A number of members had come to Madrid from different provinces to be with the Founder for the feast of the Guardian Angels, which was to be the twelfth birthday of Opus Dei. The question caught them by surprise, but they all had sufficient presence of mind to say that they would carry on, faithful to the call they had received:

I should jolly well think so! was his vigorous reply, **you would have made a sorry bargain if, instead of following Our Lord, you had come to follow this poor man.**

His genuine humility and abandonment in the hands of his Father God increased throughout his life. Maturity, holiness, real goodness, as St. Ambrose says, consists in "striving to attain the simplicity of a child".

In his last years, Msgr. Escrivá de Balaguer saw himself **like a faltering child,** who has to begin again. They were years of hope, of experiencing anew the fact of God's infinite mercy, of feeling himself to be like the prodigal son continually returning home to the loving arms of his father.

In his preaching (homilies; writings; conversations, at times in the presence of thousands of people) we catch glimpses of the immense richness of his interior life, of his close union with God which gave unity to everything he did. As we end these pages, which have scarcely begun to sketch in a few features of his life, it is as yet quite impossible to describe at all adequately the closing years of his life.

On 28 March 1975 he celebrated his Golden Jubilee as a priest. On the eve of that date, which was Maundy Thursday, he was doing his morning meditation in the oratory of the General Council of the Work. With him were the other members of the Council. He had sat down in his usual place at the back of the oratory. Shortly after the meditation had begun, he started to pray out loud. It was a simple, spontaneous prayer. It forms a fitting summary, spoken in the presence of God, of the life of Msgr. Escrivá de Balaguer. It is worth while going over some of his words, at the conclusion of these brief reflections upon his life:

Adauge nobis fidem! **Increase our faith! That is what I was saying to Our Lord. He wants me to ask for this: that he increase our faith. Tomorrow I will not be saying anything to you; even now I am not sure what I would like to say. . . . Help me to give thanks to Our Lord for this enormous accumulation of favours, of blessings, of affection . . . , of blows! which are also a sign of affection and blessing.**

Lord, increase our faith! As always, before beginning to speak intimately with you, we have turned to our Mother in Heaven, to St. Joseph, to our Guardian Angels.

Fifty years have gone by, and I am still like a faltering child. I am just beginning, beginning again, as I do each day in my interior life. And it will be so to the end of my days: always beginning anew. Our Lord wants it that way, so that none of us may ever have any reason for pride or foolish vanity. We are to live waiting upon him, upon his words: our ear attentive, our will alert and ready to follow his divine inspirations.

A glance backwards. . . . What an immense panorama, so many sorrows, so many joys. But now, all is joy, all joy . . . because experience teaches us that the sorrow is the chiseling of the divine artist, who is eager to make of each one of us, of this shapeless mass that we are, a crucifix, a Christ, that alter Christus **each one of us is called to be.**

My Lord, thank you for everything. Many, many thanks! I have given you thanks; I have been habitually thankful to you. Before repeating just now that liturgical exclamation — gratias tibi, Deus, gratias tibi! — **I was already saying it to you in my heart. And now many lips, many hearts, are together repeating the same cry to you:** gratias tibi, Deus, gratias tibi!, **for we have motives only for giving thanks.**

We must never let anything upset us. We must never let anything worry us. We must never lose our peace of mind over anything whatsoever. (. . .) Lord, grant my children peace of mind. Don't let them lose it even if they commit a serious

error. **If they realise that they have done wrong, that in itself is already a grace, a light from Heaven.**

Gratias tibi, Deus, gratias tibi! **The life of each one of us ought to be a hymn of thanksgiving; just look how Opus Dei has come about. You, Lord, have done it all, with a handful of good-for-nothings. . . .** Stulta mundi, infirma mundi, et ea quae non sunt. **St. Paul's teaching has been fulfilled to the letter. You have laid hold of instruments that were utterly illogical and in no way suitable, and you have spread the work all over the world. People are thanking you all over Europe, and in places in Asia and Africa, and in the whole of America, and in Australia. Everywhere they are giving you thanks.**

And in this Tabernacle which is so beautiful and was fashioned with such tender care by my children, and was placed here by us when we didn't have money even for food; in this display of luxury, which I think is a pittance, and really it is to shelter You, here I specified two or three special details. The most interesting one is the phrase written over the door there: consummati in unum! **Because it is as if we were all here, all of us, right close to You, never leaving you day or night, in a canticle of thanksgiving and (why not?) also of begging forgiveness. I think that you must feel a little hurt that I should say this. You have forgiven us always. You are always ready to forgive our errors or mistakes, the results of sensuality or of pride.**

Consummati in unum! **In order to atone . . . to please you . . . to give you thanks, which is a capital obligation. Not just an obligation of this instant, of today, of the anniversary we will be celebrating tomorrow, no. It is a constant duty, a sign of supernatural life, a way both human and divine of correspond-to your Love, which is both divine and human.**

(. . .) This life which, if it wishes to be human, for us must also be divine, will be so if we make much of you. We should do this even if it meant long hours spent in waiting, even if we had to make many requests for an audience. But we do not have to ask even once! You are so thoroughly almighty, in your mercy too, that though you are Lord of lords and King of those who wield dominion, you humble yourself to the point of waiting like a poor beggar who timidly approaches our half-open door. It is not us who do the waiting. You are awaiting us all the time.

You await us in Heaven, in Paradise. You await us in the Sacred Host. You await us in our prayers. You are so good that when you are there hidden for Love, hidden in the sacramental species — I believe this firmly — when you are there really, truly and substantially, with your Body and your Blood, with your Soul and your Divinity, the Blessed Trinity is there as well: Father, Son and Holy Spirit. Besides, through the indwelling of the Paraclete, God is in the centre of our souls, seeking us. The scene at Bethlehem is in some way repeated, every day. And it may be that — not with our lips, but with our deeds — we have said: non est locus in diversorio, there is no room for you, Lord, in my heart. Forgive me, Lord, I am sorry!

I adore the Father, the Son, the Holy Spirit, one God. I do not understand this marvel of the Blessed Trinity; but you have placed in my soul a yearning, a hunger to believe. I believe! I want to believe like the best. I hope! I want to hope like the best. I love! I want to love like the best.

You are what you are: perfect goodness. I am what I am: the filthiest rag in this rotten world. And yet, you look at me ... and you seek me ... and you love me. Lord, may my children look at you, and seek you, and love you. Lord, may I seek you, look at you, love you.

To look is to turn the eyes of our soul towards you, yearning to understand you, insofar as — with your grace — human reason can come to know you. I accept my littleness. When I see how little I understand of your wonder, of your goodness, of your wisdom, of your power, of your beauty ... when I see I understand so little, I am not disheartened. I am glad that you are so great that you do not fit inside my poor heart, inside my wretched head. My God! My God! ... If I can think of no other thing to say to you, this will suffice: My God! All that grandeur, all that power, all that beauty ... mine! And I ... his!

I strive to reach the Trinity in Heaven through that other "trinity" on earth: Jesus, Mary and Joseph. They are, as it were, more accessible. Jesus, who is perfectus Deus and perfectus Homo. Mary, who is a woman, the purest of creatures, the greatest: greater than her, only God. And Joseph, who is there right beside Mary: clean, manly, prudent, trustworthy. O, my God! What models for us! Just to look at them makes me want to die of sorrow, for, my Lord, I have behaved so badly. . . . I haven't lived up to my surroundings and become divinised. You gave me the means; and you are giving me them, and will go on giving them to me . . . for, to live humanly on this earth, we must strive to live in a divine way.

Sancta Maria, Spes nostra, Sedes sapientiae! **Grant us heavenly wisdom, so that we may behave in a way that is pleasing to your Son, and to the Father, and to the Holy Spirit, one God who lives and reigns world without end.**

St. Joseph, I cannot separate you from Jesus and Mary; St. Joseph to whom I have always had great devotion, but I have come to understand that I should love you more each day and proclaim this to the four winds, because this is the way we human beings express our affection, saying: I love you! St. Joseph, our Father and Lord: in how many places will they have been invoking you already by now, repeating these very words! St. Joseph, our Father and Lord, intercede for us.

We must be — and I am aware I have reminded you of this many times — in Heaven and on earth, always. Not between **Heaven and earth, because we are of the world. In the world and in Paradise at the same time! This could be the formula to express how we should go about our life while we remain** in hoc saeculo. **In Heaven and on earth, divinised; but knowing that we are of the world and made of clay, with the frailty that is typical of clay: an earthenware pot which Our Lord has deigned to use in his service. And whenever it has got broken, we have gone and riveted the bits together again, like the prodigal son: "I have sinned against heaven and against You. . . ." We have felt that way both when it was something important, and when it was a little matter. At times we have felt very, very sorry over a little failing, a lack of love, a failure to** look **at the Love of loves, a failure to smile. Because when you are in love, nothing is little: everything is important, everything is big, even in a poor and wretched person like myself, like you, my son.**

God has wished to deposit a very rich treasure in us. Am I exaggerating? No, I have said little. I have said little now, because previously I had said more. I had recalled that God Our Lord, with all his greatness, dwells within us. Heaven dwells habitually in our hearts. I need say no more.

Gratias tibi, Deus, gratias tibi: vera et una Trinitas, una et summa Deitas, sancta et una Unitas!

May the Mother of God be for us Turris civitatis, **the tower guarding the city. The city which is each one of us, with so many things coming and going inside us, with so much movement and at the same time so much quiet; with so much disorder and so much order; with so much noise and so much silence; so much war and so much peace.**

Sancta Maria, Turris civitatis: ora pro nobis!
Sancte Joseph, Pater et Domine: ora pro nobis!
Sancti Angeli Custodes: orate pro nobis!